THE KINGDOMS OF RUIN

1

story & art by
YORUHASHI

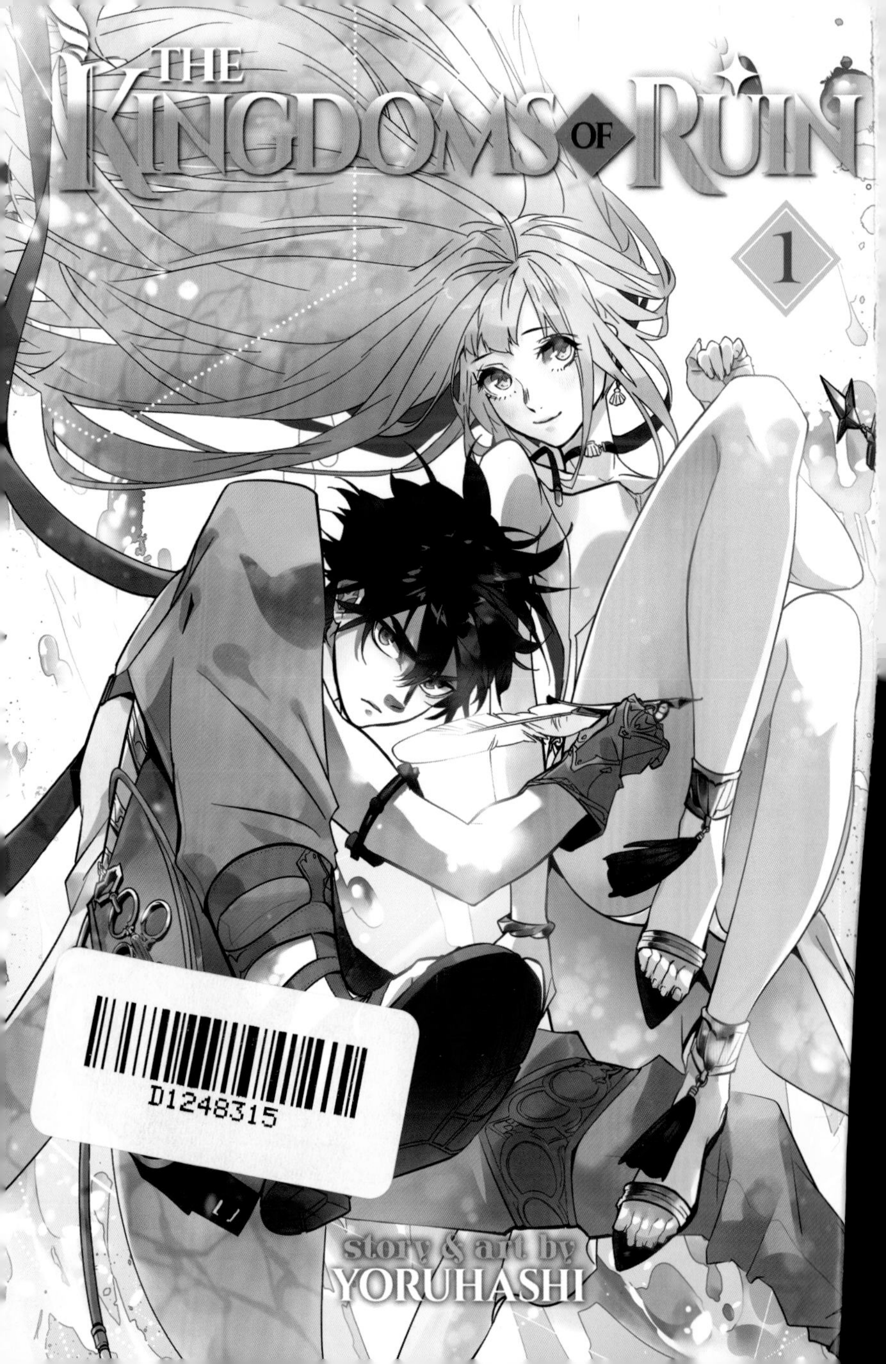

Contents

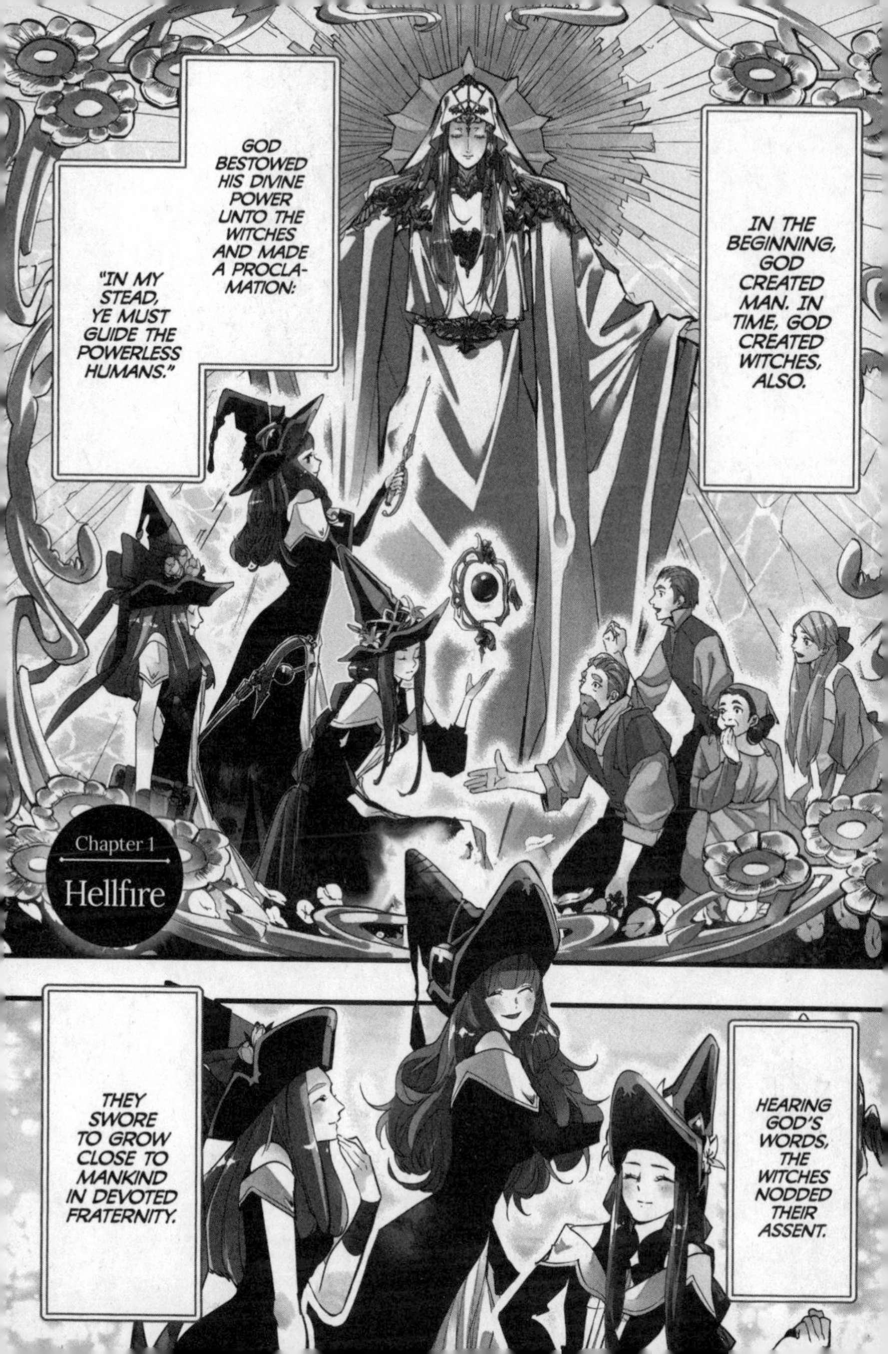
IN THE BEGINNING, GOD CREATED MAN. IN TIME, GOD CREATED WITCHES, ALSO.
GOD BESTOWED HIS DIVINE POWER UNTO THE WITCHES AND MADE A PROCLAMATION:
"IN MY STEAD, YE MUST GUIDE THE POWERLESS HUMANS."
Chapter 1
Hellfire
HEARING GOD'S WORDS, THE WITCHES NODDED THEIR ASSENT.
THEY SWORE TO GROW CLOSE TO MANKIND IN DEVOTED FRATERNITY.

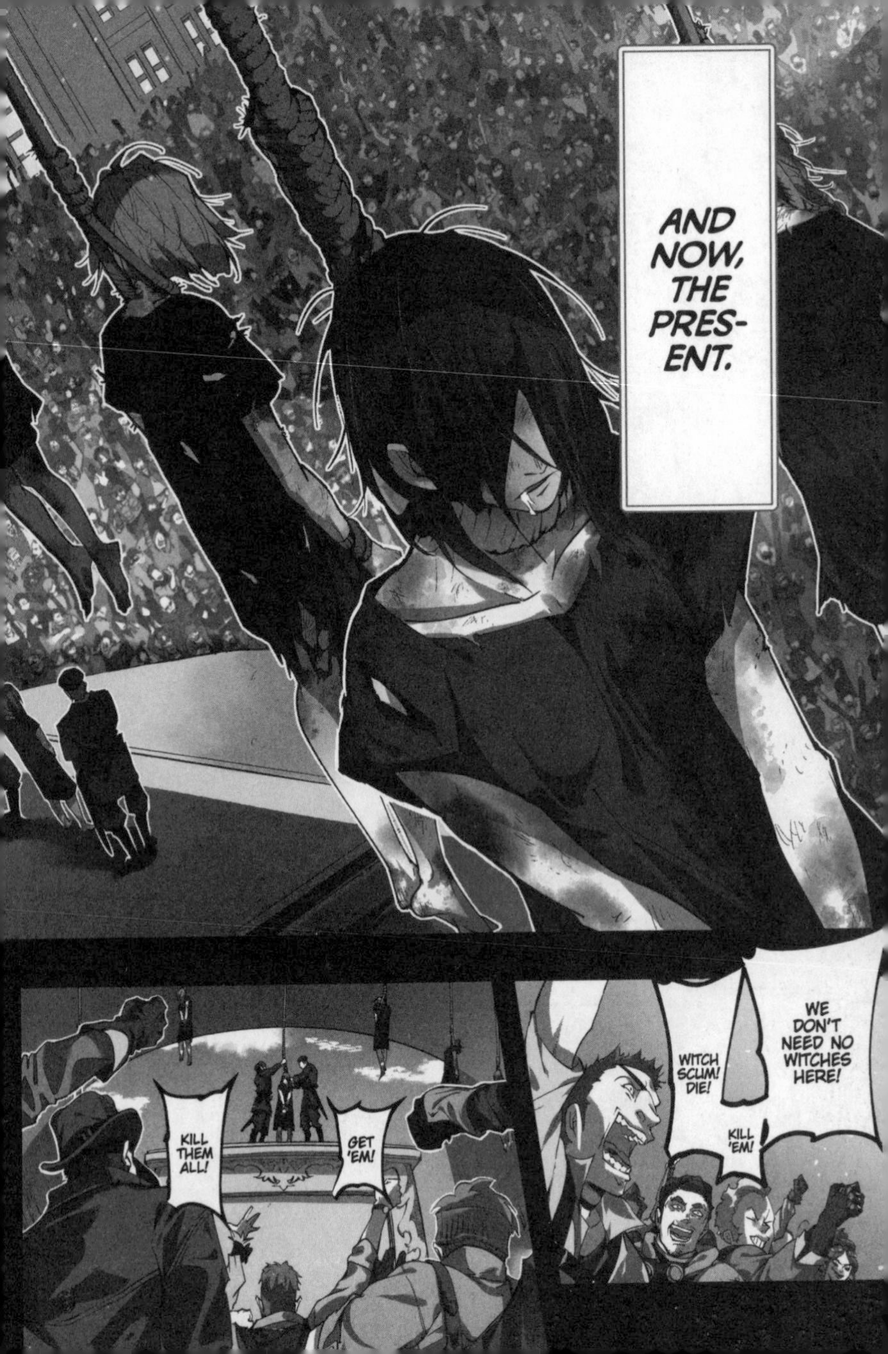
AND NOW, THE PRES- ENT.
WE DON'T NEED NO WITCHES HERE!
WITCH SCUM! DIE!
KILL 'EM!
GET 'EM!
KILL THEM ALL!

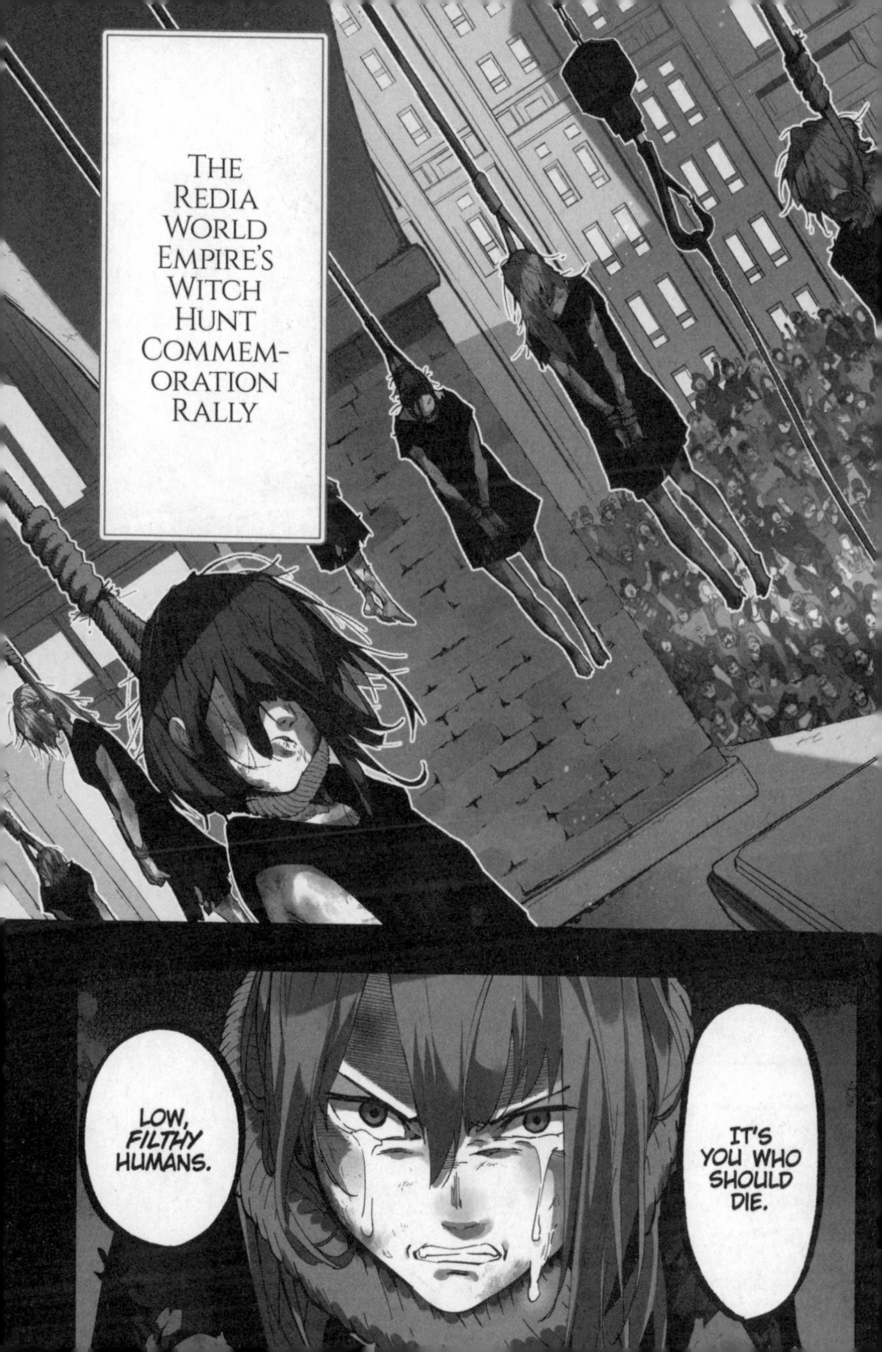
THE REDIA WORLD EMPIRE'S WITCH HUNT COMMEMORATION RALLY
IT'S YOU WHO SHOULD DIE.
LOW, FILTHY HUMANS.

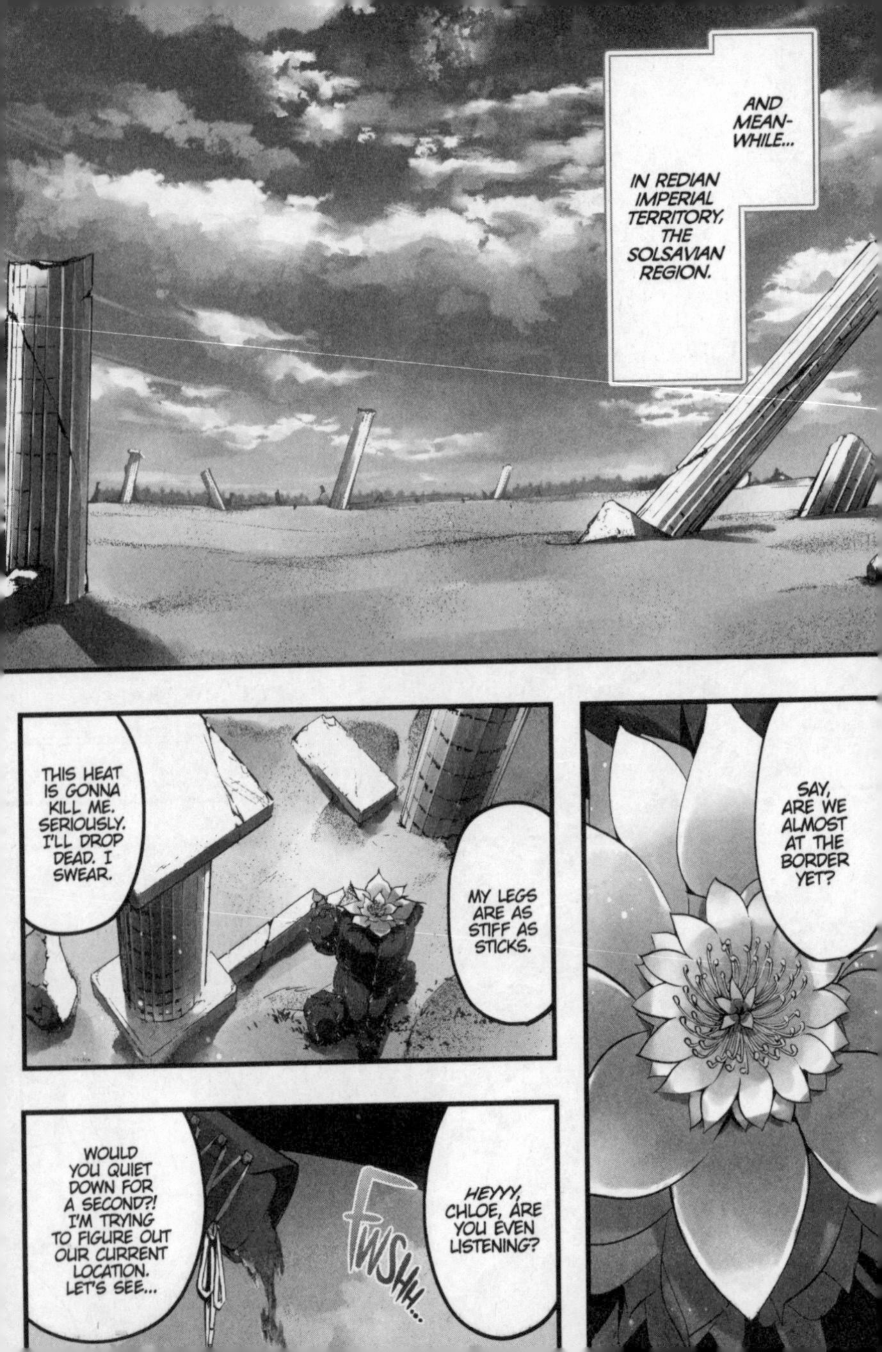
AND MEAN-WHILE...
IN REDIAN IMPERIAL TERRITORY, THE SOLSAVIAN REGION.
SAY, ARE WE ALMOST AT THE BORDER YET?
MY LEGS ARE AS STIFF AS STICKS.
THIS HEAT IS GONNA KILL ME. SERIOUSLY. I'LL DROP DEAD. I SWEAR.
HEYYY, CHLOE, ARE YOU EVEN LISTENING?
FWSHH...
WOULD YOU QUIET DOWN FOR A SECOND?! I'M TRYING TO FIGURE OUT OUR CURRENT LOCATION. LET'S SEE...

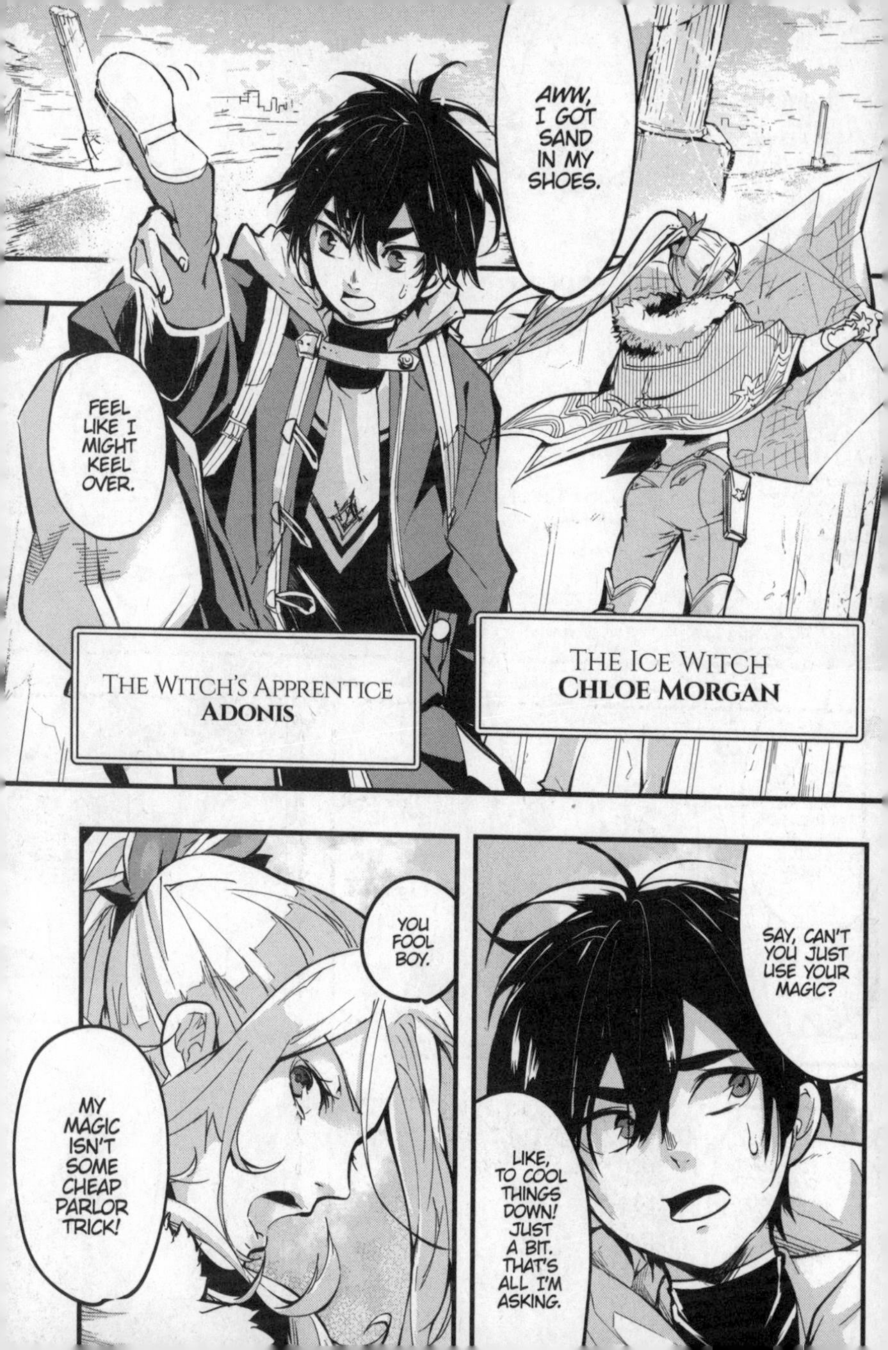
AWW, I GOT SAND IN MY SHOES.
FEEL LIKE I MIGHT KEEL OVER.
THE ICE WITCH CHLOE MORGAN
THE WITCH'S APPRENTICE ADONIS
SAY, CAN'T YOU JUST USE YOUR MAGIC?
LIKE, TO COOL THINGS DOWN! JUST A BIT. THAT'S ALL I'M ASKING.
YOU FOOL BOY.
MY MAGIC ISN'T SOME CHEAP PARLOR TRICK!

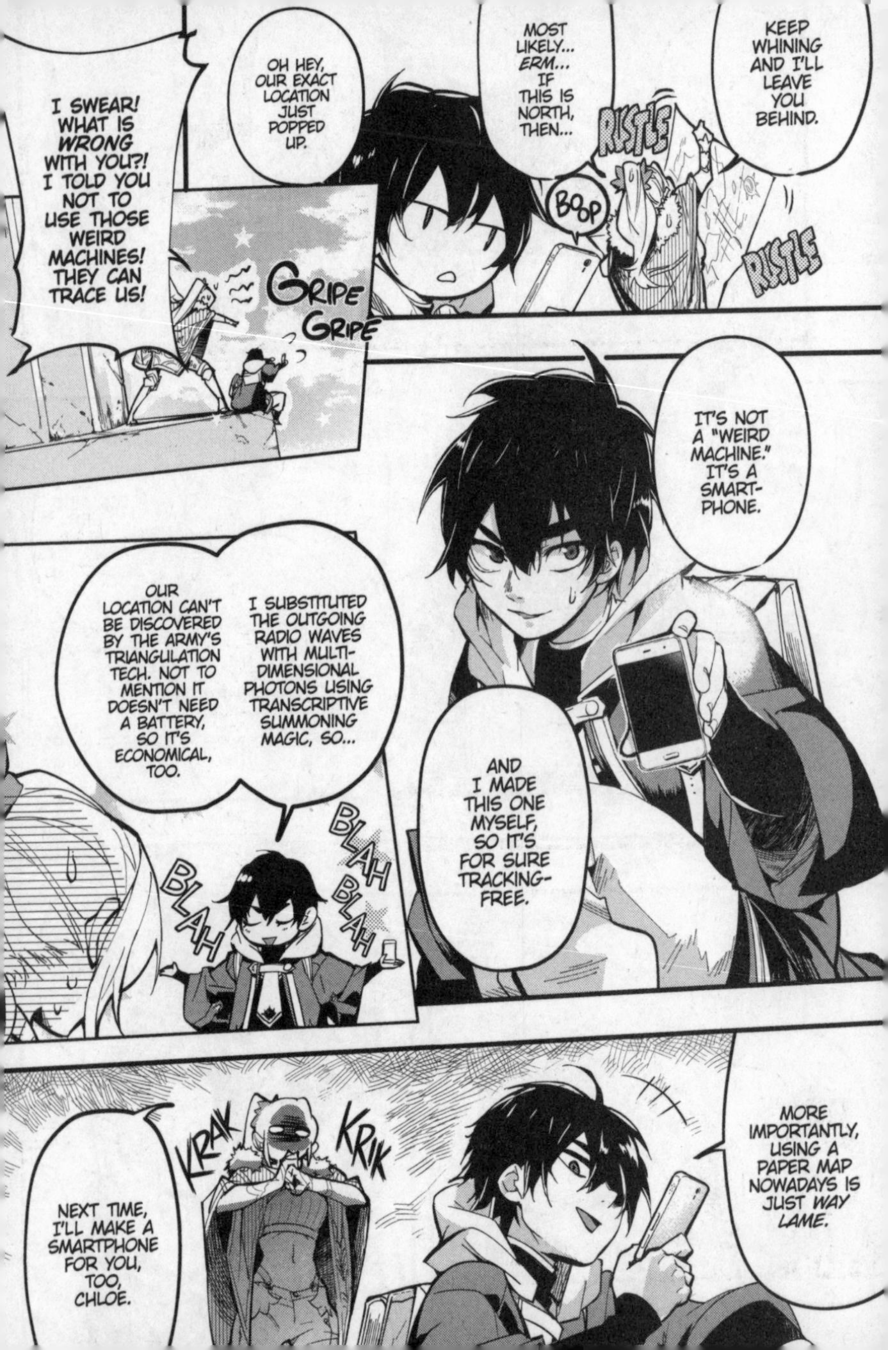
KEEP WHINING AND I'LL LEAVE YOU BEHIND.
RISTLE
MOST LIKELY... *ERM*... IF THIS IS NORTH, THEN...
BOOP
RISTLE
OH HEY, OUR EXACT LOCATION JUST POPPED UP.
I SWEAR! WHAT IS *WRONG* WITH YOU?! I TOLD YOU NOT TO USE THOSE WEIRD MACHINES! THEY CAN TRACE US!
GRIPE GRIPE
IT'S NOT A "WEIRD MACHINE." IT'S A SMART-PHONE.
AND I MADE THIS ONE MYSELF, SO IT'S FOR SURE TRACKING-FREE.
I SUBSTITUTED THE OUTGOING RADIO WAVES WITH MULTI-DIMENSIONAL PHOTONS USING TRANSCRIPTIVE SUMMONING MAGIC, SO...
OUR LOCATION CAN'T BE DISCOVERED BY THE ARMY'S TRIANGULATION TECH. NOT TO MENTION IT DOESN'T NEED A BATTERY, SO IT'S ECONOMICAL, TOO.
BLAH BLAH BLAH BLAH
MORE IMPORTANTLY, USING A PAPER MAP NOWADAYS IS JUST WAY *LAME*.
KRIK
KRAK
NEXT TIME, I'LL MAKE A SMARTPHONE FOR YOU, TOO, CHLOE.

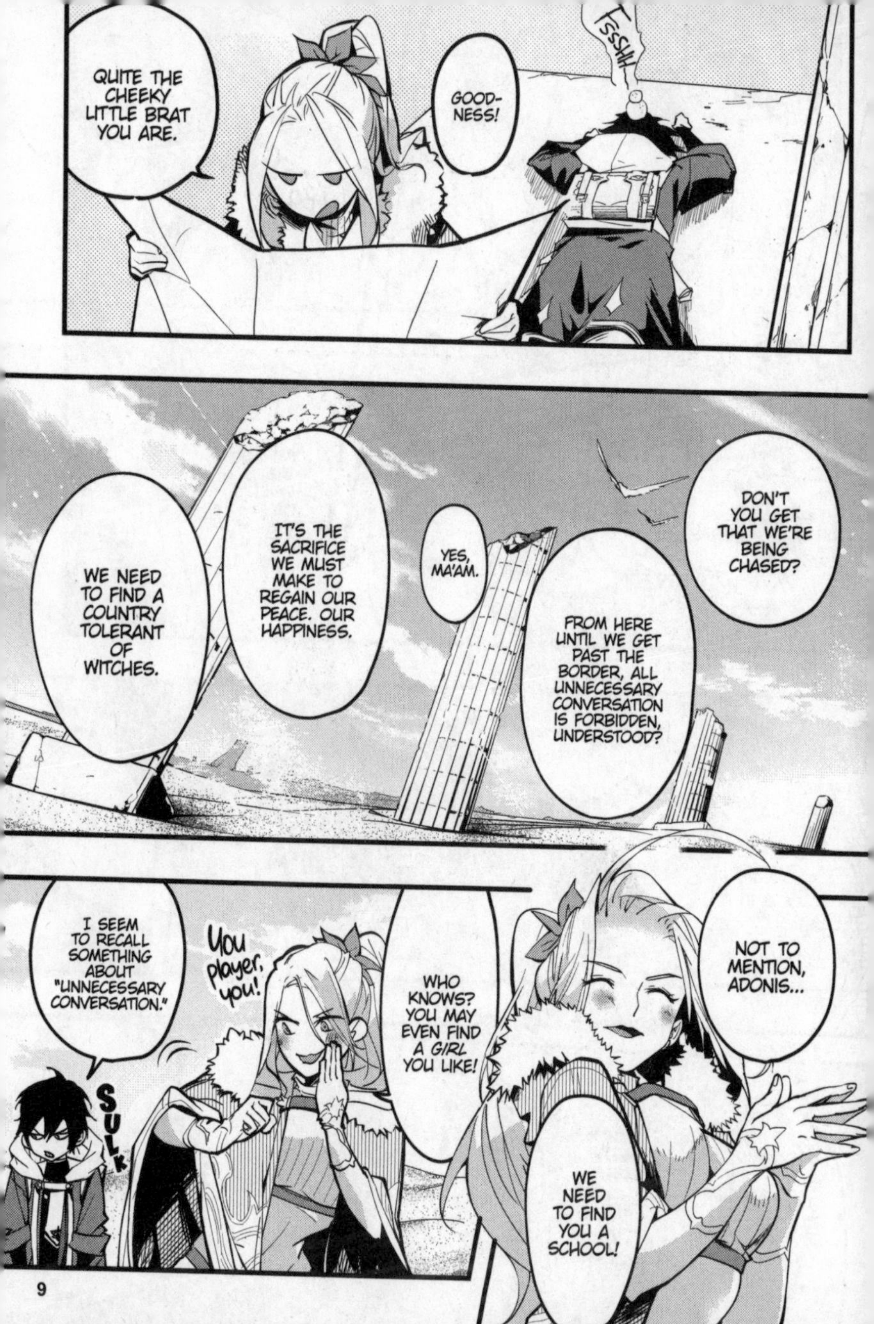
FSSSHH
GOOD-NESS!
QUITE THE CHEEKY LITTLE BRAT YOU ARE.
DON'T YOU GET THAT WE'RE BEING CHASED?
FROM HERE UNTIL WE GET PAST THE BORDER, ALL UNNECESSARY CONVERSATION IS FORBIDDEN, UNDERSTOOD?
YES, MA'AM.
IT'S THE SACRIFICE WE MUST MAKE TO REGAIN OUR PEACE. OUR HAPPINESS.
WE NEED TO FIND A COUNTRY TOLERANT OF WITCHES.
NOT TO MENTION, ADONIS...
WE NEED TO FIND YOU A SCHOOL!
WHO KNOWS? YOU MAY EVEN FIND A *GIRL* YOU LIKE!
You player, you!
I SEEM TO RECALL SOMETHING ABOUT "UNNECESSARY CONVERSATION."
SULK

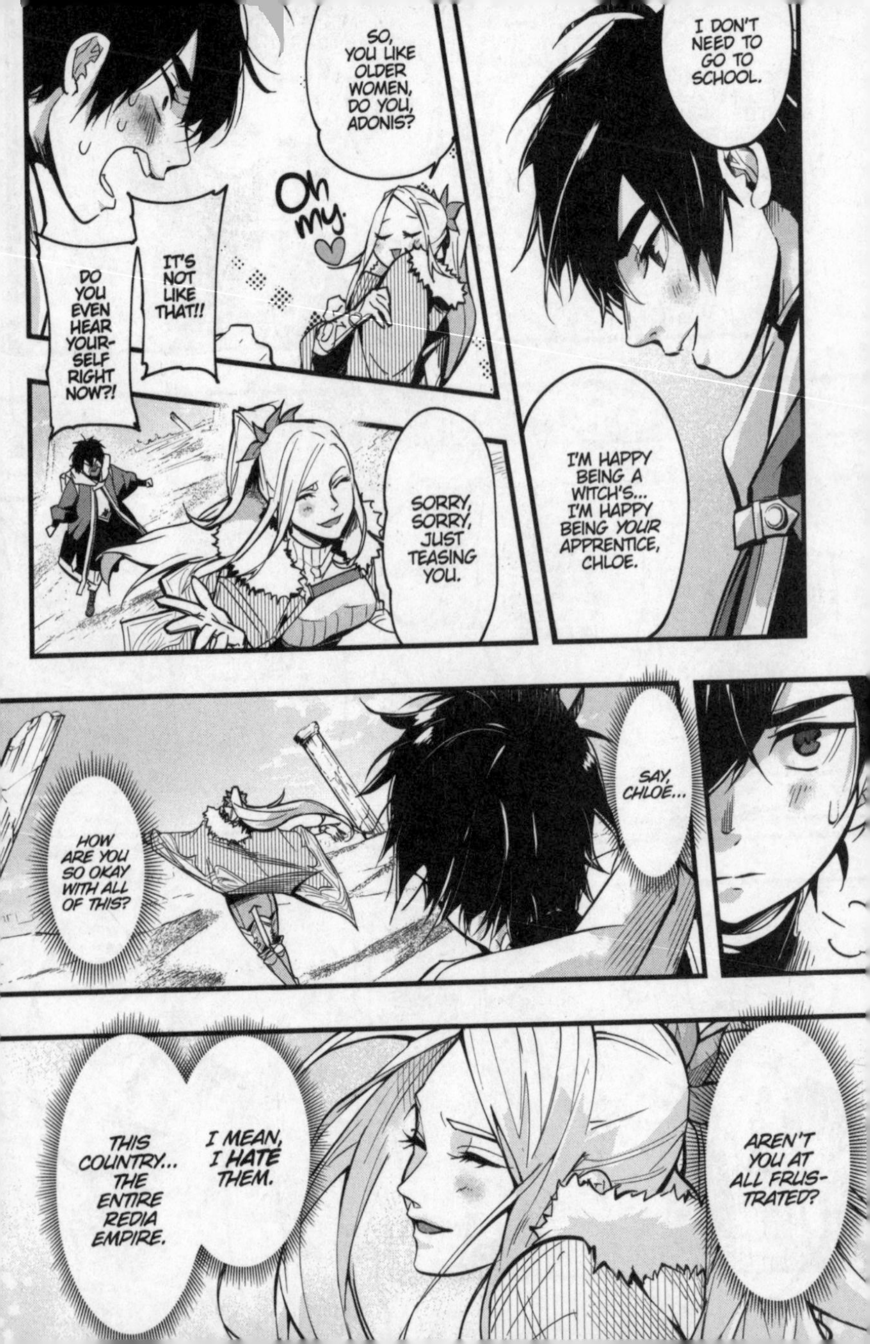
I DON'T NEED TO GO TO SCHOOL.
I'M HAPPY BEING A WITCH'S... I'M HAPPY BEING *YOUR* APPRENTICE, CHLOE.
SO, YOU LIKE OLDER WOMEN, DO YOU, ADONIS?
Oh my.
IT'S NOT LIKE THAT!!
DO YOU EVEN HEAR YOURSELF RIGHT NOW?!
SORRY, SORRY, JUST TEASING YOU.
SAY, CHLOE...
HOW ARE YOU SO OKAY WITH ALL OF THIS?
AREN'T YOU AT ALL FRUSTRATED?
I MEAN, I HATE THEM.
THIS COUNTRY... THE ENTIRE REDIA EMPIRE.

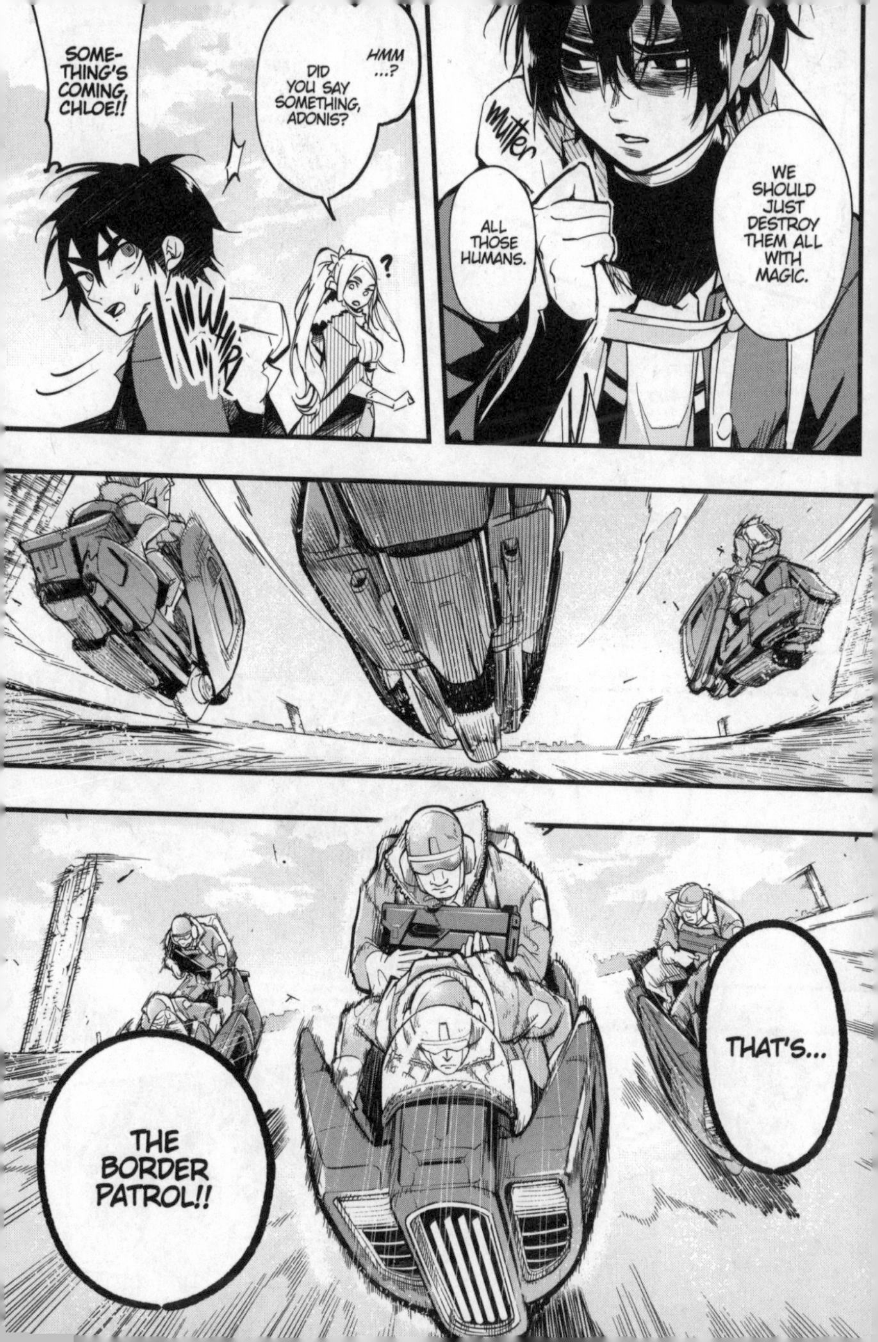
WE SHOULD JUST DESTROY THEM ALL WITH MAGIC.
mutter
ALL THOSE HUMANS.
HMM ...?
DID YOU SAY SOMETHING, ADONIS?
SOME-THING'S COMING, CHLOE!!
THAT'S...
THE BORDER PATROL!!

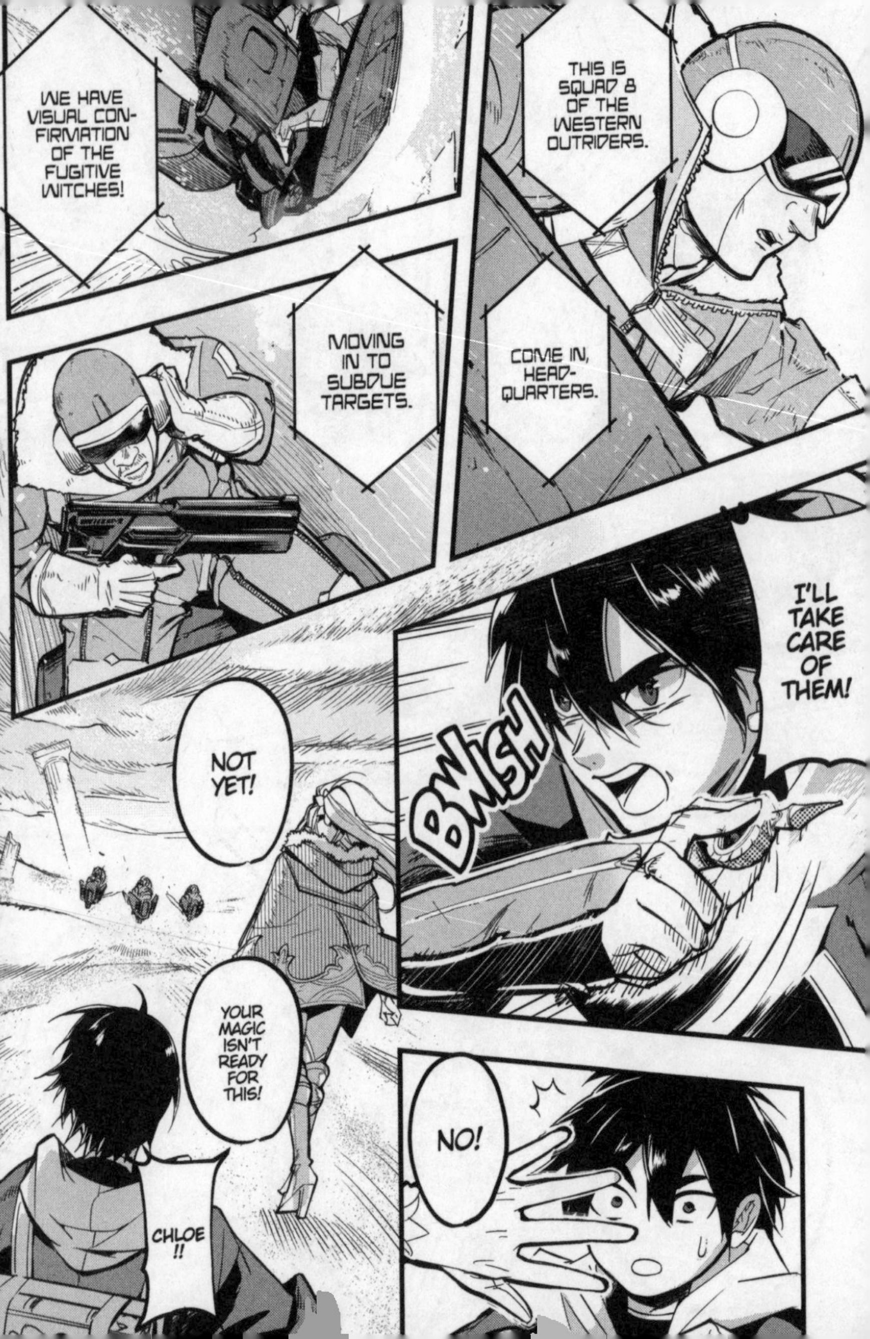
THIS IS SQUAD 8 OF THE WESTERN OUTRIDERS.
COME IN, HEAD-QUARTERS.
WE HAVE VISUAL CON-FIRMATION OF THE FUGITIVE WITCHES!
MOVING IN TO SUBDUE TARGETS.
I'LL TAKE CARE OF THEM!
BWISH
NO!
NOT YET!
YOUR MAGIC ISN'T READY FOR THIS!
CHLOE!!

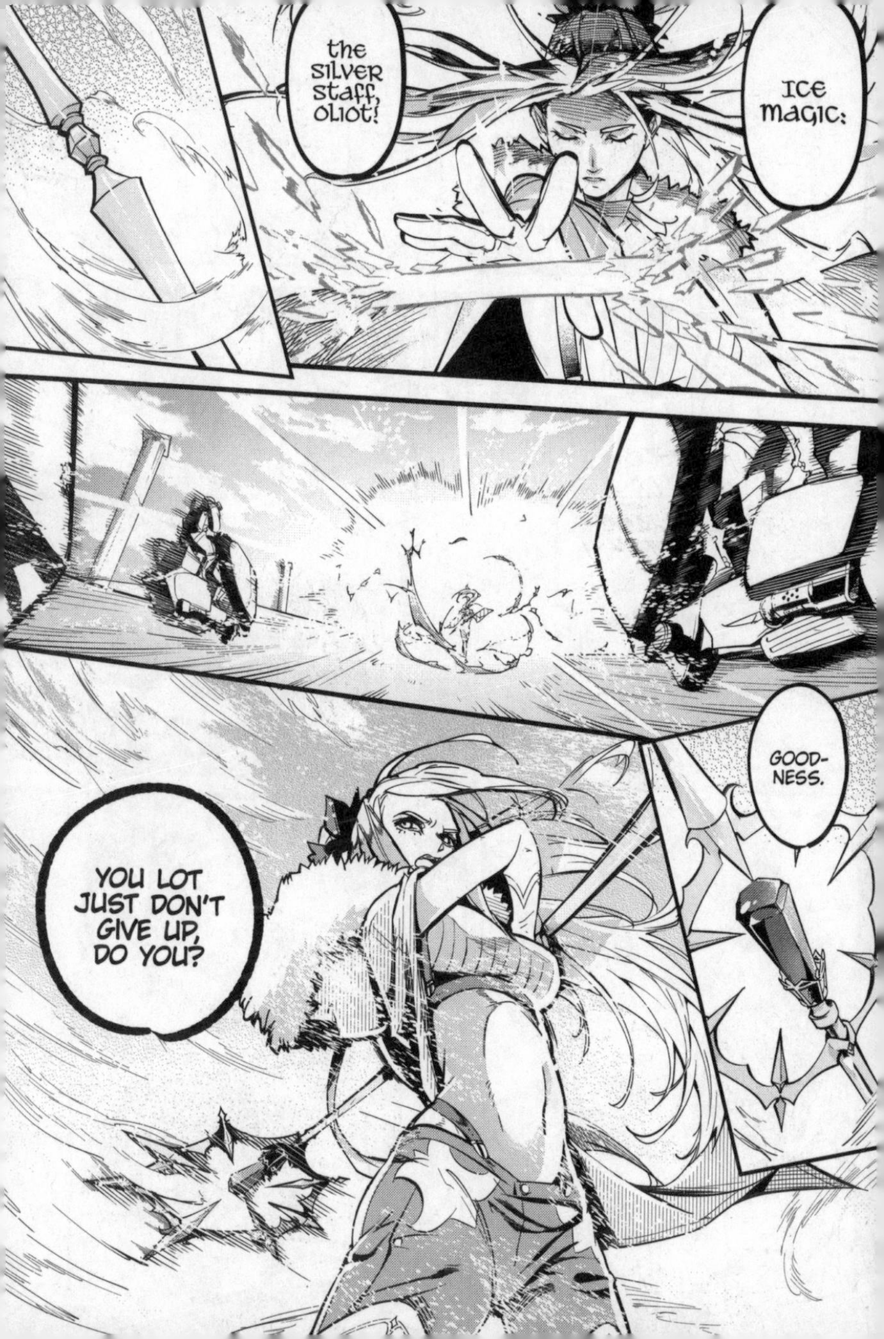
ICE MAGIC:
the SILVER staff, OLIOT!
GOODNESS.
YOU LOT JUST DON'T GIVE UP, DO YOU?

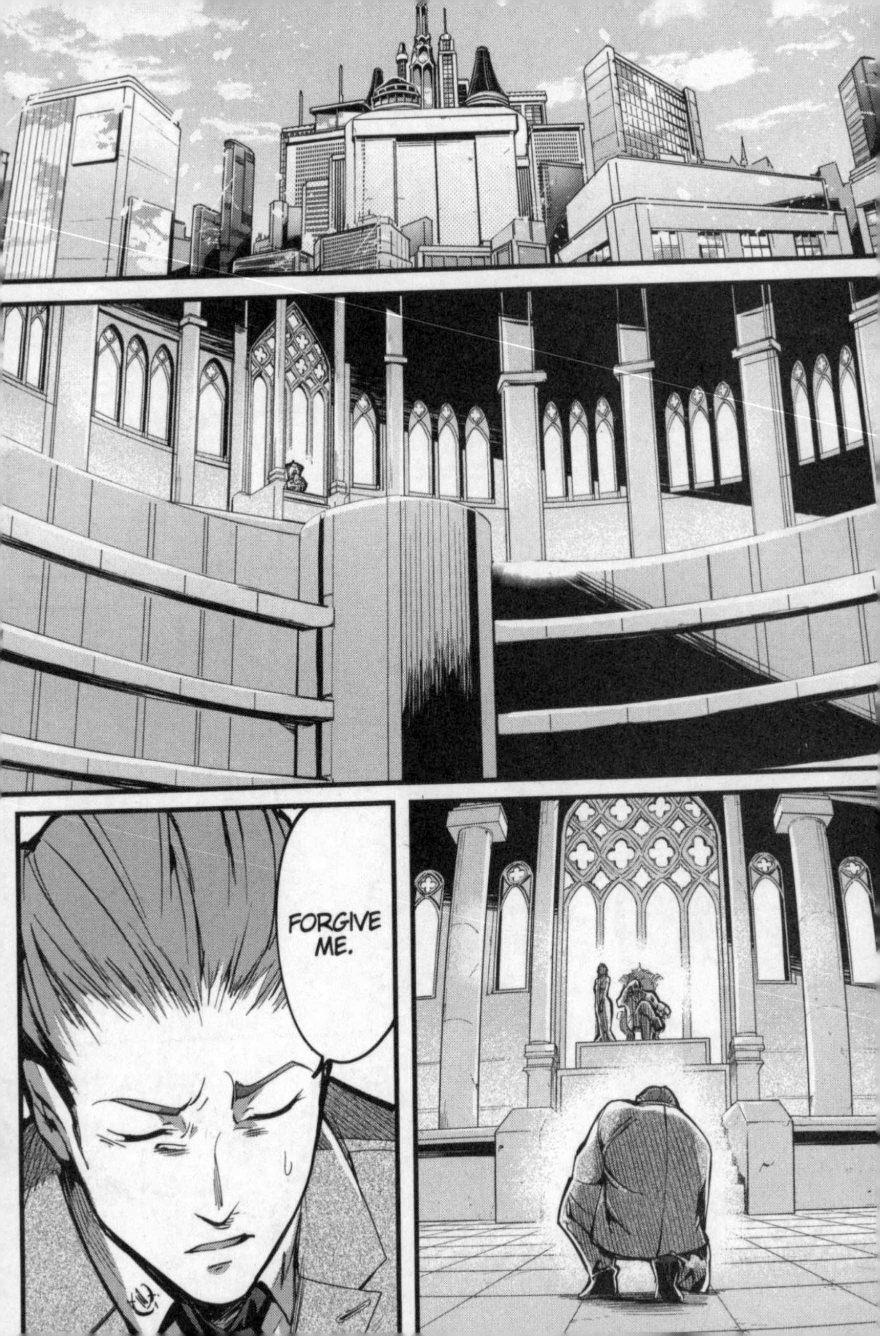
FORGIVE ME.

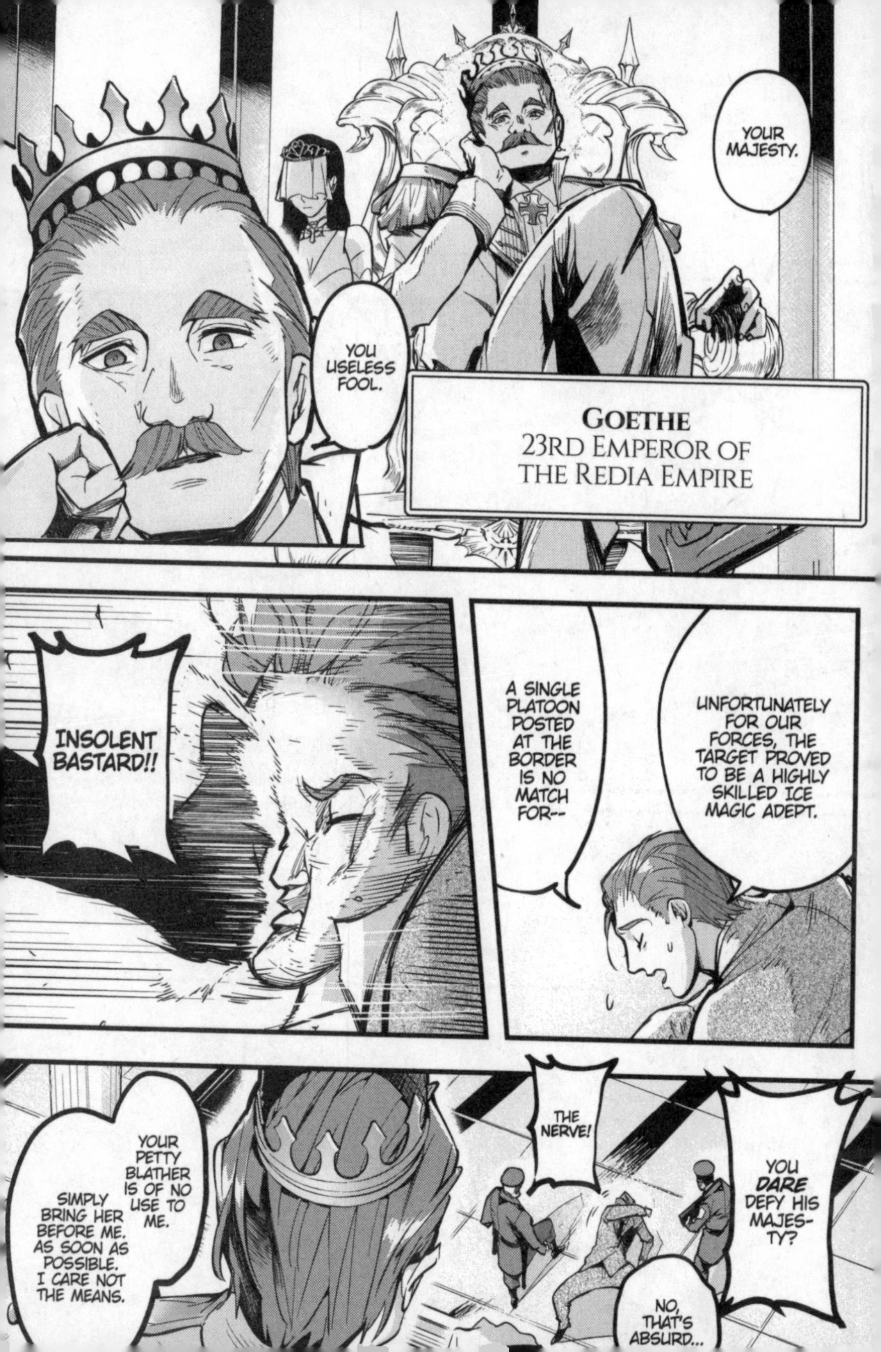

YOUR MAJESTY.
YOU USELESS FOOL.
GOETHE 23RD EMPEROR OF THE REDIA EMPIRE
UNFORTUNATELY FOR OUR FORCES, THE TARGET PROVED TO BE A HIGHLY SKILLED ICE MAGIC ADEPT.
A SINGLE PLATOON POSTED AT THE BORDER IS NO MATCH FOR--
INSOLENT BASTARD!!
YOU DARE DEFY HIS MAJESTY?
THE NERVE!
NO, THAT'S ABSURD...
YOUR PETTY BLATHER IS OF NO USE TO ME.
SIMPLY BRING HER BEFORE ME. AS SOON AS POSSIBLE. I CARE NOT THE MEANS.

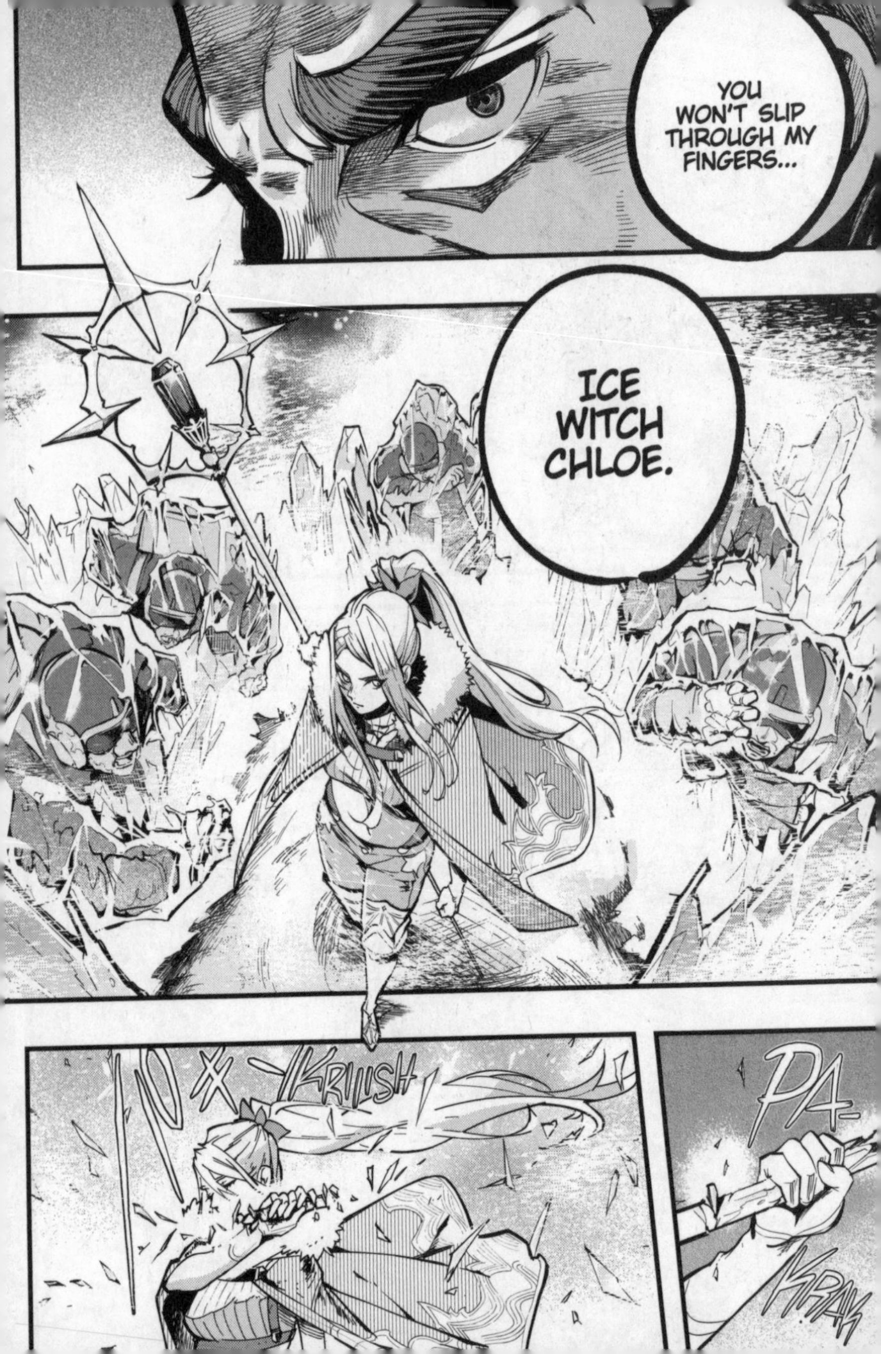
YOU WON'T SLIP THROUGH MY FINGERS...
ICE WITCH CHLOE.
PA-
KRAK
KRIIISH

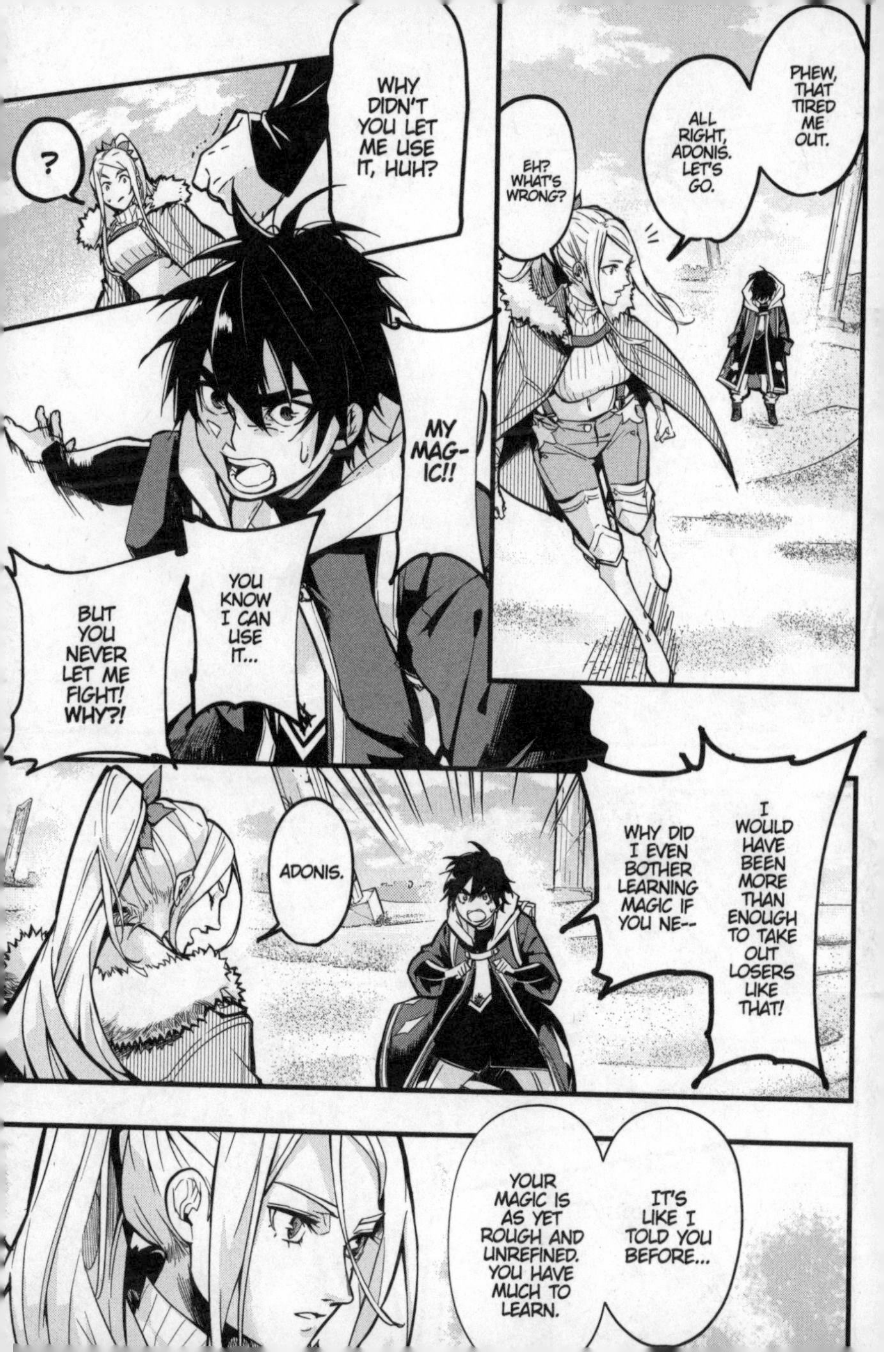
PHEW, THAT TIRED ME OUT.
ALL RIGHT, ADONIS. LET'S GO.
EH? WHAT'S WRONG?
WHY DIDN'T YOU LET ME USE IT, HUH?
?
MY MAG-IC!!
YOU KNOW I CAN USE IT...
BUT YOU NEVER LET ME FIGHT! WHY?!
I WOULD HAVE BEEN MORE THAN ENOUGH TO TAKE OUT LOSERS LIKE THAT!
WHY DID I EVEN BOTHER LEARNING MAGIC IF YOU NE--
ADONIS.
IT'S LIKE I TOLD YOU BEFORE...
YOUR MAGIC IS AS YET ROUGH AND UNREFINED. YOU HAVE MUCH TO LEARN.

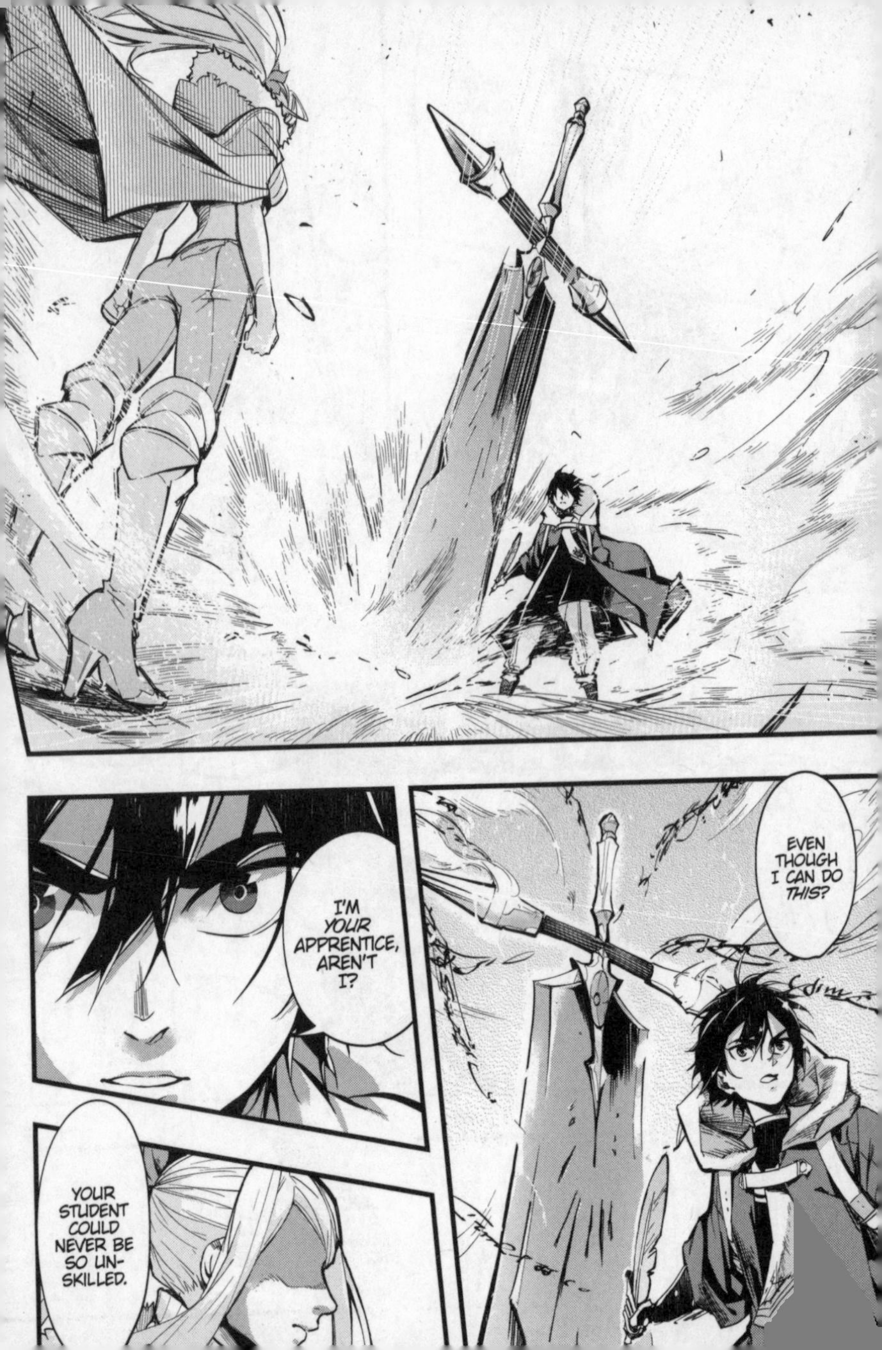
EVEN THOUGH I CAN DO *THIS*?
I'M *YOUR* APPRENTICE, AREN'T I?
YOUR STUDENT COULD NEVER BE SO UN-SKILLED.

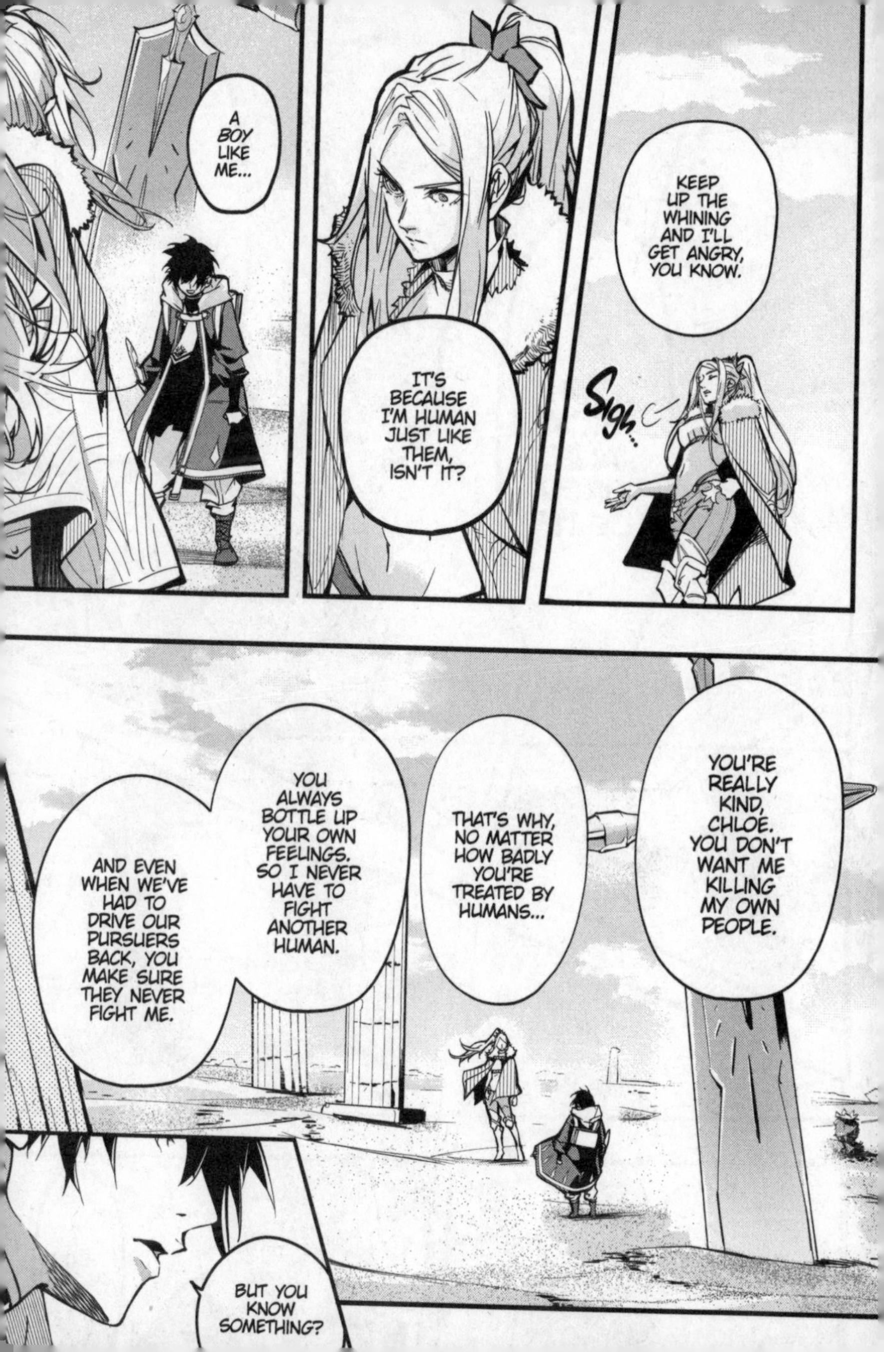
KEEP UP THE WHINING AND I'LL GET ANGRY, YOU KNOW.
Sigh...
IT'S BECAUSE I'M HUMAN JUST LIKE THEM, ISN'T IT?
A BOY LIKE ME...
YOU'RE REALLY KIND, CHLOE. YOU DON'T WANT ME KILLING MY OWN PEOPLE.
THAT'S WHY, NO MATTER HOW BADLY YOU'RE TREATED BY HUMANS...
YOU ALWAYS BOTTLE UP YOUR OWN FEELINGS. SO I NEVER HAVE TO FIGHT ANOTHER HUMAN.
AND EVEN WHEN WE'VE HAD TO DRIVE OUR PURSUERS BACK, YOU MAKE SURE THEY NEVER FIGHT ME.
BUT YOU KNOW SOMETHING?

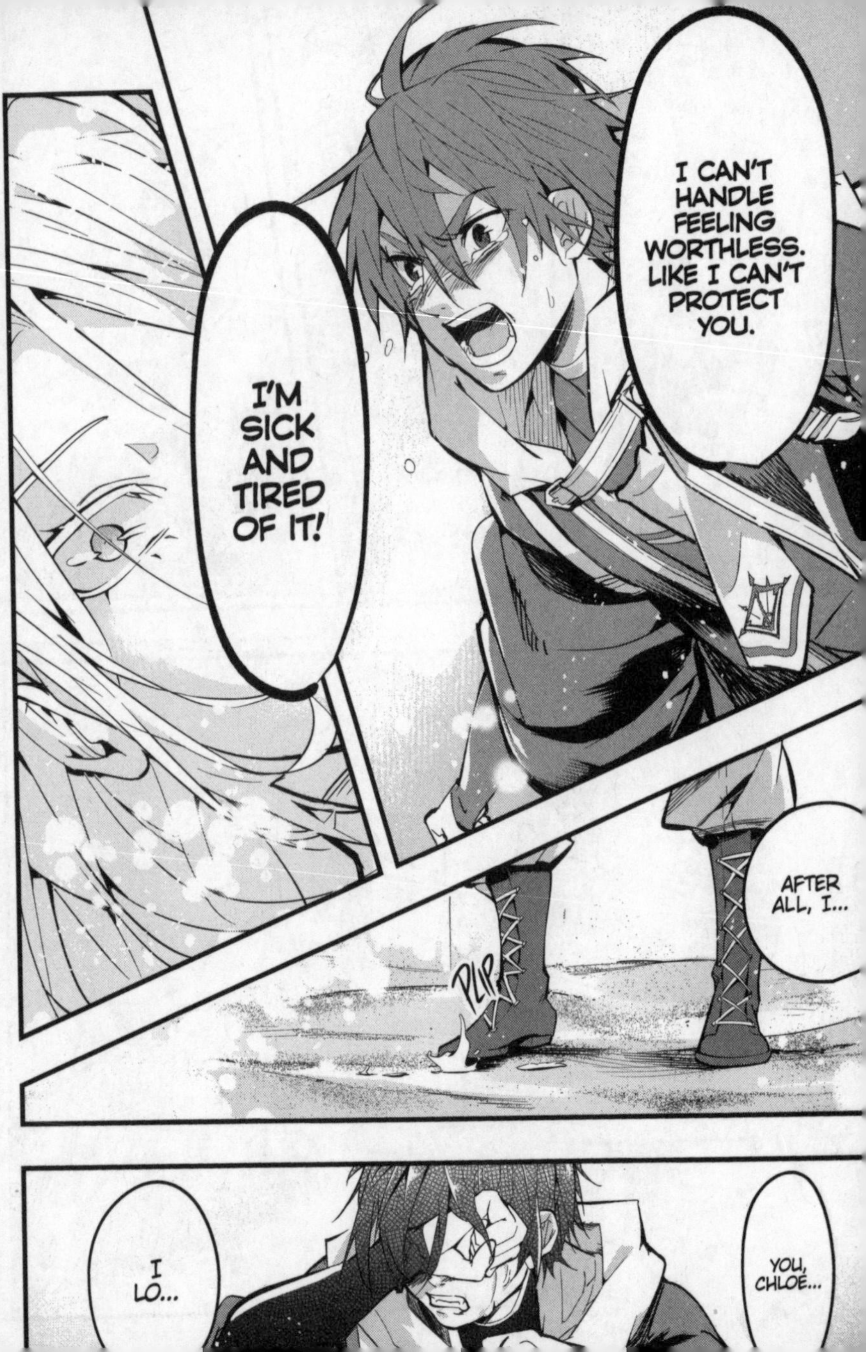
I CAN'T HANDLE FEELING WORTHLESS. LIKE I CAN'T PROTECT YOU.
I'M SICK AND TIRED OF IT!
AFTER ALL, I...
PLIP
YOU, CHLOE...
I LO...

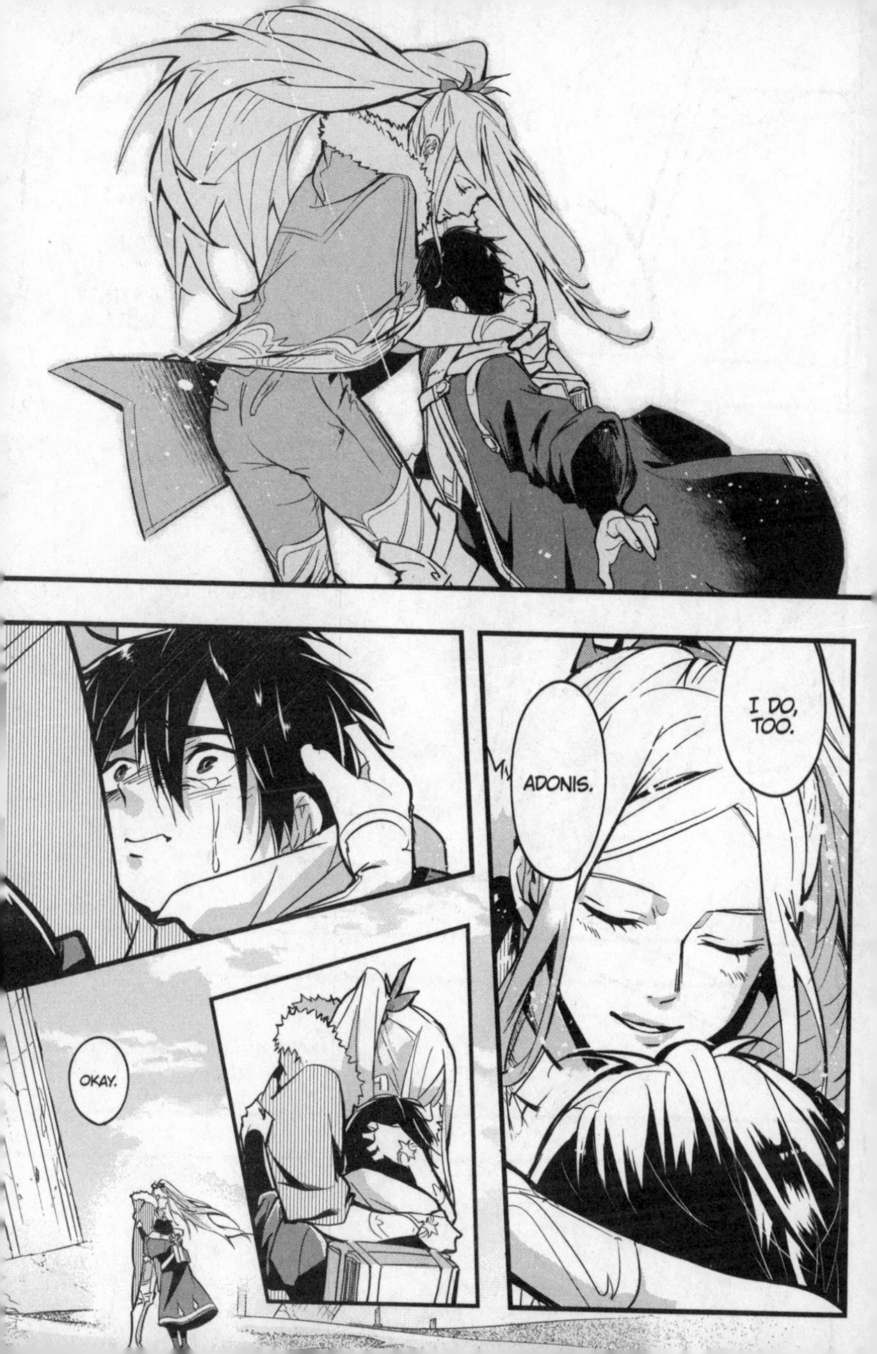
I DO, TOO.
ADONIS.
OKAY.

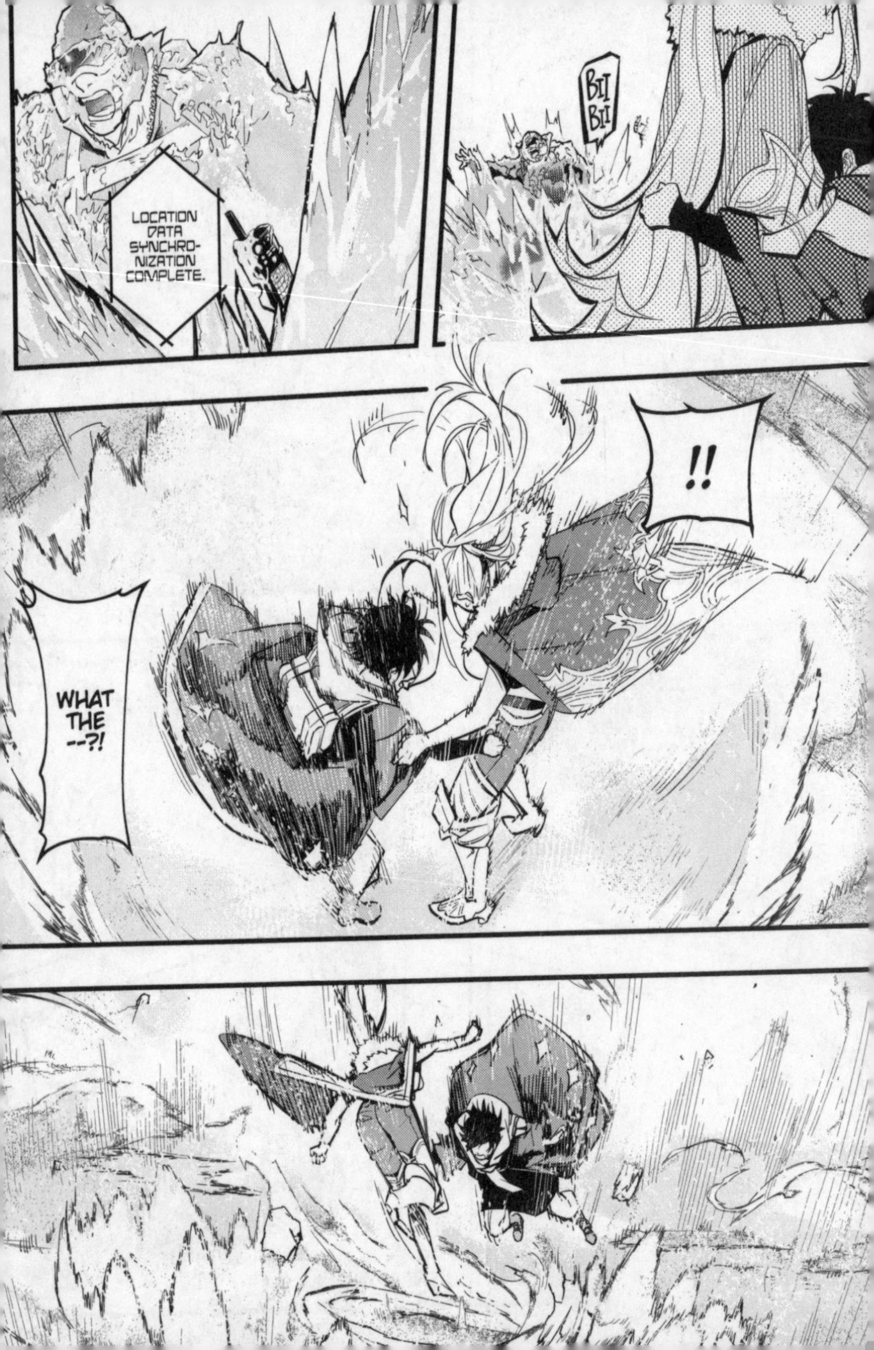
BII BII
LOCATION DATA SYNCHRO-NIZATION COMPLETE.
!!
WHAT THE --?!

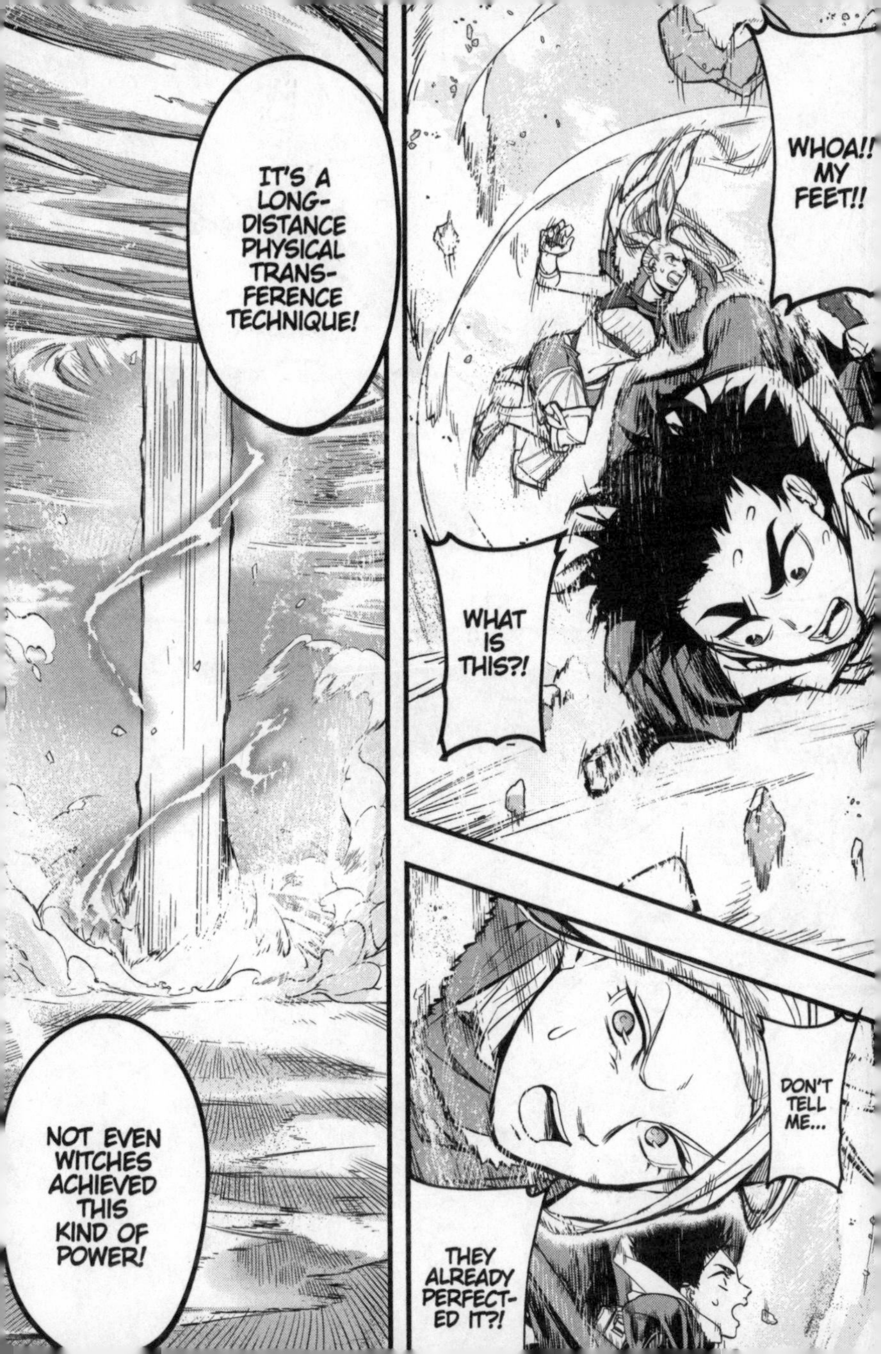
WHOA!! MY FEET!!
WHAT IS THIS?!
DON'T TELL ME...
THEY ALREADY PERFECTED IT?!
IT'S A LONG-DISTANCE PHYSICAL TRANSFERENCE TECHNIQUE!
NOT EVEN WITCHES ACHIEVED THIS KIND OF POWER!

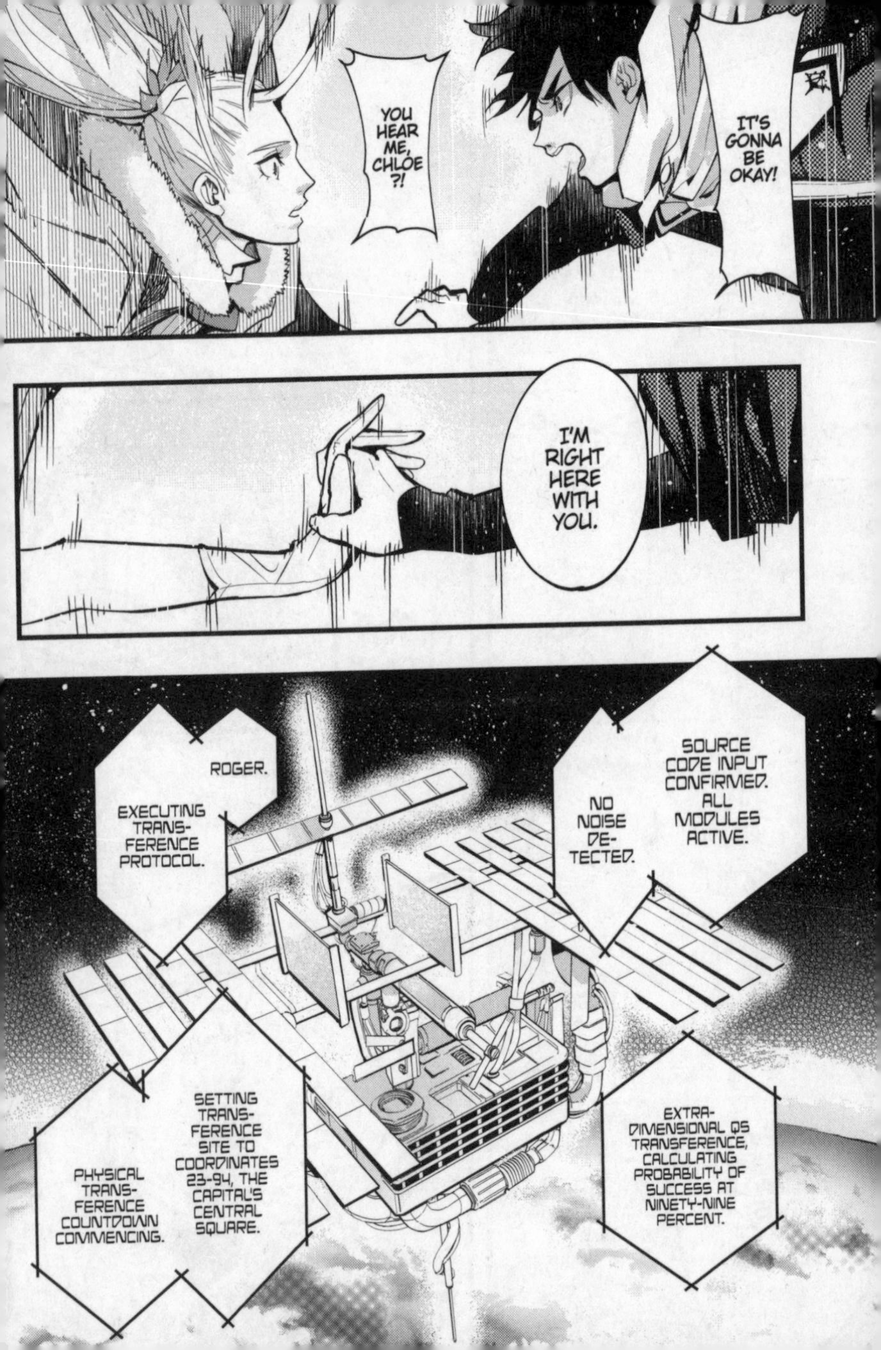
IT'S GONNA BE OKAY!
YOU HEAR ME, CHLOE?!
I'M RIGHT HERE WITH YOU.
SOURCE CODE INPUT CONFIRMED. ALL MODULES ACTIVE.
NO NOISE DETECTED.
ROGER.
EXECUTING TRANSFERENCE PROTOCOL.
EXTRA-DIMENSIONAL QS TRANSFERENCE, CALCULATING PROBABILITY OF SUCCESS AT NINETY-NINE PERCENT.
SETTING TRANSFERENCE SITE TO COORDINATES 23-94, THE CAPITAL'S CENTRAL SQUARE.
PHYSICAL TRANSFERENCE COUNTDOWN COMMENCING.

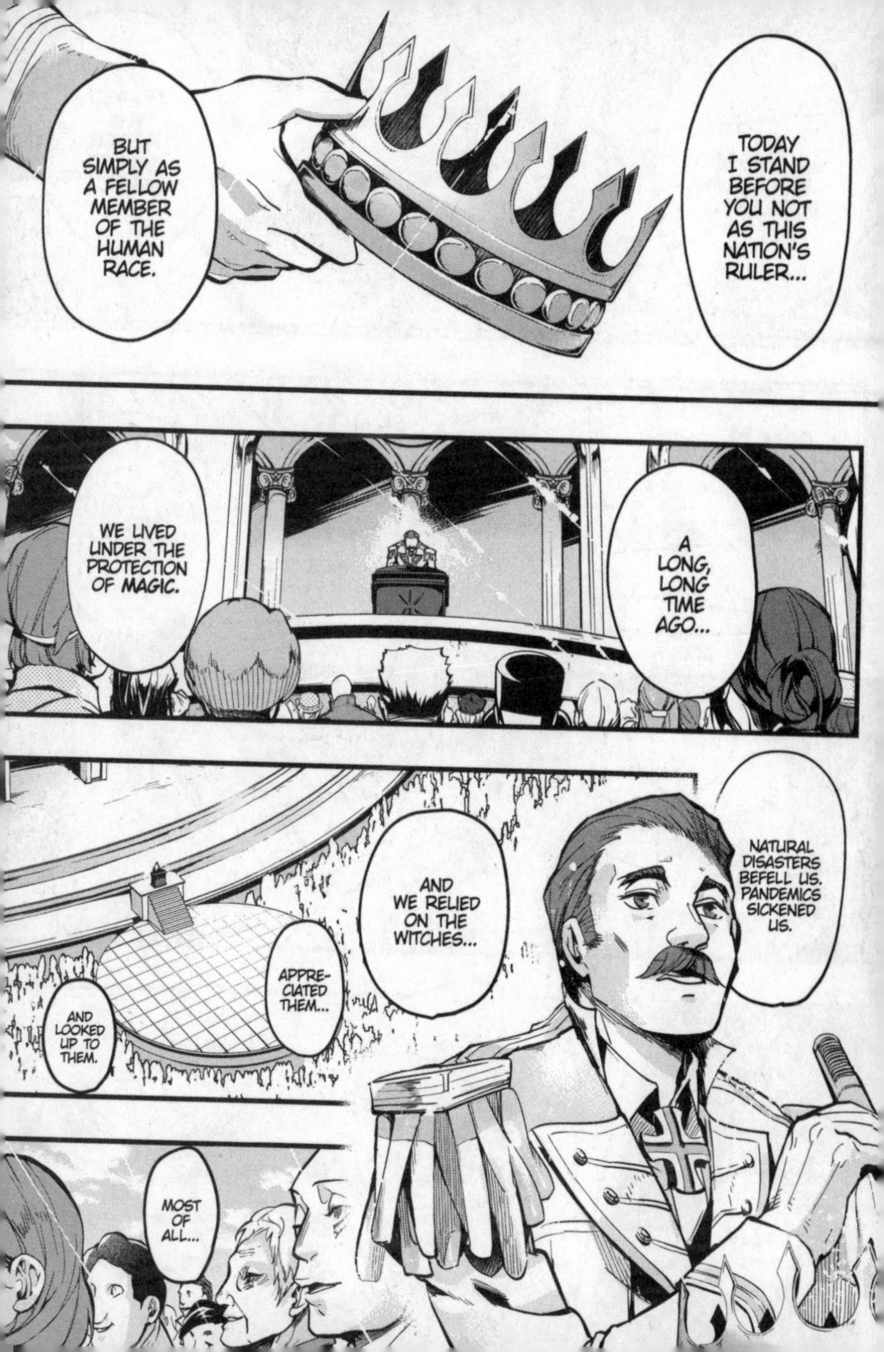
TODAY I STAND BEFORE YOU NOT AS THIS NATION'S RULER...
BUT SIMPLY AS A FELLOW MEMBER OF THE HUMAN RACE.
A LONG, LONG TIME AGO...
WE LIVED UNDER THE PROTECTION OF MAGIC.
NATURAL DISASTERS BEFELL US. PANDEMICS SICKENED US.
AND WE RELIED ON THE WITCHES...
APPRE-CIATED THEM...
AND LOOKED UP TO THEM.
MOST OF ALL...

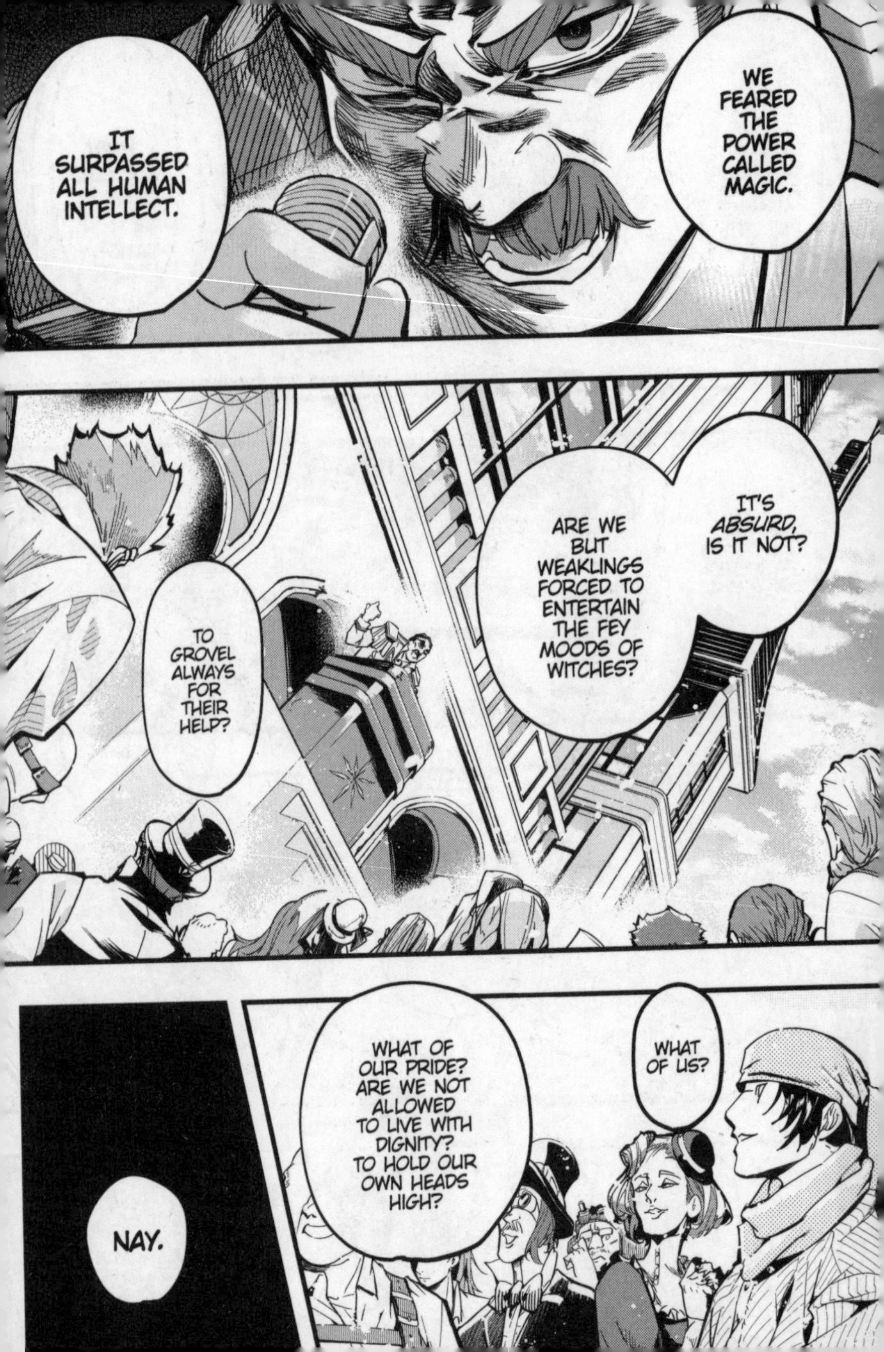
WE FEARED THE POWER CALLED MAGIC.
IT SURPASSED ALL HUMAN INTELLECT.
IT'S *ABSURD*, IS IT NOT?
ARE WE BUT WEAKLINGS FORCED TO ENTERTAIN THE FEY MOODS OF WITCHES?
TO GROVEL ALWAYS FOR THEIR HELP?
WHAT OF US?
WHAT OF OUR PRIDE? ARE WE NOT ALLOWED TO LIVE WITH DIGNITY? TO HOLD OUR OWN HEADS HIGH?
NAY.

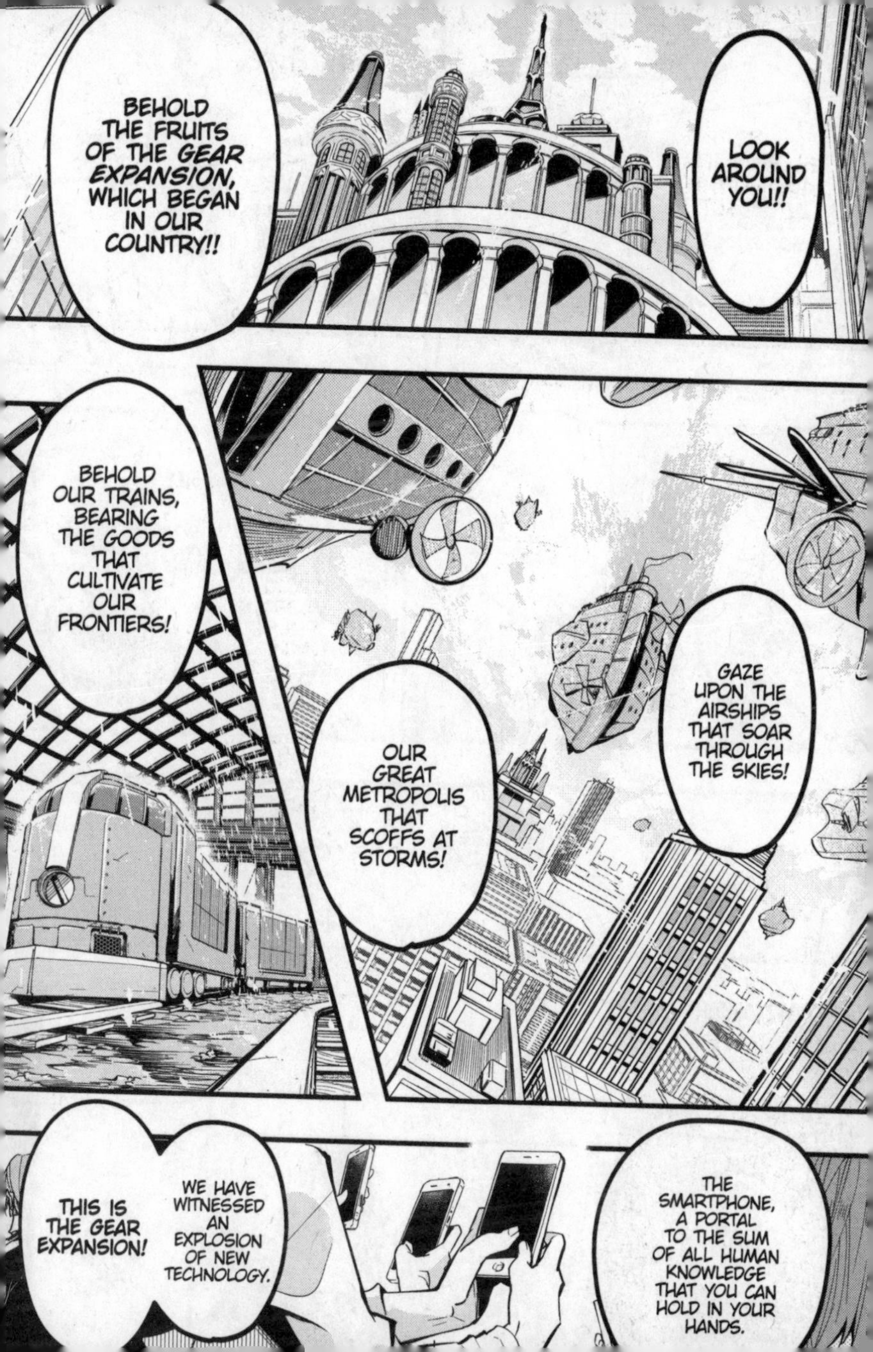
LOOK AROUND YOU!!
BEHOLD THE FRUITS OF THE *GEAR EXPANSION*, WHICH BEGAN IN OUR COUNTRY!!
GAZE UPON THE AIRSHIPS THAT SOAR THROUGH THE SKIES!
OUR GREAT METROPOLIS THAT SCOFFS AT STORMS!
BEHOLD OUR TRAINS, BEARING THE GOODS THAT CULTIVATE OUR FRONTIERS!
THE SMARTPHONE, A PORTAL TO THE SUM OF ALL HUMAN KNOWLEDGE THAT YOU CAN HOLD IN YOUR HANDS.
WE HAVE WITNESSED AN EXPLOSION OF NEW TECHNOLOGY.
THIS IS THE GEAR EXPANSION!

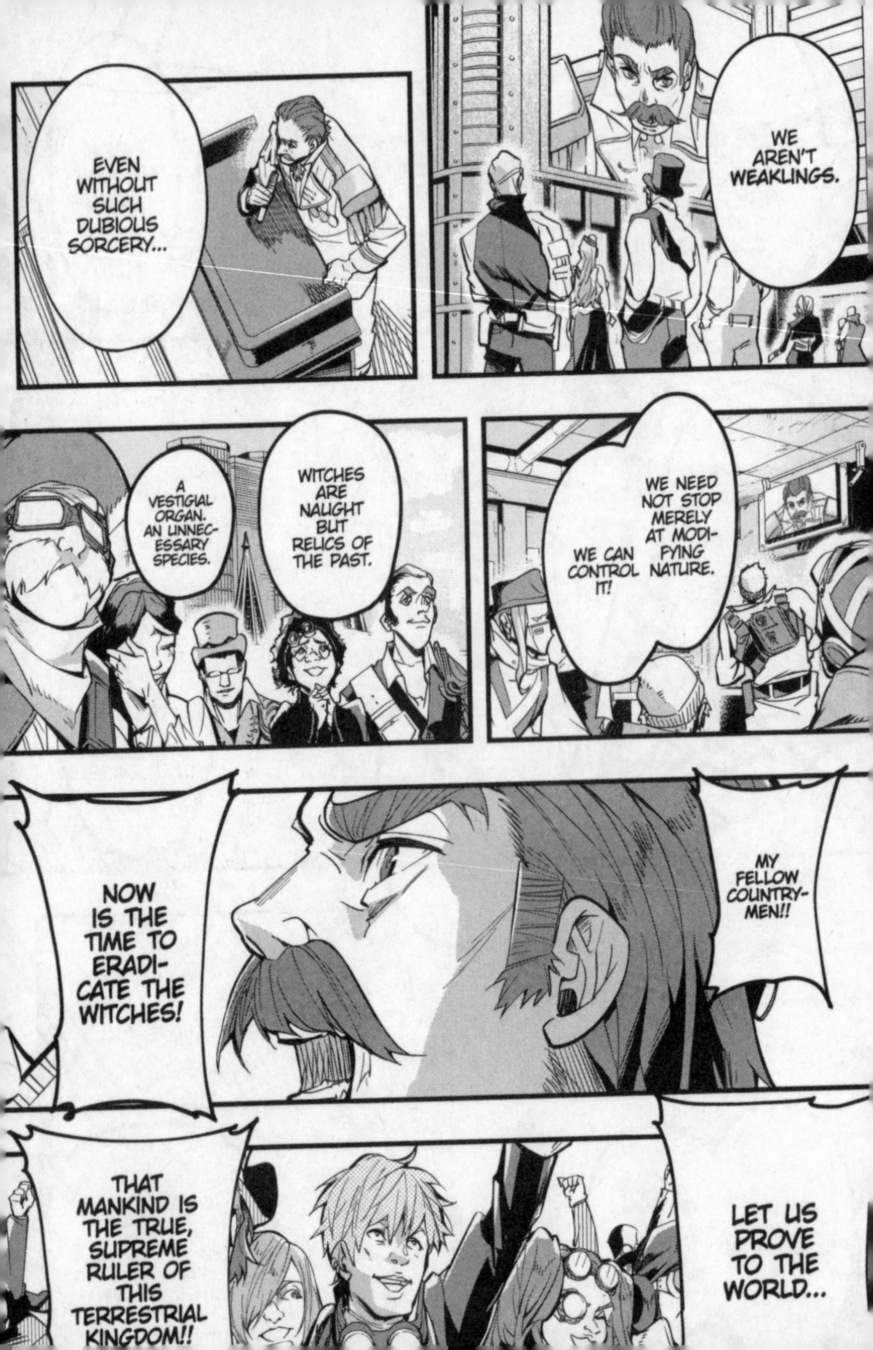
WE AREN'T WEAKLINGS.
EVEN WITHOUT SUCH DUBIOUS SORCERY...
WE NEED NOT STOP MERELY AT MODIFYING NATURE.
WE CAN CONTROL IT!
WITCHES ARE NAUGHT BUT RELICS OF THE PAST.
A VESTIGIAL ORGAN. AN UNNECESSARY SPECIES.
MY FELLOW COUNTRYMEN!!
NOW IS THE TIME TO ERADICATE THE WITCHES!
LET US PROVE TO THE WORLD...
THAT MANKIND IS THE TRUE, SUPREME RULER OF THIS TERRESTRIAL KINGDOM!!

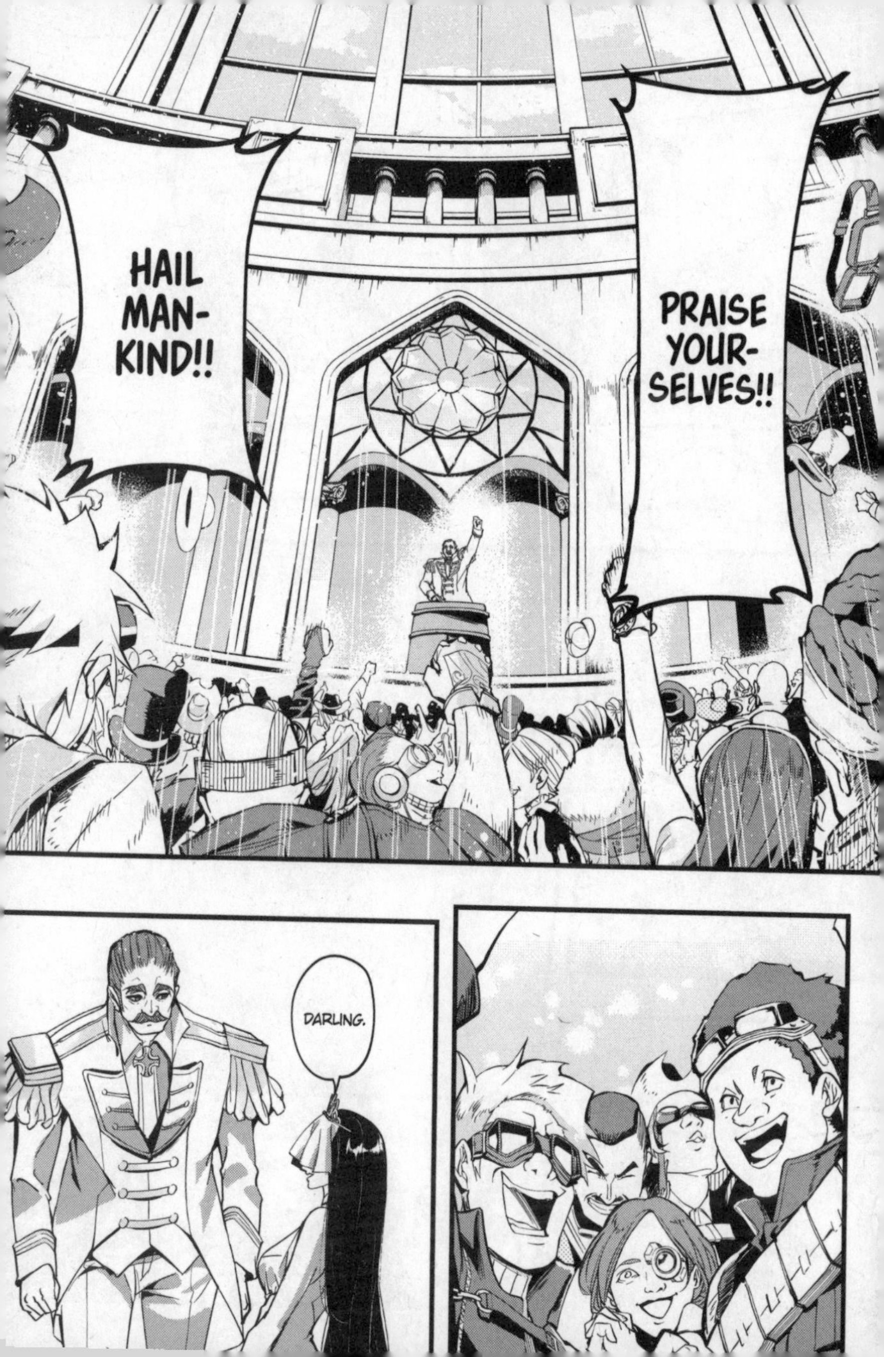
PRAISE YOUR-SELVES!!
HAIL MAN-KIND!!
DARLING.

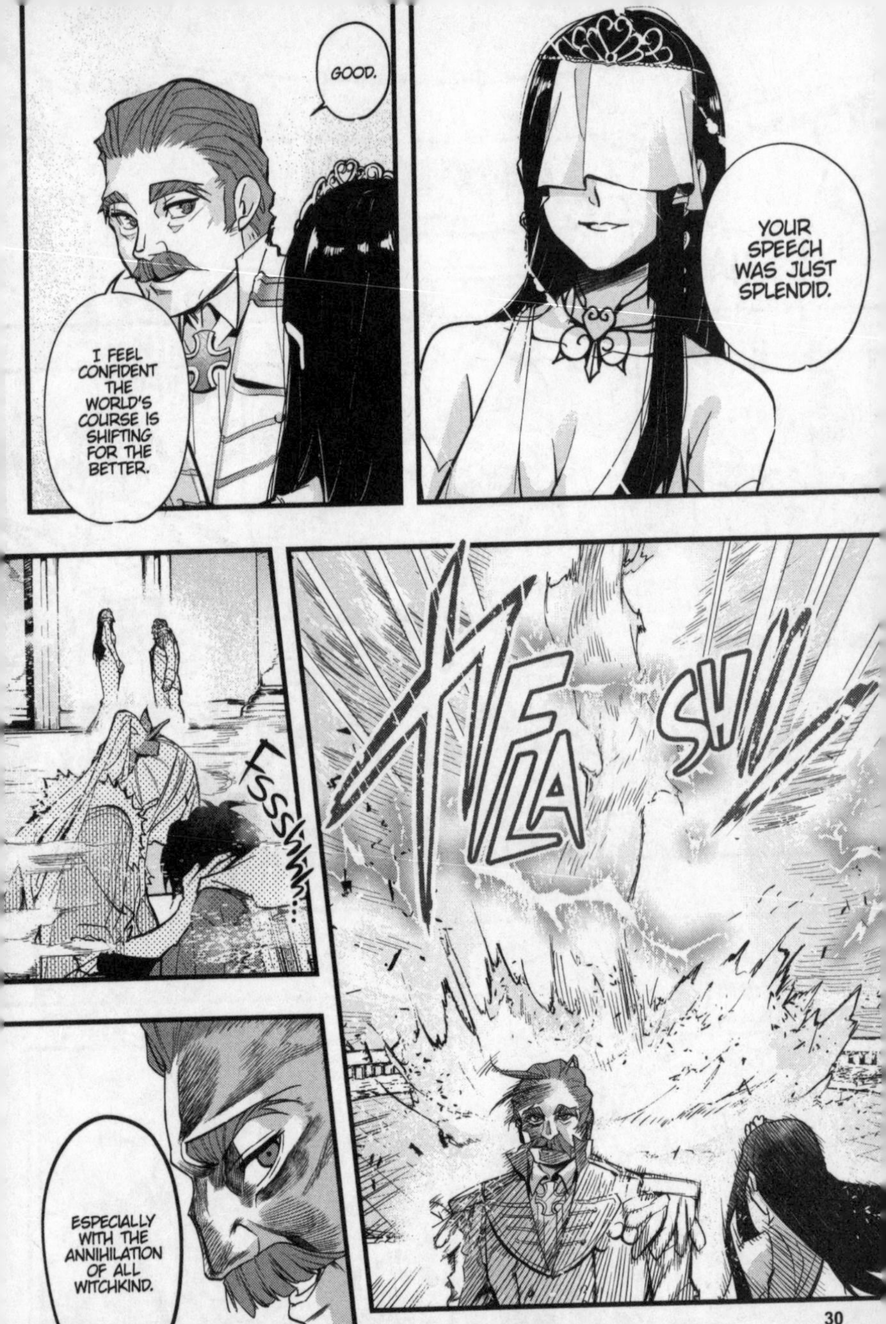
YOUR SPEECH WAS JUST SPLENDID.
GOOD.
I FEEL CONFIDENT THE WORLD'S COURSE IS SHIFTING FOR THE BETTER.
FLASH
Fssshhh...
ESPECIALLY WITH THE ANNIHILATION OF ALL WITCHKIND.

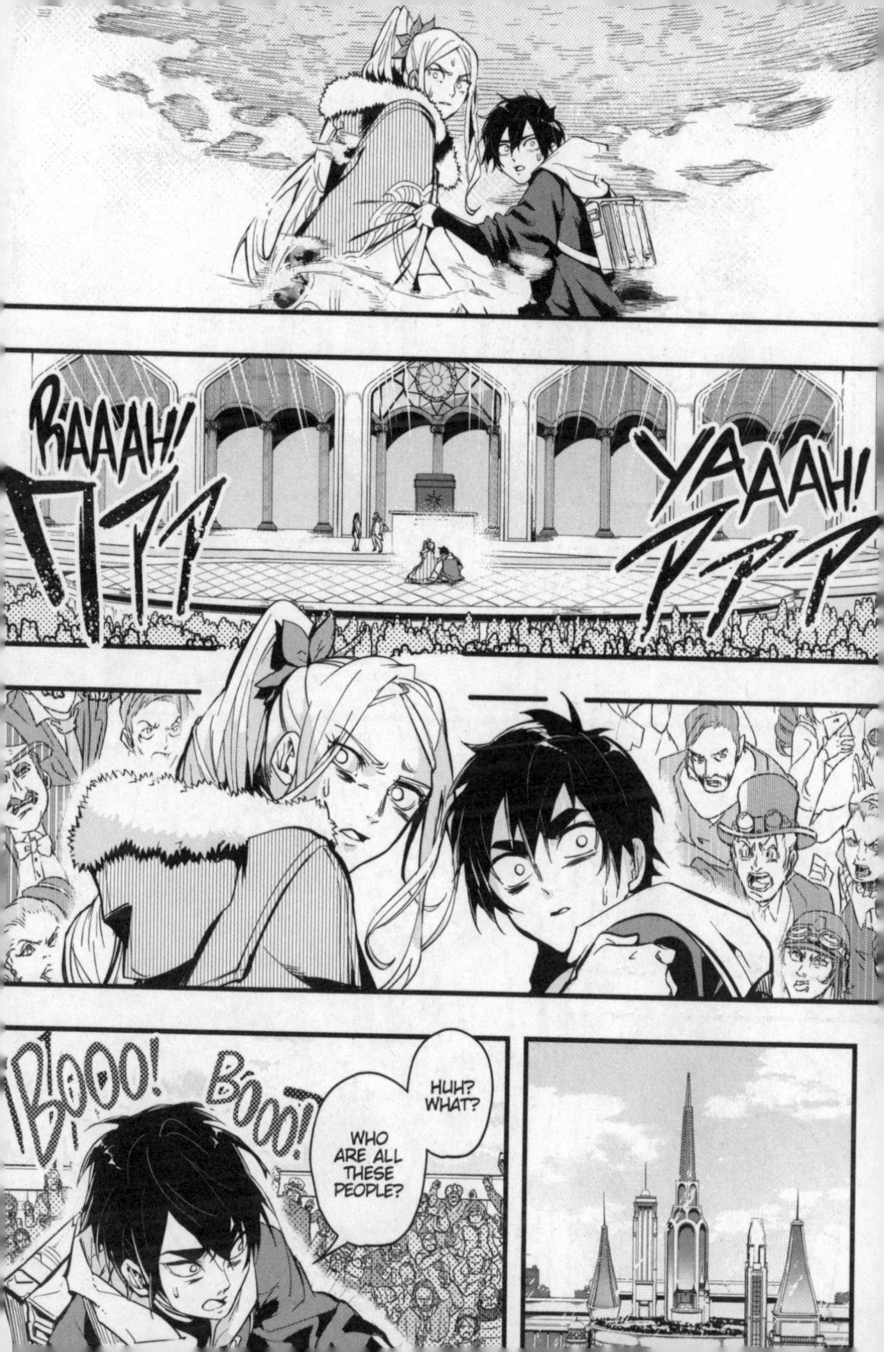
YAAAH!
アァァ
RAAAH!
ワァァ
HUH? WHAT?
WHO ARE ALL THESE PEOPLE?
BOOO!
BOOO!

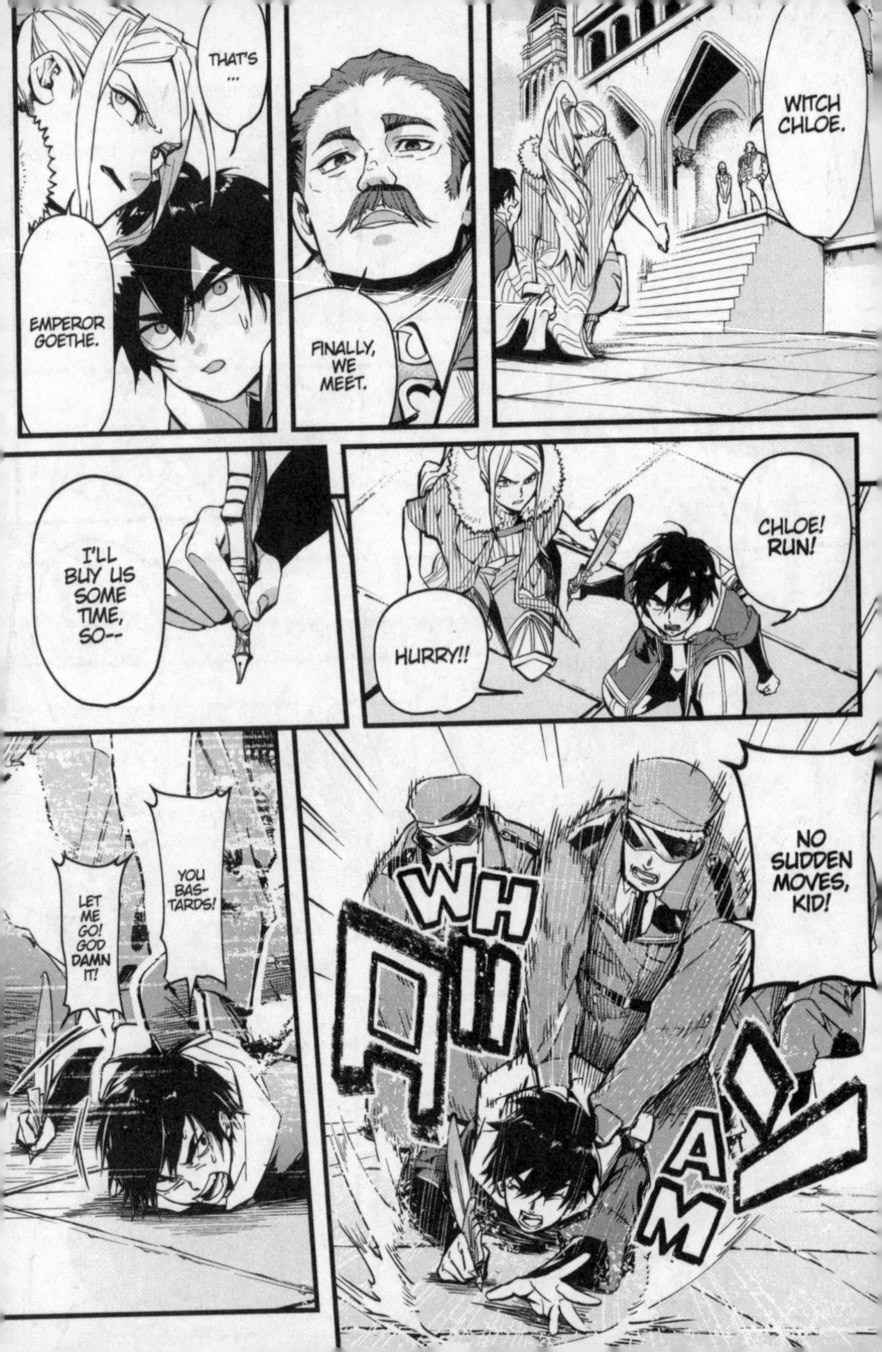
WITCH CHLOE.
FINALLY, WE MEET.
THAT'S ...
EMPEROR GOETHE.
CHLOE! RUN!
HURRY!!
I'LL BUY US SOME TIME, SO--
NO SUDDEN MOVES, KID!
WHAM
YOU BAS-TARDS!
LET ME GO! GOD DAMN IT!

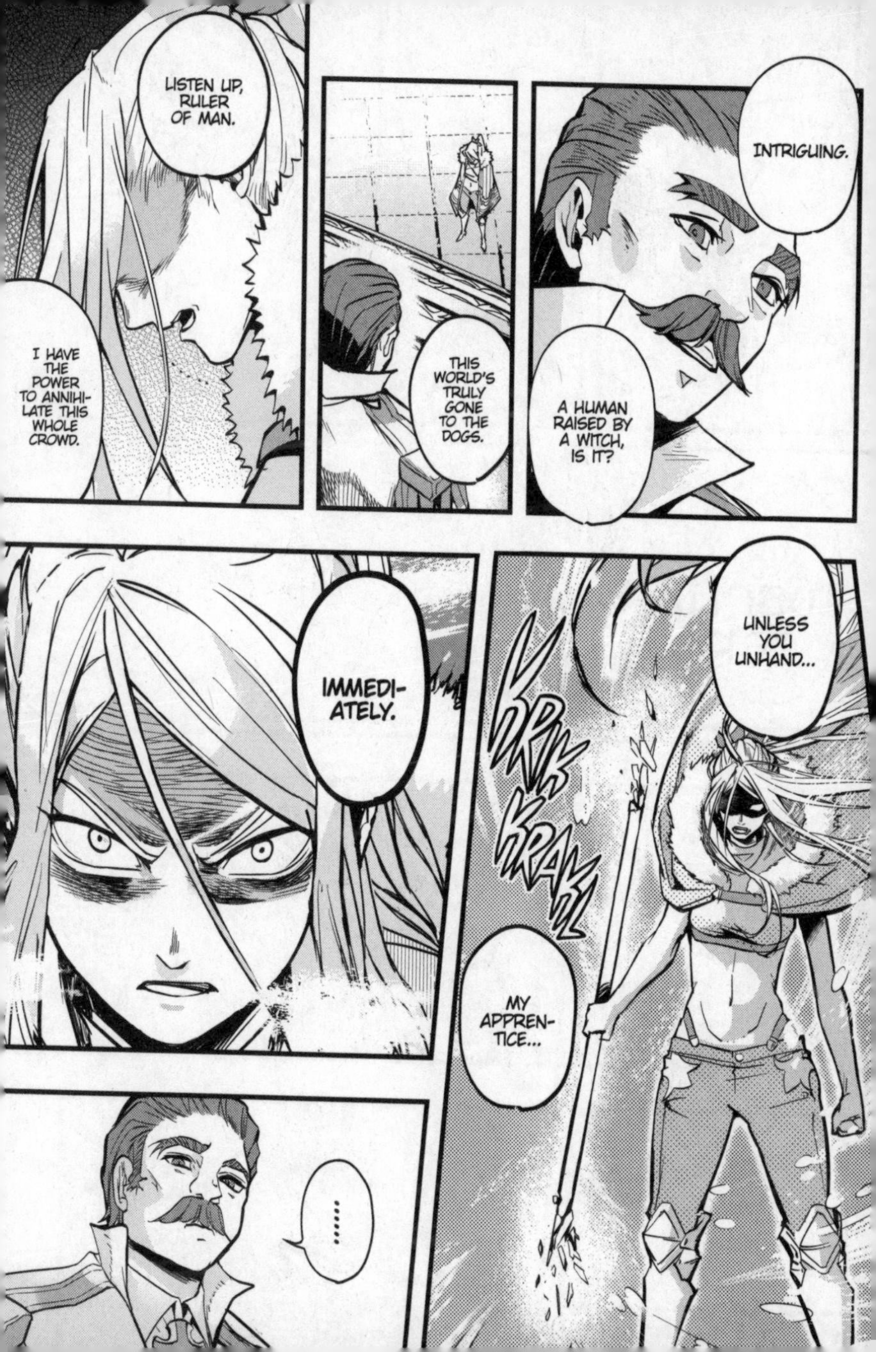
INTRIGUING.
A HUMAN RAISED BY A WITCH, IS IT?
THIS WORLD'S TRULY GONE TO THE DOGS.
LISTEN UP, RULER OF MAN.
I HAVE THE POWER TO ANNIHILATE THIS WHOLE CROWD.
UNLESS YOU UNHAND...
KRIK KRAK
MY APPRENTICE...
IMMEDIATELY.
......

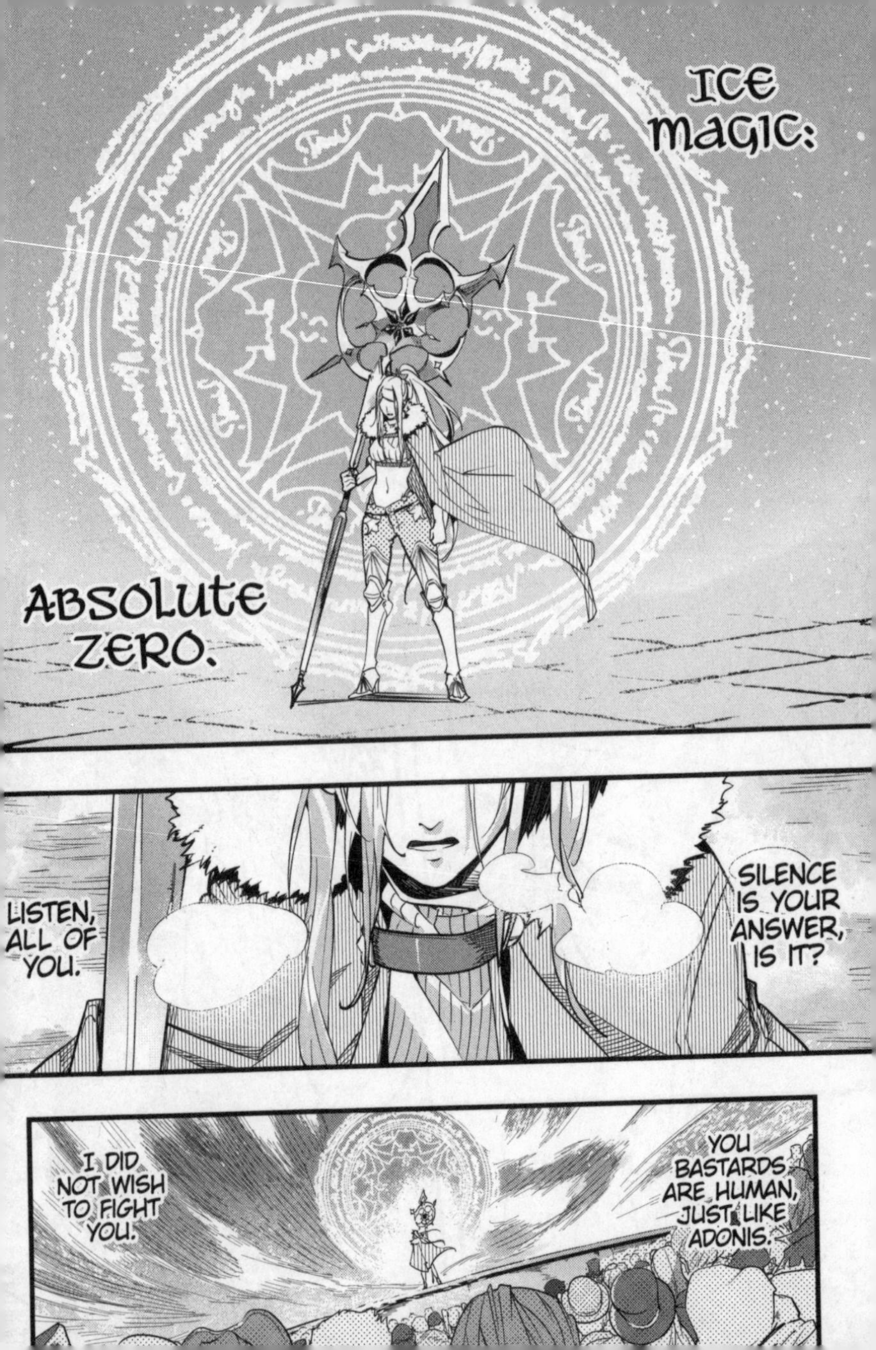
ICE MAGIC:
ABSOLUTE ZERO.
SILENCE IS YOUR ANSWER, IS IT?
LISTEN, ALL OF YOU.
YOU BASTARDS ARE HUMAN, JUST LIKE ADONIS.
I DID NOT WISH TO FIGHT YOU.

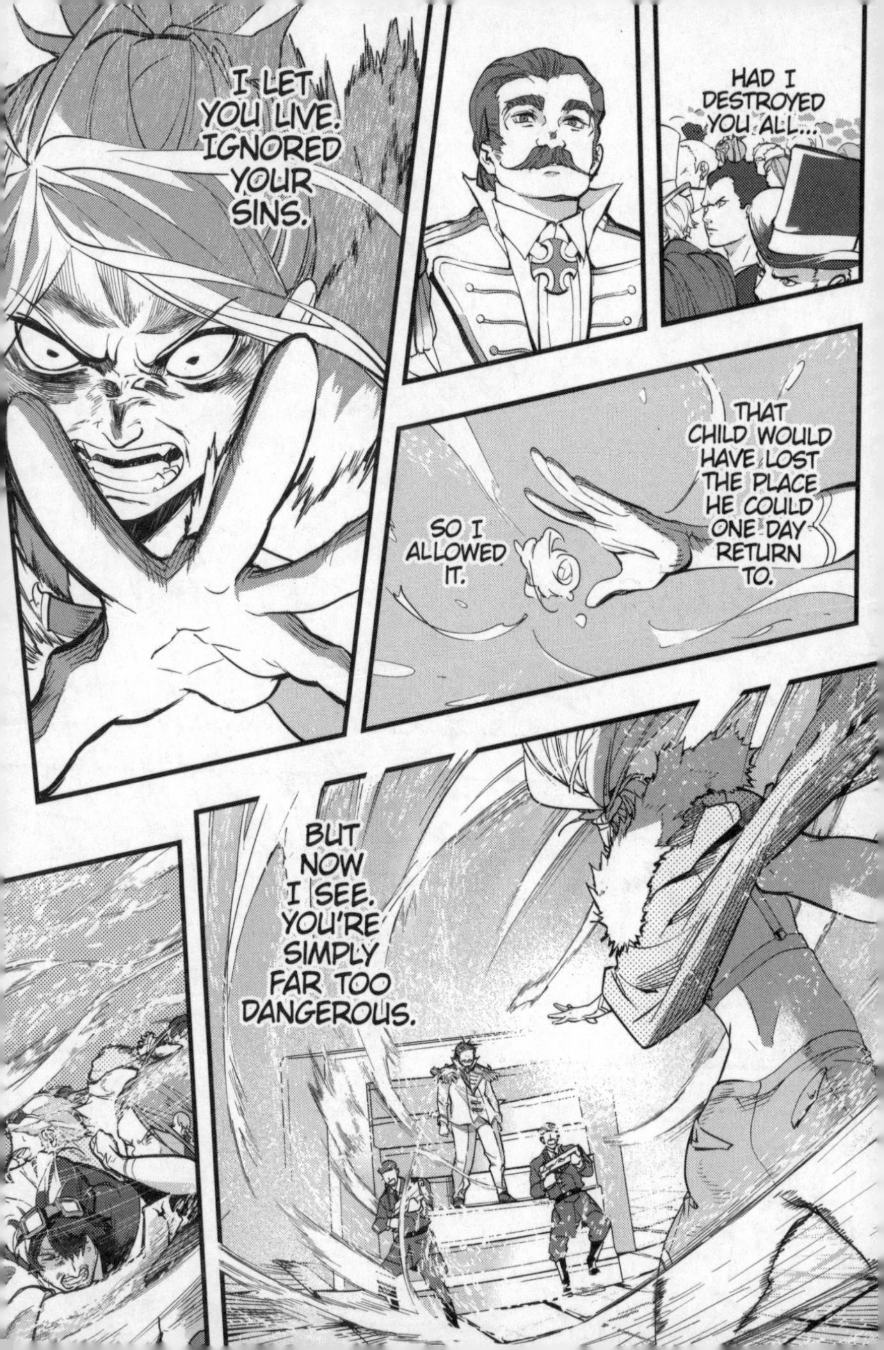
HAD I DESTROYED YOU ALL...
THAT CHILD WOULD HAVE LOST THE PLACE HE COULD ONE DAY RETURN TO.
SO I ALLOWED IT.
I LET YOU LIVE. IGNORED YOUR SINS.
BUT NOW I SEE. YOU'RE SIMPLY FAR TOO DANGEROUS.

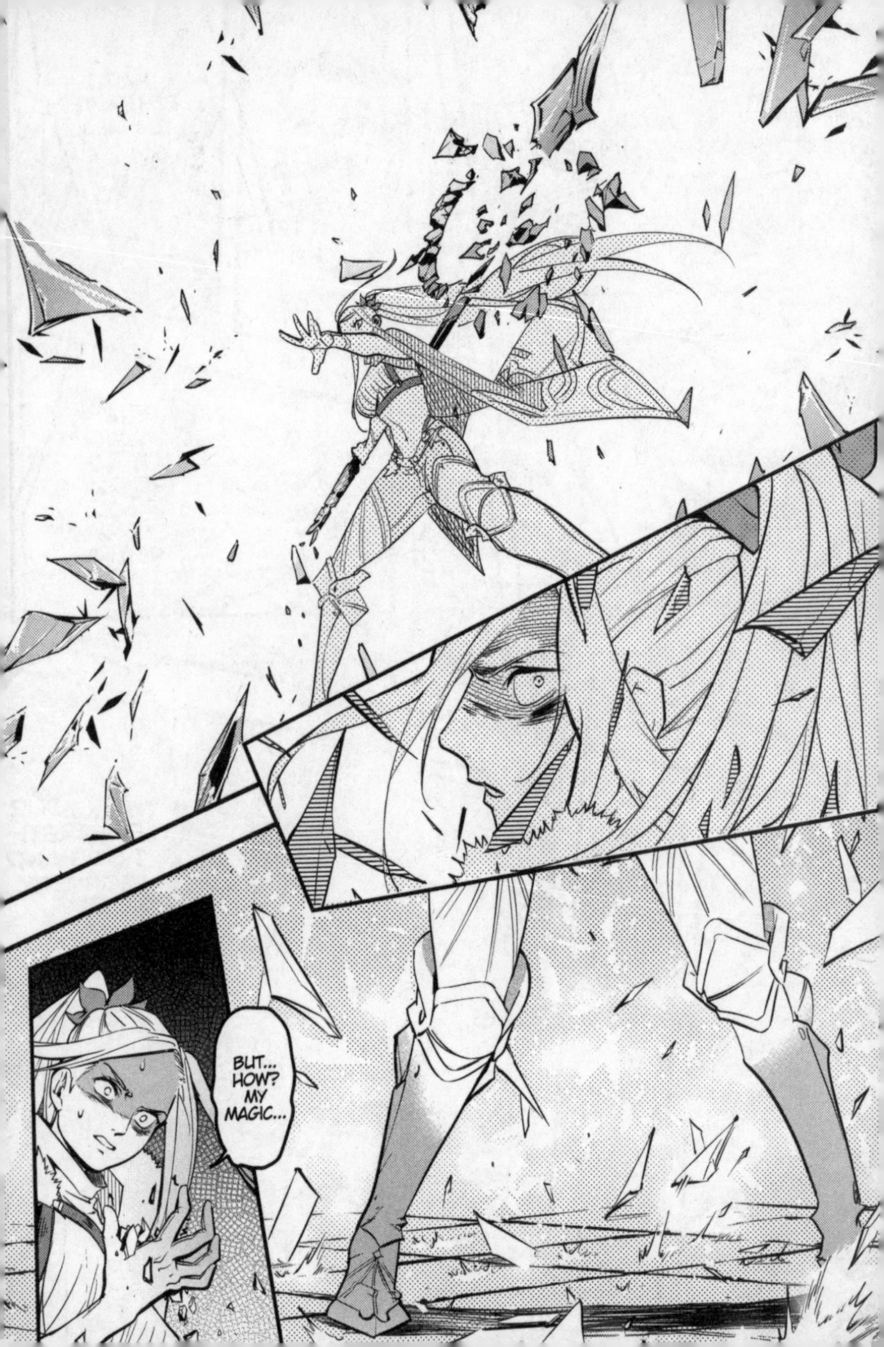
BUT... HOW? MY MAGIC...

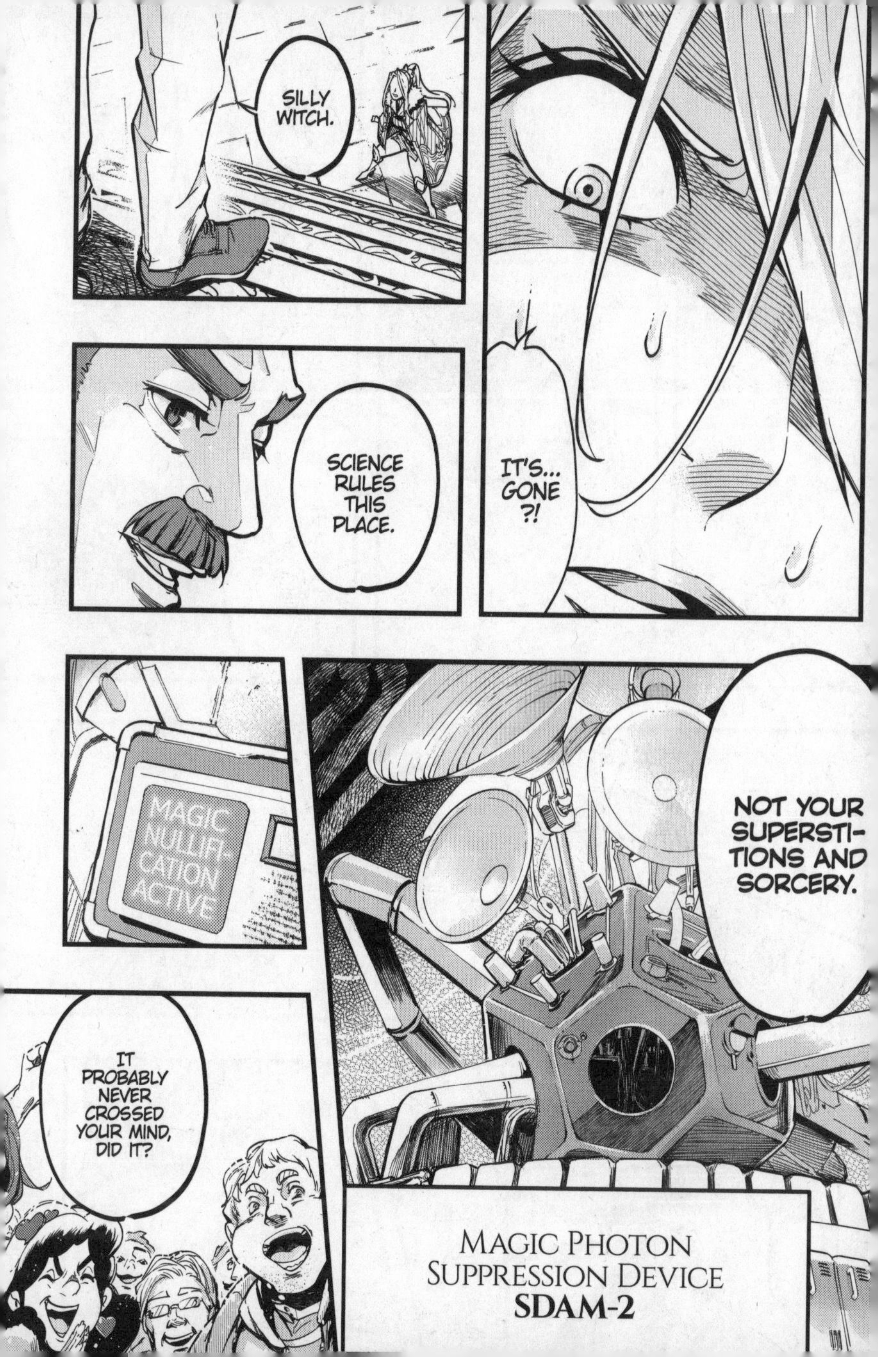
IT'S... GONE?!
SILLY WITCH.
SCIENCE RULES THIS PLACE.
NOT YOUR SUPERSTITIONS AND SORCERY.
MAGIC PHOTON SUPPRESSION DEVICE SDAM-2
MAGIC NULLIFICATION ACTIVE
IT PROBABLY NEVER CROSSED YOUR MIND, DID IT?

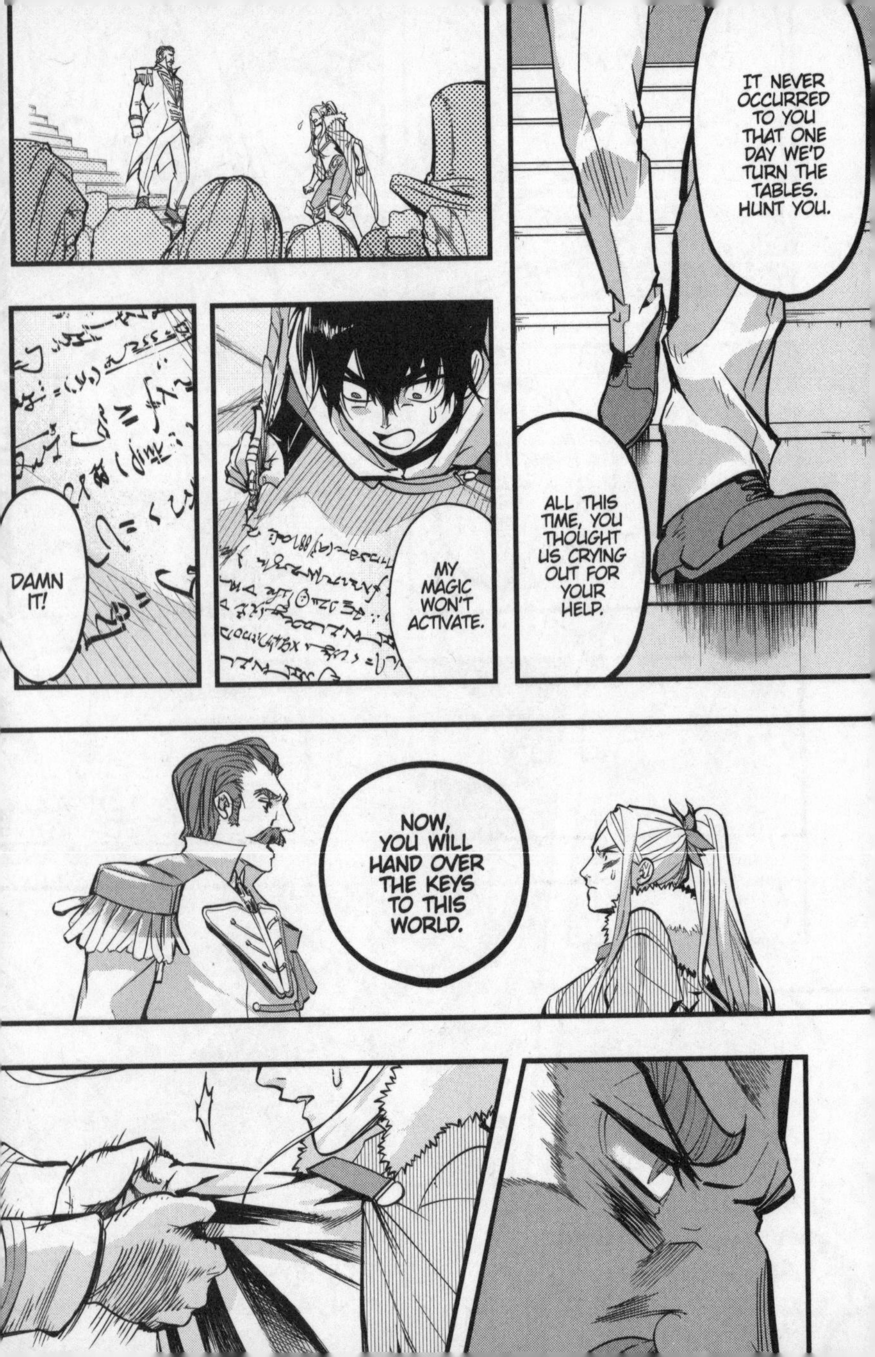
IT NEVER OCCURRED TO YOU THAT ONE DAY WE'D TURN THE TABLES. HUNT YOU.
ALL THIS TIME, YOU THOUGHT US CRYING OUT FOR YOUR HELP.
MY MAGIC WON'T ACTIVATE.
DAMN IT!
NOW, YOU WILL HAND OVER THE KEYS TO THIS WORLD.

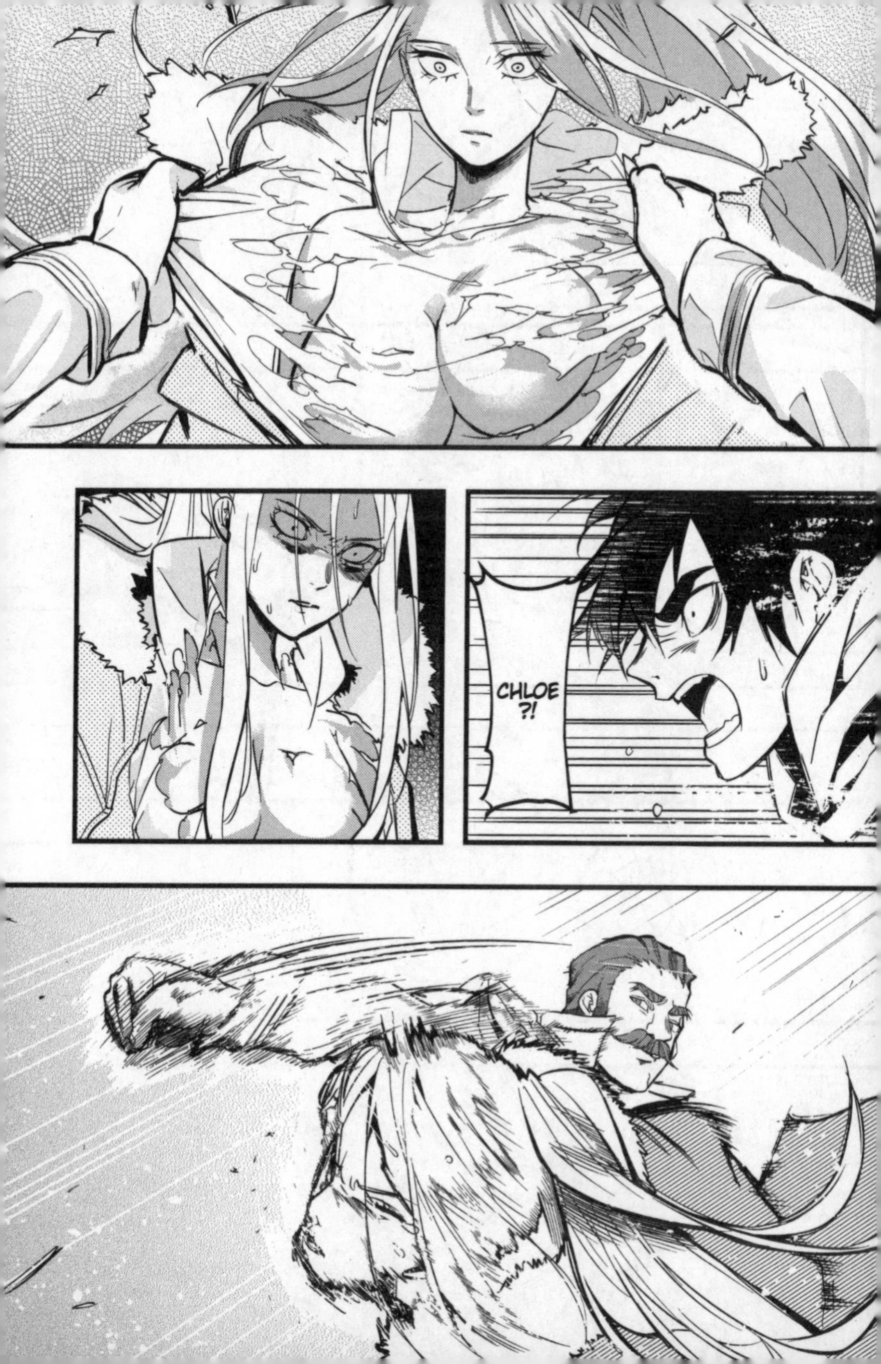
CHLOE ?!

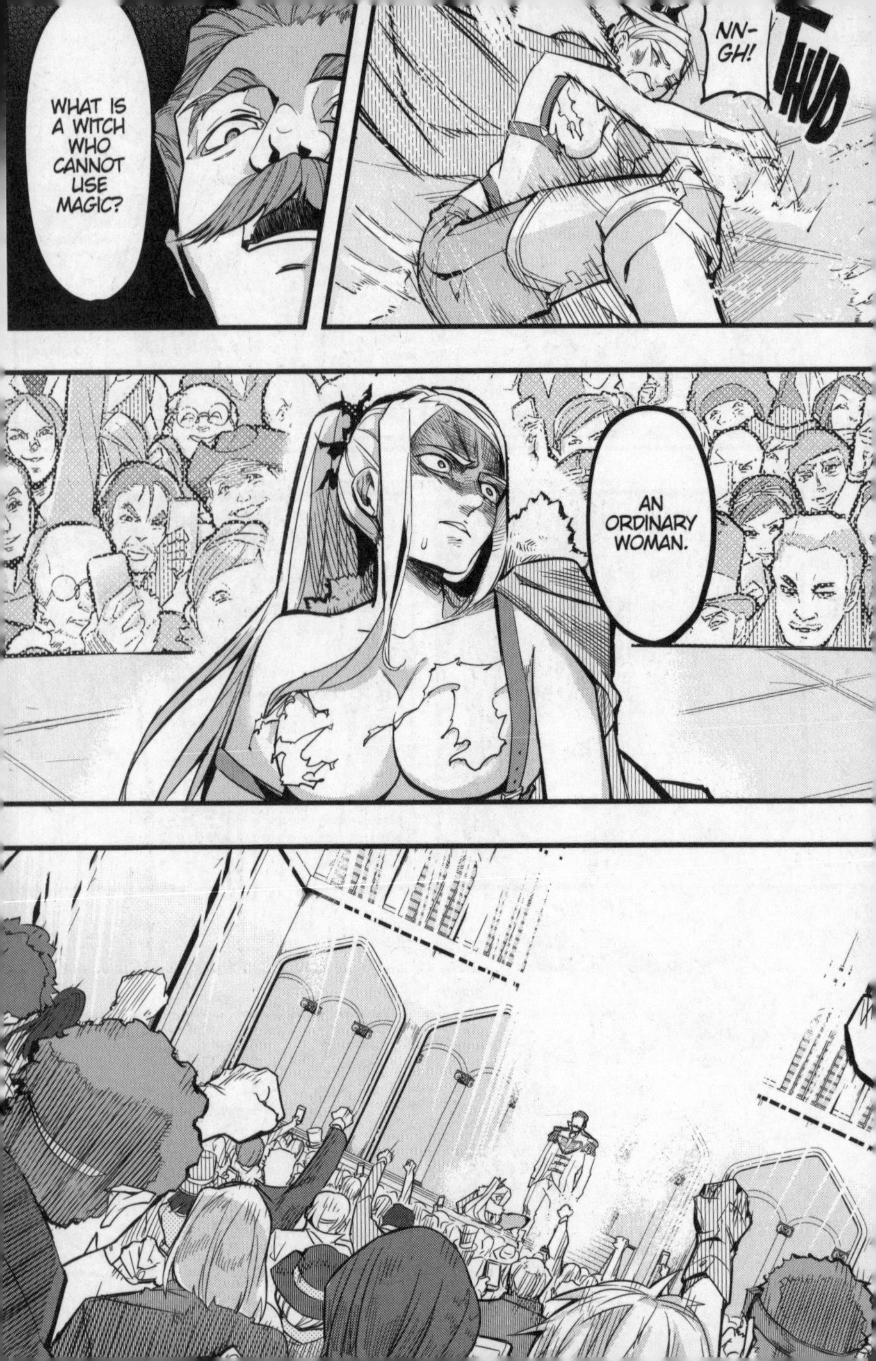
NN-GH!
THUD
WHAT IS A WITCH WHO CANNOT USE MAGIC?
AN ORDINARY WOMAN.

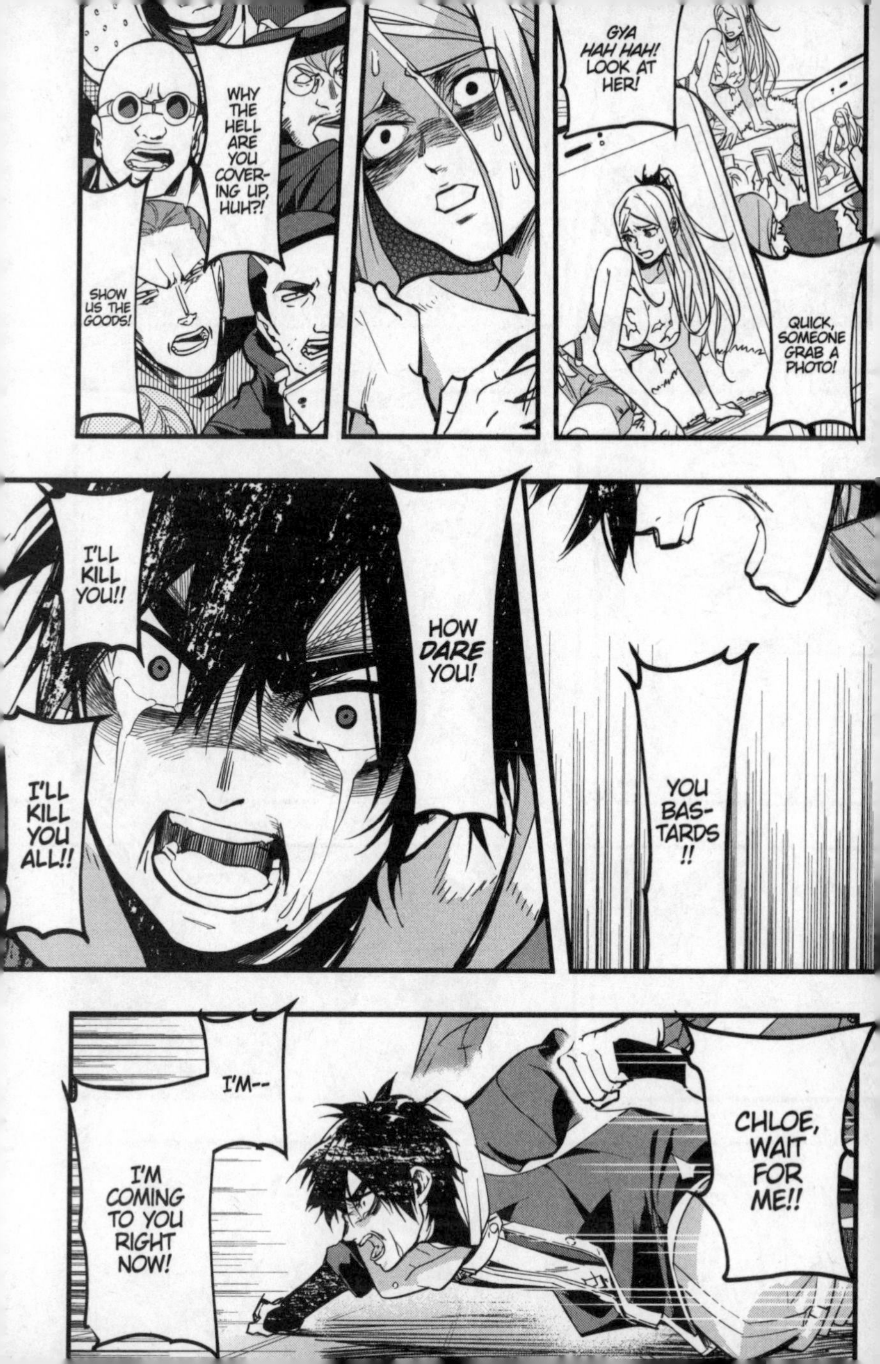
GYA HAH HAH! LOOK AT HER!
QUICK, SOMEONE GRAB A PHOTO!
WHY THE HELL ARE YOU COVERING UP, HUH?!
SHOW US THE GOODS!
YOU BASTARDS!!
HOW DARE YOU!
I'LL KILL YOU!!
I'LL KILL YOU ALL!!
CHLOE, WAIT FOR ME!!
I'M--
I'M COMING TO YOU RIGHT NOW!

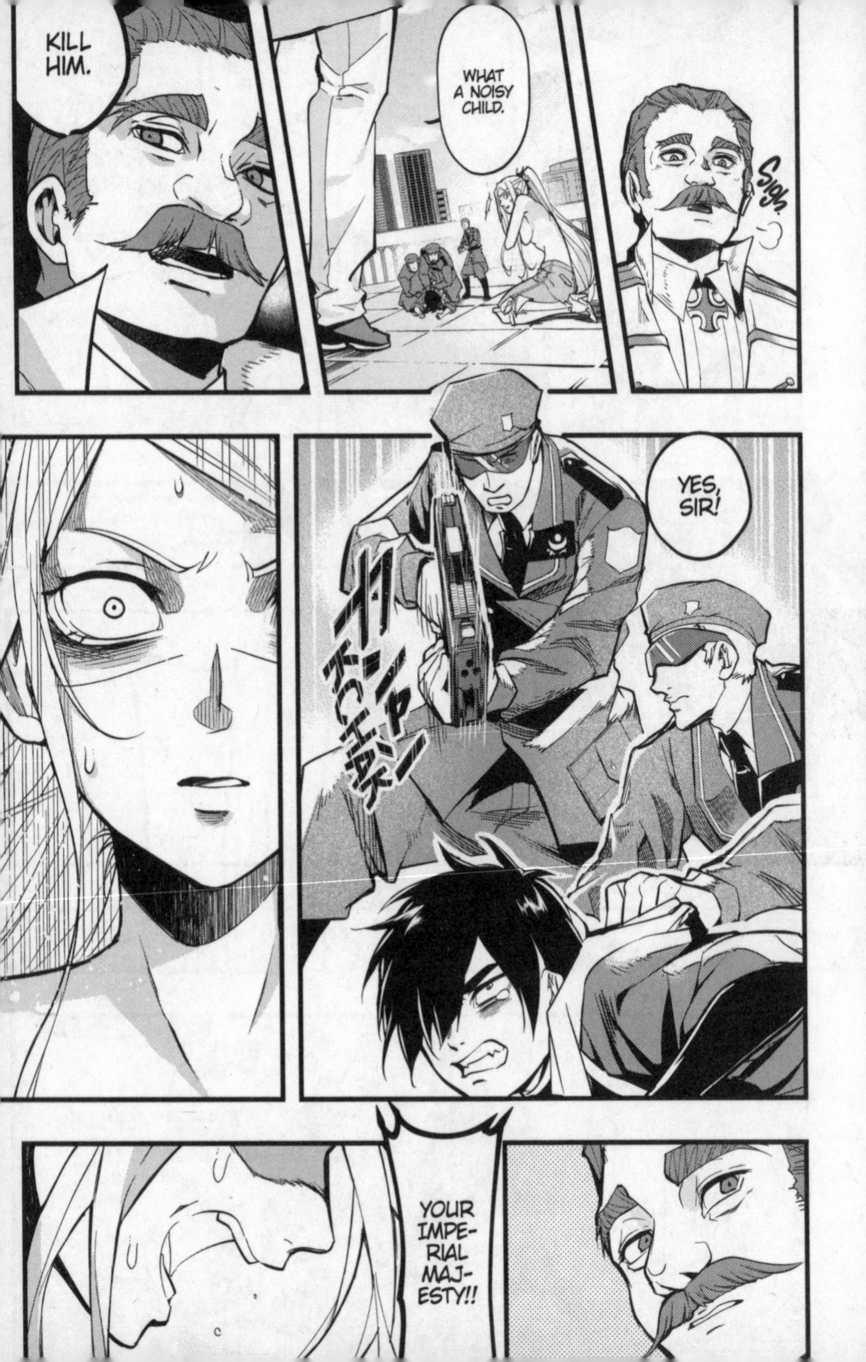
Sigh.
WHAT A NOISY CHILD.
KILL HIM.
YES, SIR!
KCHAK
YOUR IMPERIAL MAJESTY!!

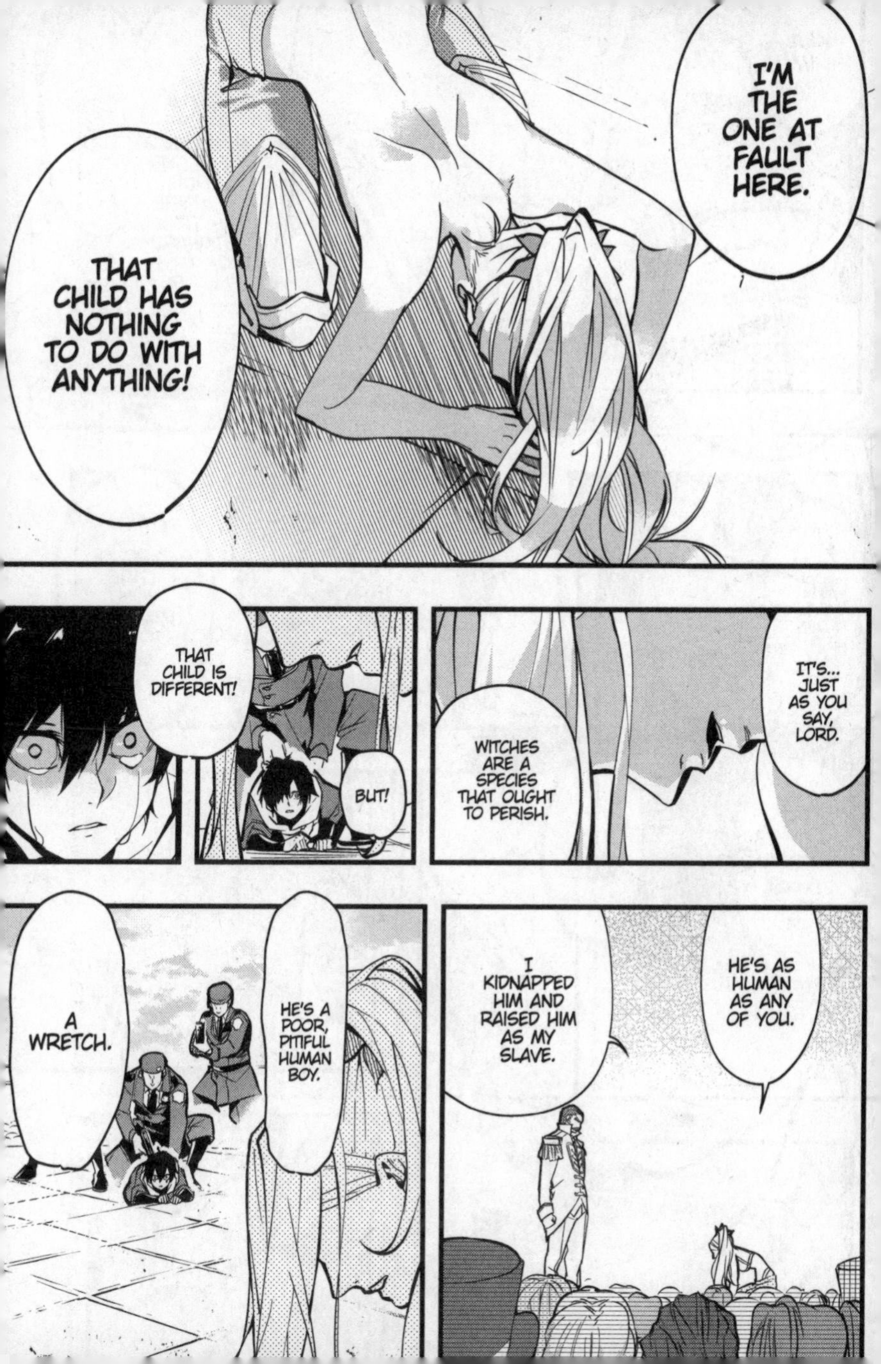
I'M THE ONE AT FAULT HERE.
THAT CHILD HAS NOTHING TO DO WITH ANYTHING!
IT'S... JUST AS YOU SAY, LORD.
WITCHES ARE A SPECIES THAT OUGHT TO PERISH.
BUT!
THAT CHILD IS DIFFERENT!
HE'S AS HUMAN AS ANY OF YOU.
I KIDNAPPED HIM AND RAISED HIM AS MY SLAVE.
HE'S A POOR, PITIFUL HUMAN BOY.
A WRETCH.

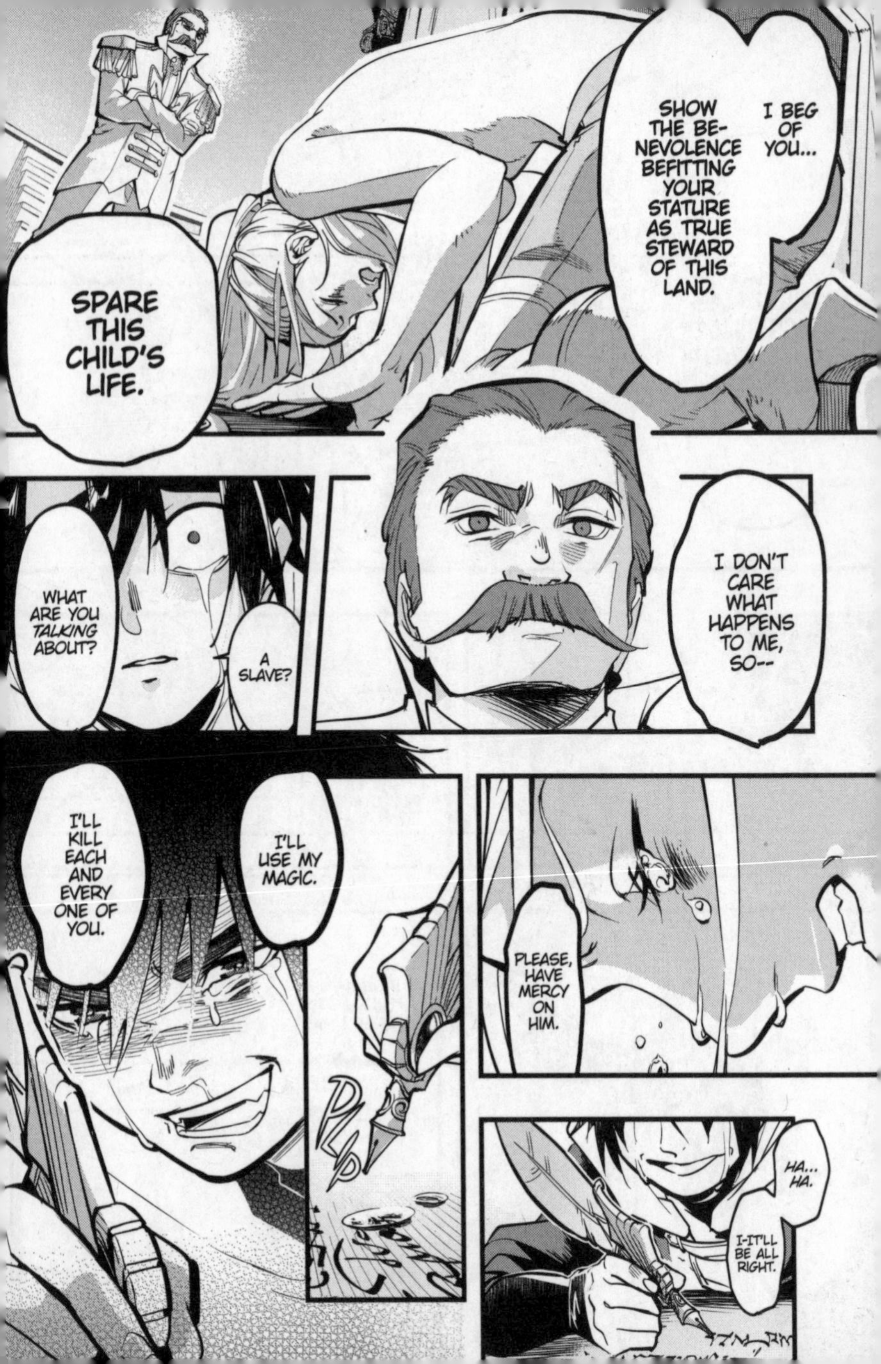

I BEG OF YOU...
SHOW THE BENEVOLENCE BEFITTING YOUR STATURE AS TRUE STEWARD OF THIS LAND.
SPARE THIS CHILD'S LIFE.
I DON'T CARE WHAT HAPPENS TO ME, SO--
A SLAVE?
WHAT ARE YOU *TALKING* ABOUT?
PLEASE, HAVE MERCY ON HIM.
HA... HA.
I-IT'LL BE ALL RIGHT.
PLIP
I'LL USE MY MAGIC.
I'LL KILL EACH AND EVERY ONE OF YOU.

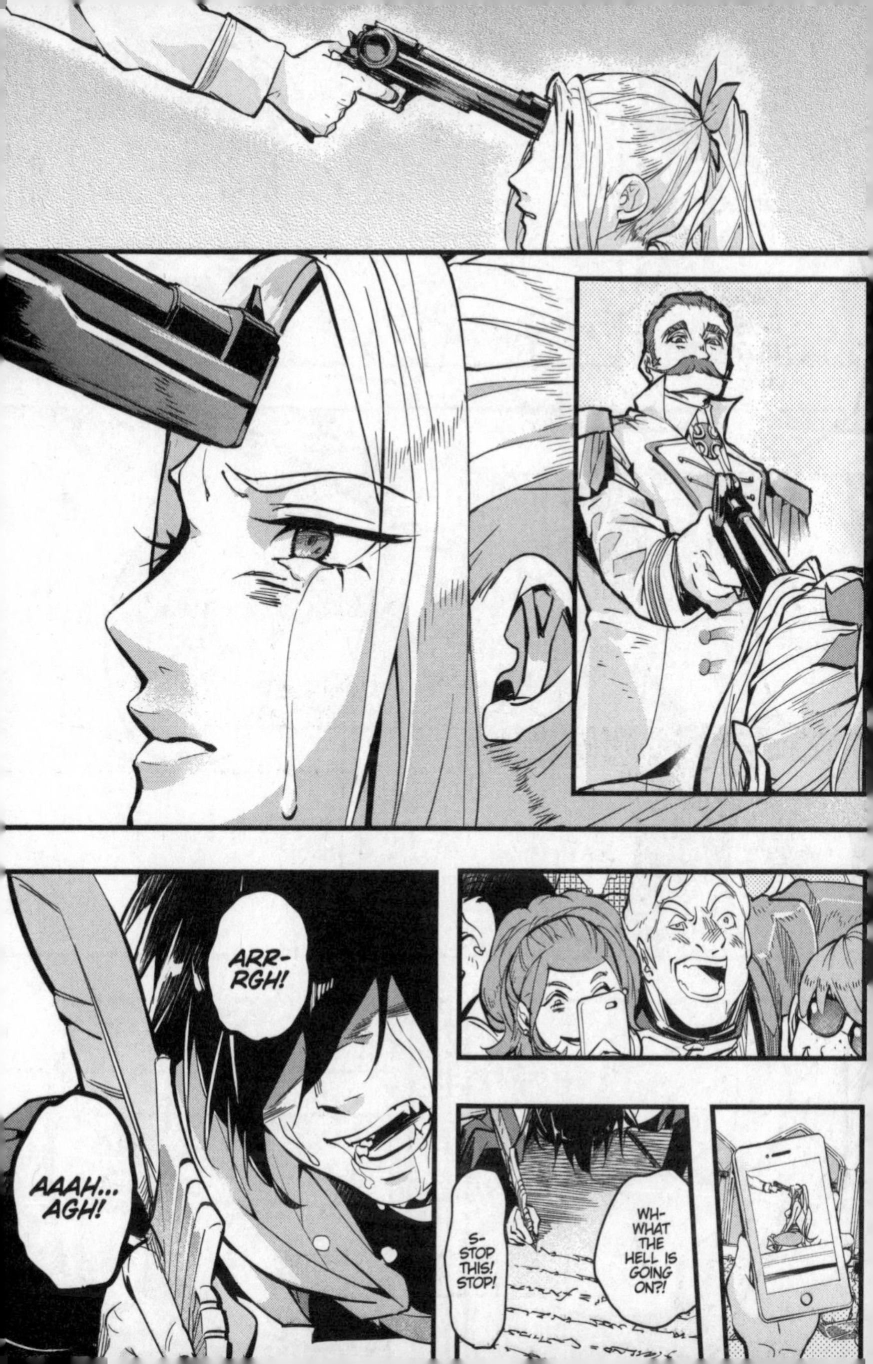
WH-WHAT THE HELL IS GOING ON?!
S-STOP THIS! STOP!
ARR-RGH!
AAAH... AGH!

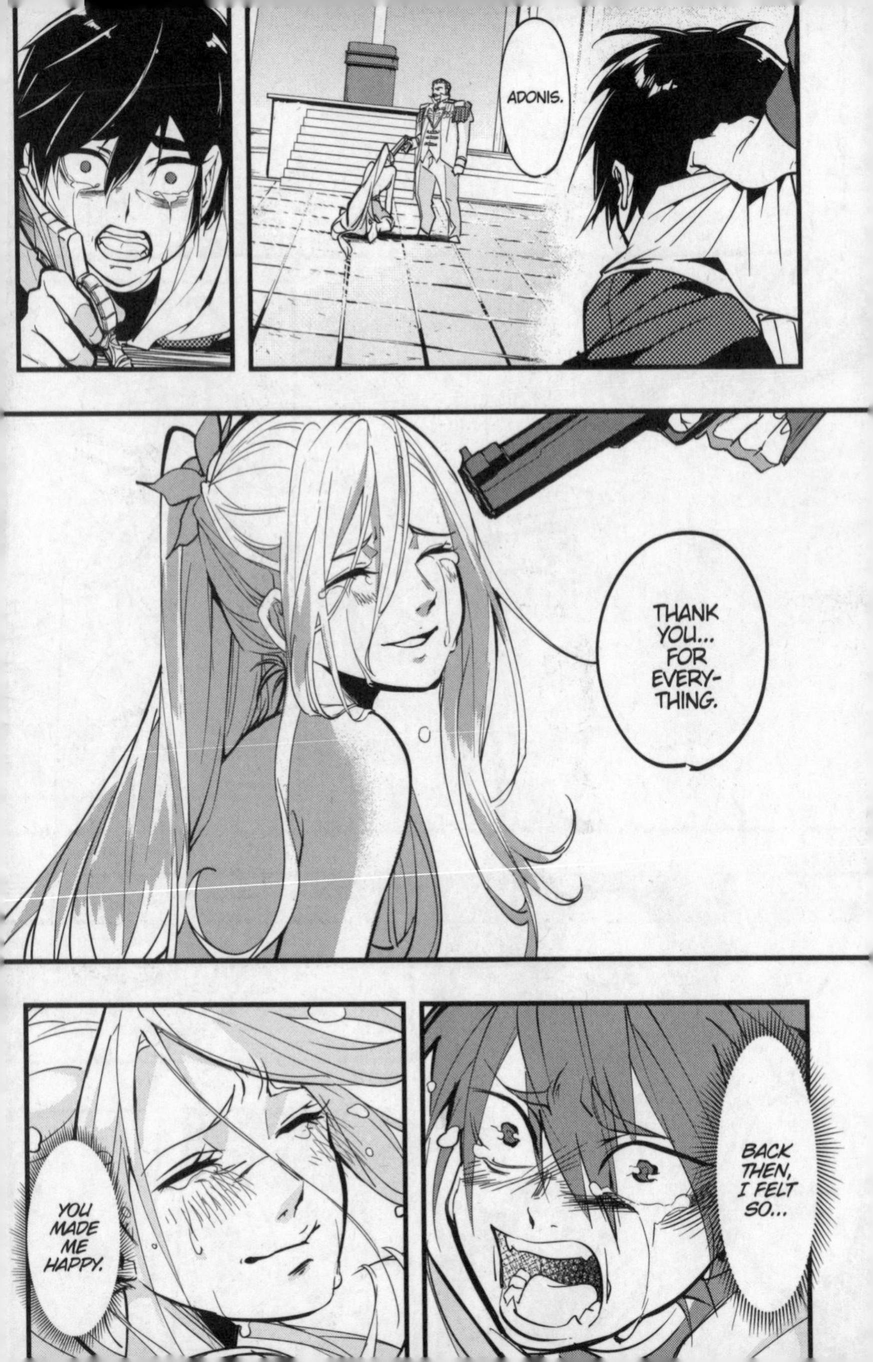
ADONIS.
THANK YOU... FOR EVERYTHING.
BACK THEN, I FELT SO...
YOU MADE ME HAPPY.

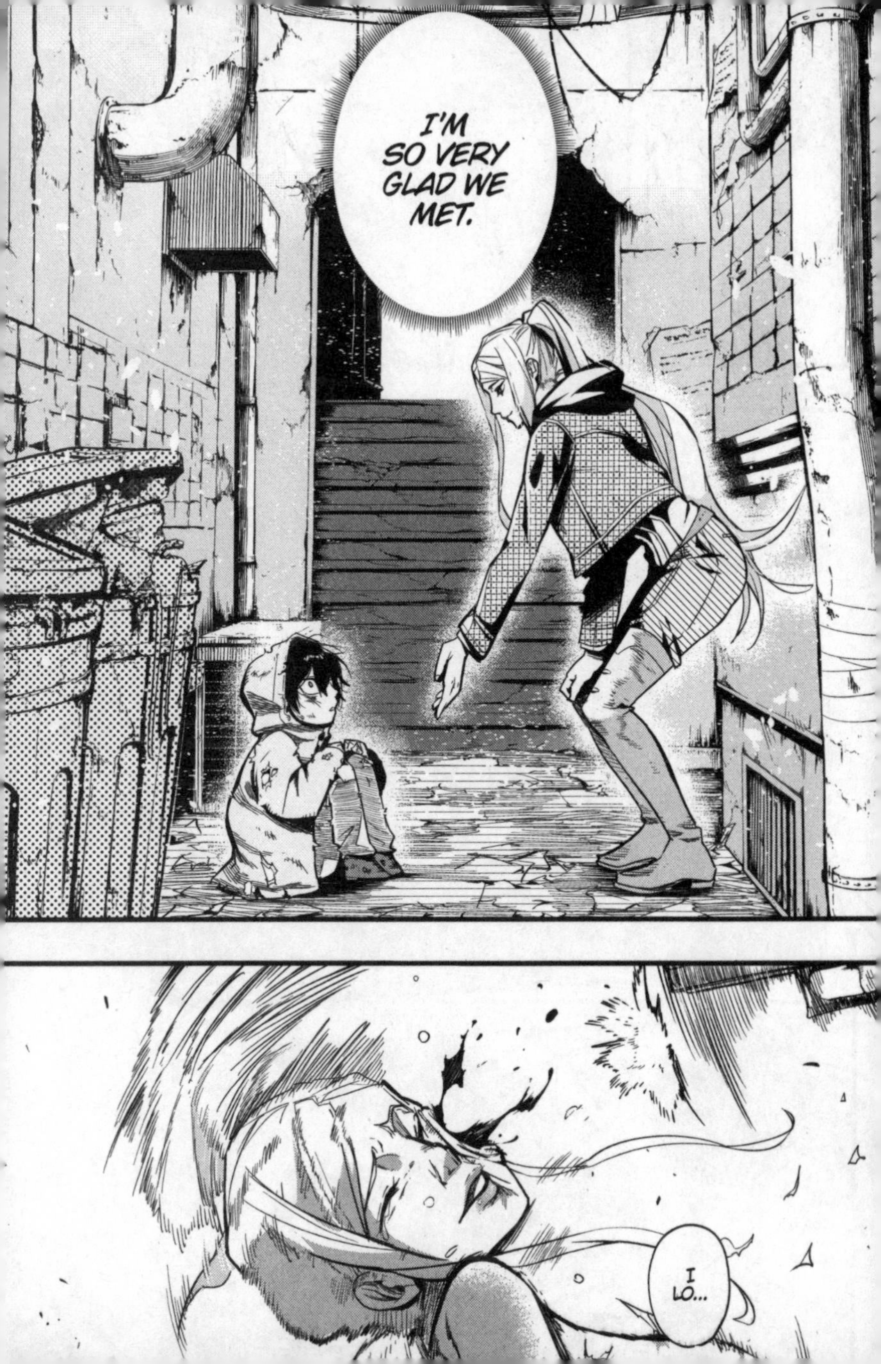
I'M SO VERY GLAD WE MET.
I LO...

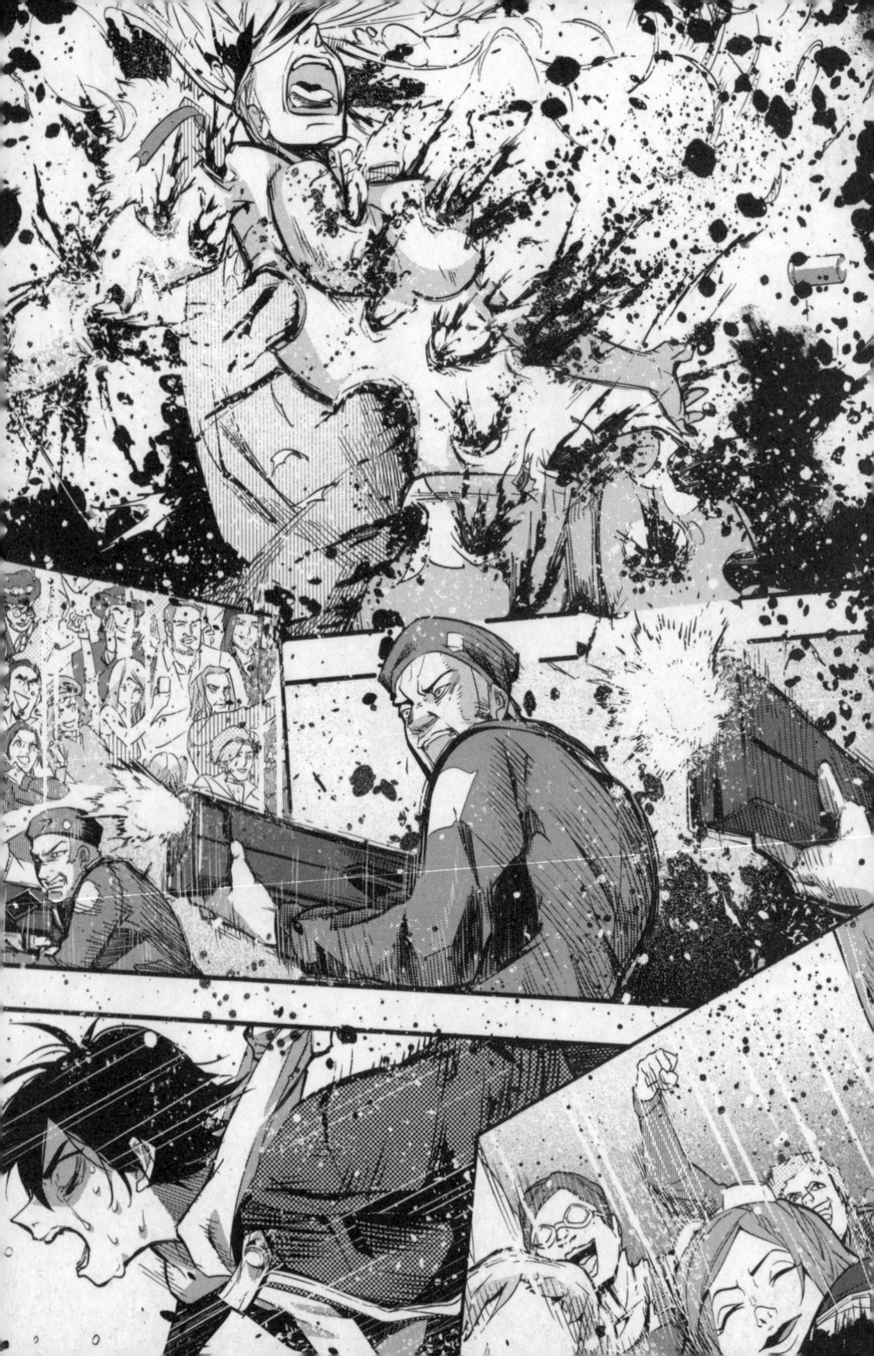

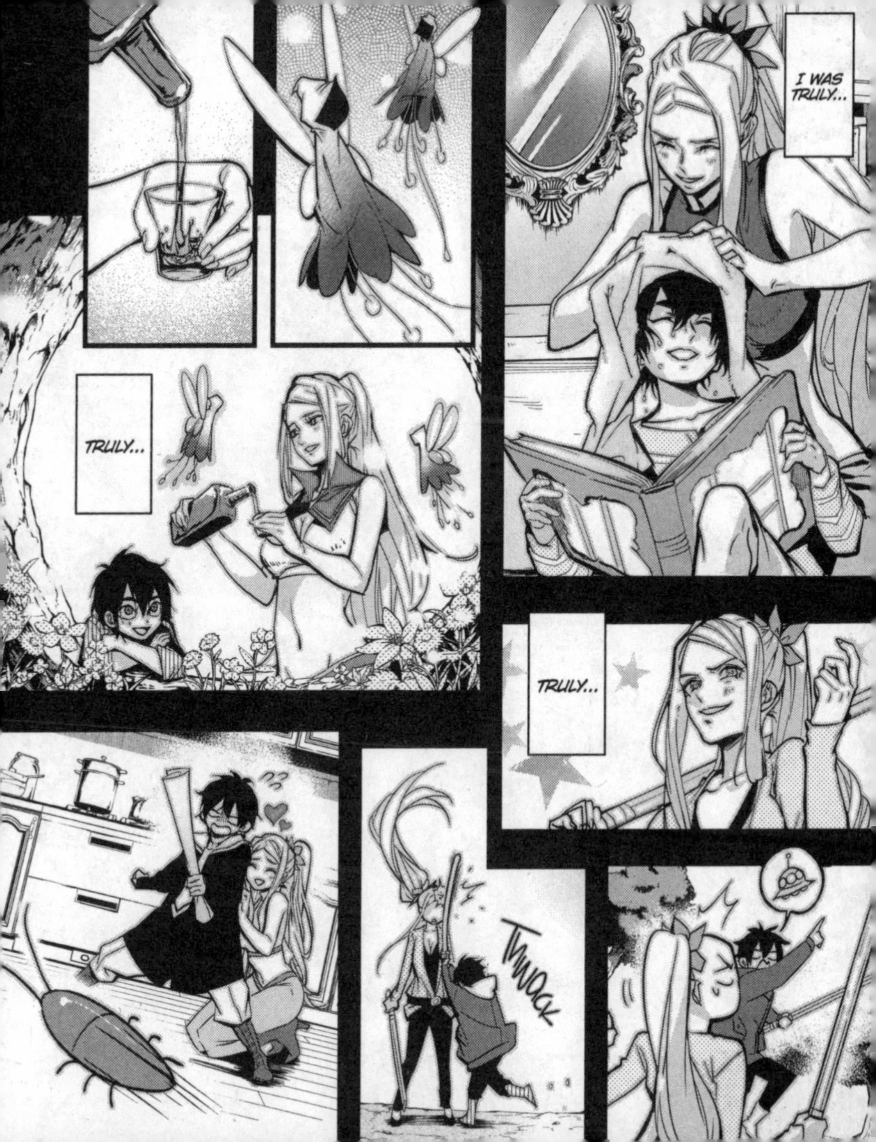
I WAS TRULY...
TRULY...
TRULY...
THWACK

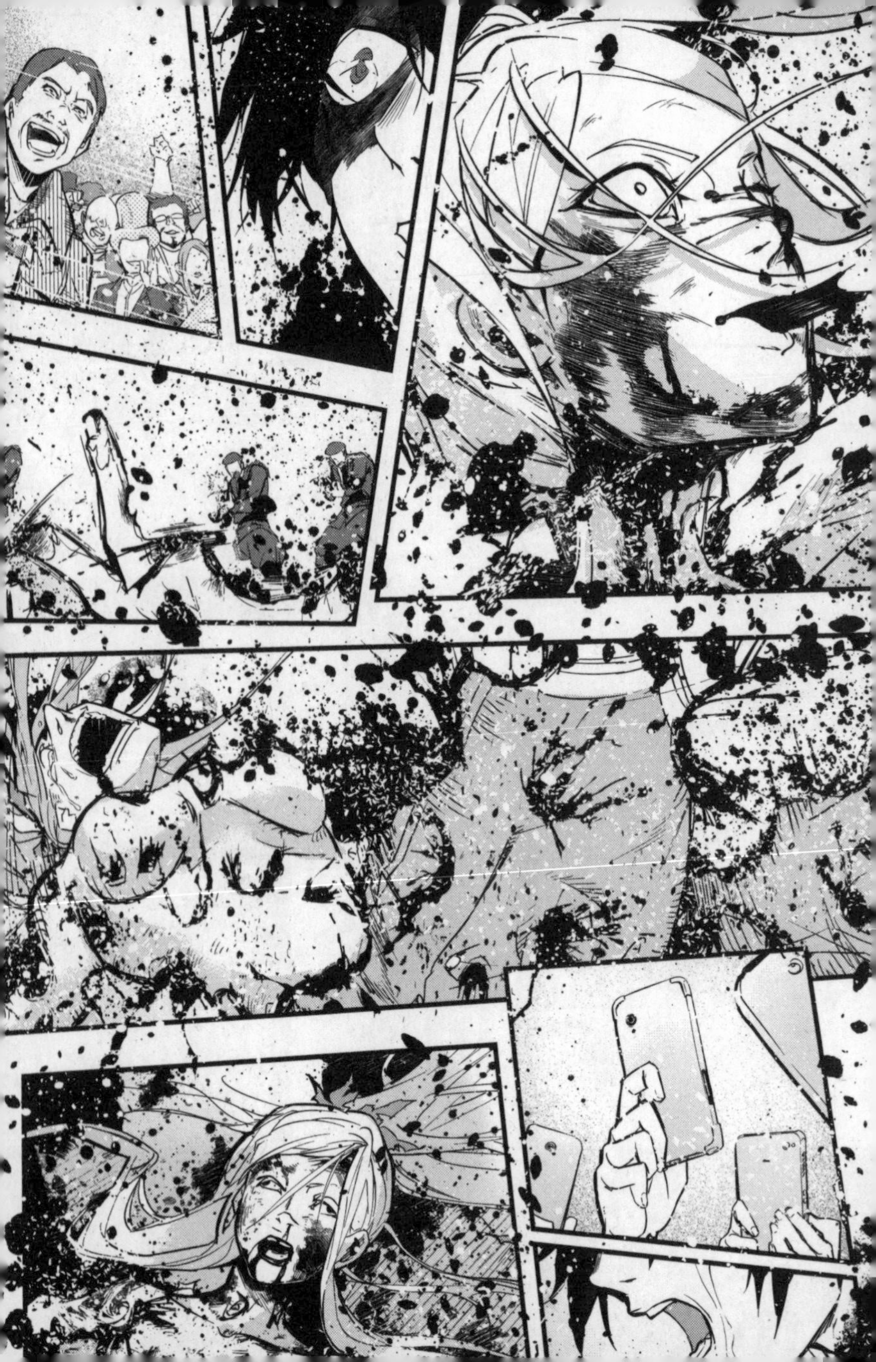

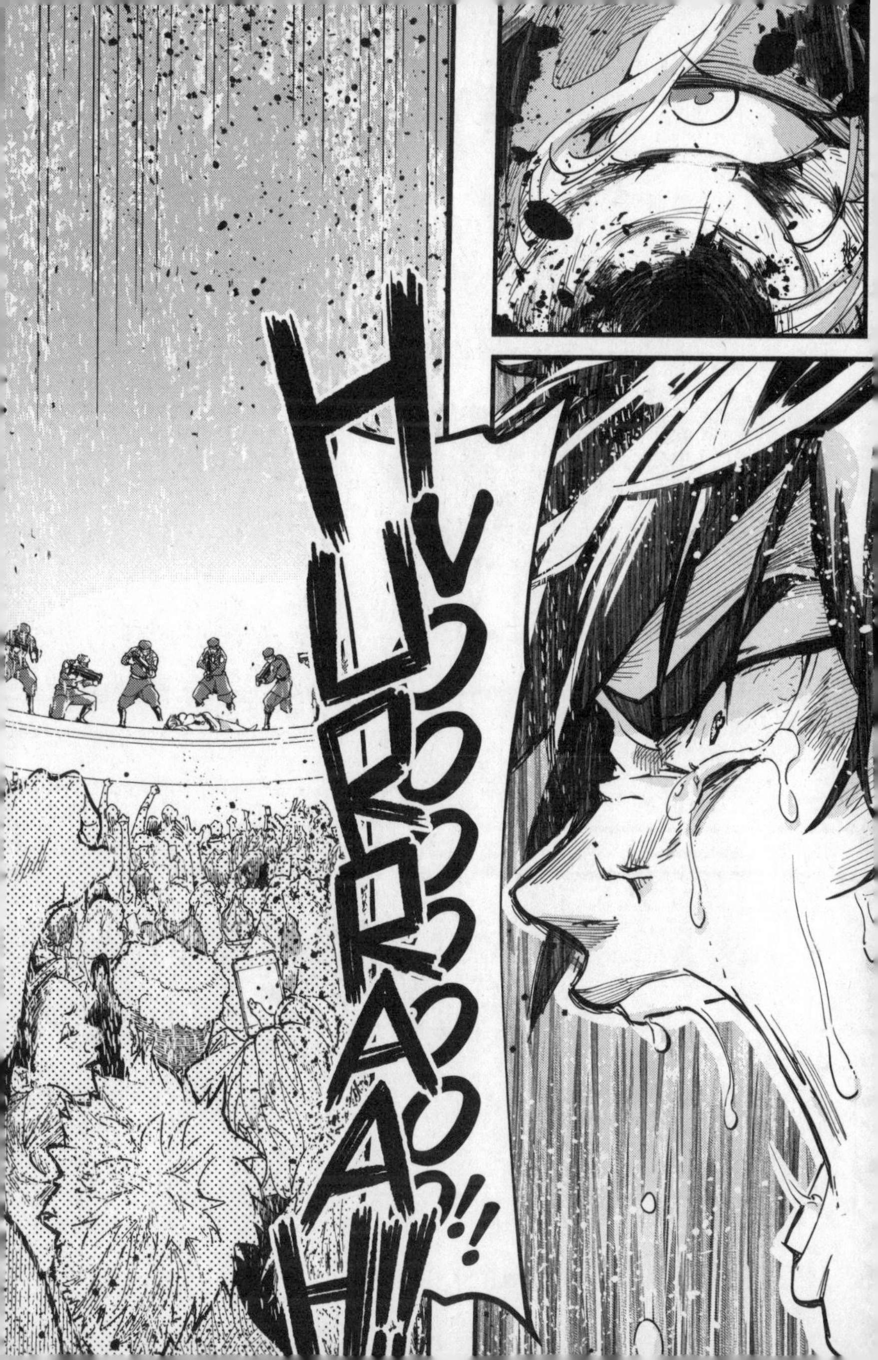
HURRAAH!!

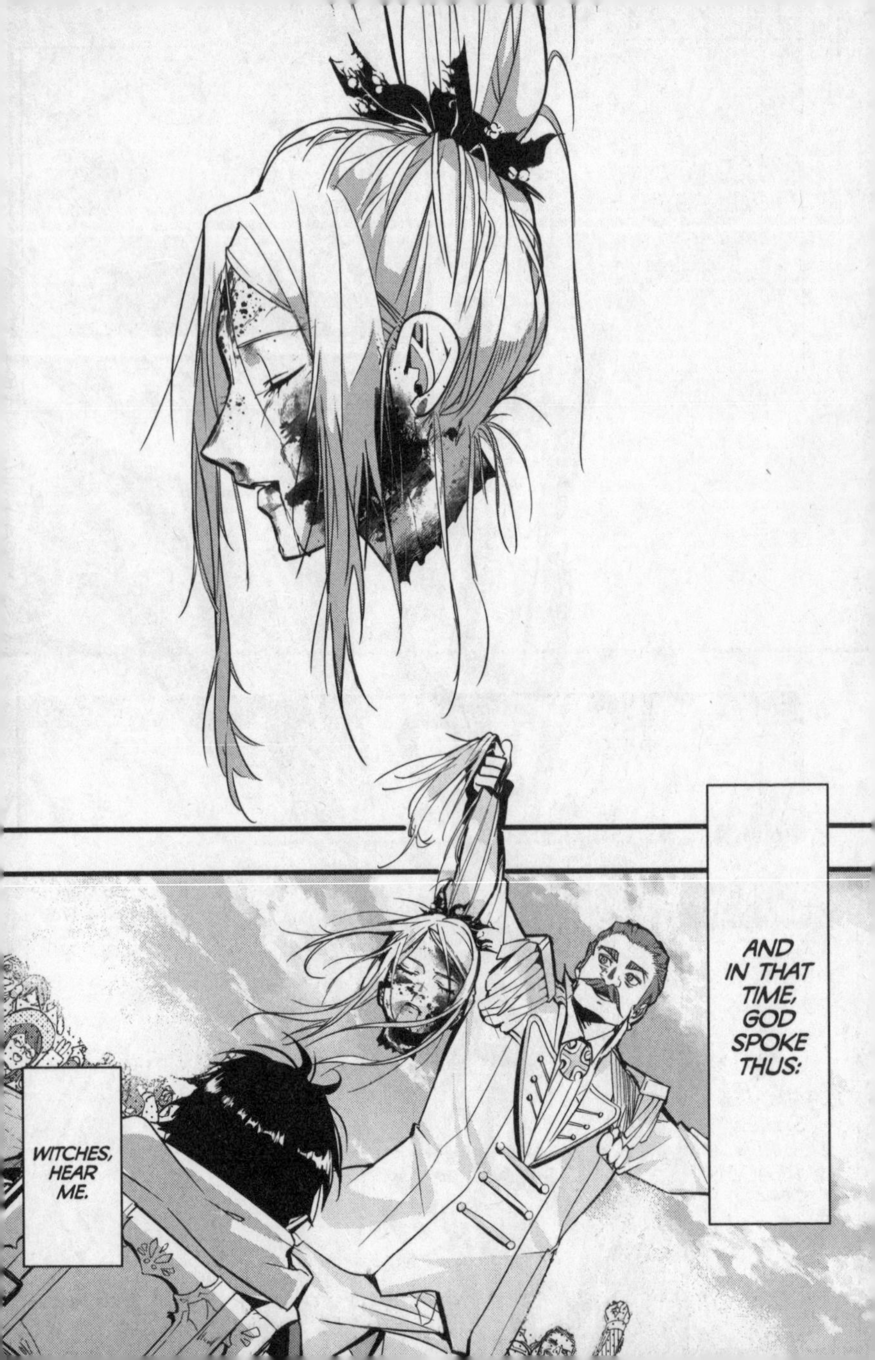
AND IN THAT TIME, GOD SPOKE THUS:
WITCHES, HEAR ME.

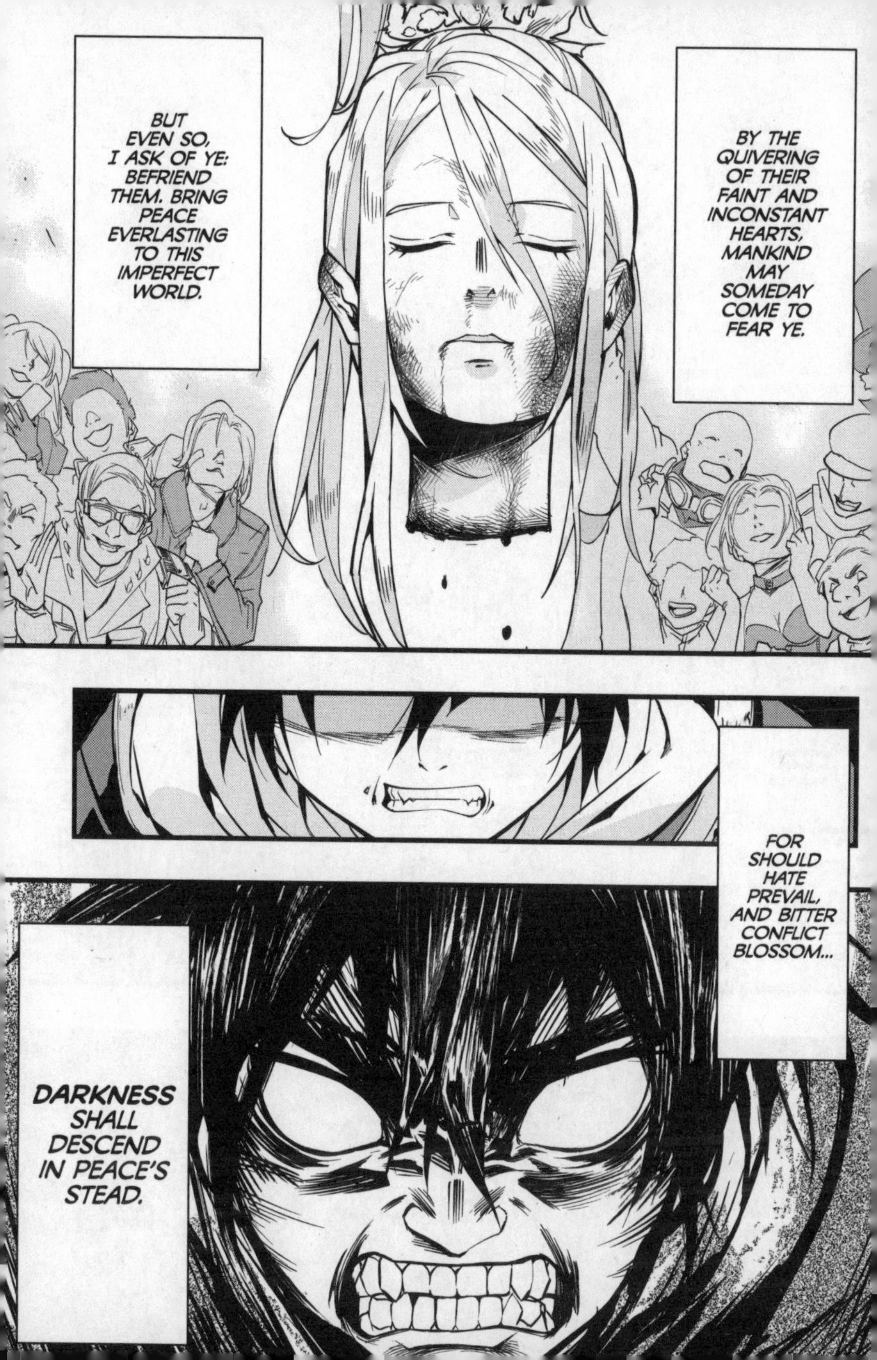
BY THE QUIVERING OF THEIR FAINT AND INCONSTANT HEARTS, MANKIND MAY SOMEDAY COME TO FEAR YE.
BUT EVEN SO, I ASK OF YE: BEFRIEND THEM. BRING PEACE EVERLASTING TO THIS IMPERFECT WORLD.
FOR SHOULD HATE PREVAIL, AND BITTER CONFLICT BLOSSOM...
DARKNESS SHALL DESCEND IN PEACE'S STEAD.

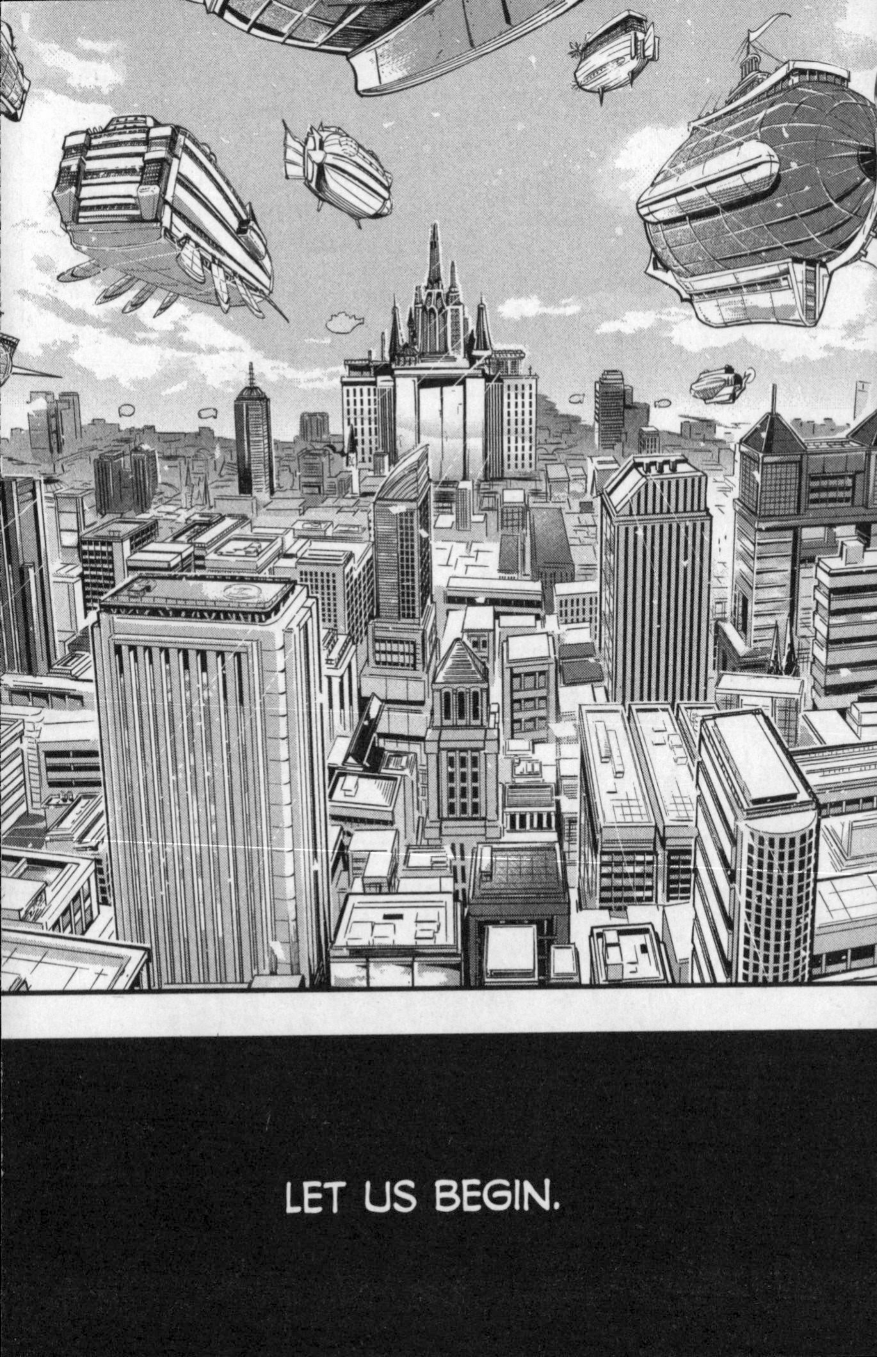
LET US BEGIN.

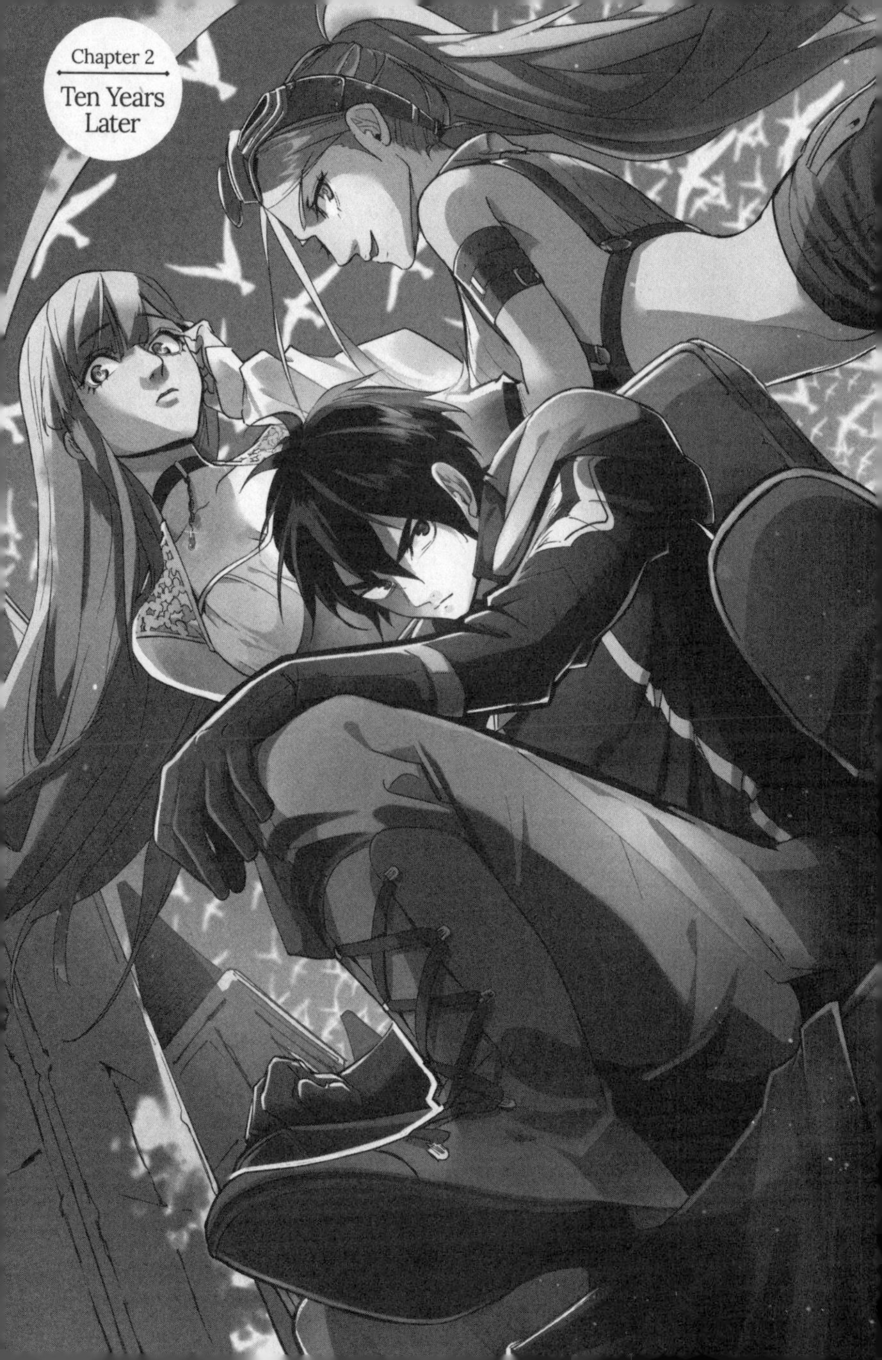
Chapter 2
Ten Years Later

THE
KINGDOMS
OF RUIN

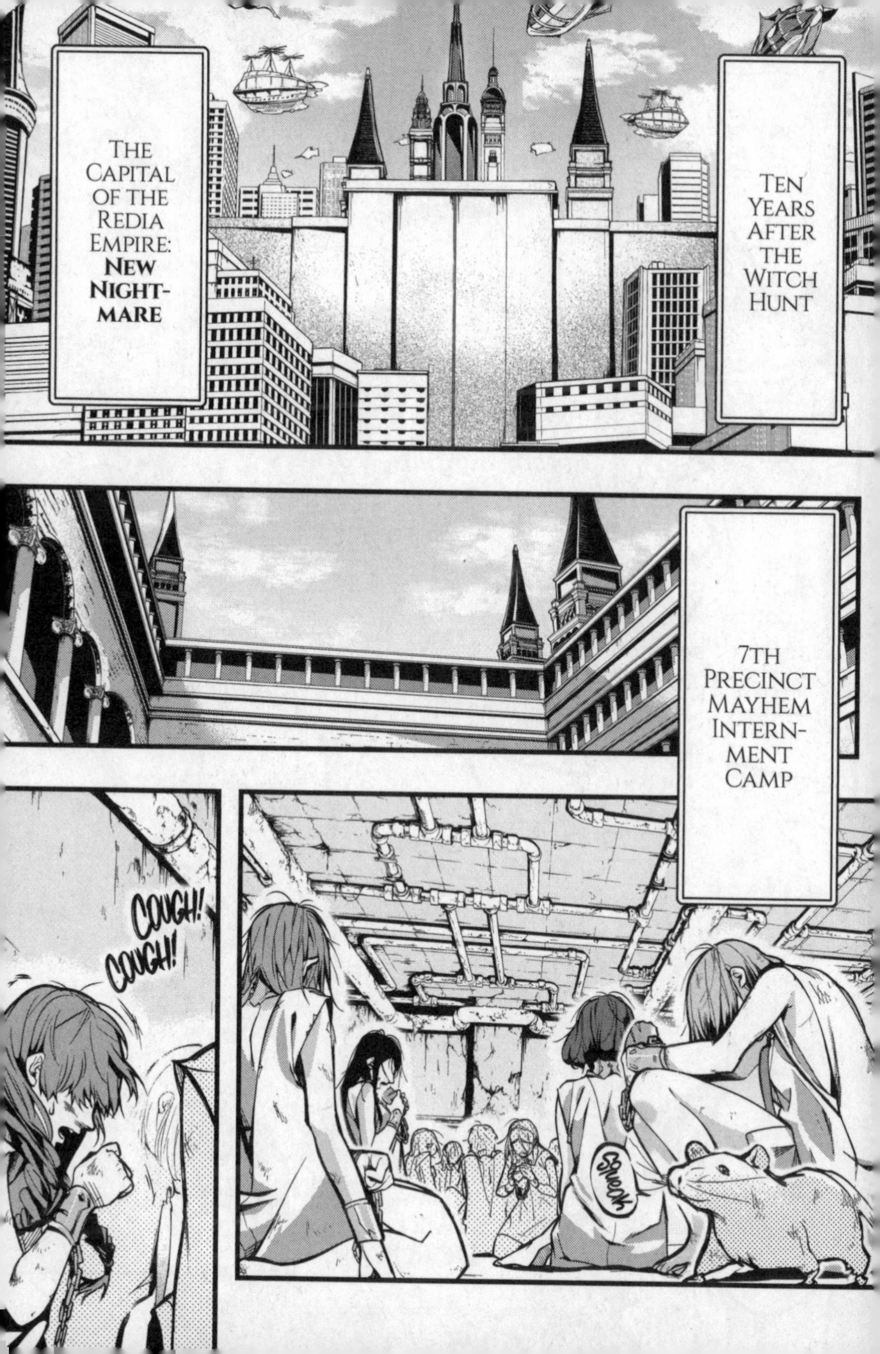
Ten Years After the Witch Hunt
The Capital of the Redia Empire: **New Nightmare**
7th Precinct Mayhem Internment Camp
Squeak
Cough! Cough!

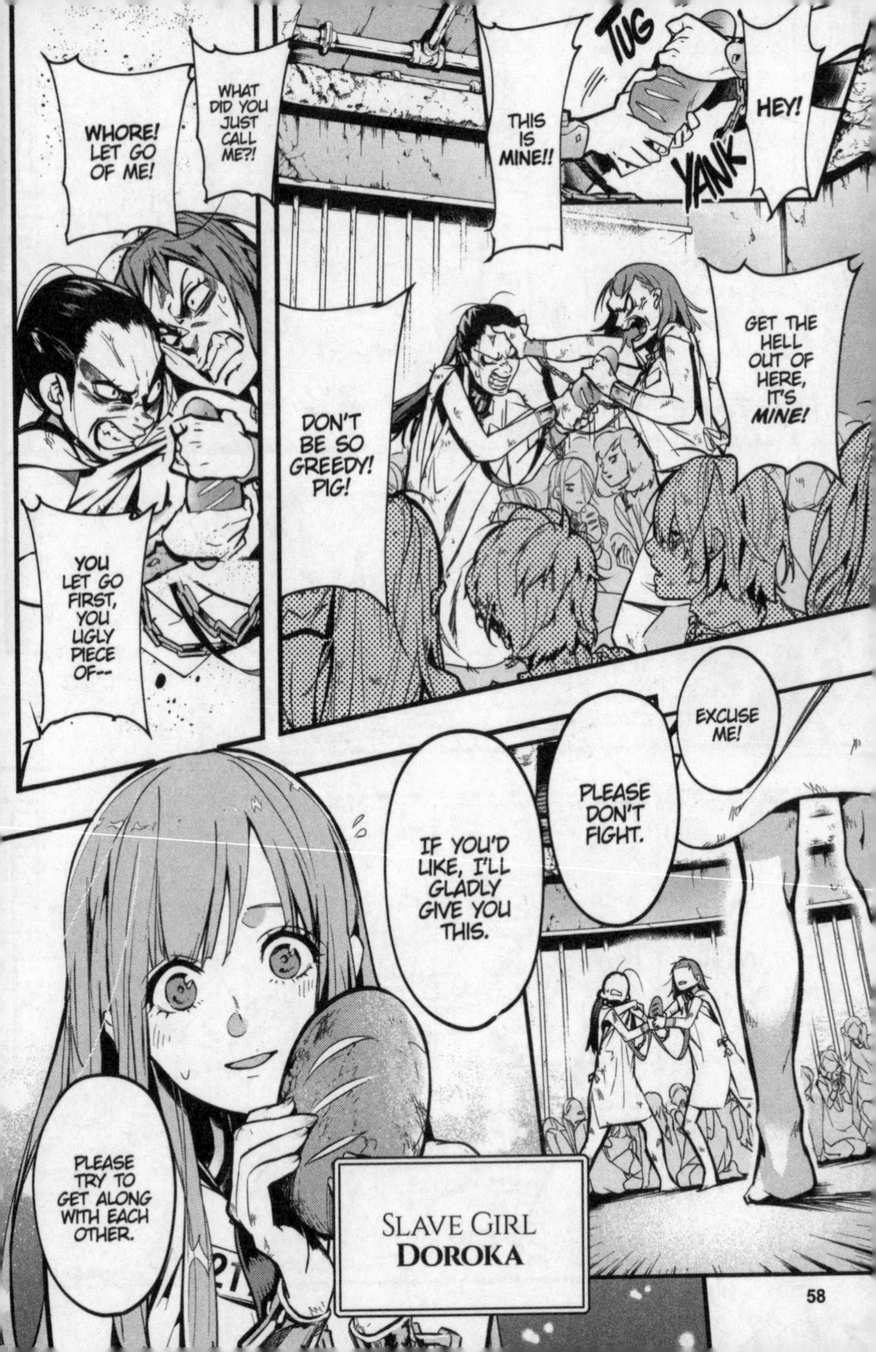
HEY!
TUG
YANK
THIS IS MINE!!
GET THE HELL OUT OF HERE, IT'S *MINE!*
DON'T BE SO GREEDY! PIG!
WHAT DID YOU JUST CALL ME?!
WHORE! LET GO OF ME!
YOU LET GO FIRST, YOU UGLY PIECE OF--
EXCUSE ME!
PLEASE DON'T FIGHT.
IF YOU'D LIKE, I'LL GLADLY GIVE YOU THIS.
PLEASE TRY TO GET ALONG WITH EACH OTHER.
SLAVE GIRL
DOROKA

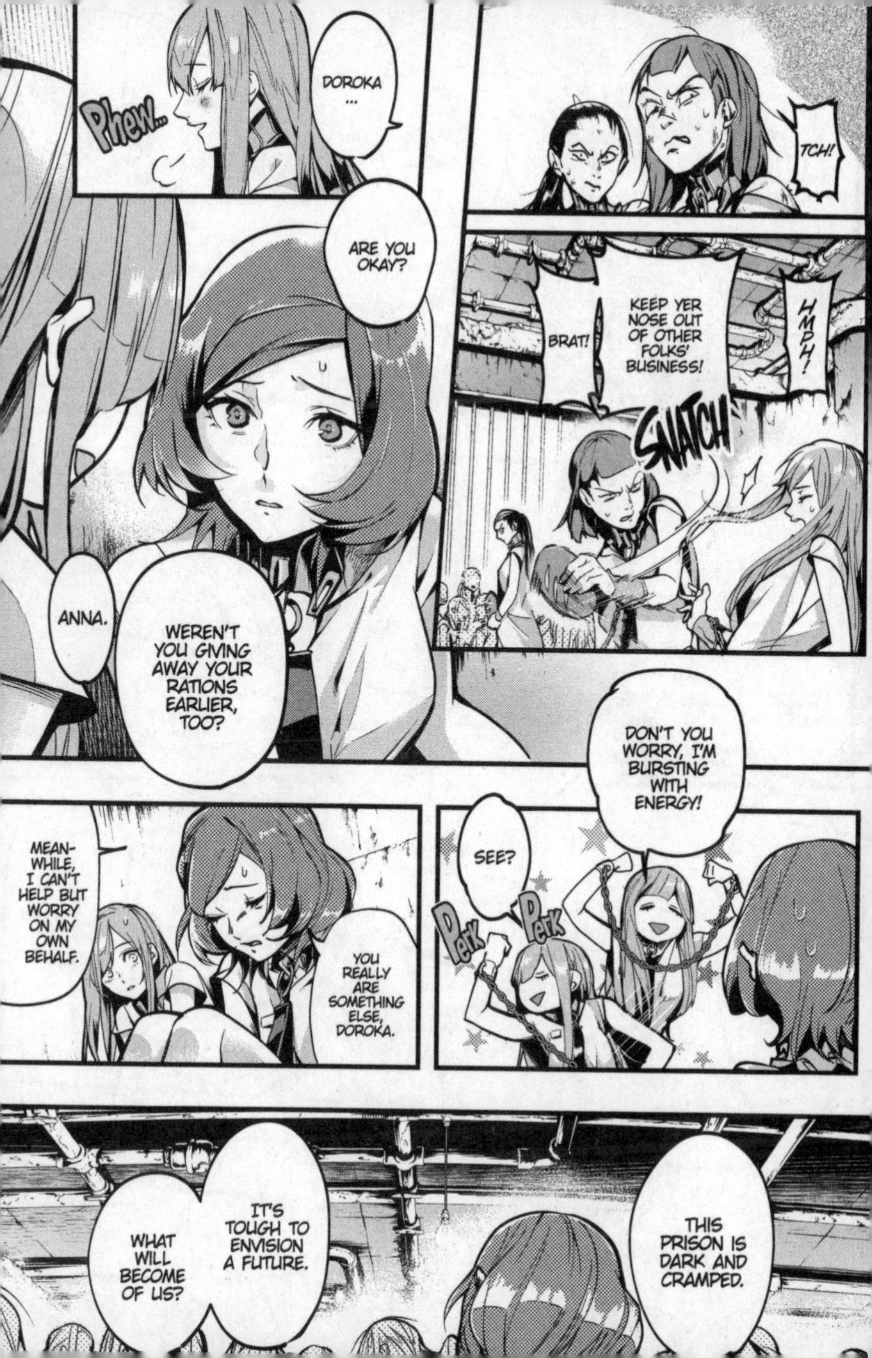
TCH!
Phew...
DOROKA ...
HMPH!
KEEP YER NOSE OUT OF OTHER FOLKS' BUSINESS!
BRAT!
SNATCH
ARE YOU OKAY?
ANNA.
WEREN'T YOU GIVING AWAY YOUR RATIONS EARLIER, TOO?
DON'T YOU WORRY, I'M BURSTING WITH ENERGY!
SEE?
Perk Perk
YOU REALLY ARE SOMETHING ELSE, DOROKA.
MEAN-WHILE, I CAN'T HELP BUT WORRY ON MY OWN BEHALF.
THIS PRISON IS DARK AND CRAMPED.
IT'S TOUGH TO ENVISION A FUTURE.
WHAT WILL BECOME OF US?

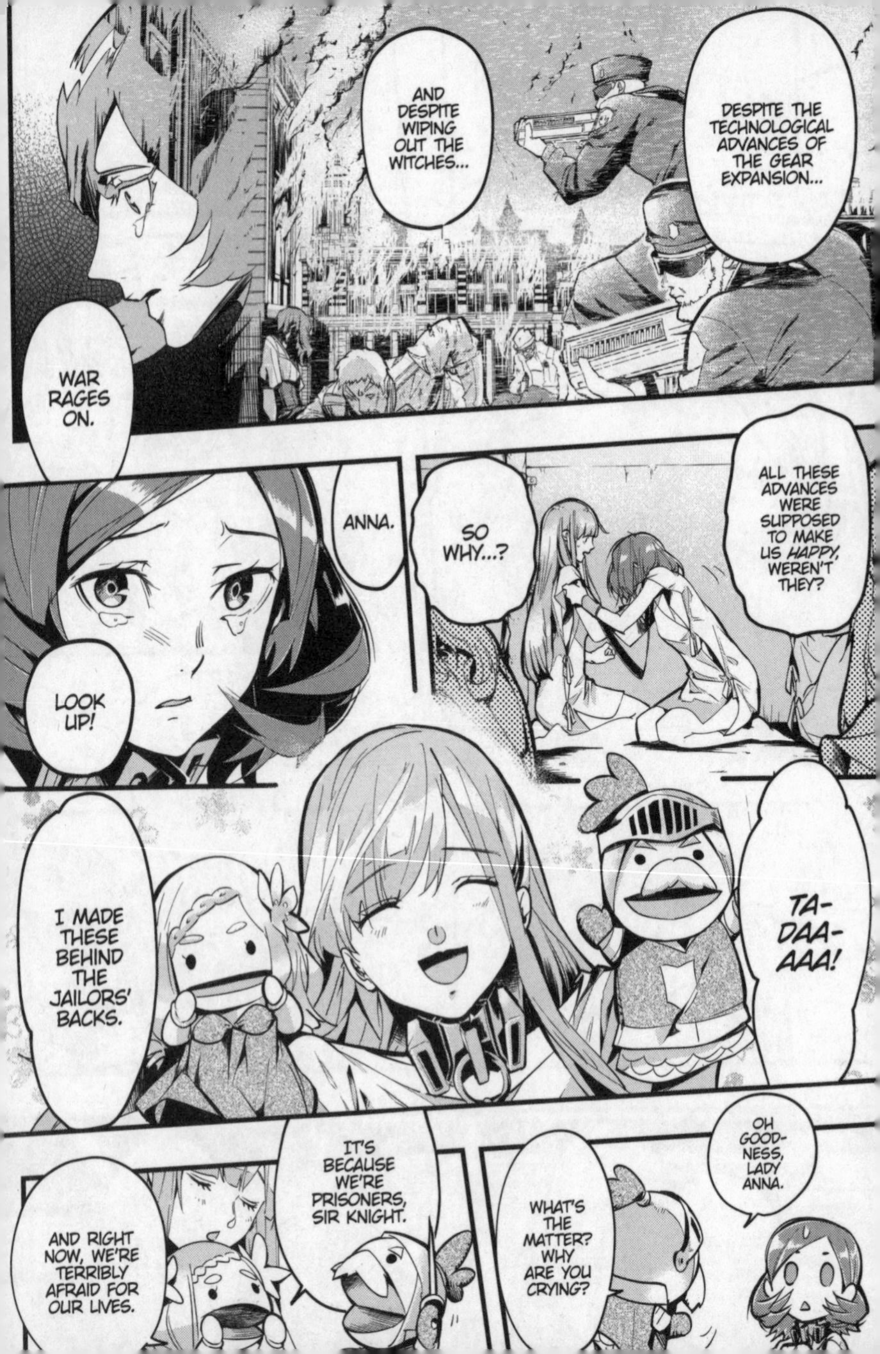
DESPITE THE TECHNOLOGICAL ADVANCES OF THE GEAR EXPANSION...
AND DESPITE WIPING OUT THE WITCHES...
WAR RAGES ON.
ALL THESE ADVANCES WERE SUPPOSED TO MAKE US *HAPPY,* WEREN'T THEY?
SO WHY...?
ANNA.
LOOK UP!
TA-DAAAAA!
I MADE THESE BEHIND THE JAILORS' BACKS.
OH GOODNESS, LADY ANNA.
WHAT'S THE MATTER? WHY ARE YOU CRYING?
IT'S BECAUSE WE'RE PRISONERS, SIR KNIGHT.
AND RIGHT NOW, WE'RE TERRIBLY AFRAID FOR OUR LIVES.

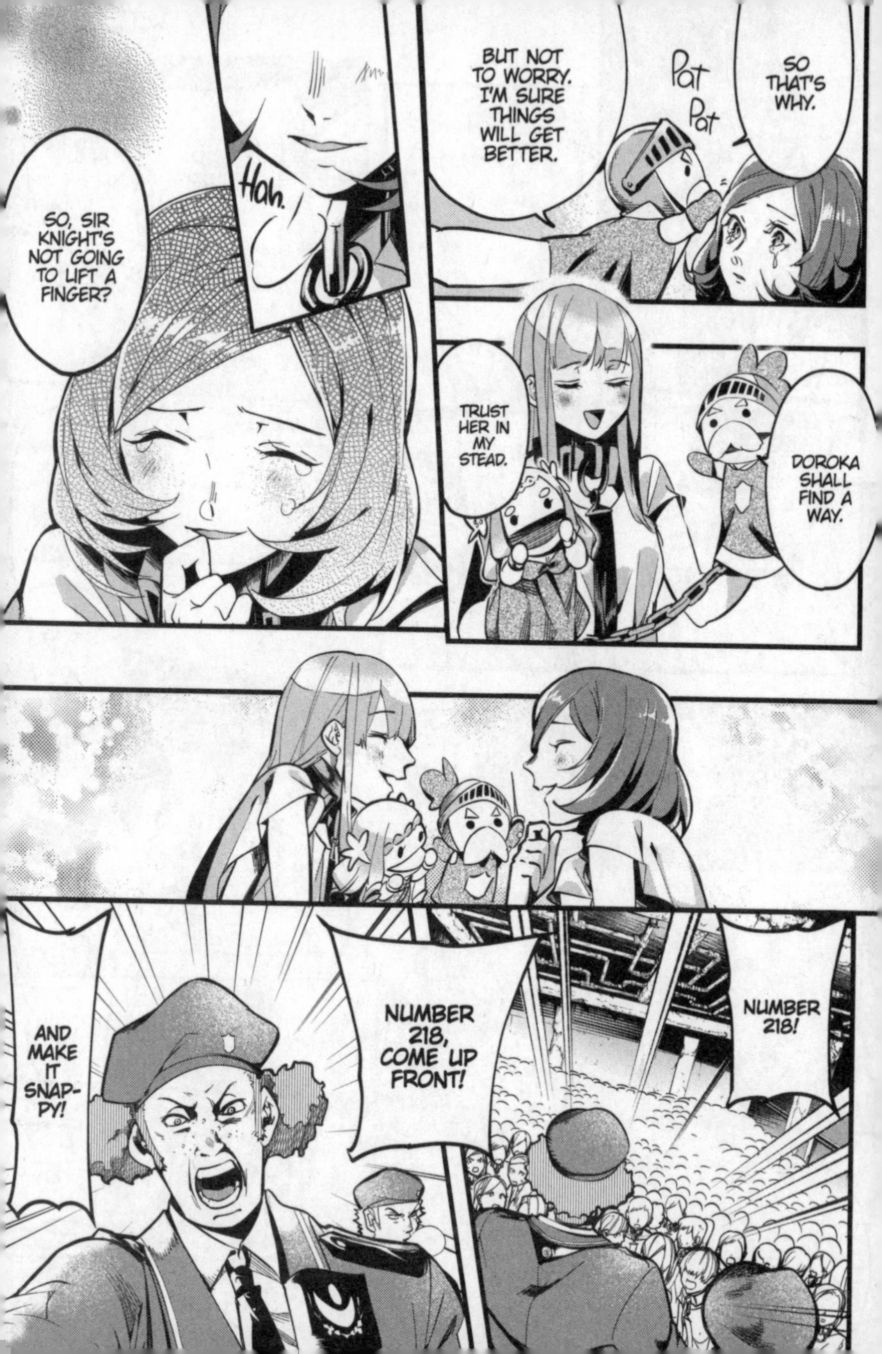
SO THAT'S WHY.
Pat Pat
BUT NOT TO WORRY. I'M SURE THINGS WILL GET BETTER.
DOROKA SHALL FIND A WAY.
TRUST HER IN MY STEAD.
Hah.
SO, SIR KNIGHT'S NOT GOING TO LIFT A FINGER?
NUMBER 218!
NUMBER 218, COME UP FRONT!
AND MAKE IT SNAP-PY!

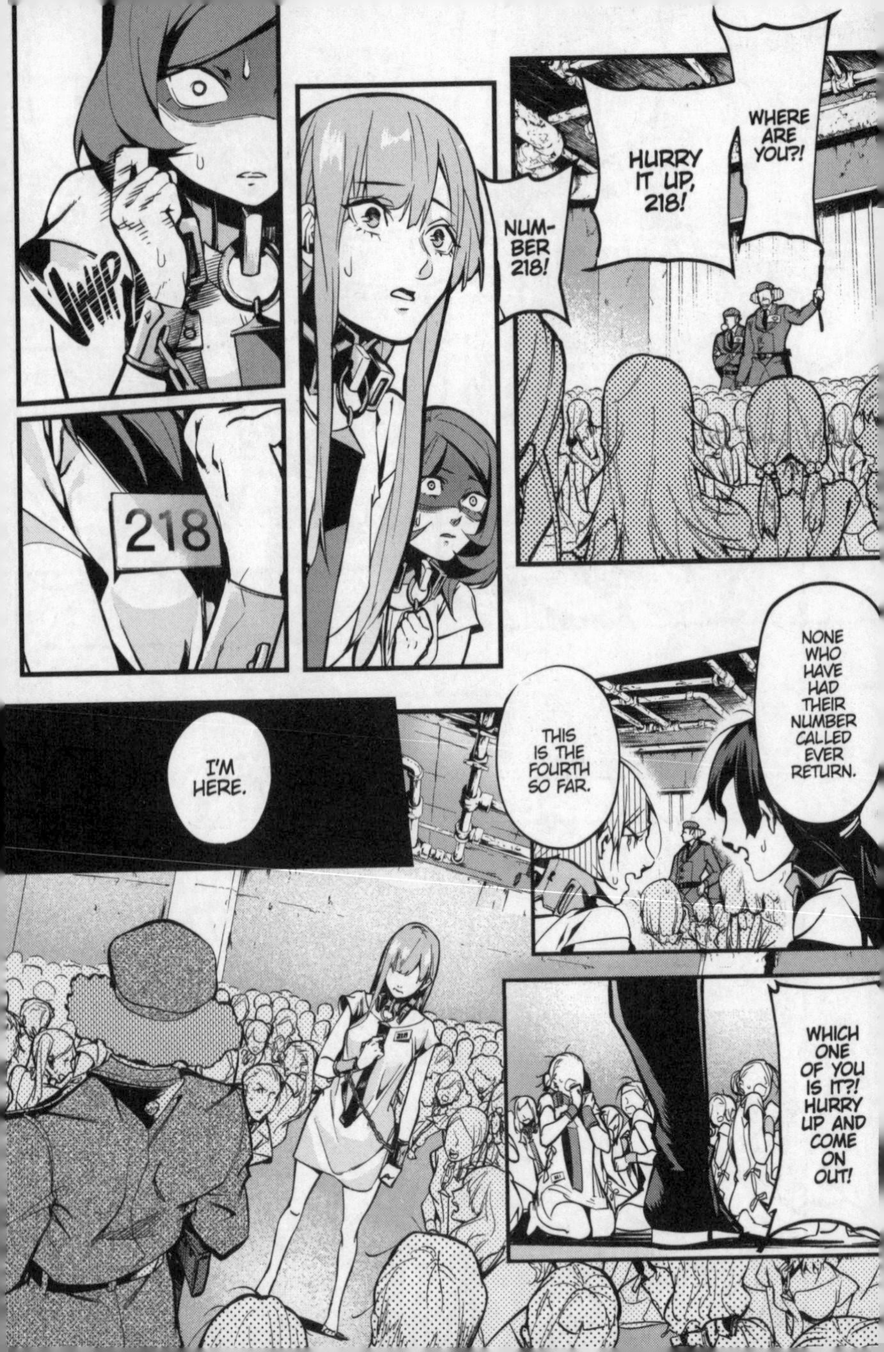
WHERE ARE YOU?!
HURRY IT UP, 218!
NUM-BER 218!
VWIP
218
NONE WHO HAVE HAD THEIR NUMBER CALLED EVER RETURN.
THIS IS THE FOURTH SO FAR.
WHICH ONE OF YOU IS IT?! HURRY UP AND COME ON OUT!
I'M HERE.

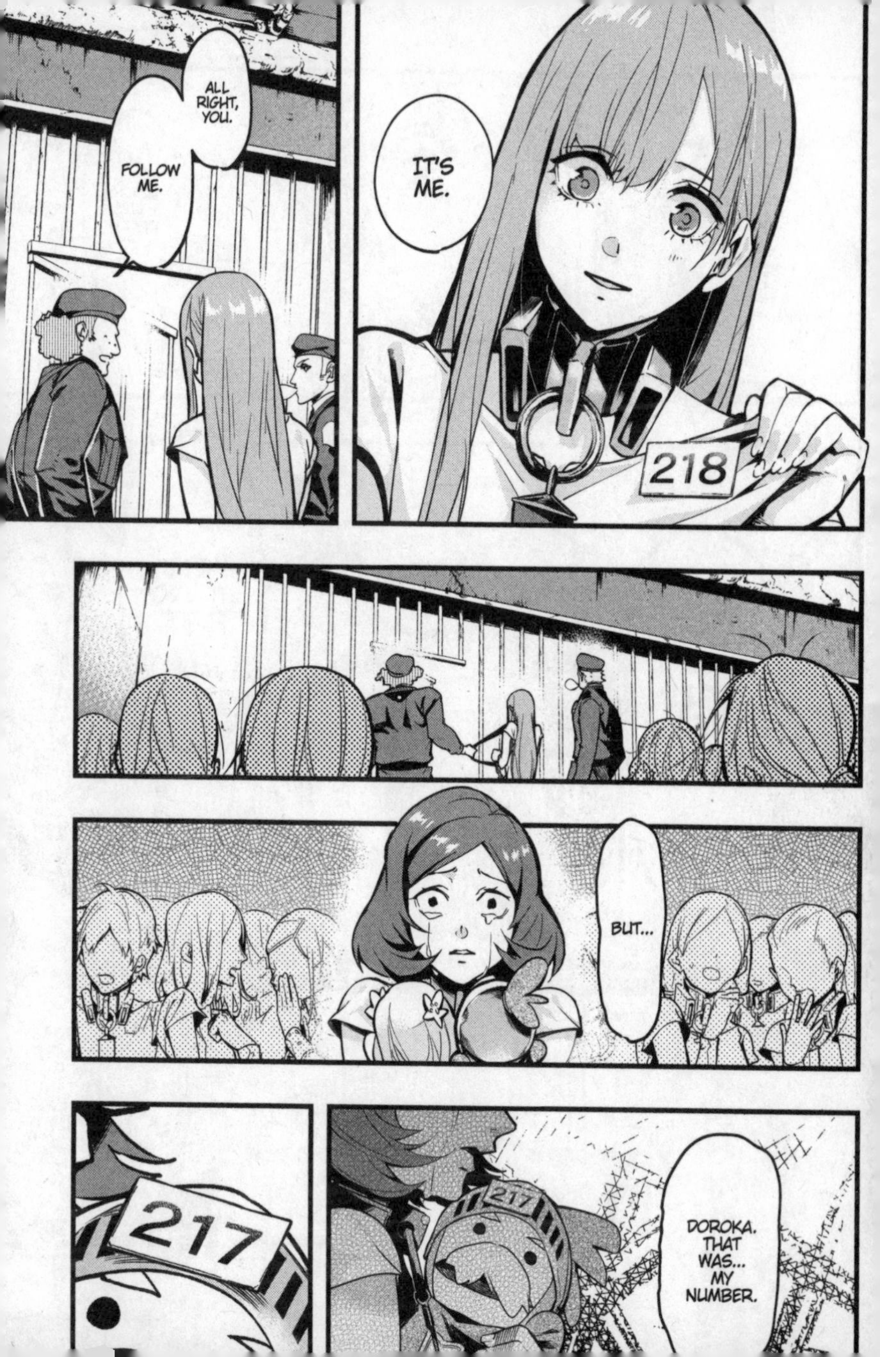
IT'S ME.
218
ALL RIGHT, YOU.
FOLLOW ME.
BUT...
DOROKA. THAT WAS... MY NUMBER.
217
217

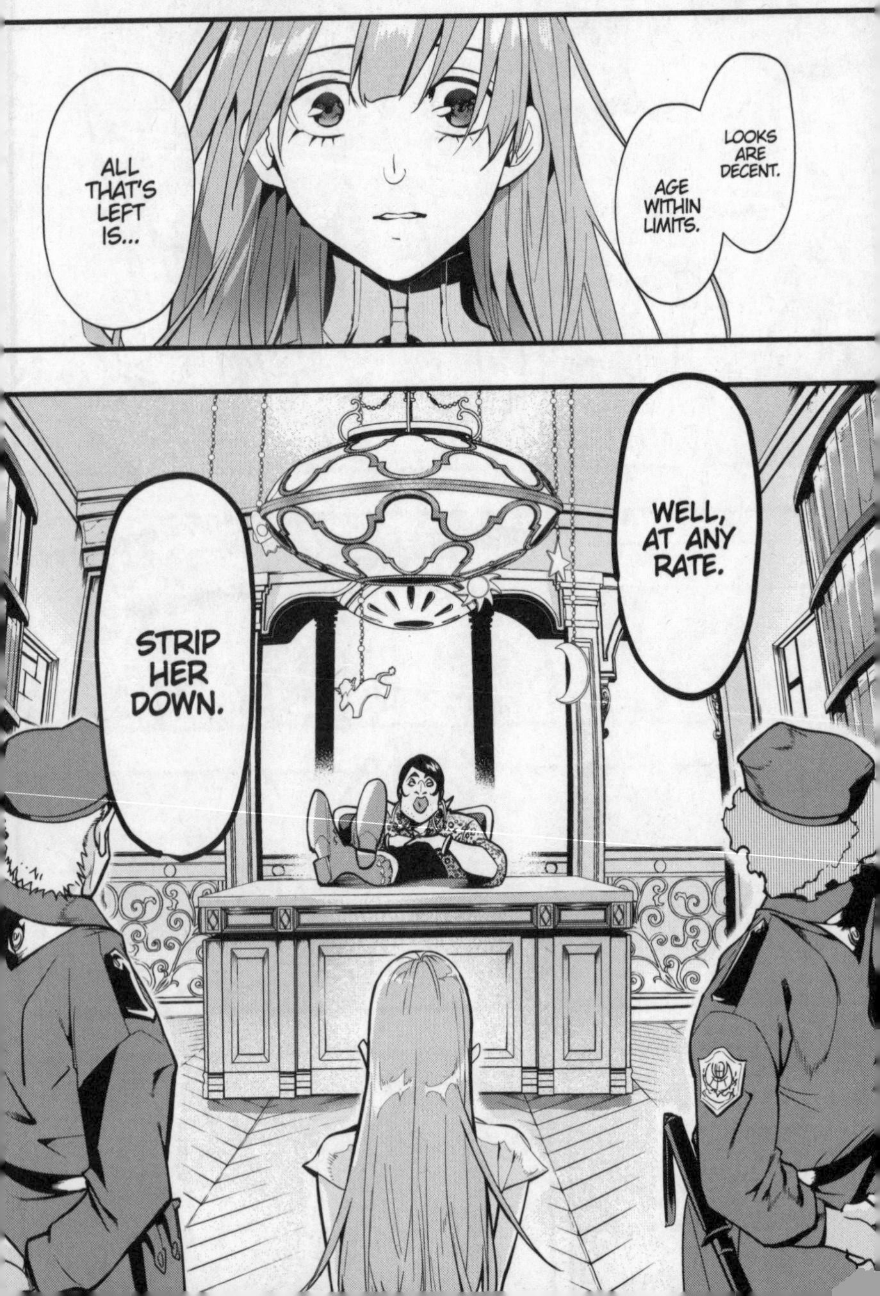
LOOKS ARE DECENT.
AGE WITHIN LIMITS.
ALL THAT'S LEFT IS...
WELL, AT ANY RATE.
STRIP HER DOWN.

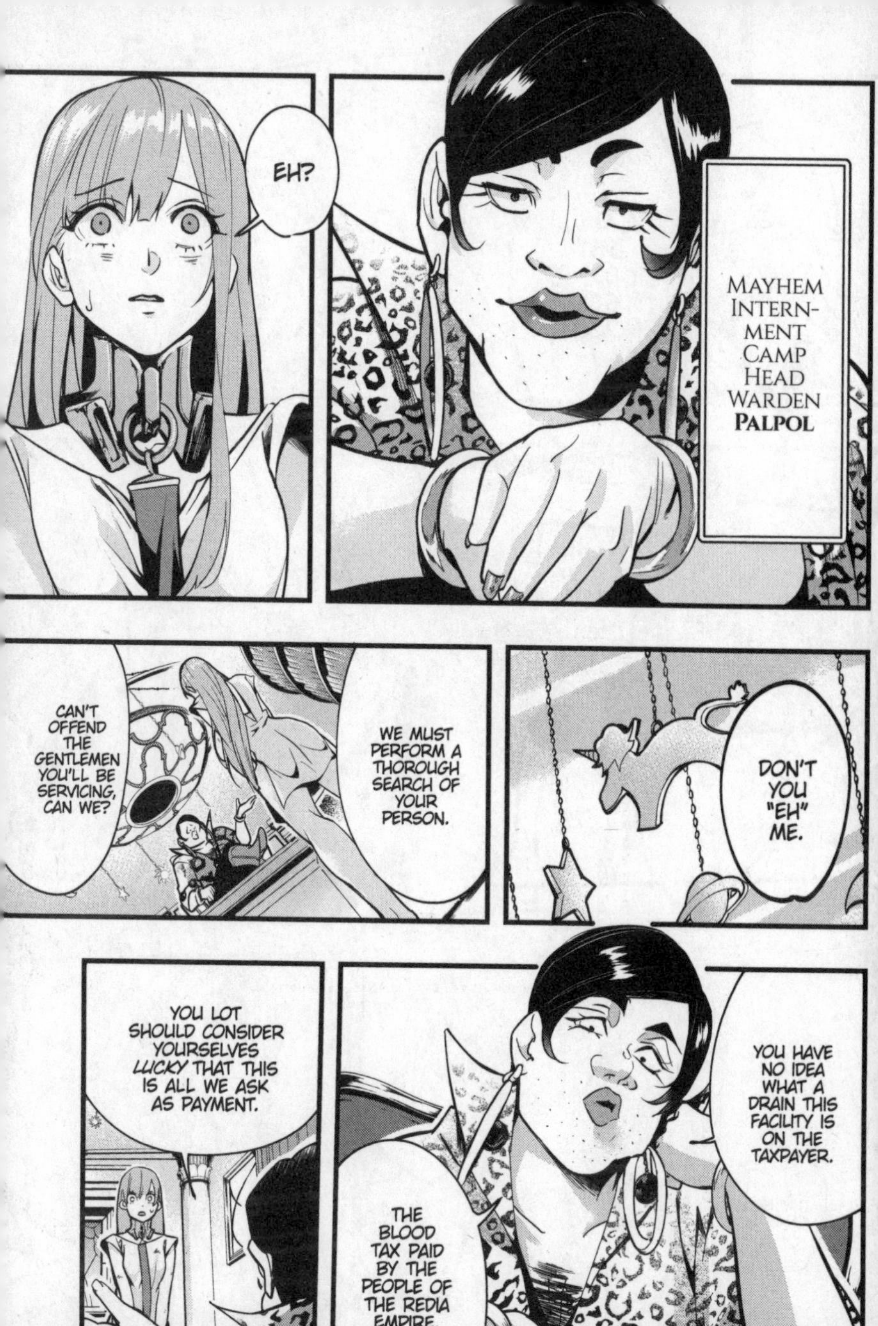
MAYHEM INTERNMENT CAMP HEAD WARDEN **PALPOL**
EH?
DON'T YOU "EH" ME.
WE MUST PERFORM A THOROUGH SEARCH OF YOUR PERSON.
CAN'T OFFEND THE GENTLEMEN YOU'LL BE SERVICING, CAN WE?
YOU HAVE NO IDEA WHAT A DRAIN THIS FACILITY IS ON THE TAXPAYER.
THE BLOOD TAX PAID BY THE PEOPLE OF THE REDIA EMPIRE.
YOU LOT SHOULD CONSIDER YOURSELVES *LUCKY* THAT THIS IS ALL WE ASK AS PAYMENT.

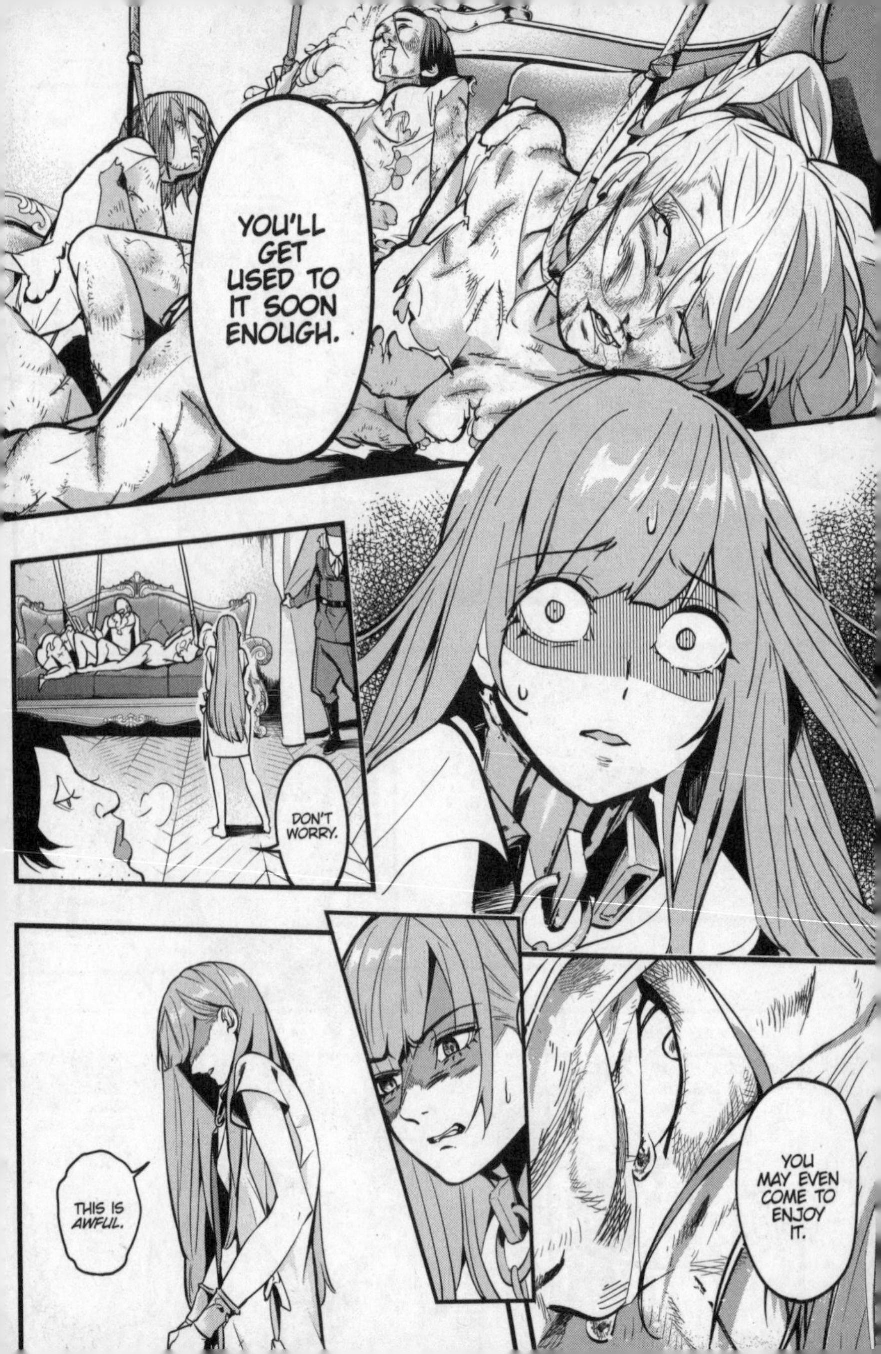

YOU'LL GET USED TO IT SOON ENOUGH.
DON'T WORRY.
YOU MAY EVEN COME TO ENJOY IT.
THIS IS *AWFUL.*

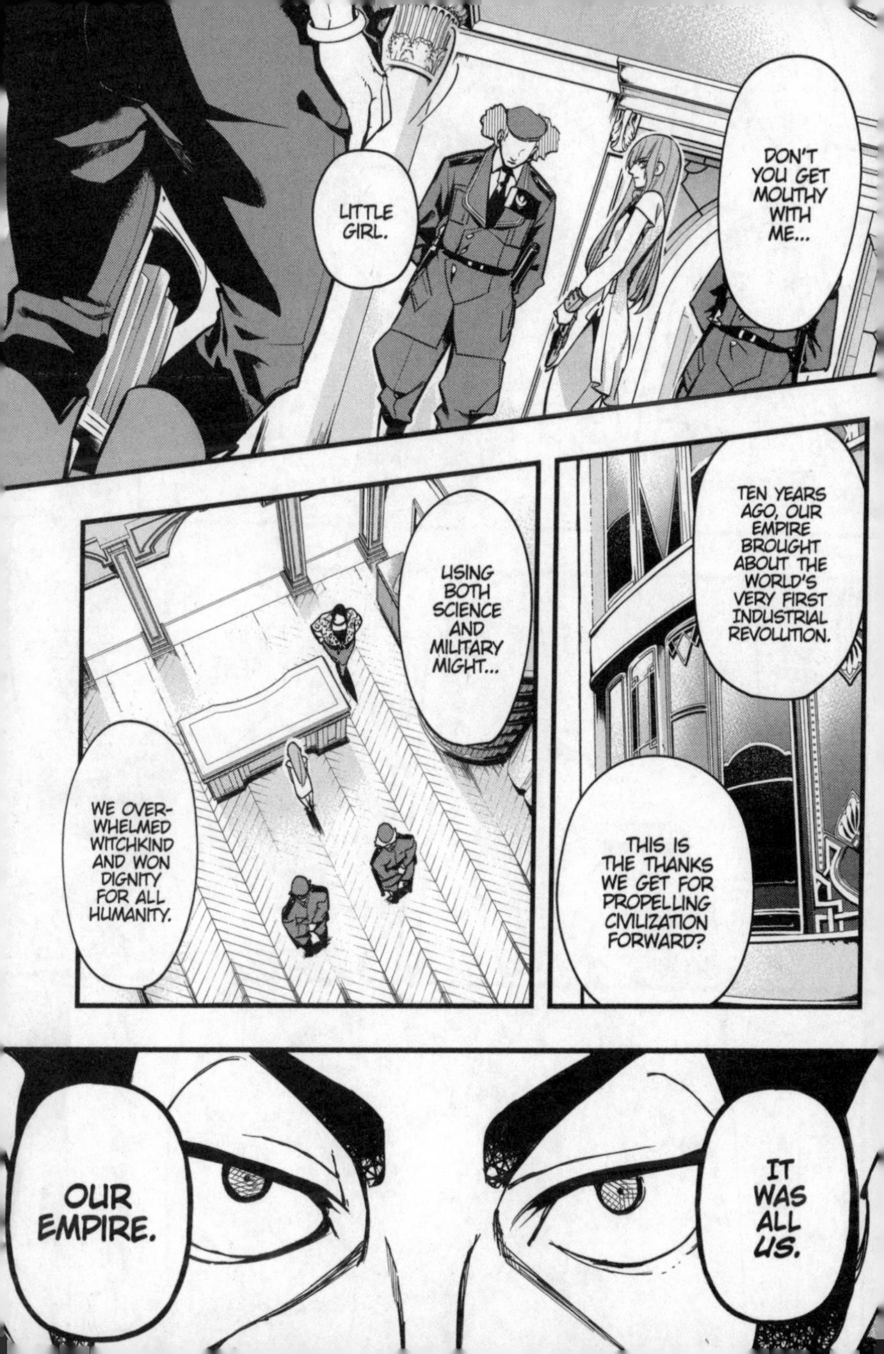
DON'T YOU GET MOUTHY WITH ME...
LITTLE GIRL.
TEN YEARS AGO, OUR EMPIRE BROUGHT ABOUT THE WORLD'S VERY FIRST INDUSTRIAL REVOLUTION.
THIS IS THE THANKS WE GET FOR PROPELLING CIVILIZATION FORWARD?
USING BOTH SCIENCE AND MILITARY MIGHT...
WE OVER-WHELMED WITCHKIND AND WON DIGNITY FOR ALL HUMANITY.
IT WAS ALL US.
OUR EMPIRE.

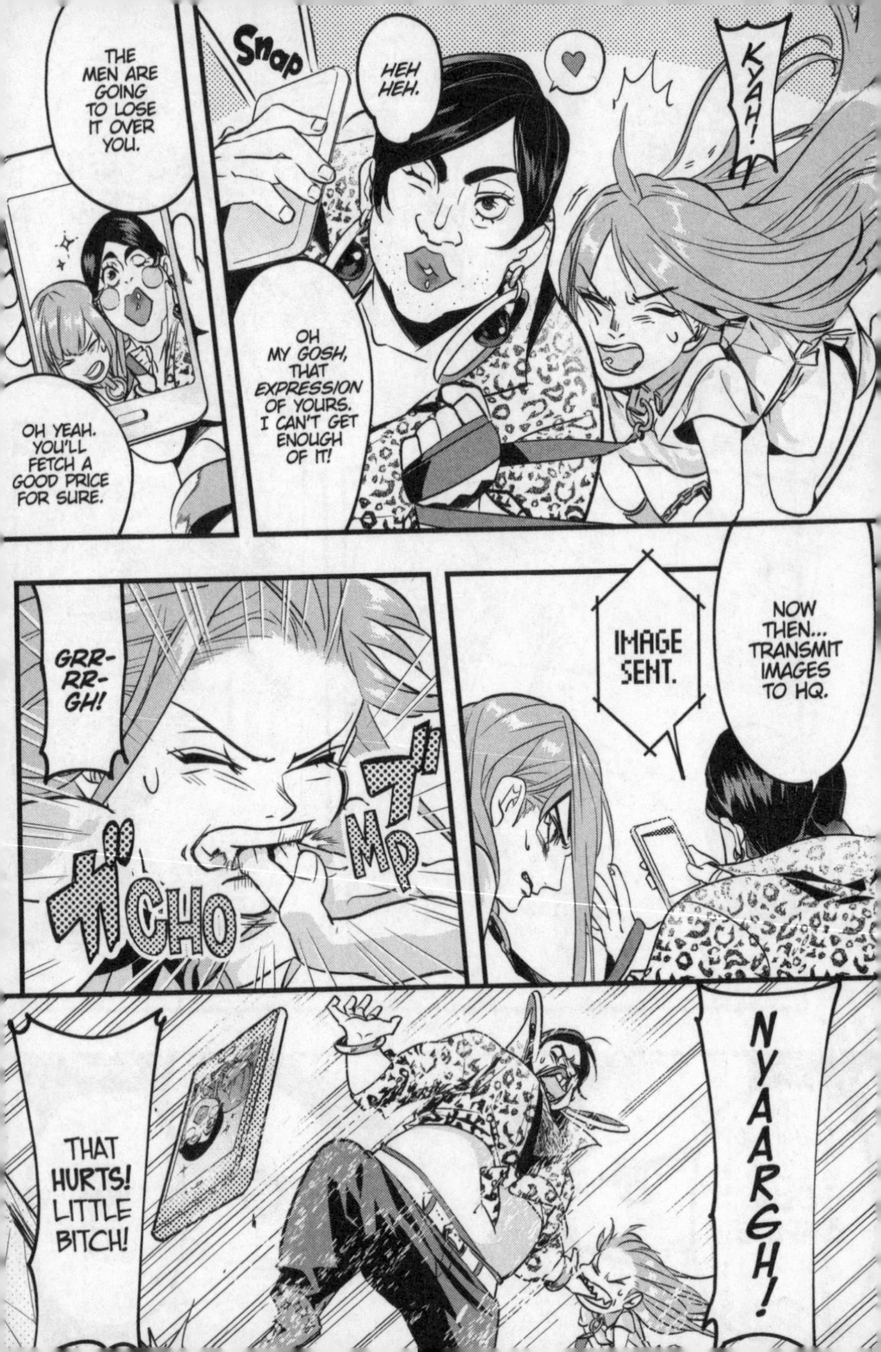
KYAH!!
♥
HEH HEH.
Snap
OH MY GOSH, THAT EXPRESSION OF YOURS. I CAN'T GET ENOUGH OF IT!
THE MEN ARE GOING TO LOSE IT OVER YOU.
OH YEAH. YOU'LL FETCH A GOOD PRICE FOR SURE.
NOW THEN... TRANSMIT IMAGES TO HQ.
IMAGE SENT.
GRR-RR-GH!
CHOMP
NYAARGH!
THAT HURTS! LITTLE BITCH!

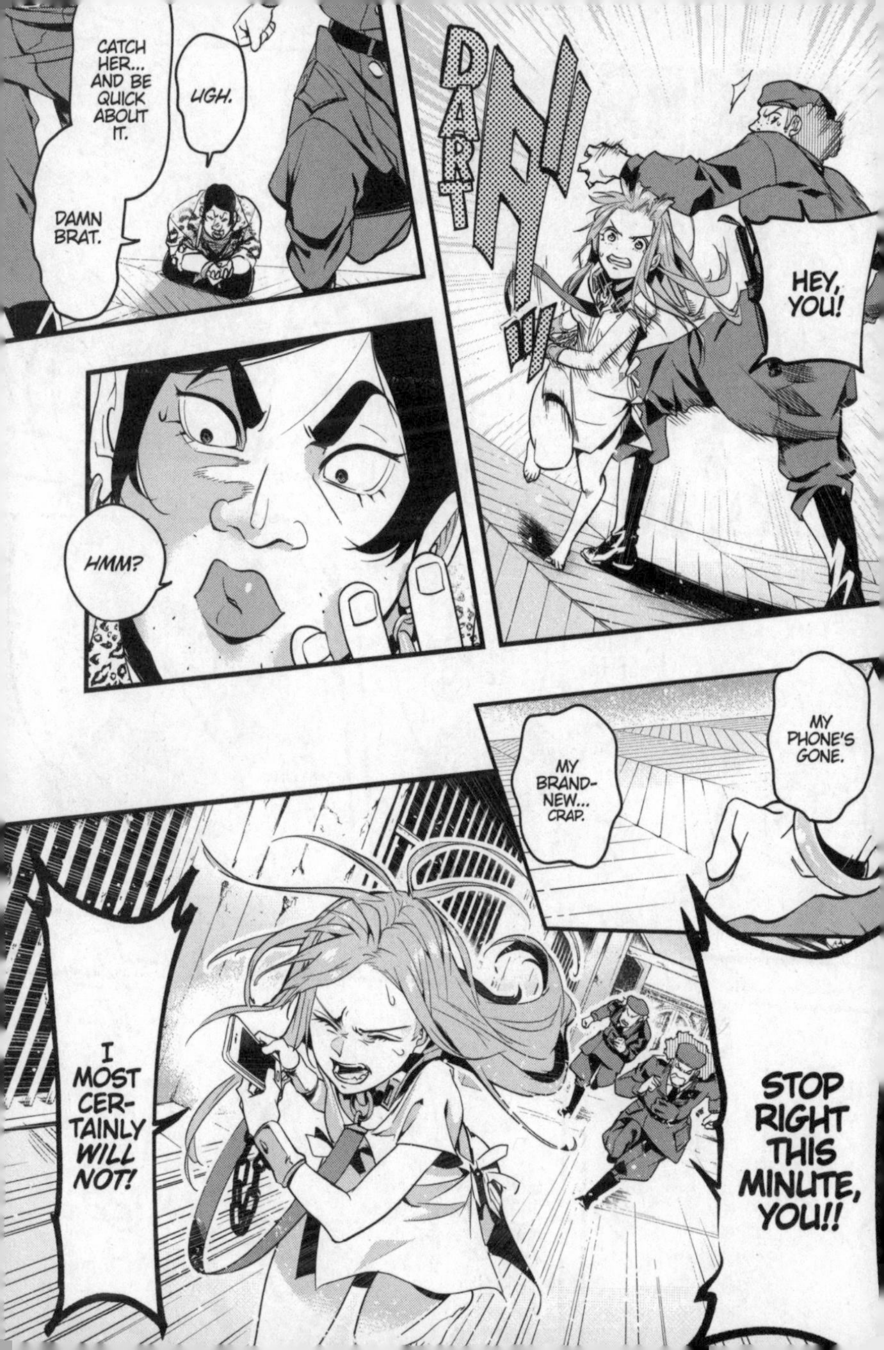
DART
HEY, YOU!
UGH.
CATCH HER... AND BE QUICK ABOUT IT.
DAMN BRAT.
HMM?
MY PHONE'S GONE.
MY BRAND-NEW... CRAP.
STOP RIGHT THIS MINUTE, YOU!!
I MOST CER-TAINLY WILL NOT!

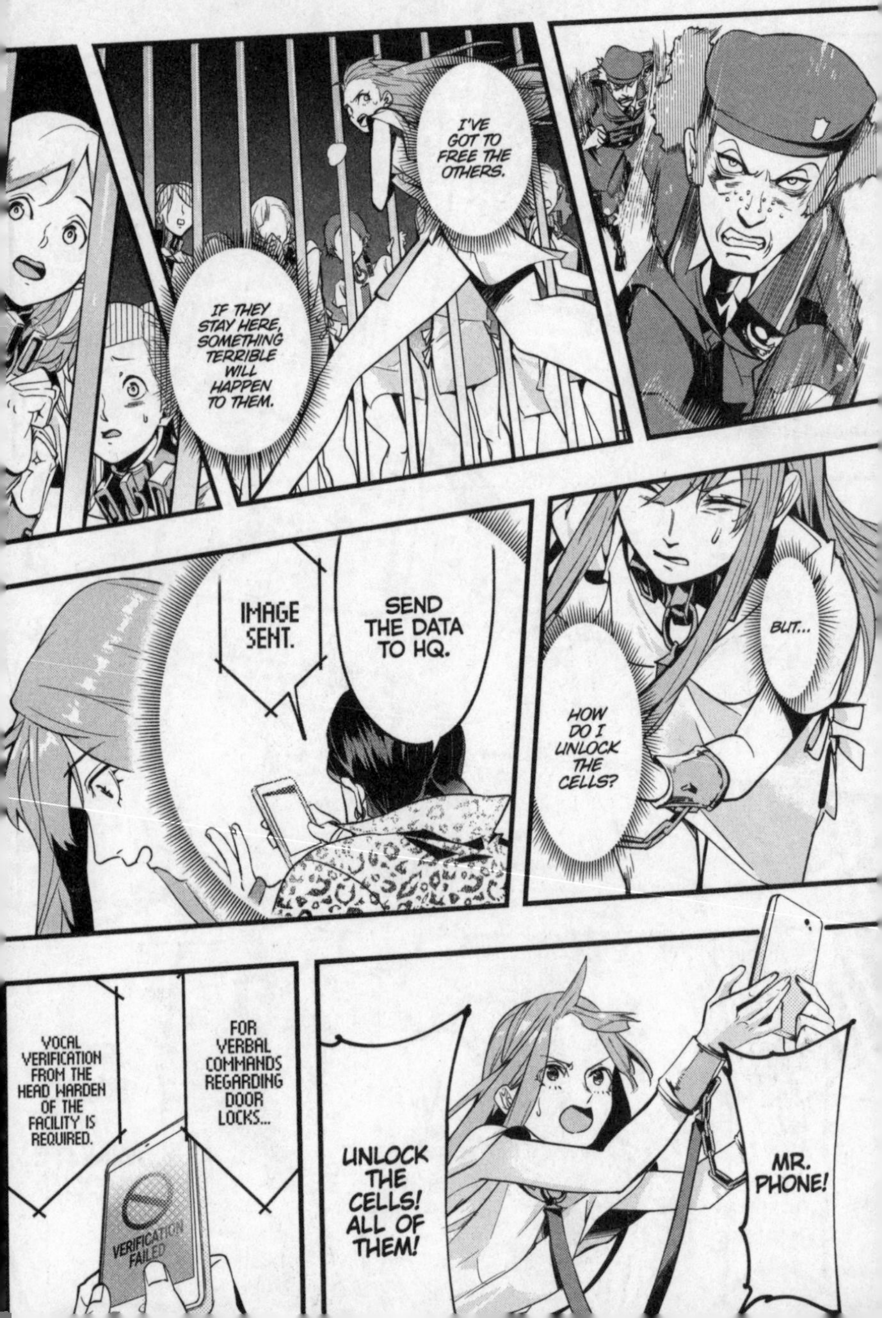
I'VE GOT TO FREE THE OTHERS.
IF THEY STAY HERE, SOMETHING TERRIBLE WILL HAPPEN TO THEM.
BUT...
HOW DO I UNLOCK THE CELLS?
SEND THE DATA TO HQ.
IMAGE SENT.
MR. PHONE!
UNLOCK THE CELLS! ALL OF THEM!
FOR VERBAL COMMANDS REGARDING DOOR LOCKS...
VOCAL VERIFICATION FROM THE HEAD WARDEN OF THE FACILITY IS REQUIRED.
VERIFICATION FAILED

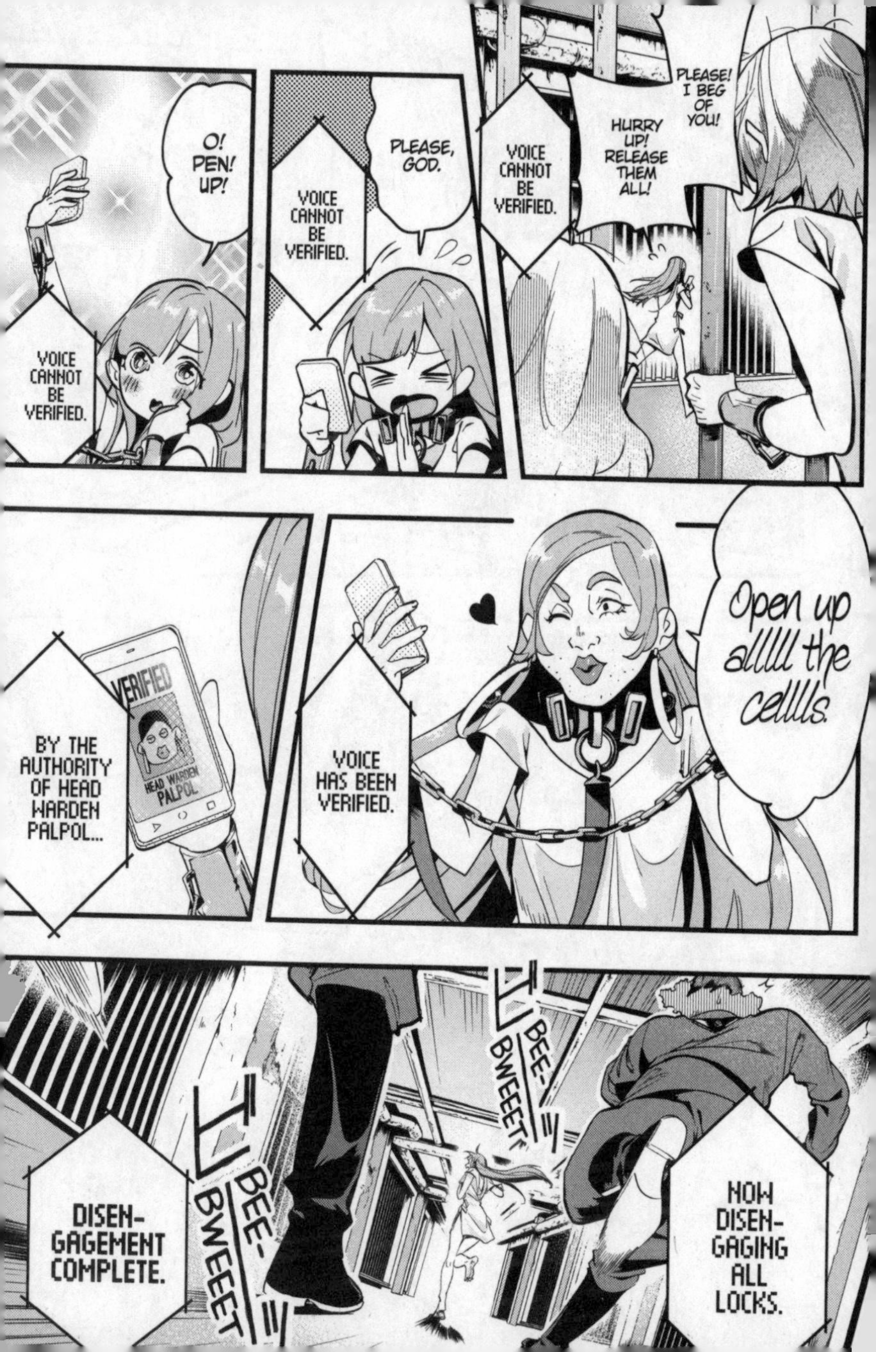
PLEASE! I BEG OF YOU!
HURRY UP! RELEASE THEM ALL!
VOICE CANNOT BE VERIFIED.
PLEASE, GOD.
VOICE CANNOT BE VERIFIED.
O! PEN! UP!
VOICE CANNOT BE VERIFIED.
Open up alllll the cellls.
VOICE HAS BEEN VERIFIED.
VERIFIED
HEAD WARDEN PALPOL
BY THE AUTHORITY OF HEAD WARDEN PALPOL...
NOW DISEN-GAGING ALL LOCKS.
BEE-BWEEET
BEE-BWEEET
DISEN-GAGEMENT COMPLETE.

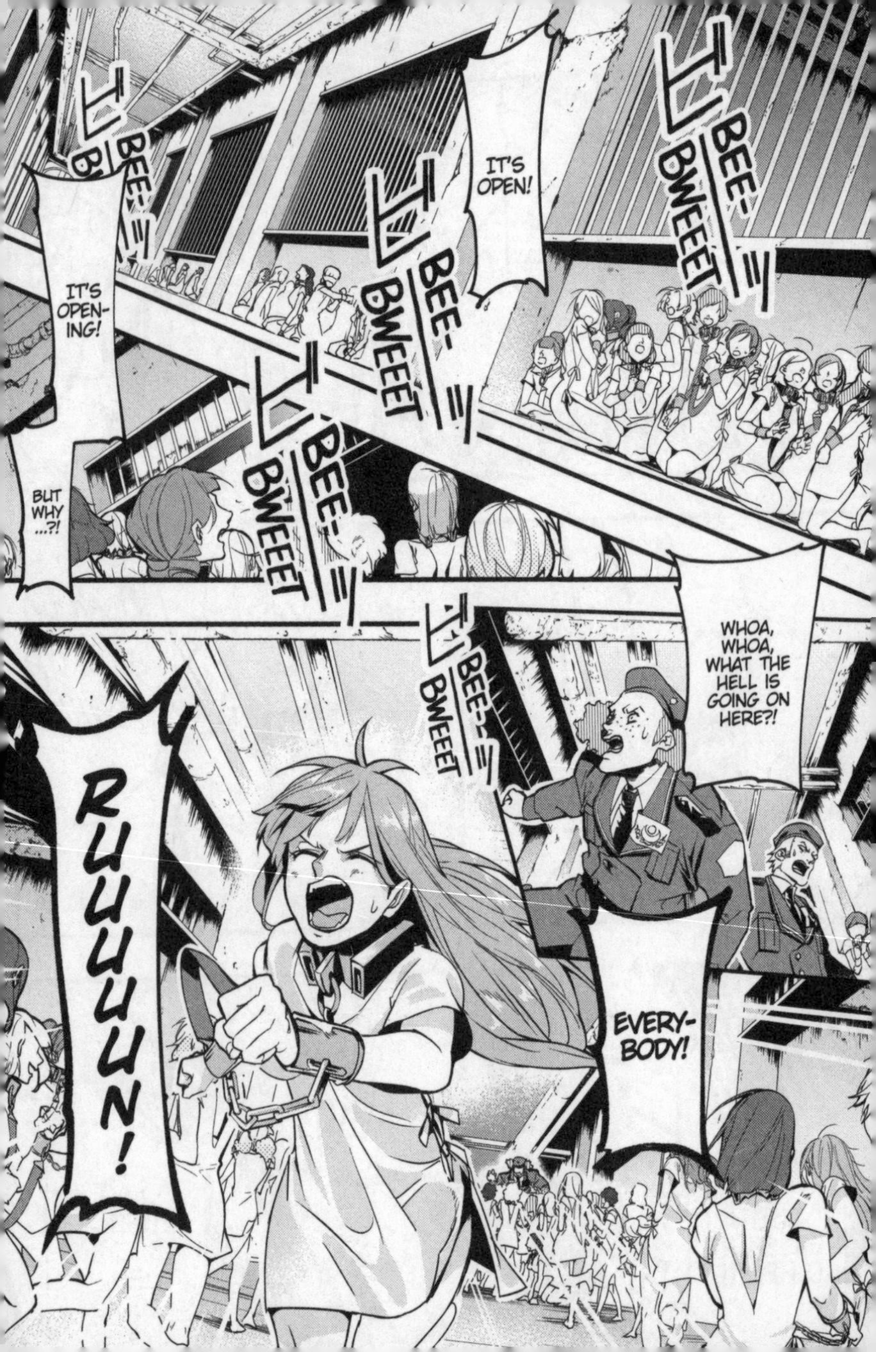
BEE-BWEEET
IT'S OPEN!
BEE-BWEEET
IT'S OPENING!
BEE-B
BEE-BWEEET
BUT WHY...?!
BEE-BWEEET
WHOA, WHOA, WHAT THE HELL IS GOING ON HERE?!
EVERYBODY!
RUUUUUN!

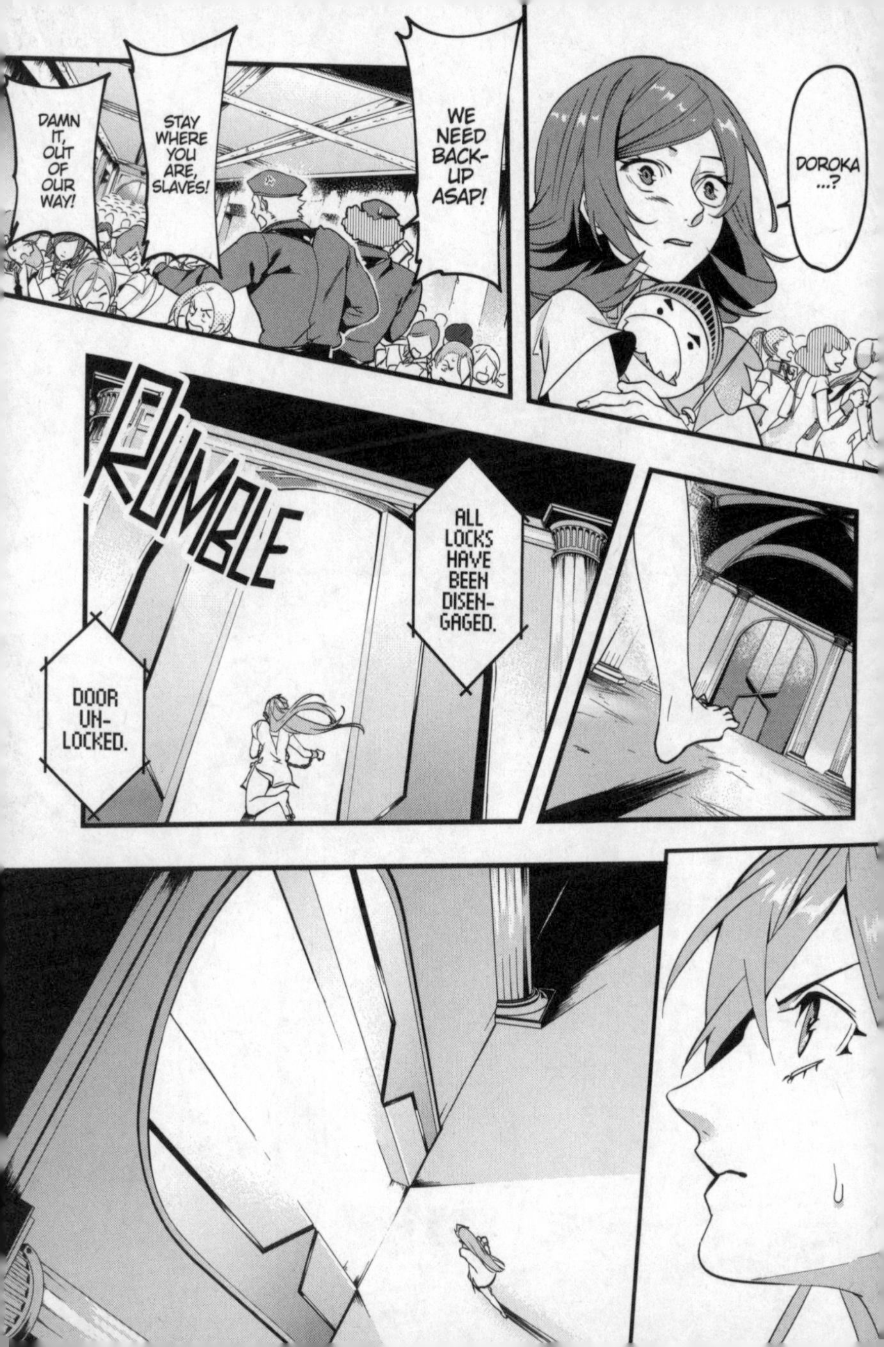
DOROKA ...?
WE NEED BACK-UP ASAP!
STAY WHERE YOU ARE, SLAVES!
DAMN IT, OUT OF OUR WAY!
RUMBLE
ALL LOCKS HAVE BEEN DISENGAGED.
DOOR UNLOCKED.

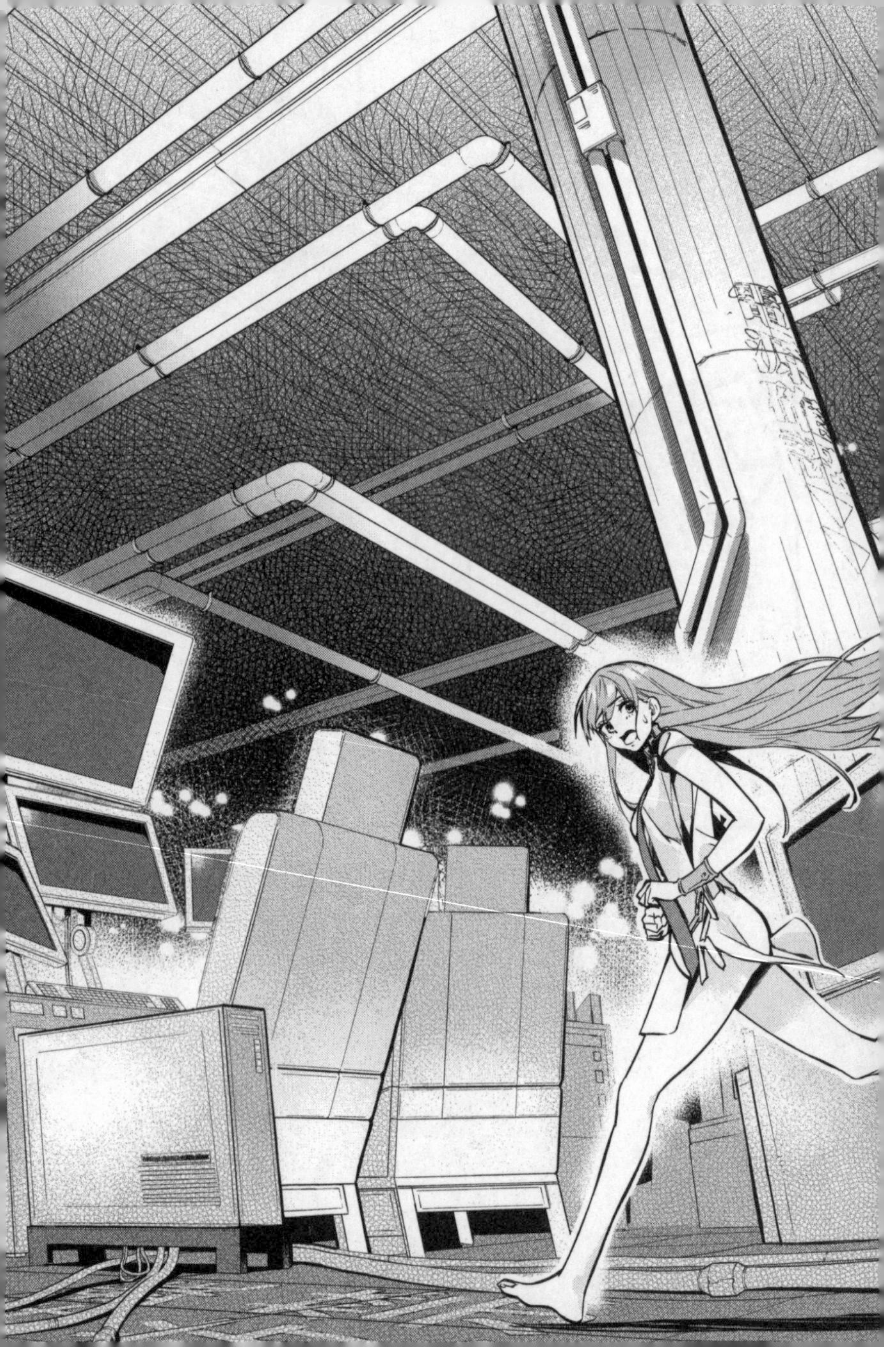

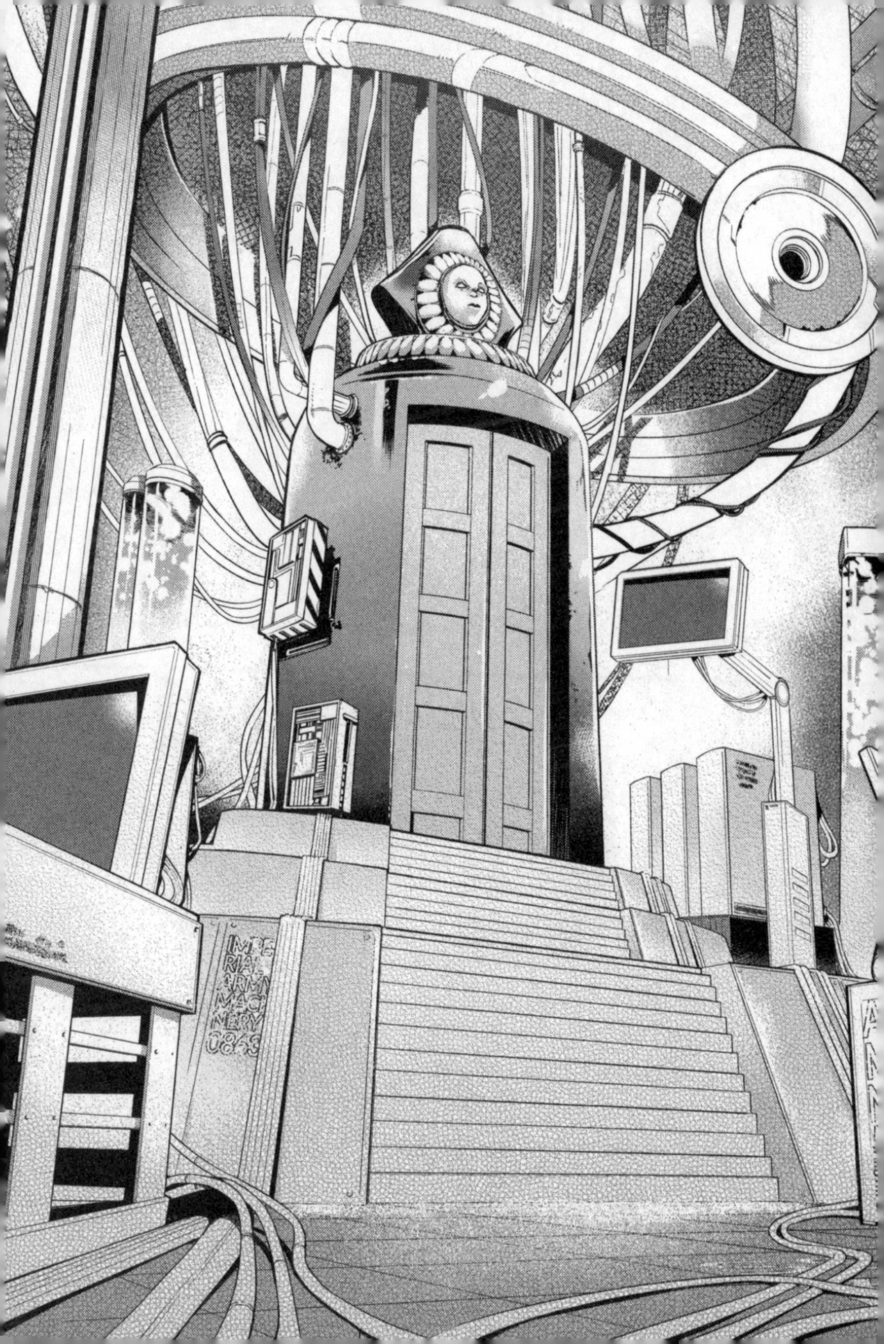

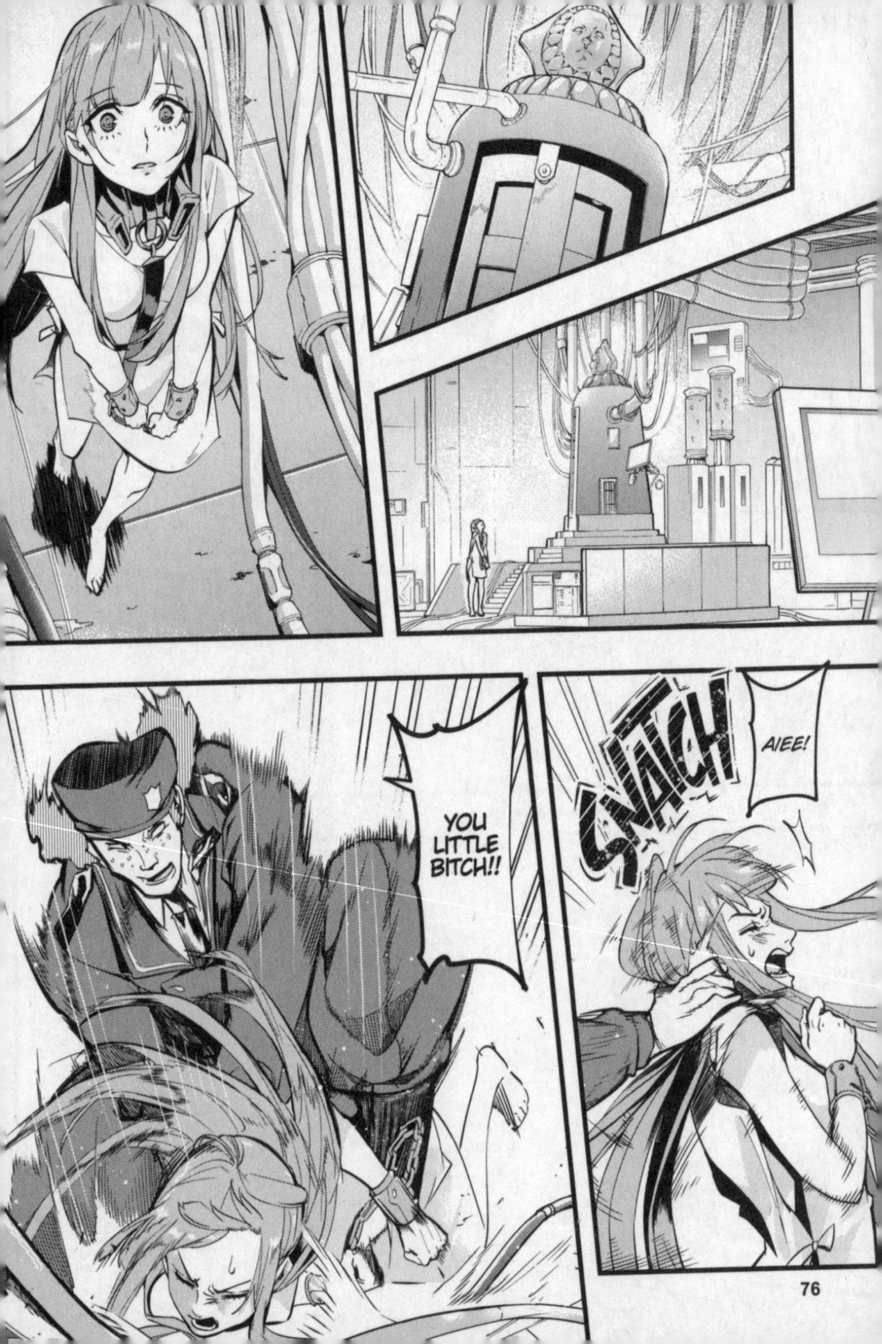
SNATCH
AIEE!
YOU LITTLE BITCH!!

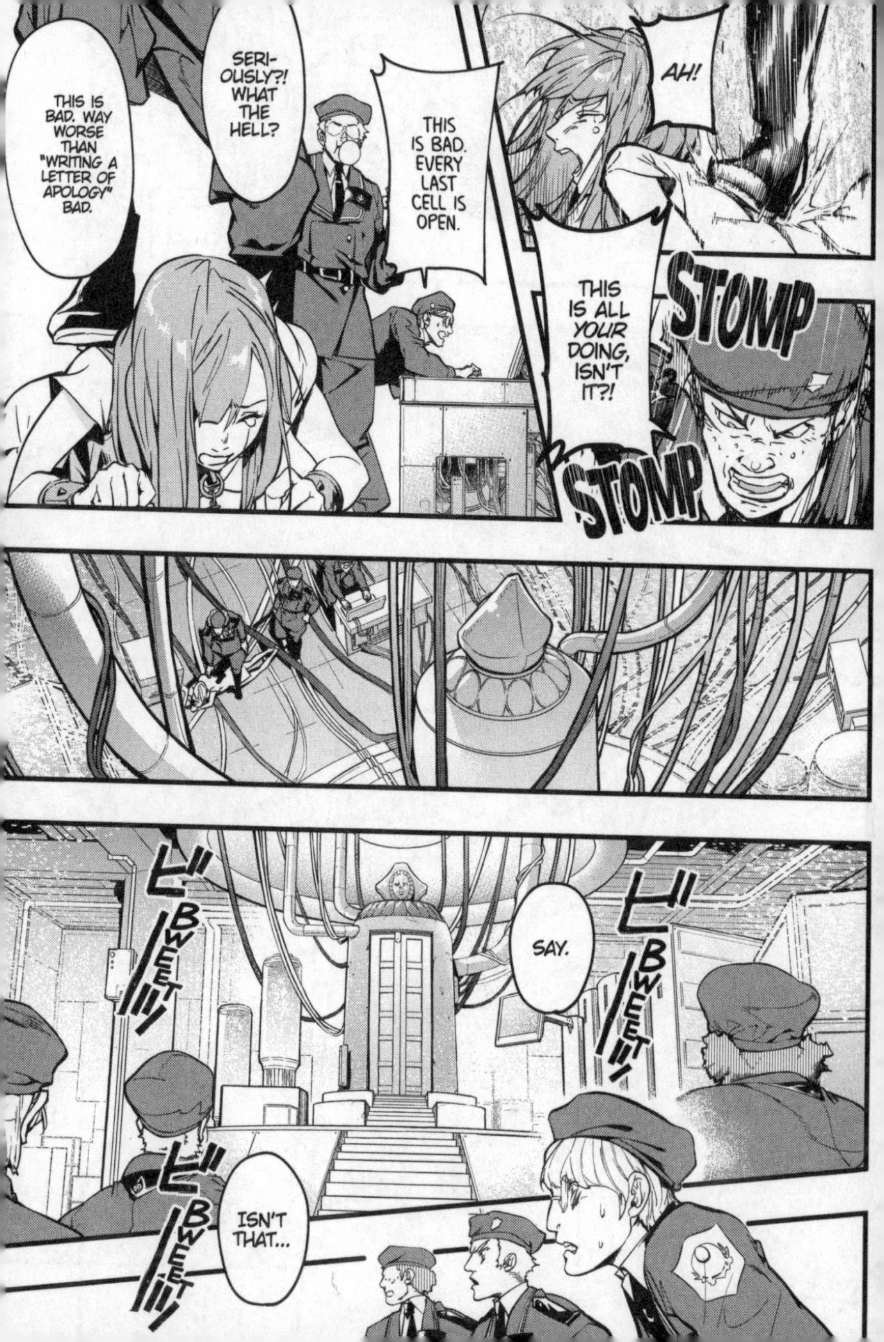
AH!
STOMP
THIS IS ALL YOUR DOING, ISN'T IT?!
STOMP
THIS IS BAD. EVERY LAST CELL IS OPEN.
SERIOUSLY?! WHAT THE HELL?
THIS IS BAD. WAY WORSE THAN "WRITING A LETTER OF APOLOGY" BAD.
ビ BWEET!!!
SAY.
ビ BWEET!!!
ISN'T THAT...
ビ BWEET!!!

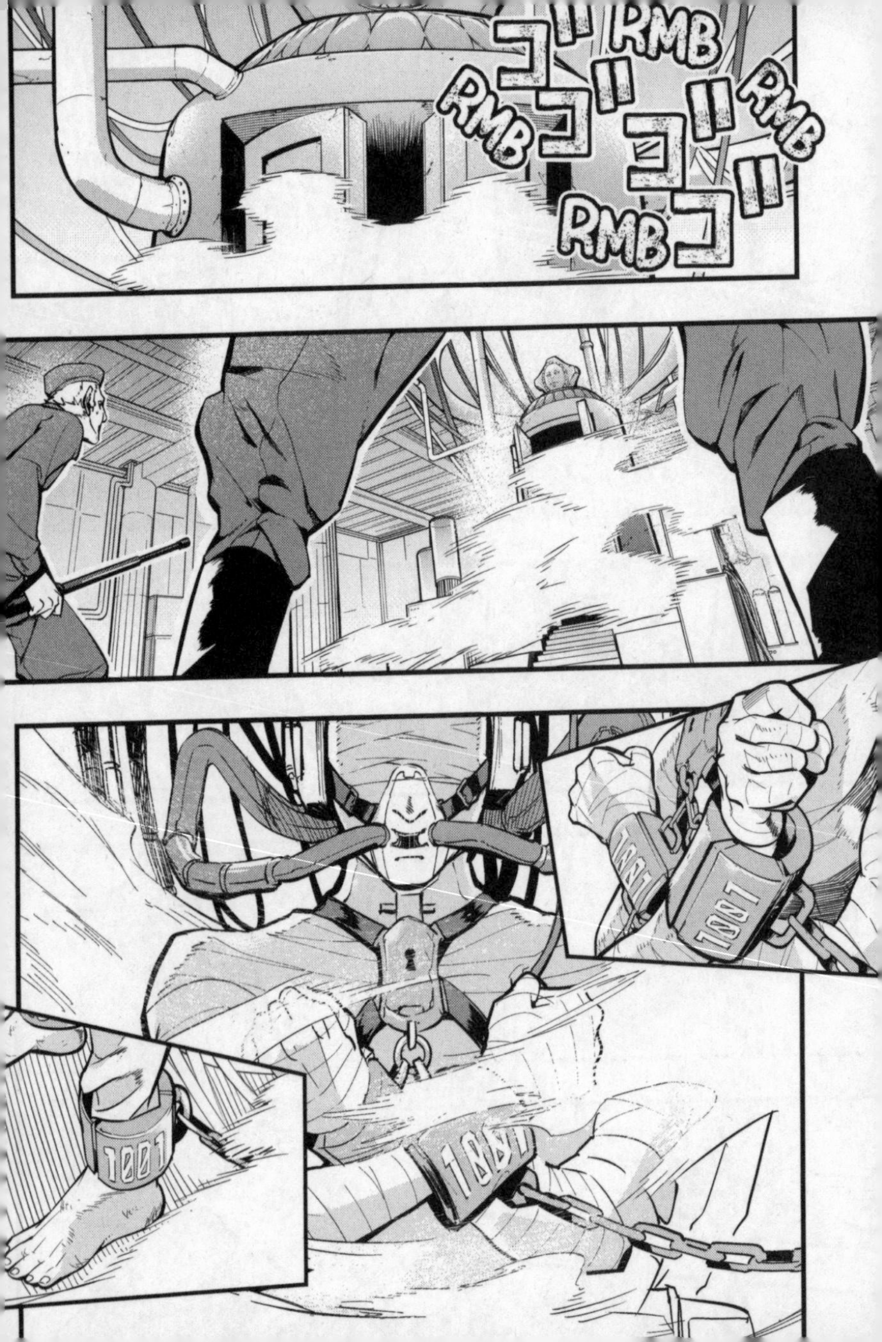
RMB
ゴ
RMB
ゴ
RMB
ゴ
RMB
ゴ
1001

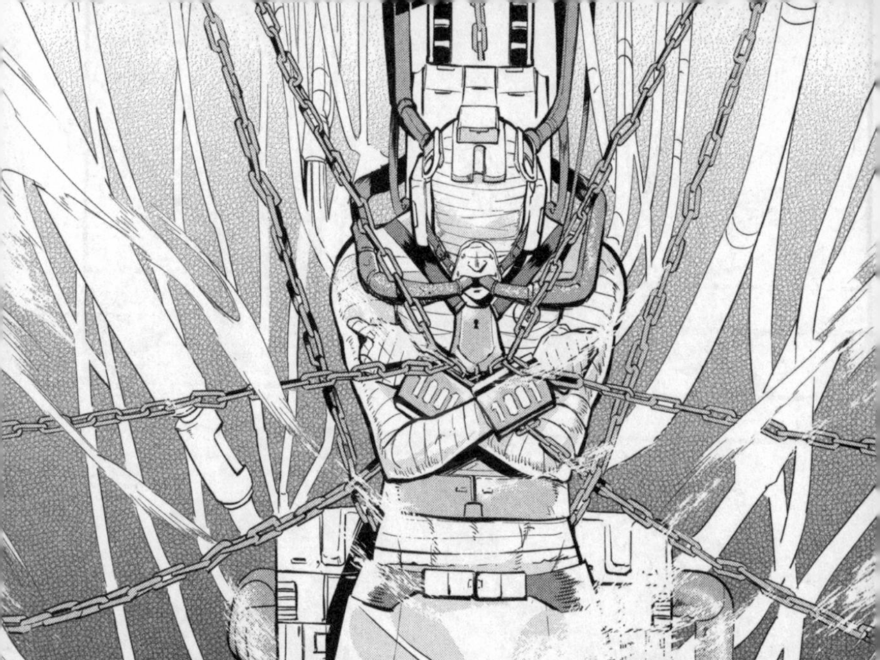
1001
1001

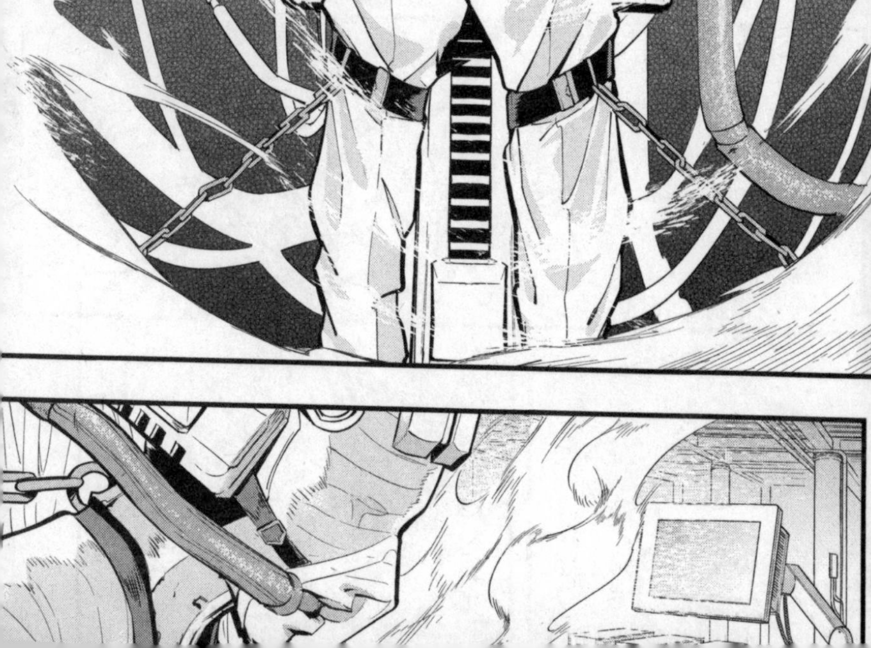

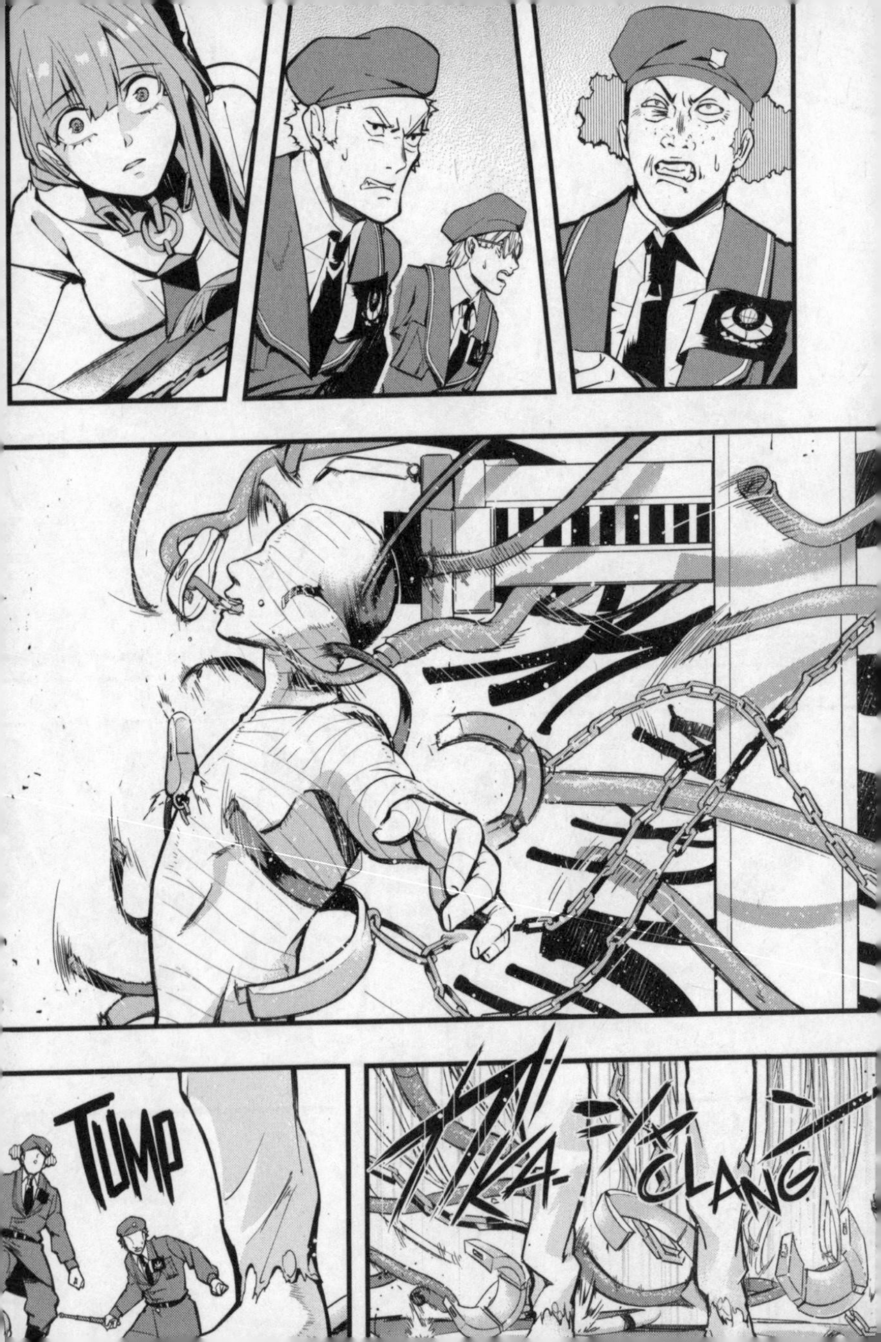
KA-
CLANG
TUMP

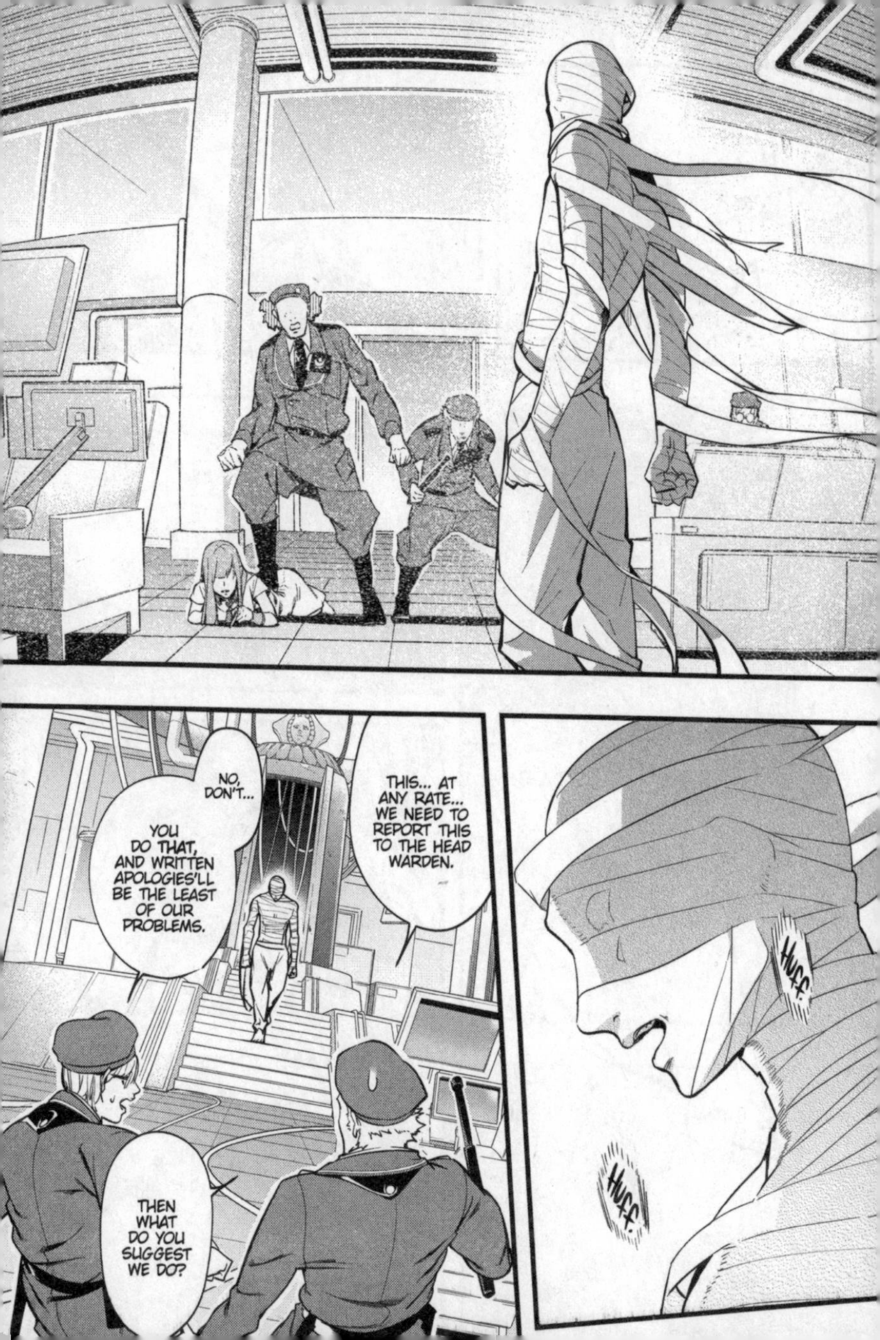
HUFF.
HUFF.
THIS... AT ANY RATE... WE NEED TO REPORT THIS TO THE HEAD WARDEN.
NO, DON'T...
YOU DO THAT, AND WRITTEN APOLOGIES'LL BE THE LEAST OF OUR PROBLEMS.
THEN WHAT DO YOU SUGGEST WE DO?

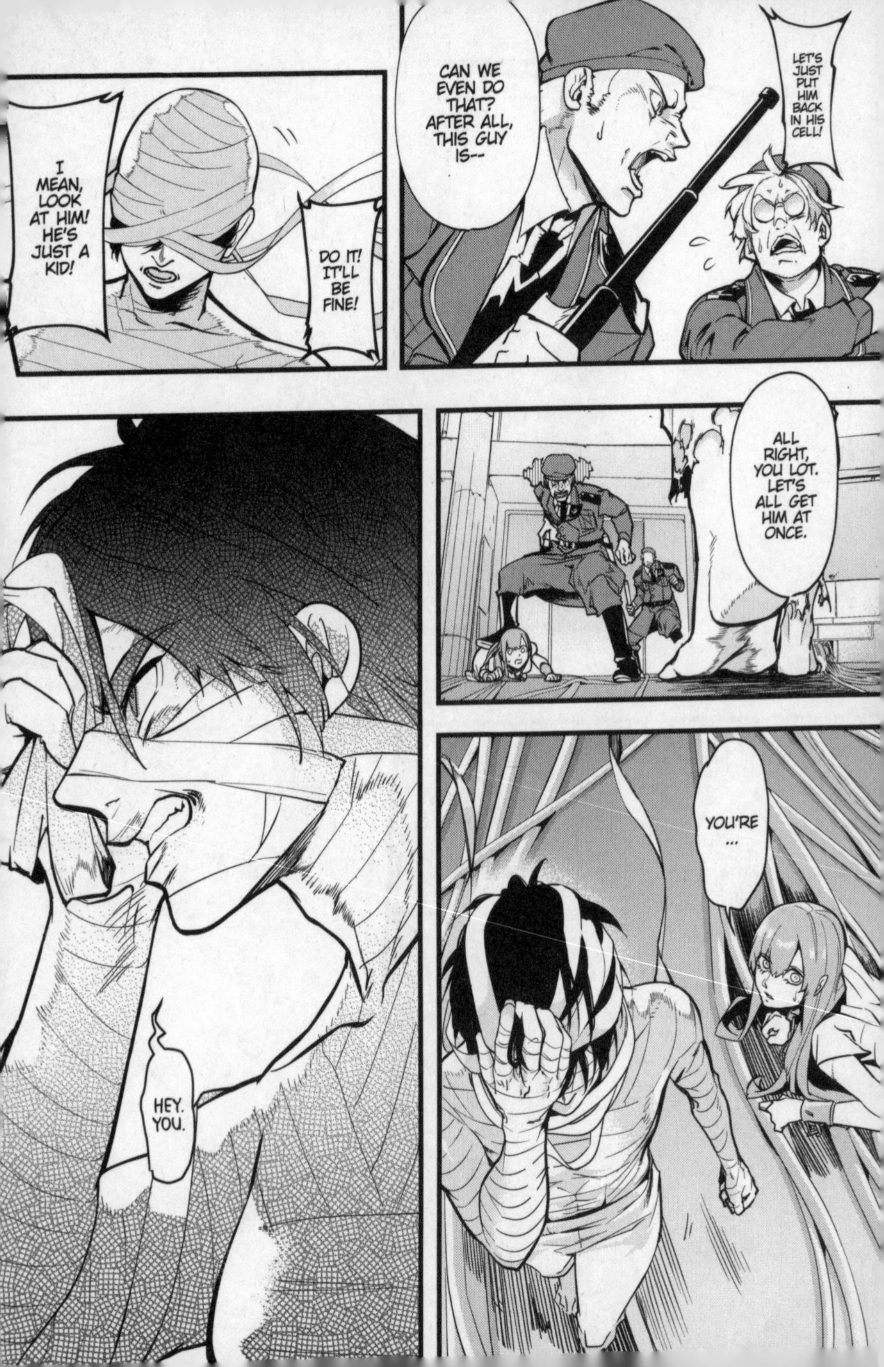
LET'S JUST PUT HIM BACK IN HIS CELL!
CAN WE EVEN DO THAT? AFTER ALL, THIS GUY IS--
I MEAN, LOOK AT HIM! HE'S JUST A KID!
DO IT! IT'LL BE FINE!
ALL RIGHT, YOU LOT. LET'S ALL GET HIM AT ONCE.
YOU'RE ...
HEY. YOU.

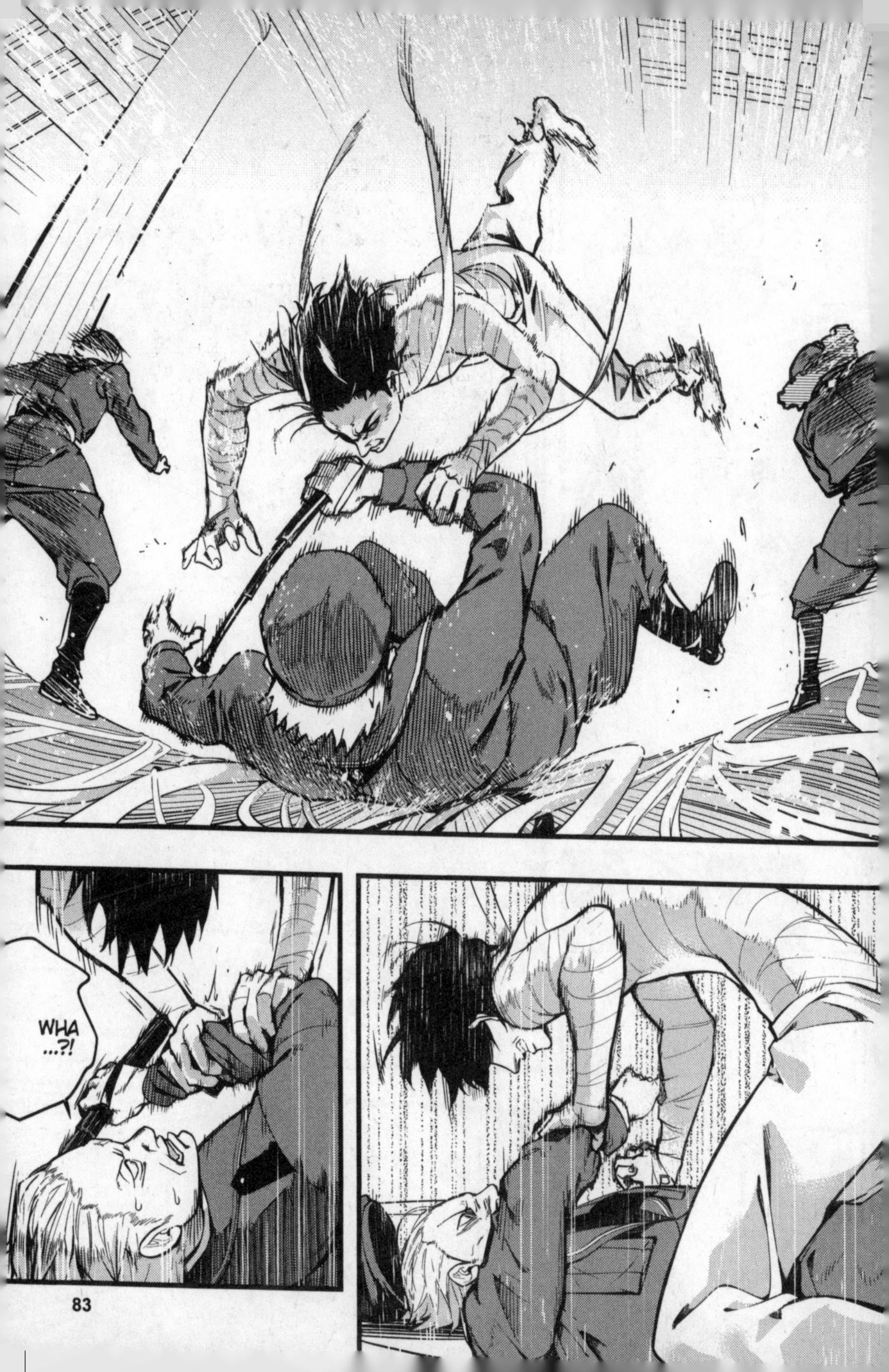
WHA ...?!

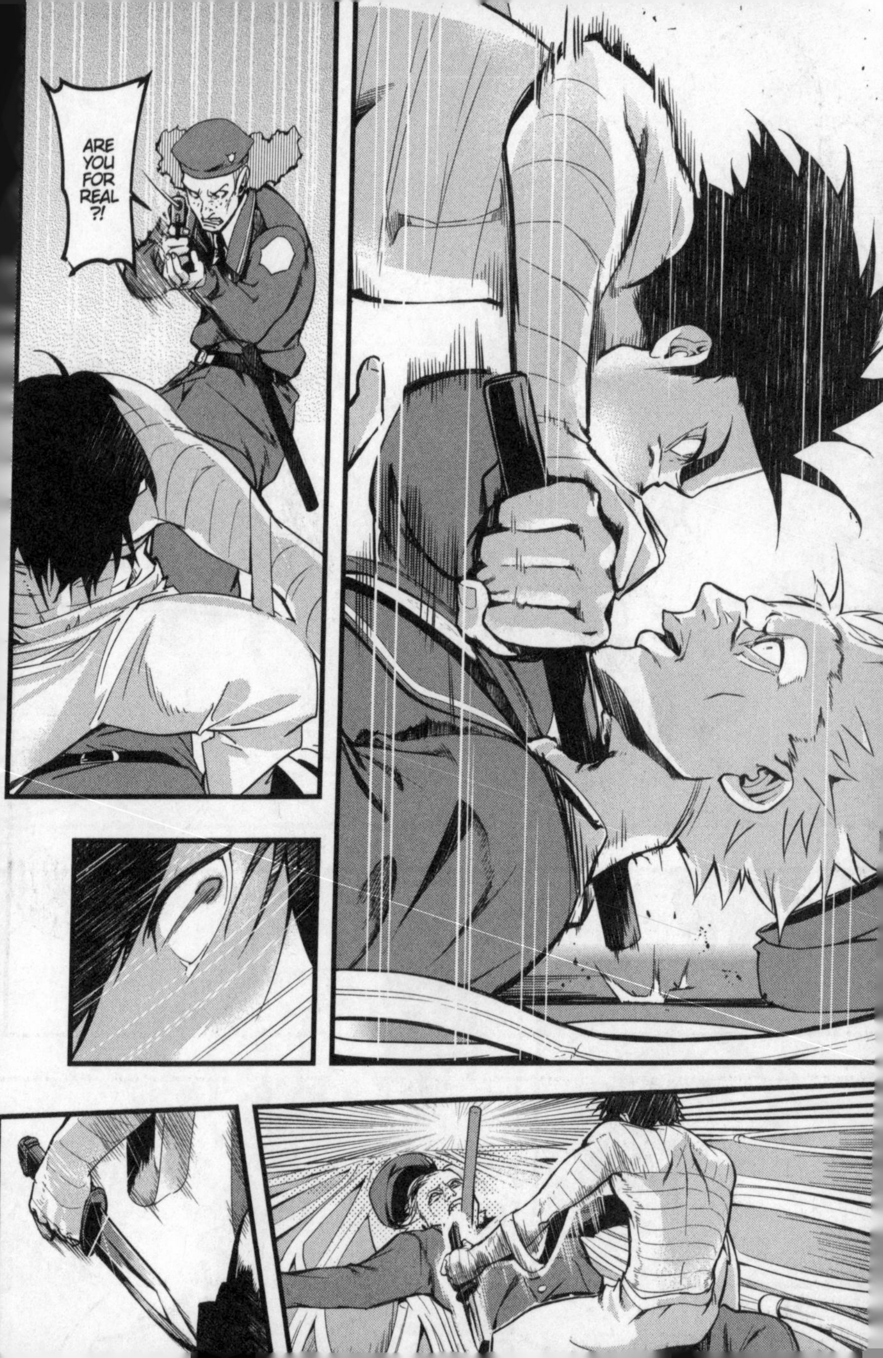
ARE YOU FOR REAL ?!

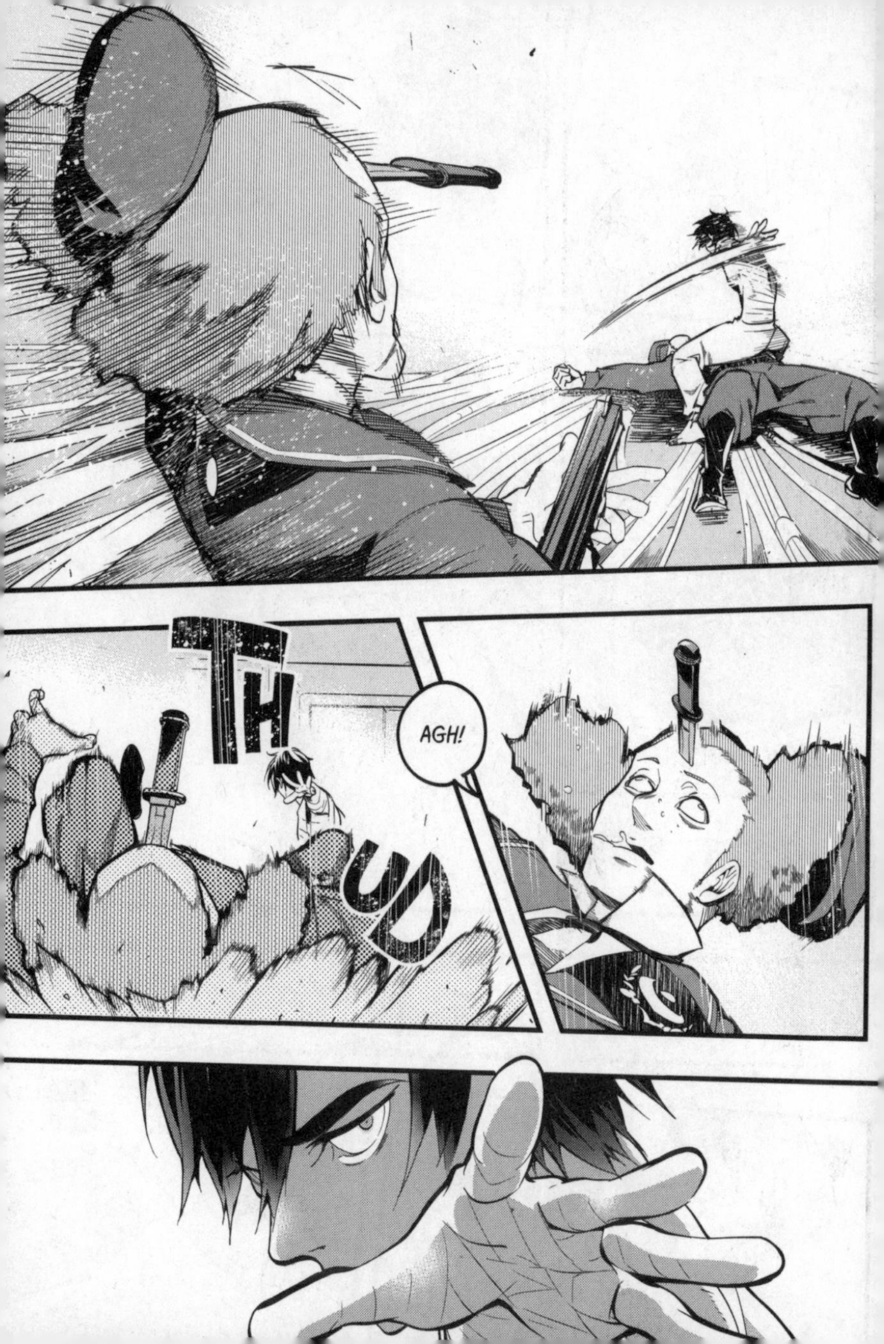
AGH!
THUD

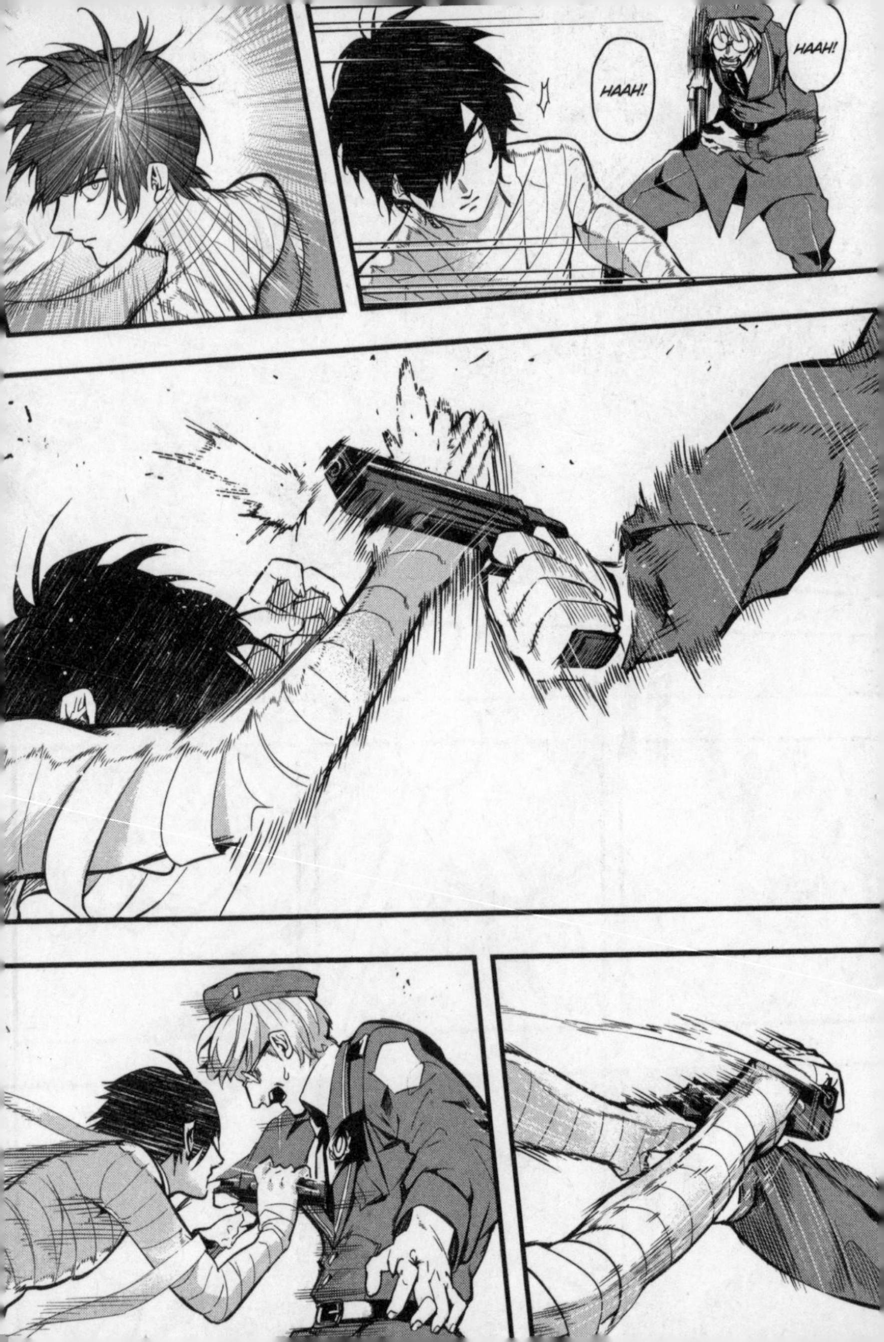
HAAH!
HAAH!

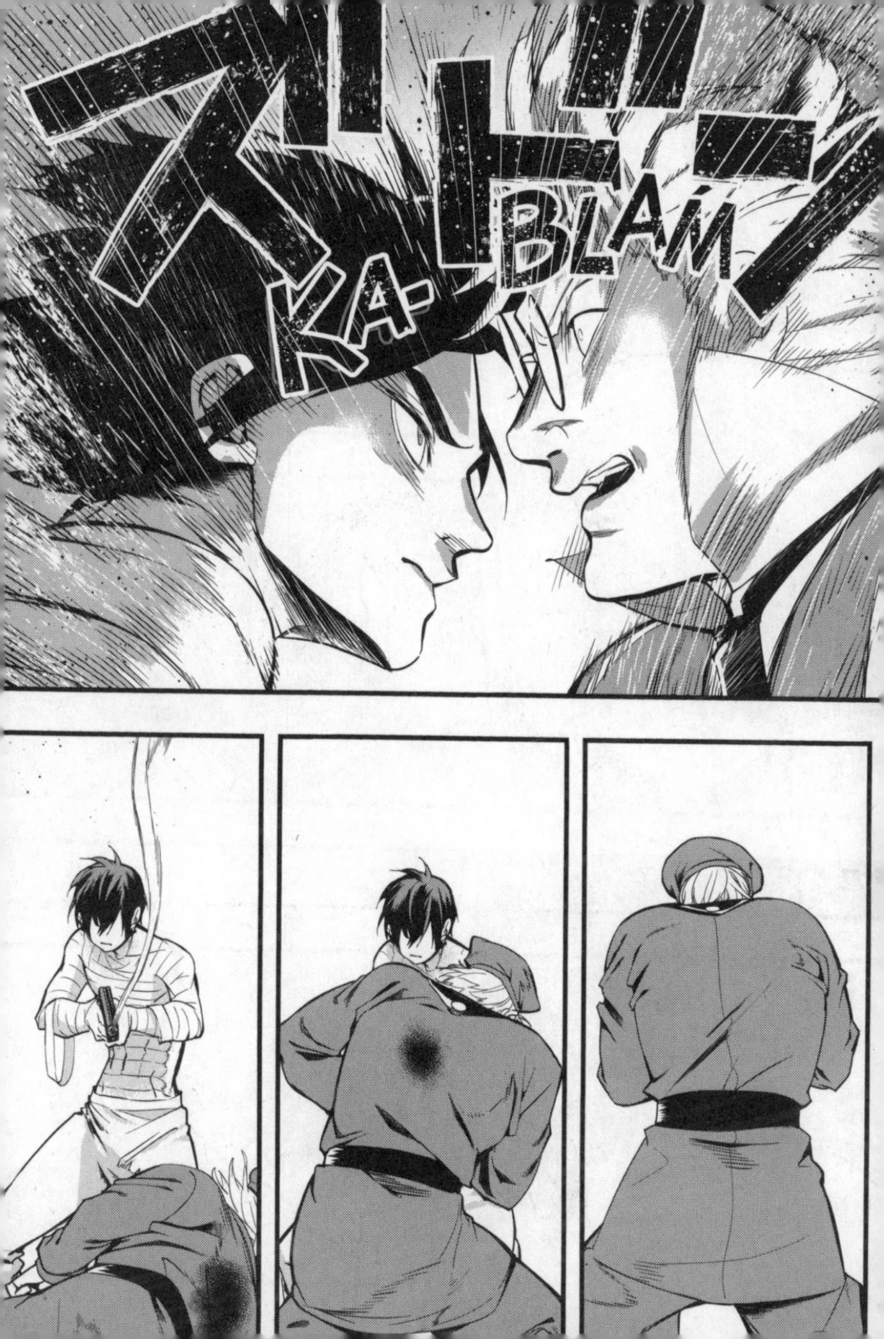
KA-BLAM

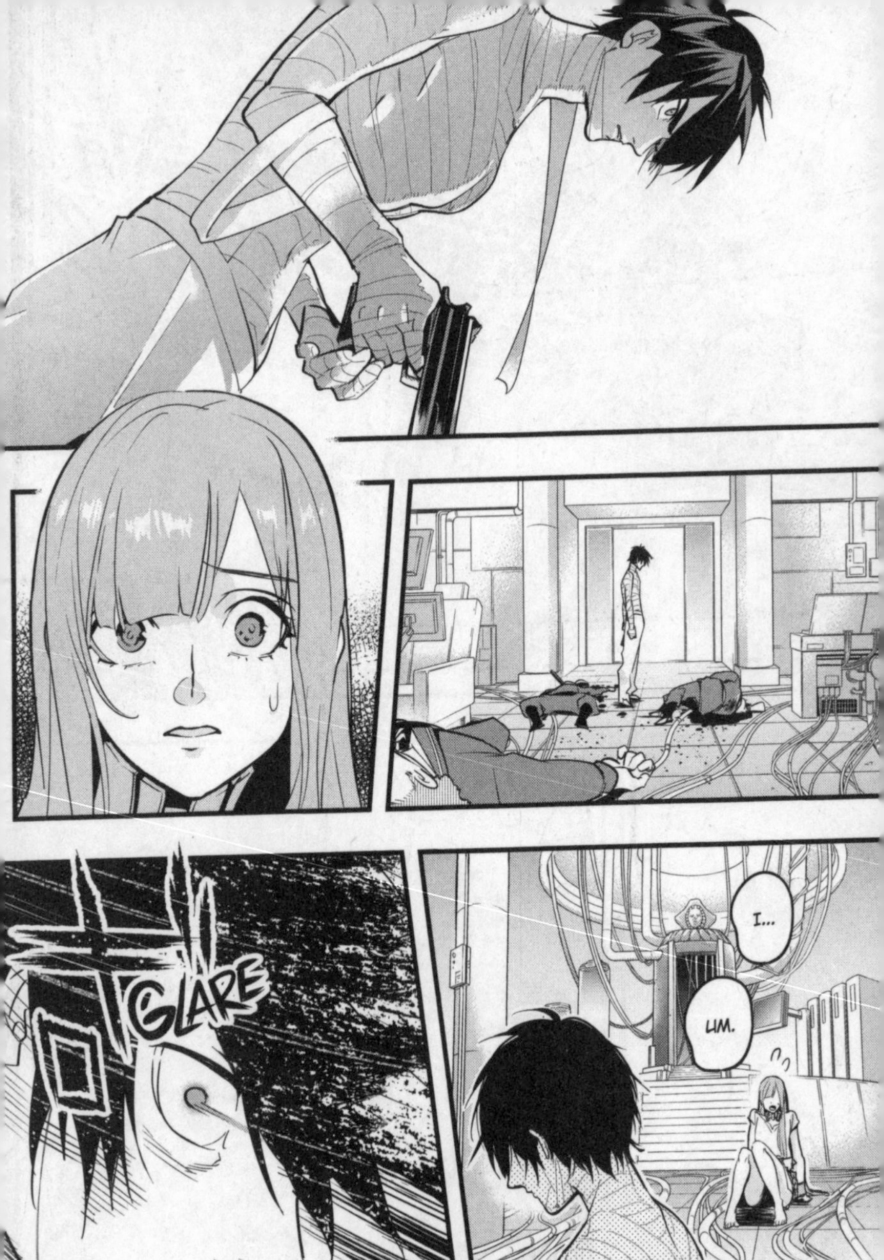
I...
UM.
GLARE

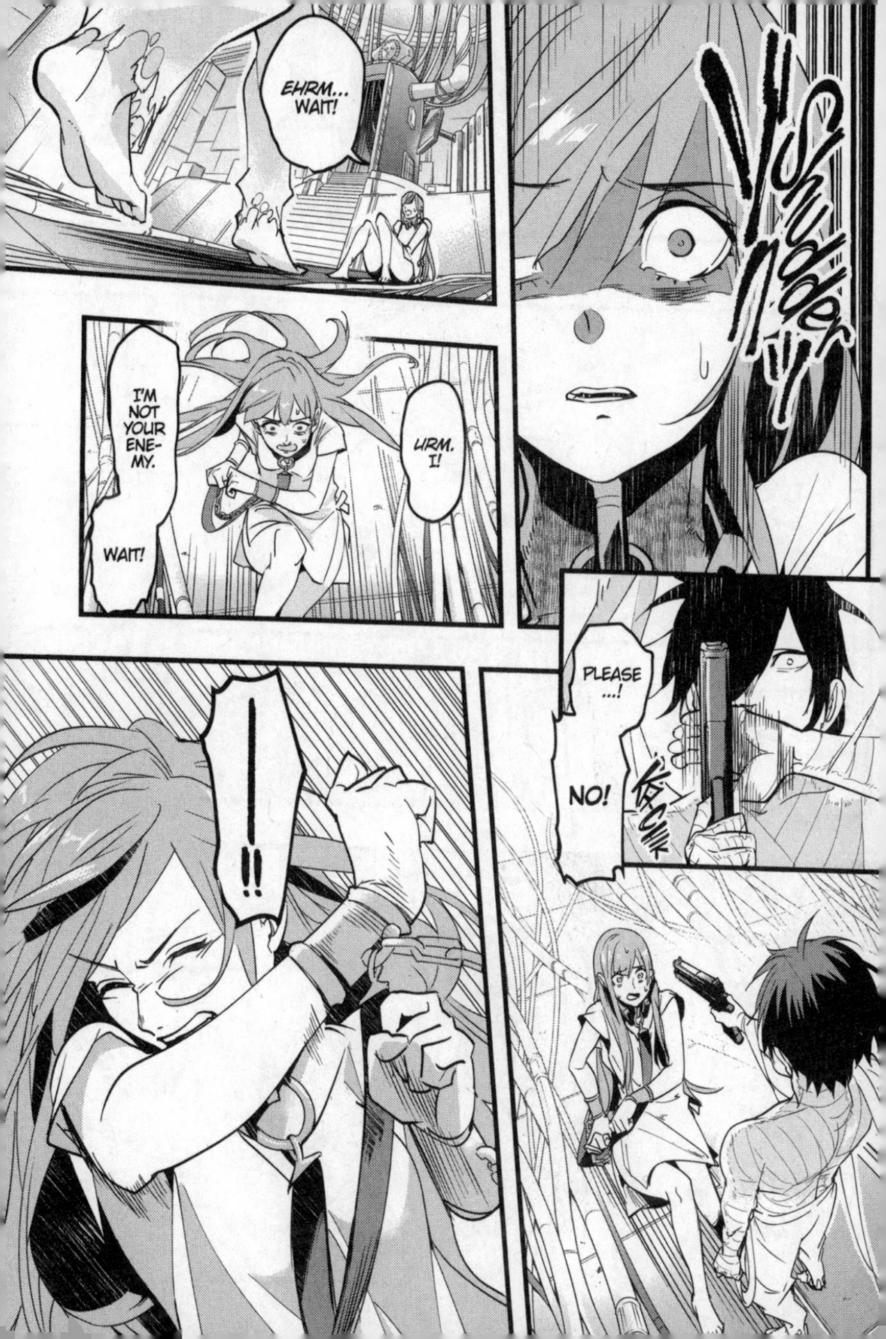
Shudder!!
EHRM... WAIT!
URM. I!
I'M NOT YOUR ENE-MY.
WAIT!
KA-CHIK
PLEASE ...!
NO!
!!!

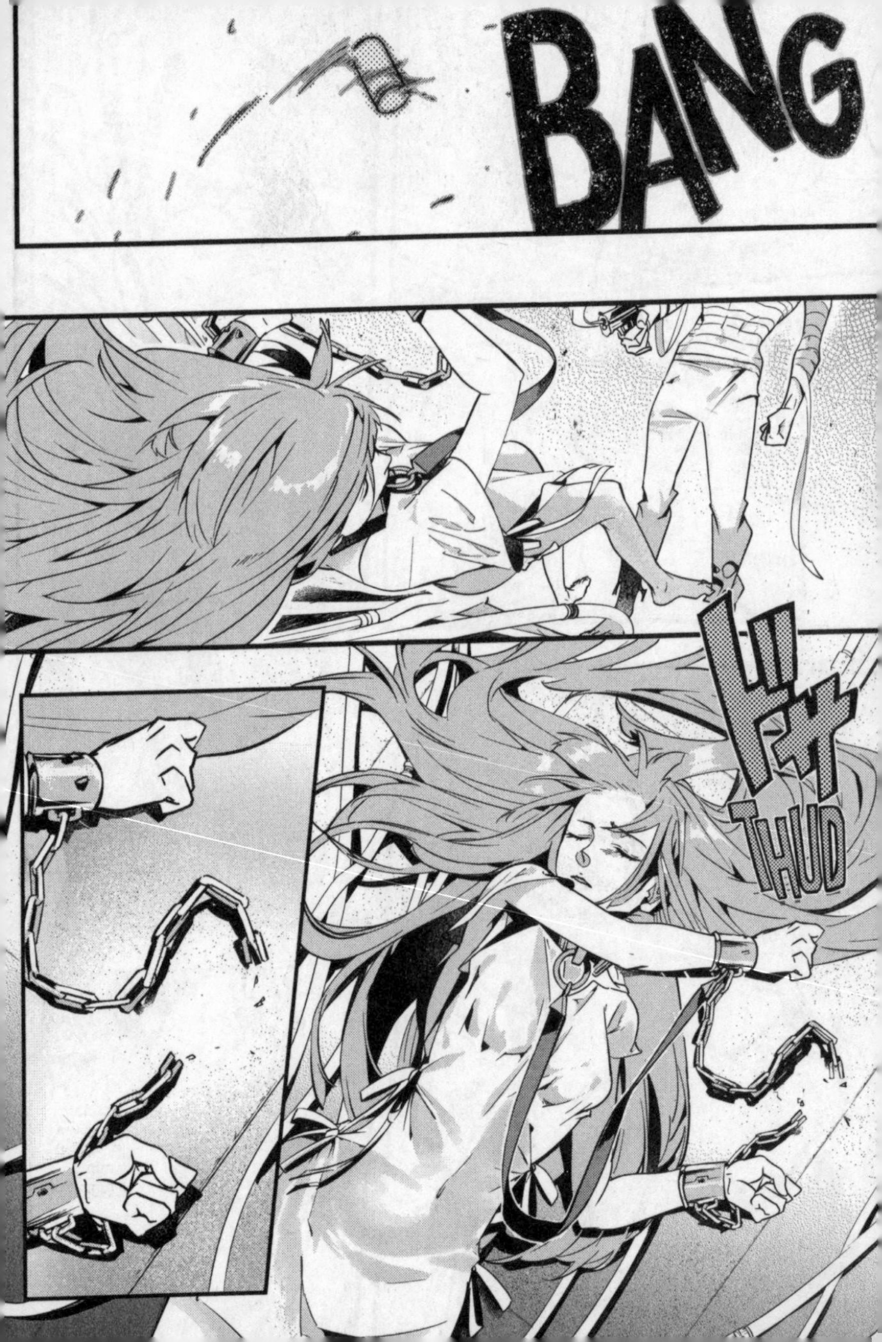
BANG
THUD

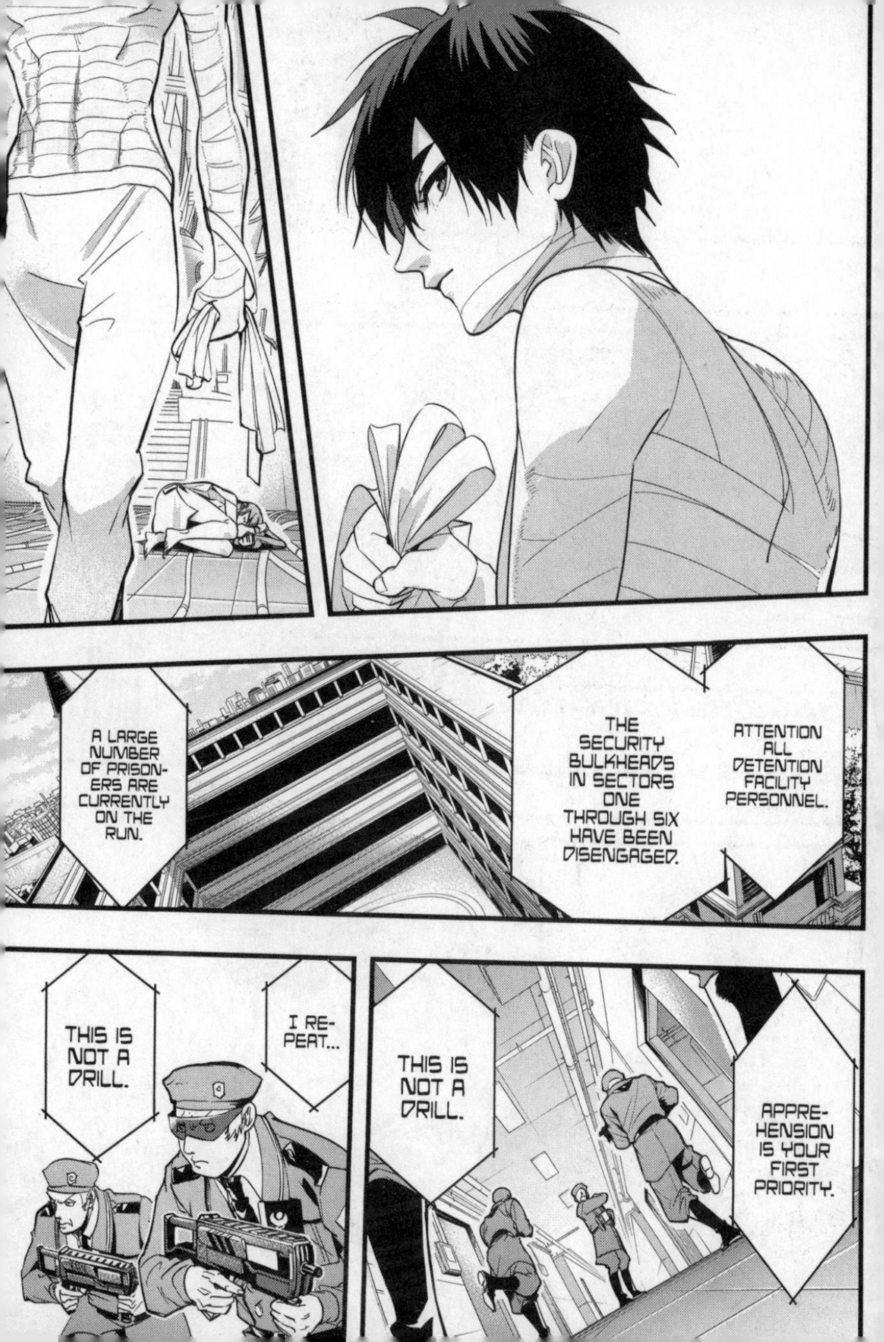
ATTENTION ALL DETENTION FACILITY PERSONNEL.
THE SECURITY BULKHEADS IN SECTORS ONE THROUGH SIX HAVE BEEN DISENGAGED.
A LARGE NUMBER OF PRISONERS ARE CURRENTLY ON THE RUN.
APPREHENSION IS YOUR FIRST PRIORITY.
THIS IS NOT A DRILL.
I REPEAT...
THIS IS NOT A DRILL.

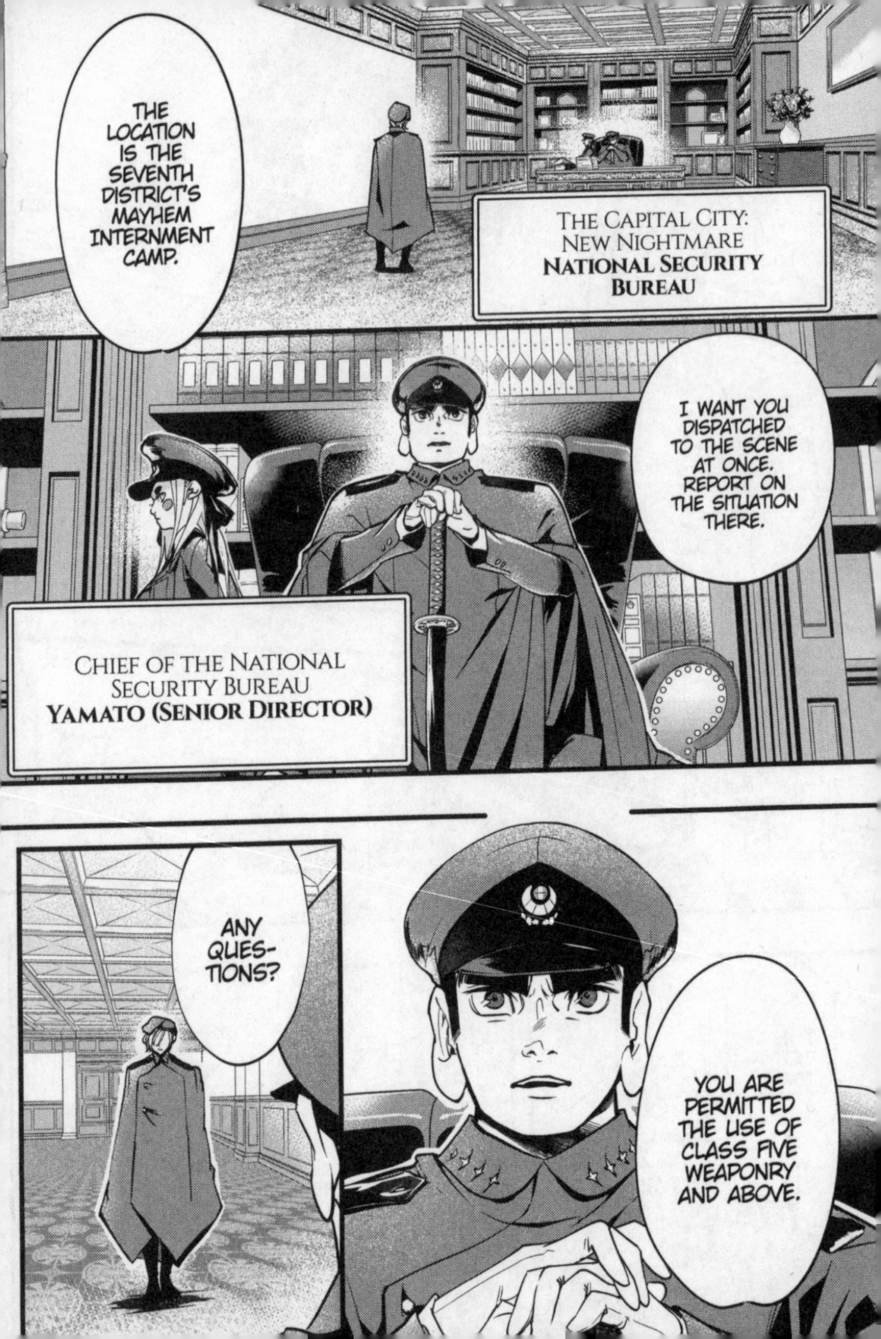
THE CAPITAL CITY: NEW NIGHTMARE NATIONAL SECURITY BUREAU
THE LOCATION IS THE SEVENTH DISTRICT'S MAYHEM INTERNMENT CAMP.
I WANT YOU DISPATCHED TO THE SCENE AT ONCE. REPORT ON THE SITUATION THERE.
CHIEF OF THE NATIONAL SECURITY BUREAU YAMATO (SENIOR DIRECTOR)
YOU ARE PERMITTED THE USE OF CLASS FIVE WEAPONRY AND ABOVE.
ANY QUES-TIONS?

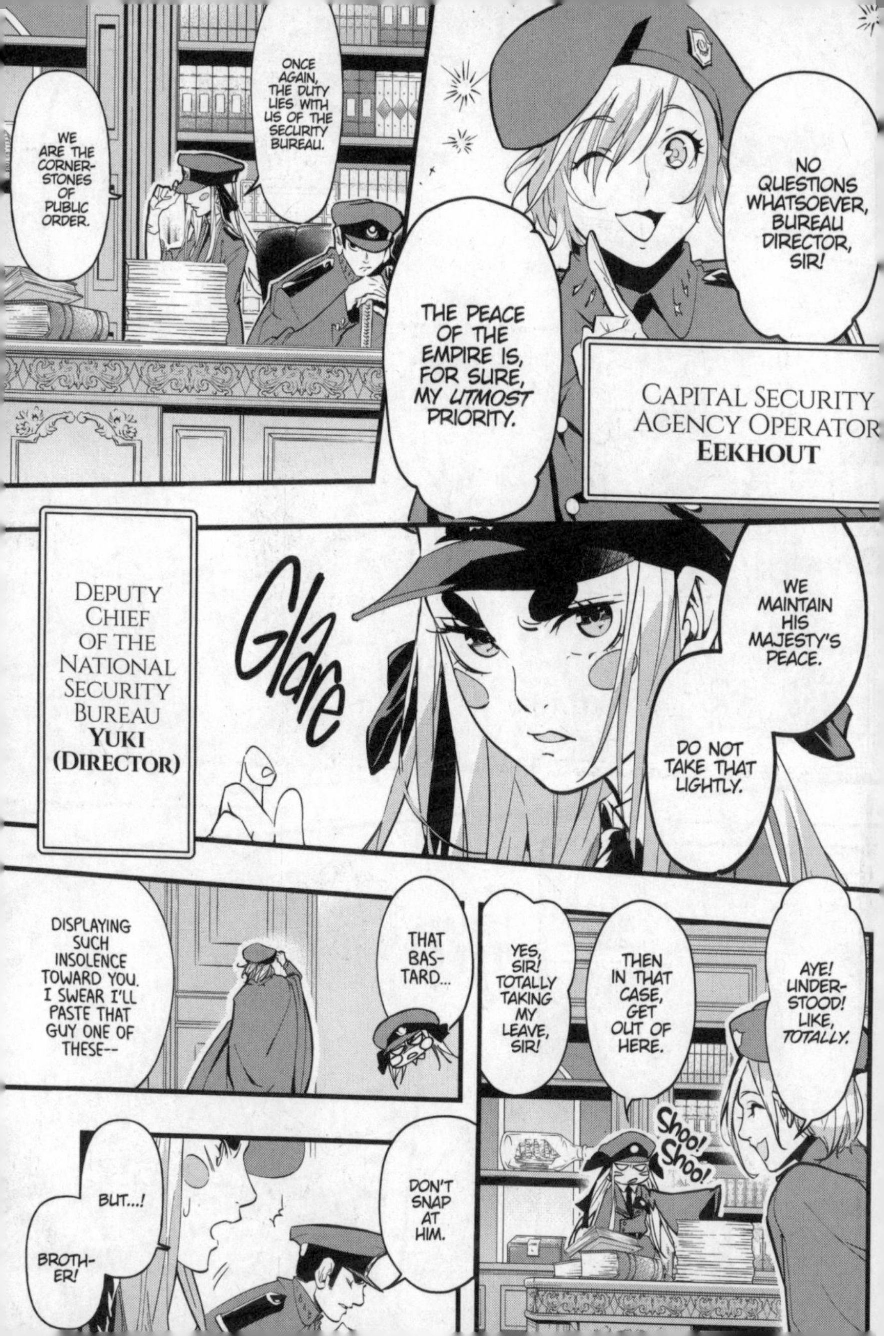
NO QUESTIONS WHATSOEVER, BUREAU DIRECTOR, SIR!
THE PEACE OF THE EMPIRE IS, FOR SURE, MY *UTMOST* PRIORITY.
CAPITAL SECURITY AGENCY OPERATOR **EEKHOUT**
ONCE AGAIN, THE DUTY LIES WITH US OF THE SECURITY BUREAU.
WE ARE THE CORNERSTONES OF PUBLIC ORDER.
WE MAINTAIN HIS MAJESTY'S PEACE.
DO NOT TAKE THAT LIGHTLY.
Glare
DEPUTY CHIEF OF THE NATIONAL SECURITY BUREAU **YUKI (DIRECTOR)**
AYE! UNDERSTOOD! LIKE, *TOTALLY.*
THEN IN THAT CASE, GET OUT OF HERE.
YES, SIR! TOTALLY TAKING MY LEAVE, SIR!
Shoo! Shoo!
THAT BASTARD...
DISPLAYING SUCH INSOLENCE TOWARD YOU. I SWEAR I'LL PASTE THAT GUY ONE OF THESE--
DON'T SNAP AT HIM.
BUT...!
BROTHER!

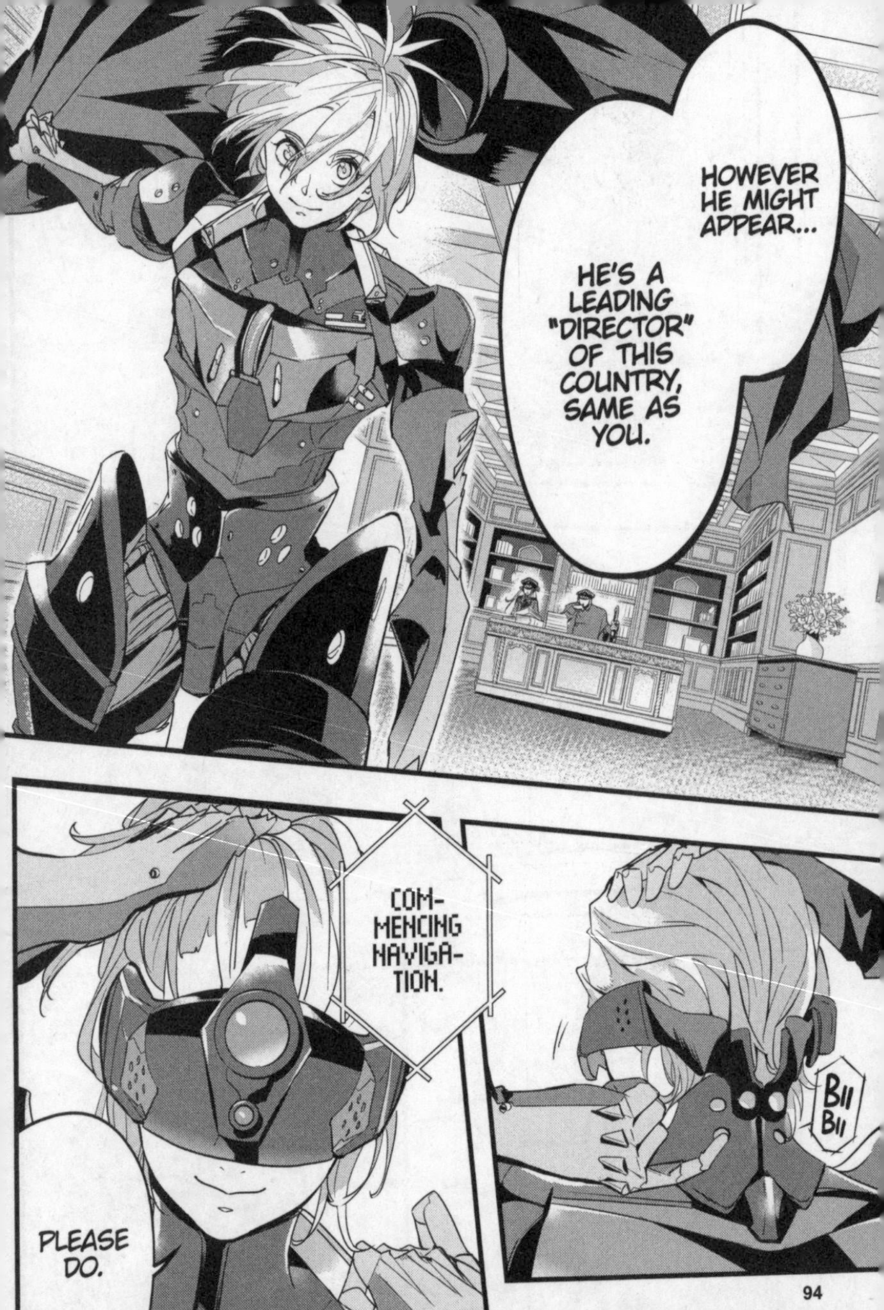
HOWEVER HE MIGHT APPEAR...
HE'S A LEADING "DIRECTOR" OF THIS COUNTRY, SAME AS YOU.
BII BII
COM-MENCING NAVIGA-TION.
PLEASE DO.

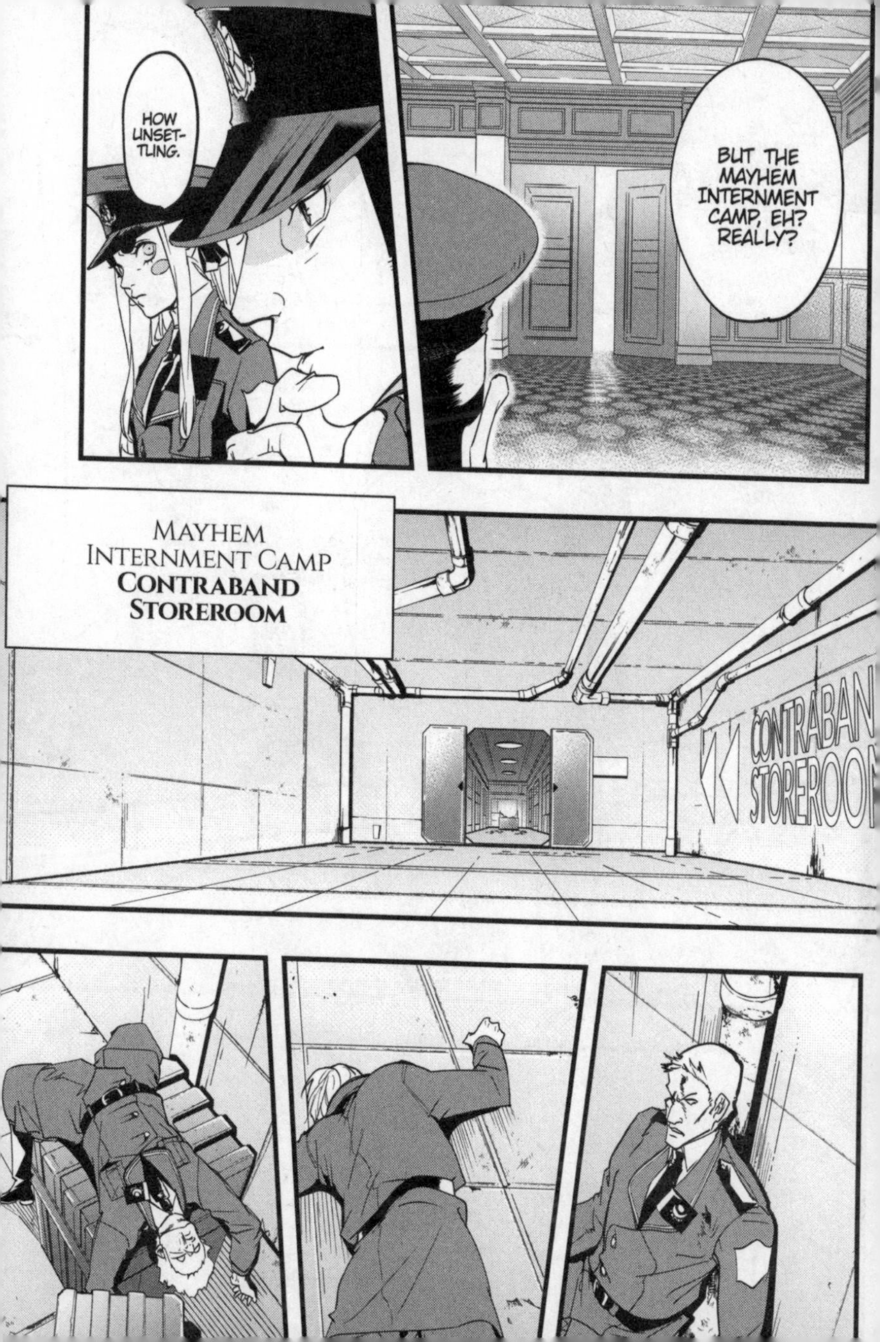
BUT THE MAYHEM INTERNMENT CAMP, EH? REALLY?
HOW UNSET-TLING.
MAYHEM INTERNMENT CAMP **CONTRABAND STOREROOM**
CONTRABAN STOREROOM

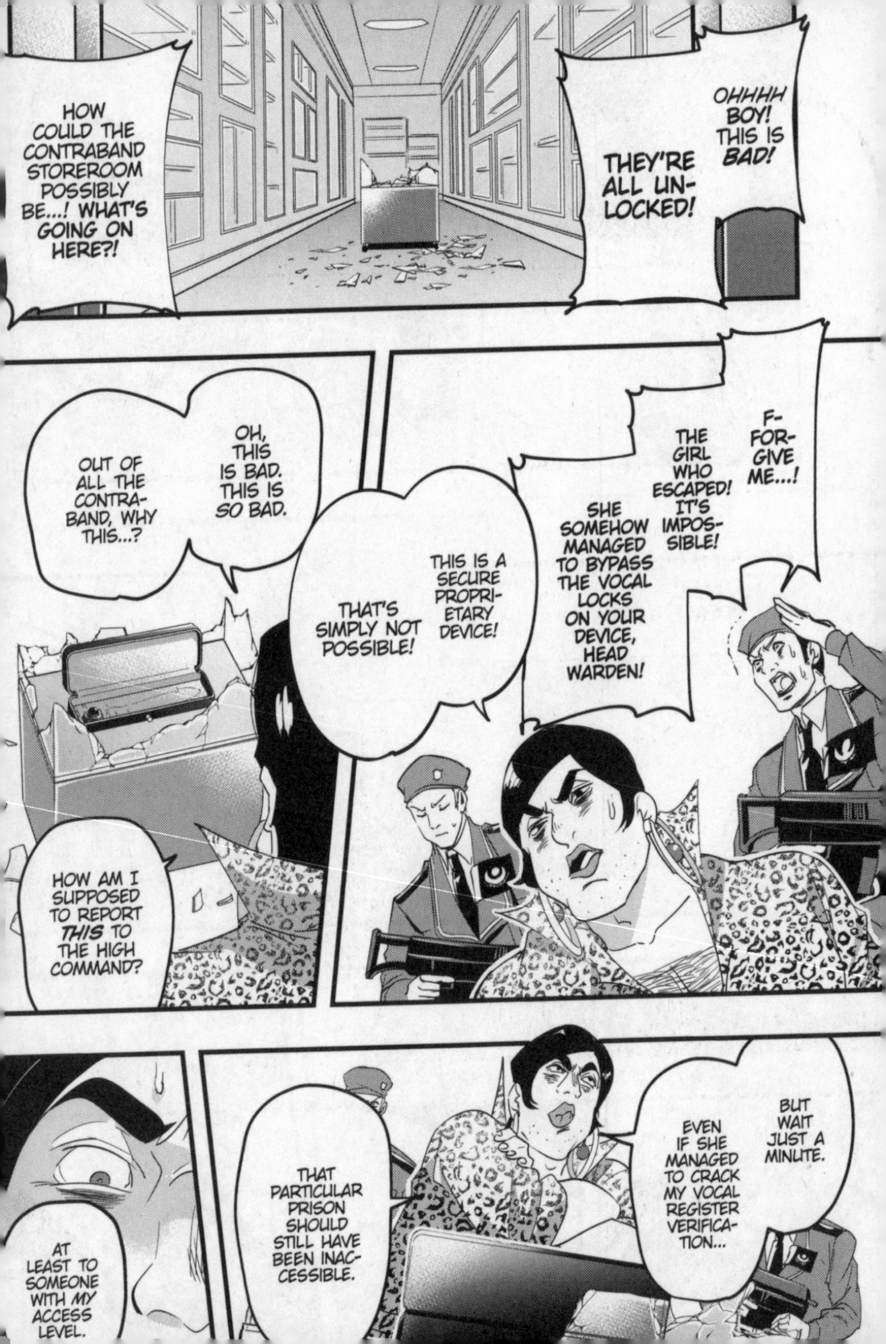
OHHHH BOY! THIS IS BAD!
THEY'RE ALL UN-LOCKED!
HOW COULD THE CONTRABAND STOREROOM POSSIBLY BE...! WHAT'S GOING ON HERE?!
F-FORGIVE ME...!
THE GIRL WHO ESCAPED! IT'S IMPOSSIBLE!
SHE SOMEHOW MANAGED TO BYPASS THE VOCAL LOCKS ON YOUR DEVICE, HEAD WARDEN!
THIS IS A SECURE PROPRIETARY DEVICE!
THAT'S SIMPLY NOT POSSIBLE!
OH, THIS IS BAD. THIS IS SO BAD.
OUT OF ALL THE CONTRABAND, WHY THIS...?
HOW AM I SUPPOSED TO REPORT *THIS* TO THE HIGH COMMAND?
BUT WAIT JUST A MINUTE.
EVEN IF SHE MANAGED TO CRACK MY VOCAL REGISTER VERIFICATION...
THAT PARTICULAR PRISON SHOULD STILL HAVE BEEN INACCESSIBLE.
AT LEAST TO SOMEONE WITH *MY* ACCESS LEVEL.

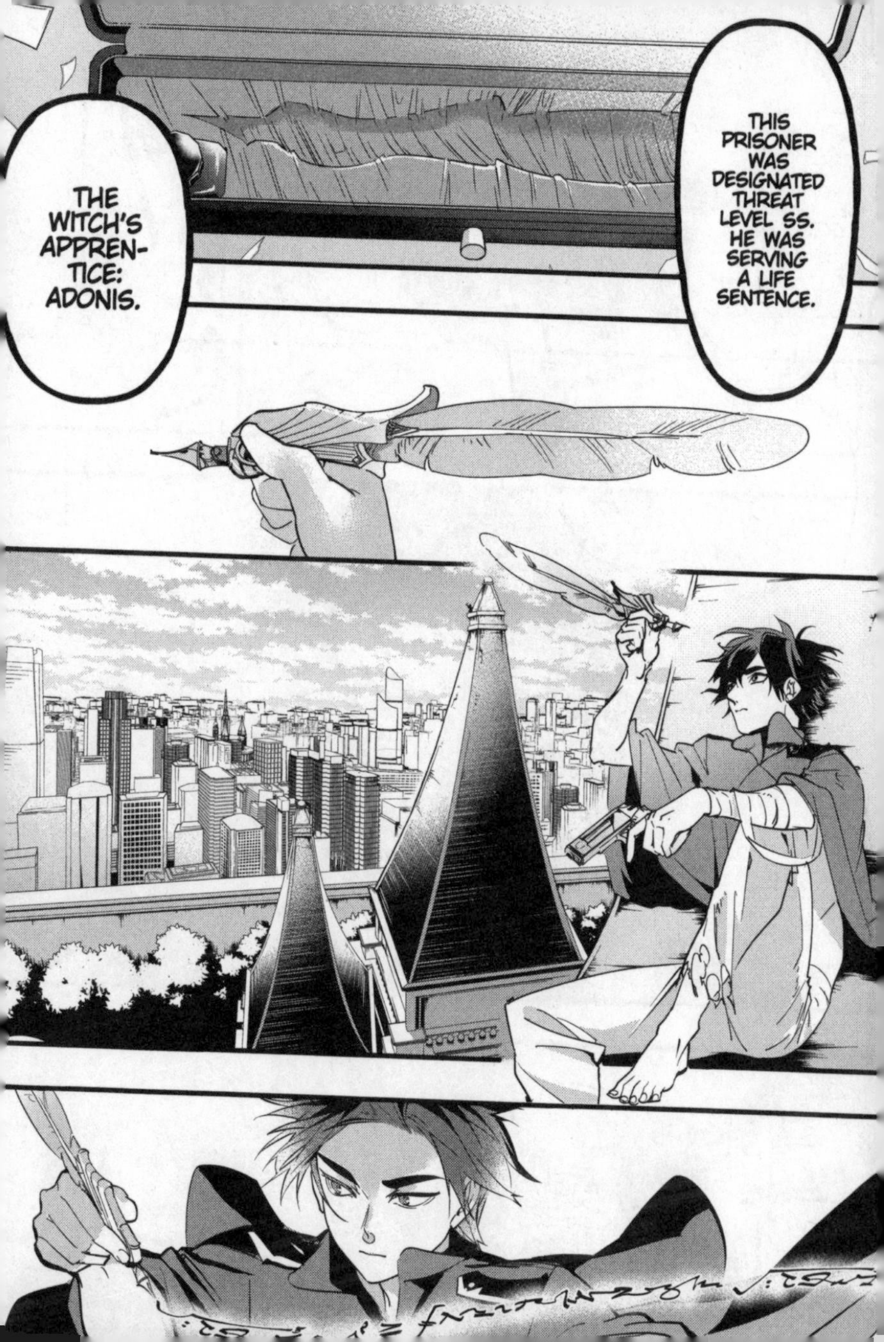
THIS PRISONER WAS DESIGNATED THREAT LEVEL SS. HE WAS SERVING A LIFE SENTENCE.
THE WITCH'S APPREN-TICE: ADONIS.

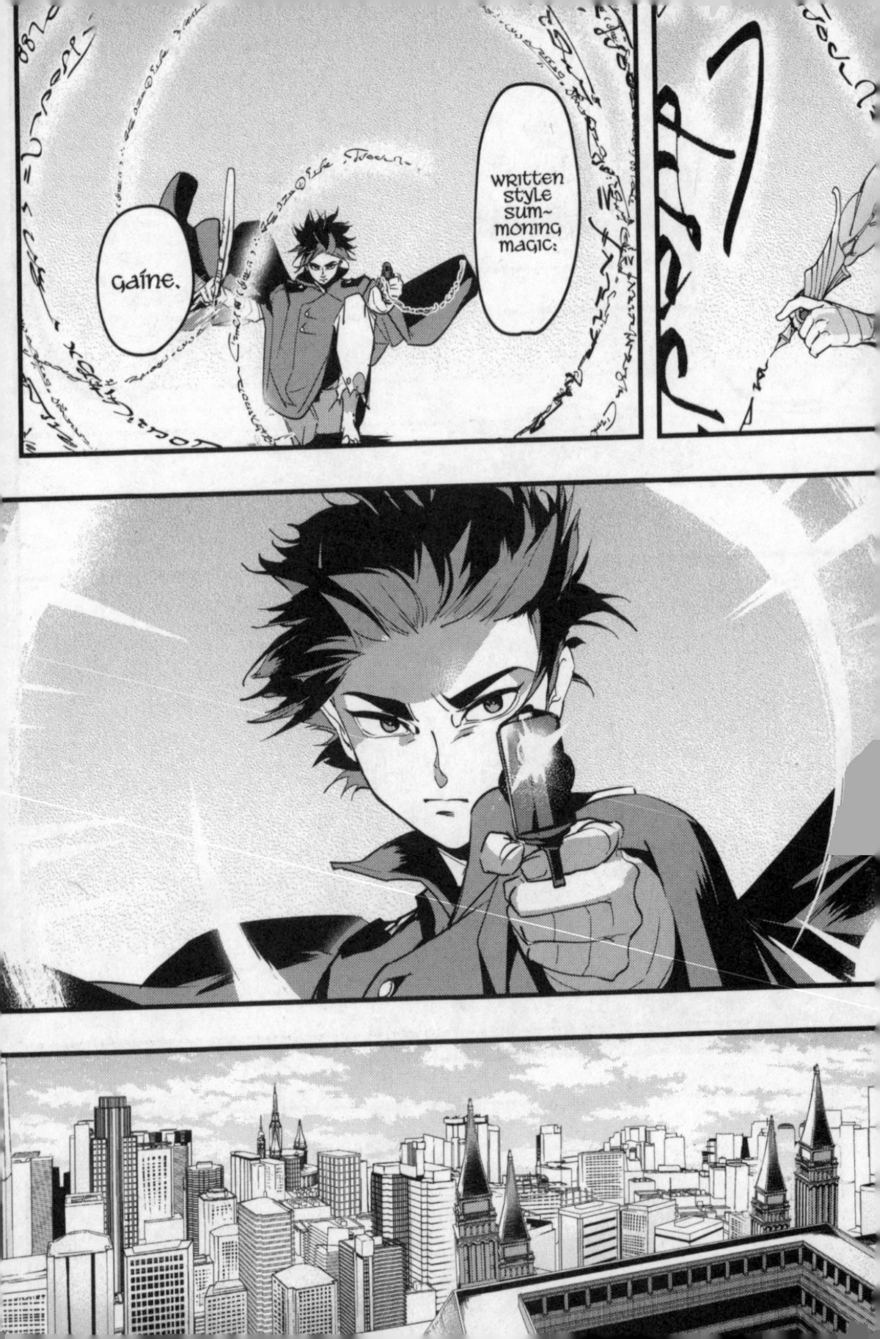
Written style sum-moning magic:
Gaine.

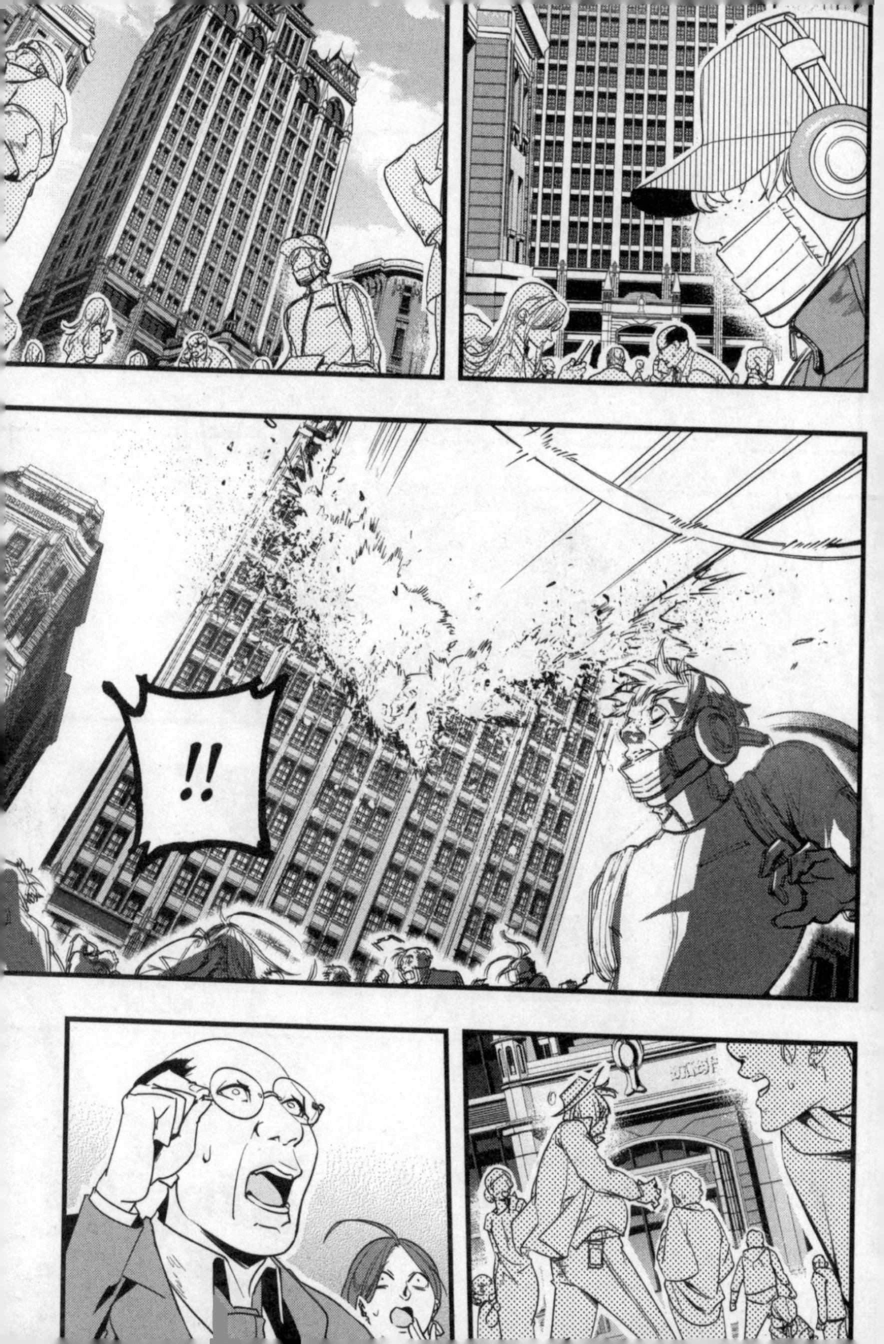
!!

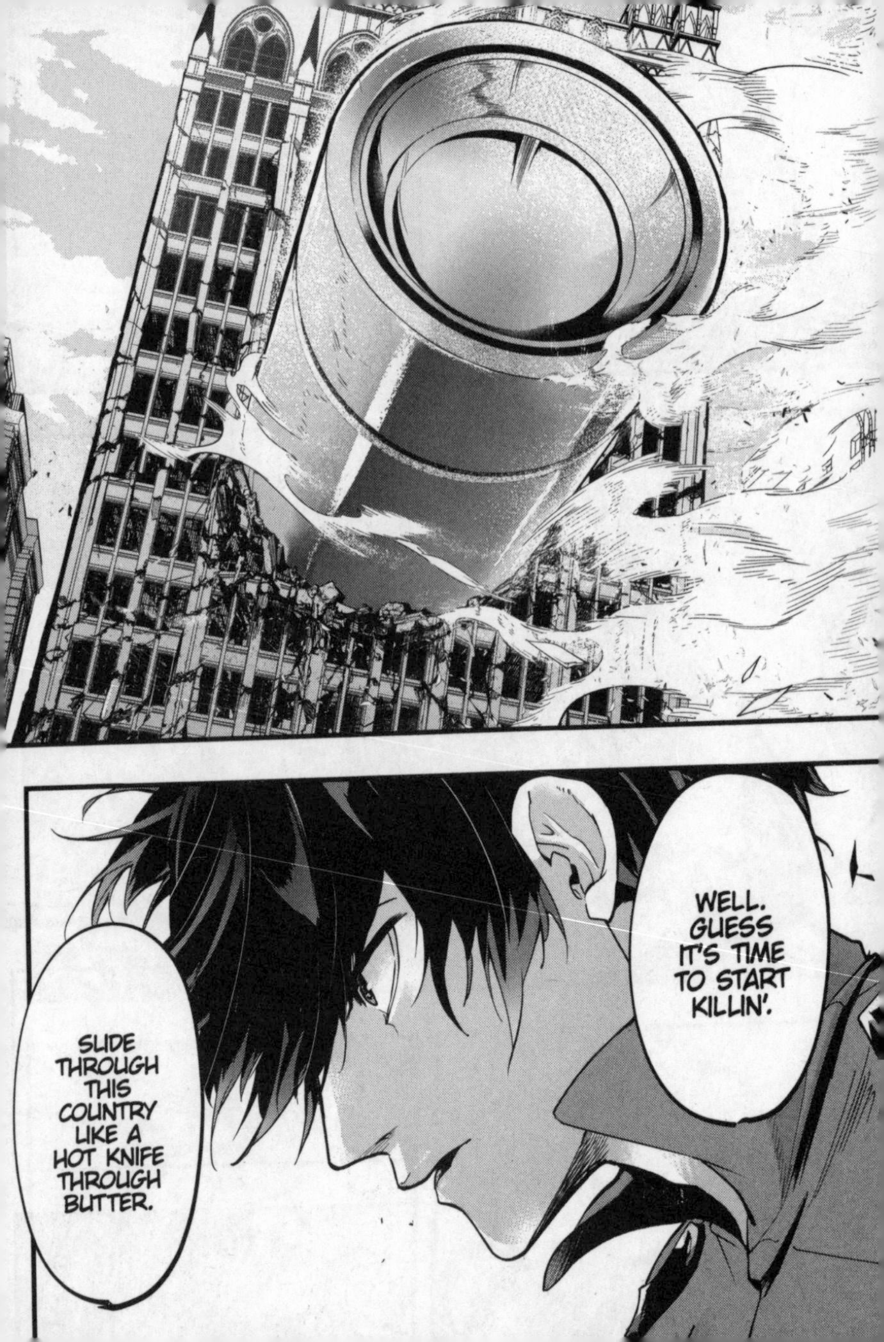
WELL. GUESS IT'S TIME TO START KILLIN'.
SLIDE THROUGH THIS COUNTRY LIKE A HOT KNIFE THROUGH BUTTER.

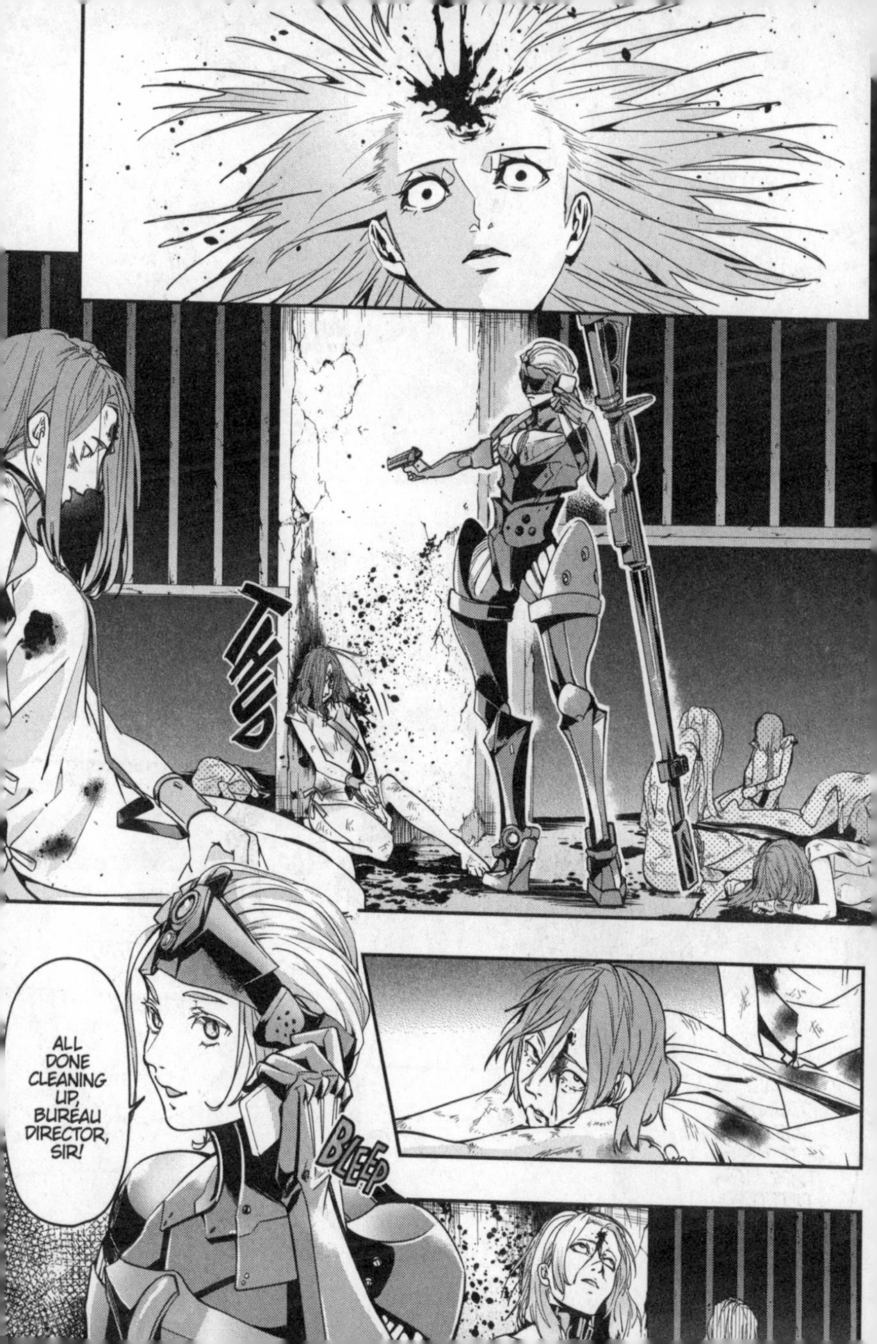
THUD
BLEEP
ALL DONE CLEANING UP, BUREAU DIRECTOR, SIR!

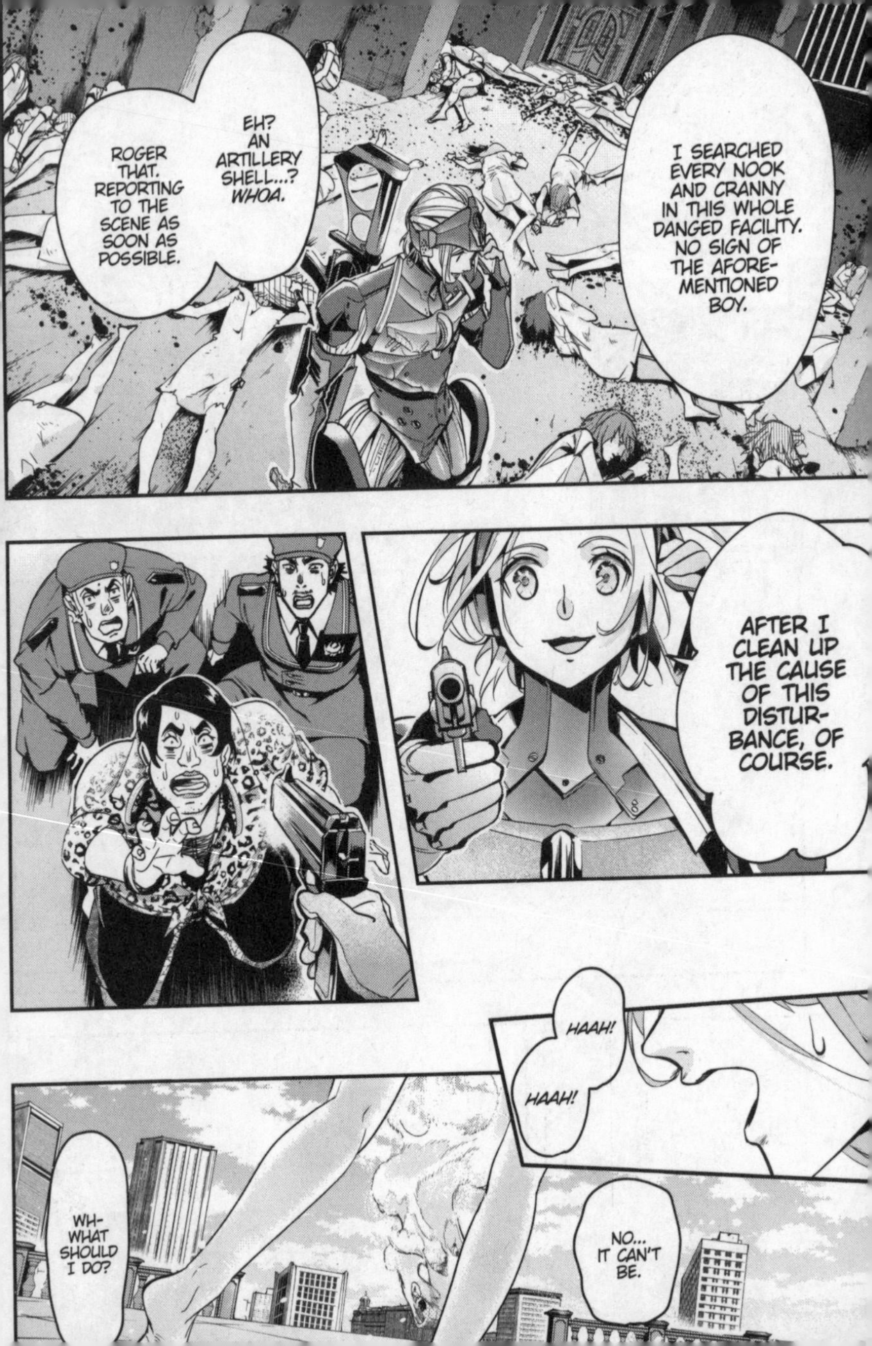
I SEARCHED EVERY NOOK AND CRANNY IN THIS WHOLE DANGED FACILITY. NO SIGN OF THE AFORE-MENTIONED BOY.
EH? AN ARTILLERY SHELL...? *WHOA.*
ROGER THAT. REPORTING TO THE SCENE AS SOON AS POSSIBLE.
AFTER I CLEAN UP THE CAUSE OF THIS DISTUR-BANCE, OF COURSE.
HAAH!
HAAH!
NO... IT CAN'T BE.
WH-WHAT SHOULD I DO?

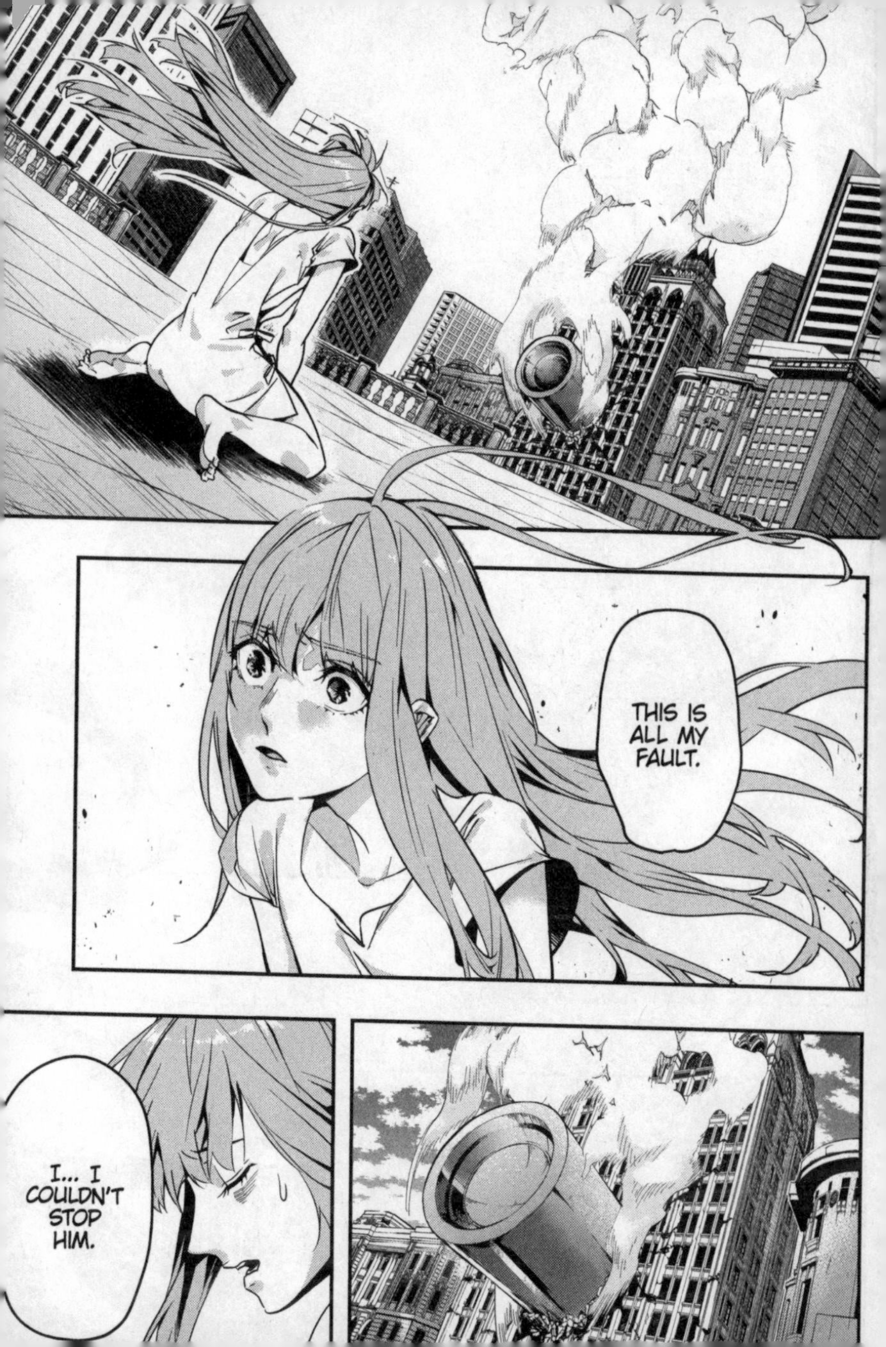
THIS IS ALL MY FAULT.
I... I COULDN'T STOP HIM.

Chapter 3
The Kingdom of Ruin

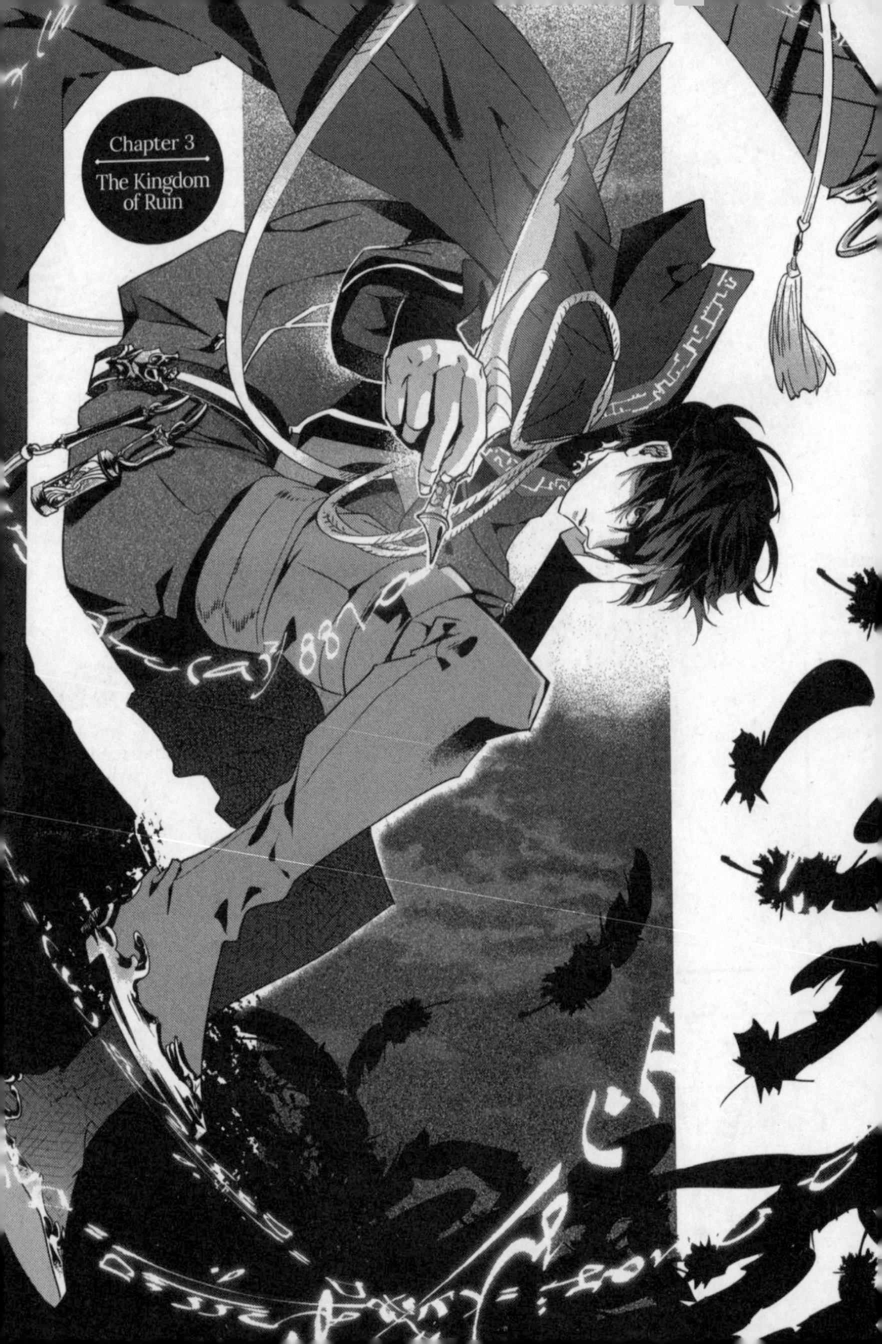

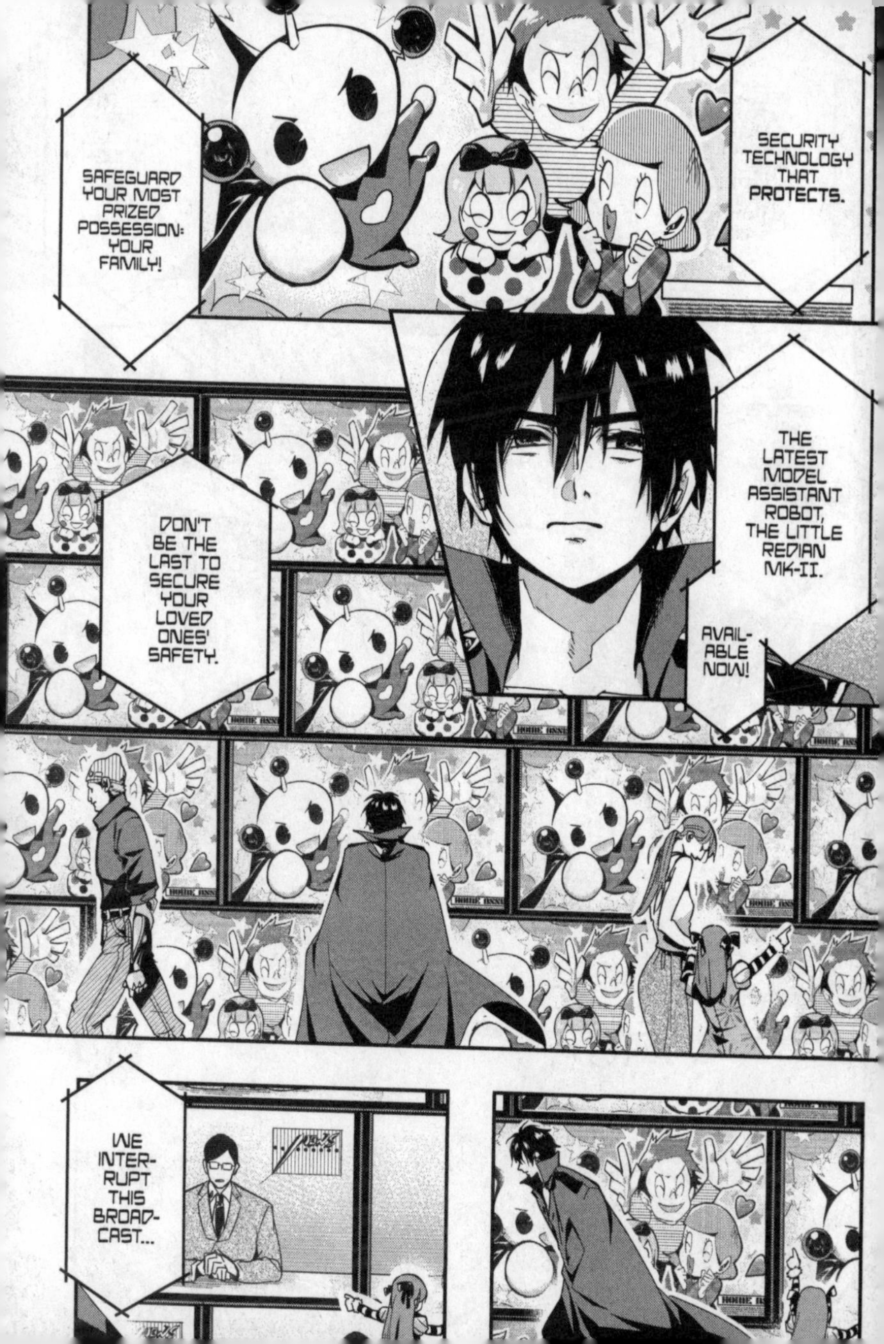
SECURITY TECHNOLOGY THAT PROTECTS.
SAFEGUARD YOUR MOST PRIZED POSSESSION: YOUR FAMILY!
THE LATEST MODEL ASSISTANT ROBOT, THE LITTLE REDIAN MK-II.
AVAIL-ABLE NOW!
DON'T BE THE LAST TO SECURE YOUR LOVED ONES' SAFETY.
WE INTER-RUPT THIS BROAD-CAST...

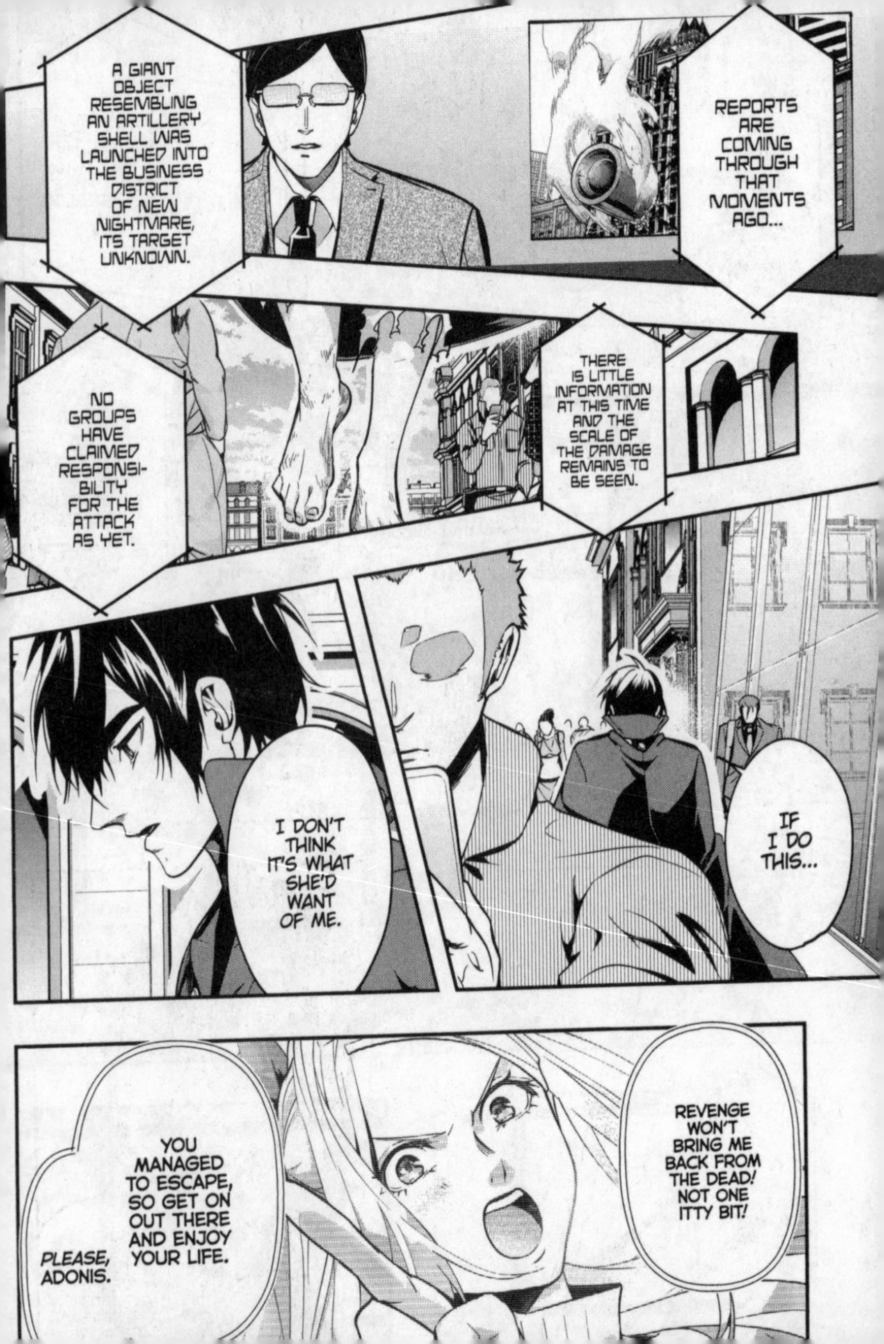
REPORTS ARE COMING THROUGH THAT MOMENTS AGO...
A GIANT OBJECT RESEMBLING AN ARTILLERY SHELL WAS LAUNCHED INTO THE BUSINESS DISTRICT OF NEW NIGHTMARE, ITS TARGET UNKNOWN.
THERE IS LITTLE INFORMATION AT THIS TIME AND THE SCALE OF THE DAMAGE REMAINS TO BE SEEN.
NO GROUPS HAVE CLAIMED RESPONSI-BILITY FOR THE ATTACK AS YET.
IF I DO THIS...
I DON'T THINK IT'S WHAT SHE'D WANT OF ME.
REVENGE WON'T BRING ME BACK FROM THE DEAD! NOT ONE ITTY BIT!
YOU MANAGED TO ESCAPE, SO GET ON OUT THERE AND ENJOY YOUR LIFE.
PLEASE, ADONIS.

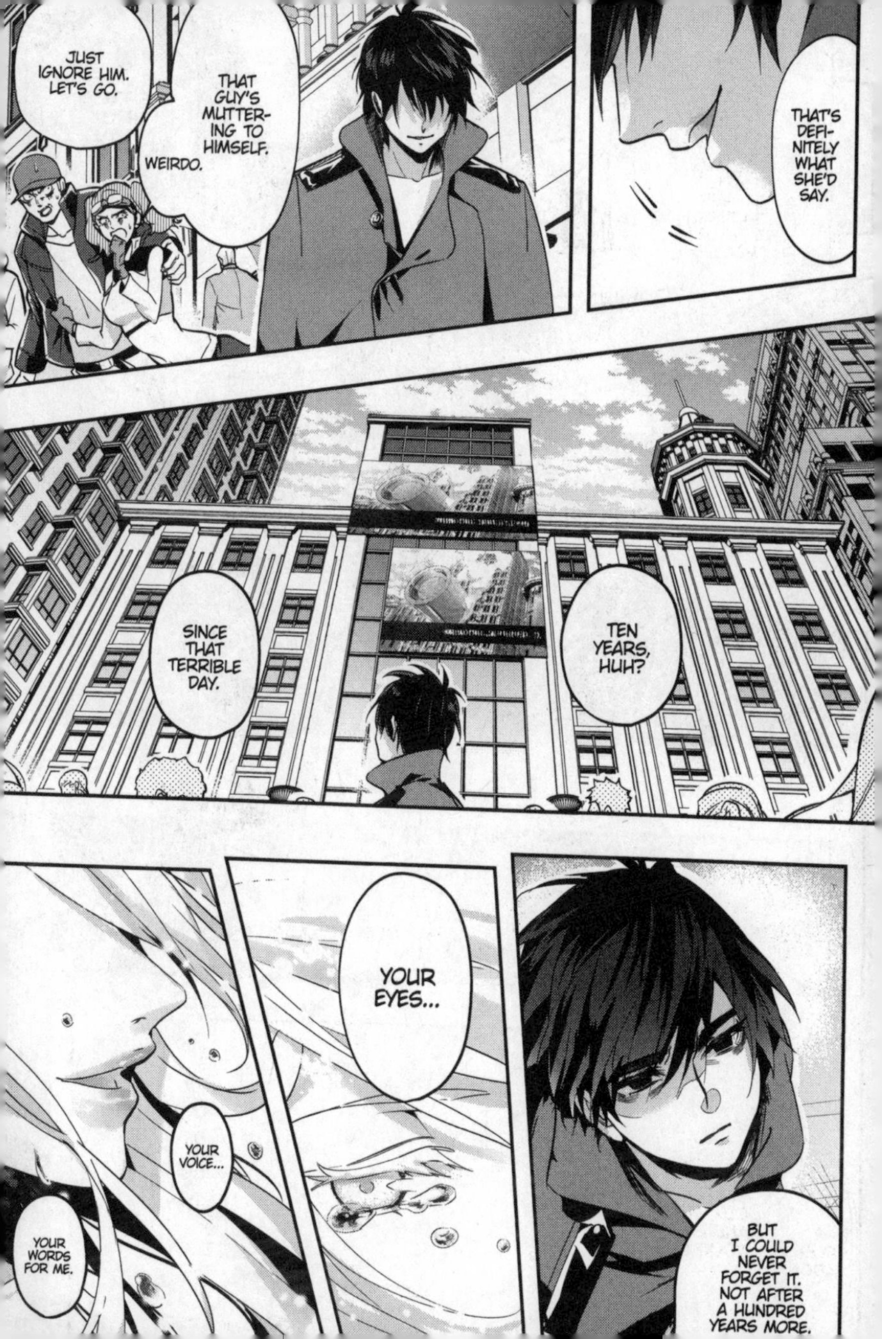
THAT'S DEFINITELY WHAT SHE'D SAY.
THAT GUY'S MUTTERING TO HIMSELF.
WEIRDO.
JUST IGNORE HIM. LET'S GO.
TEN YEARS, HUH?
SINCE THAT TERRIBLE DAY.
BUT I COULD NEVER FORGET IT. NOT AFTER A HUNDRED YEARS MORE.
YOUR EYES...
YOUR VOICE...
YOUR WORDS FOR ME.

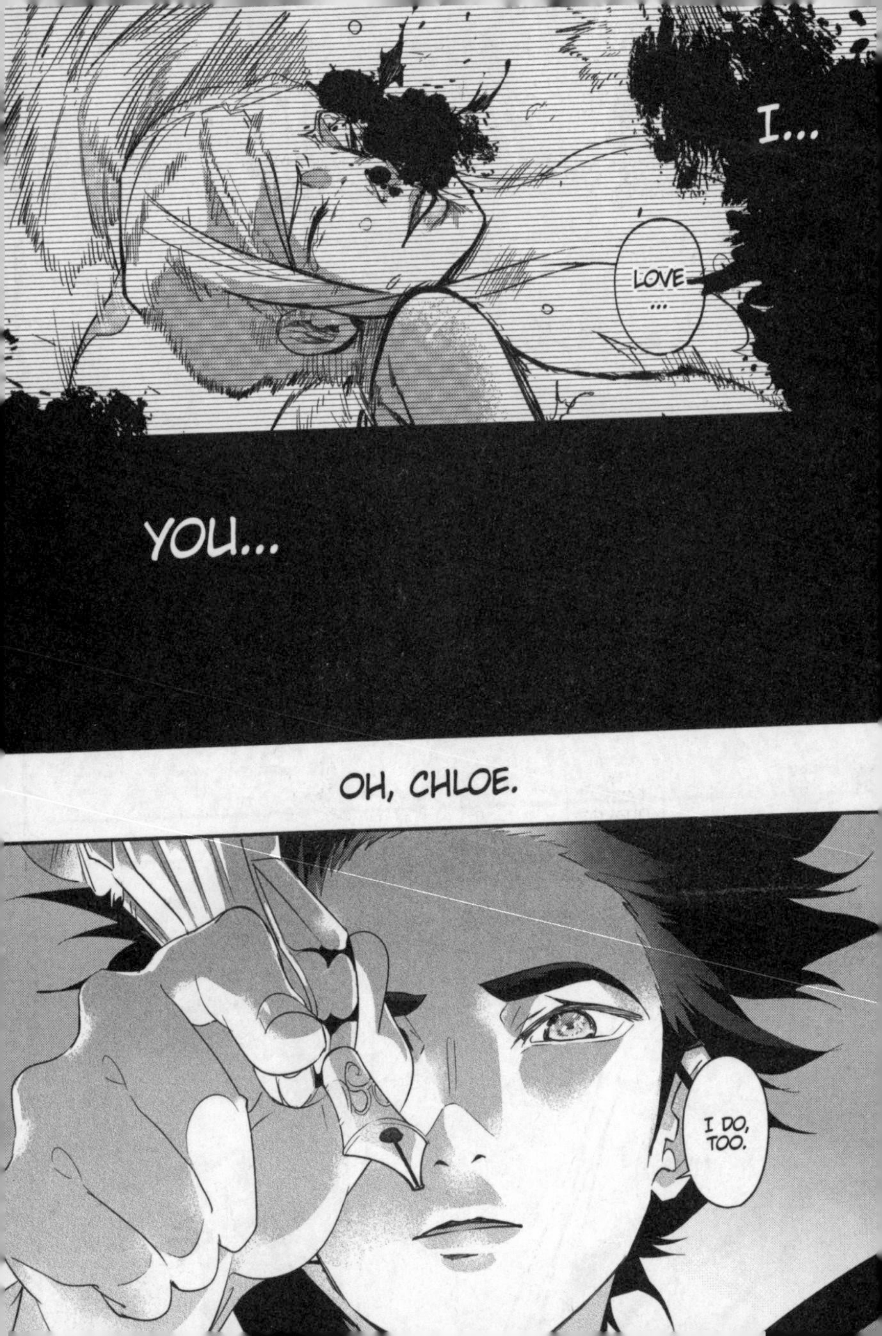
I...
LOVE ...
YOU...
OH, CHLOE.
I DO, TOO.

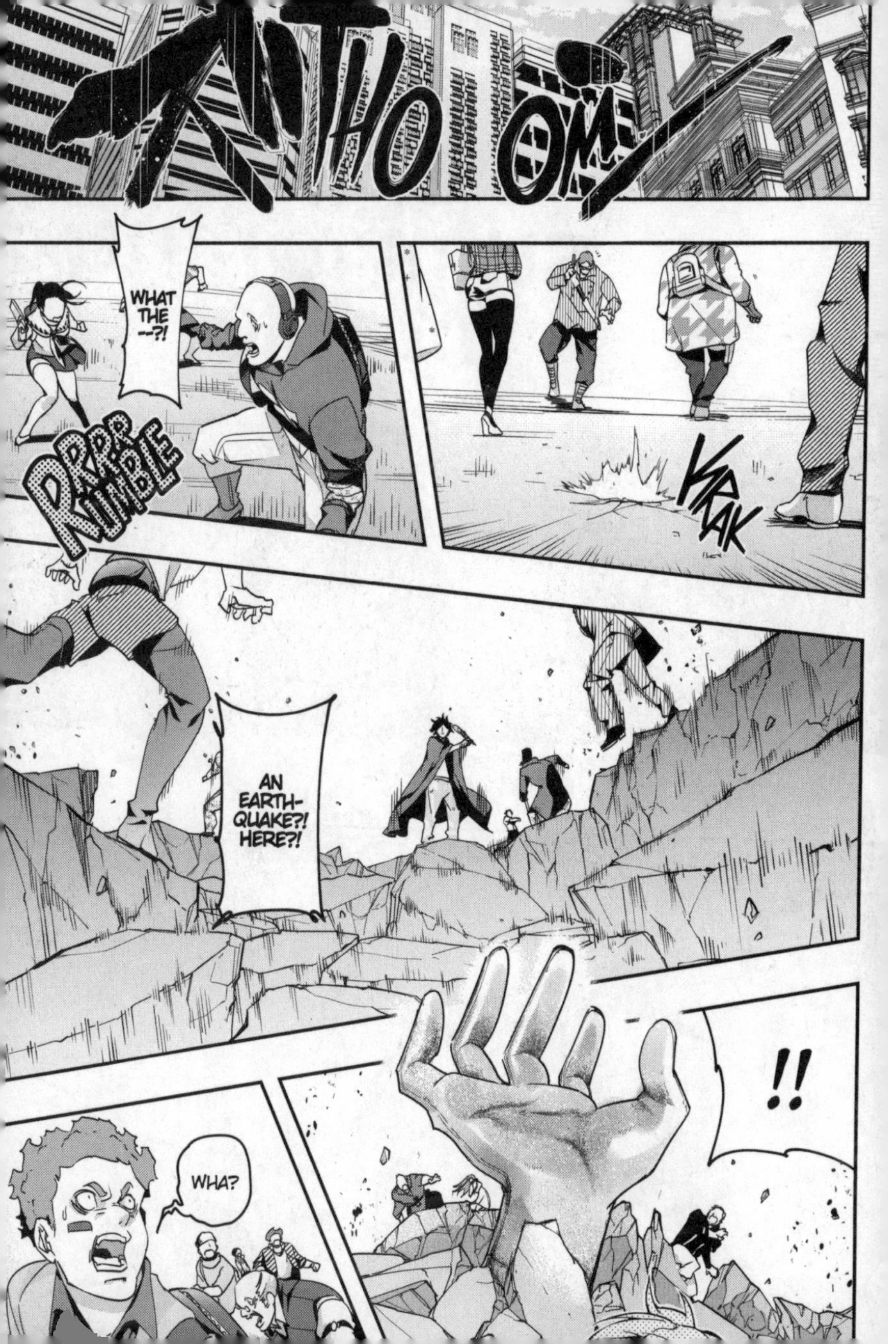
KATHOOM
KRAK
WHAT THE --?!
RRRR RUMBLE
AN EARTH-QUAKE?! HERE?!
!!
WHA?

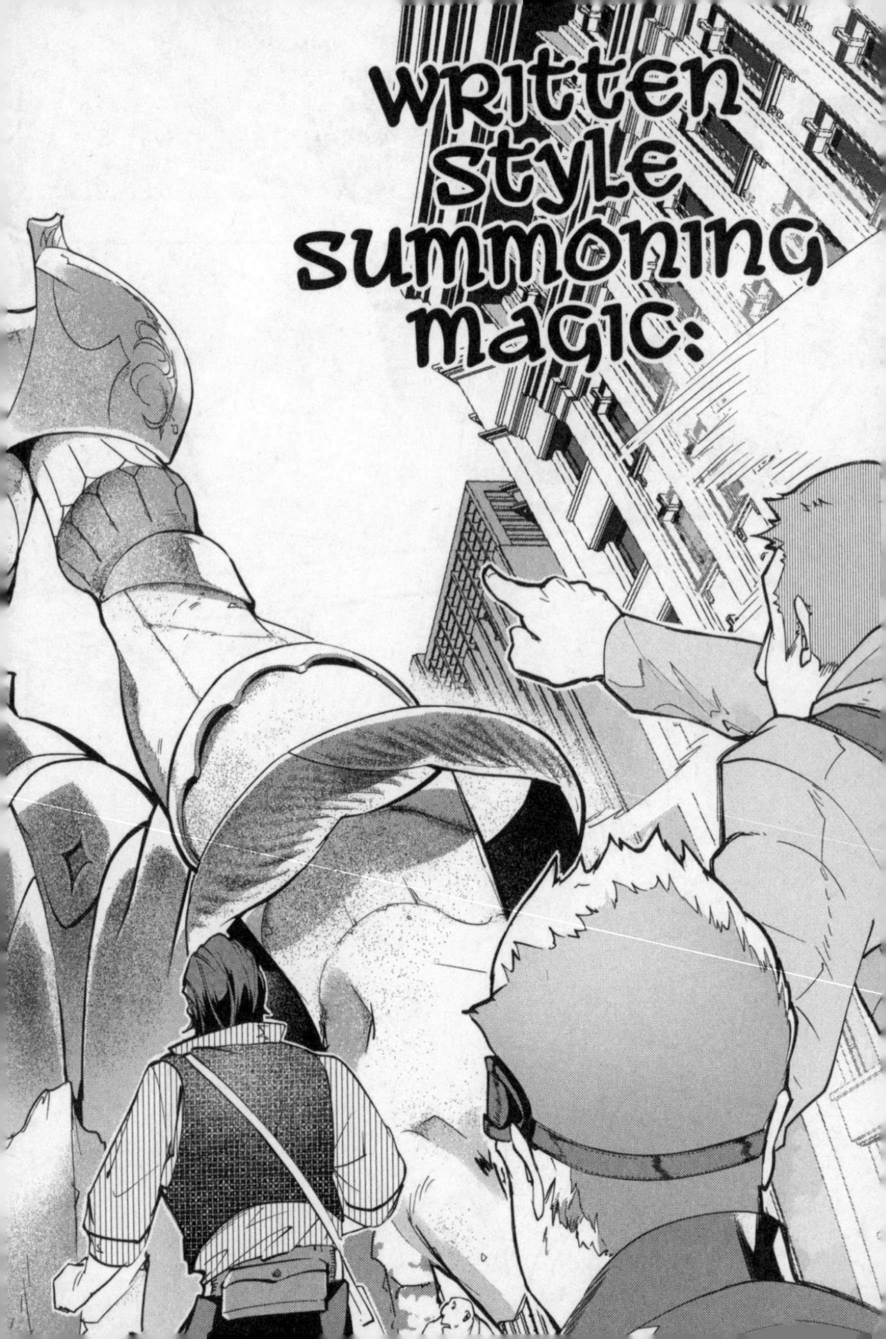
WRITTEN STYLE SUMMONING MAGIC:

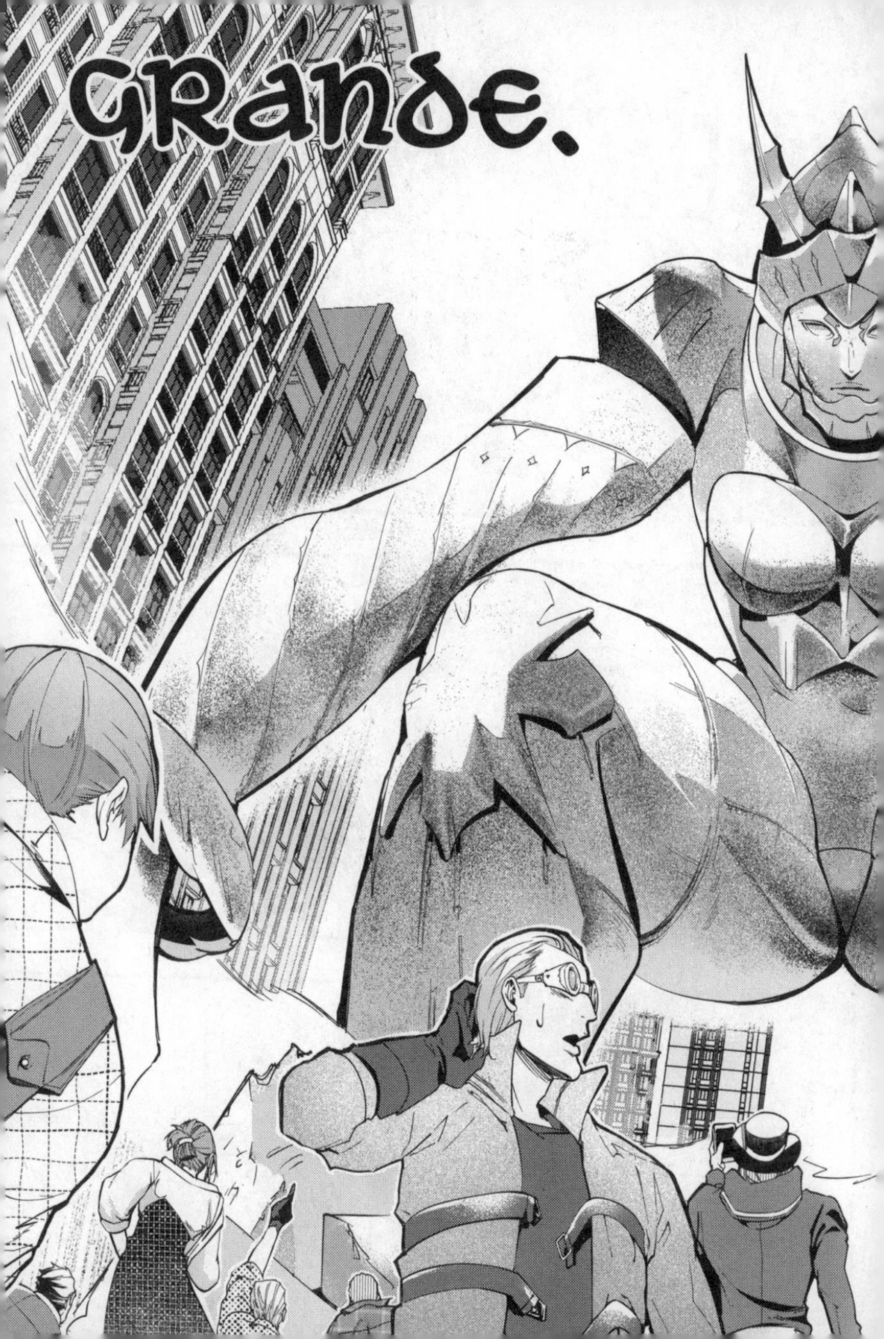
GRANDE.

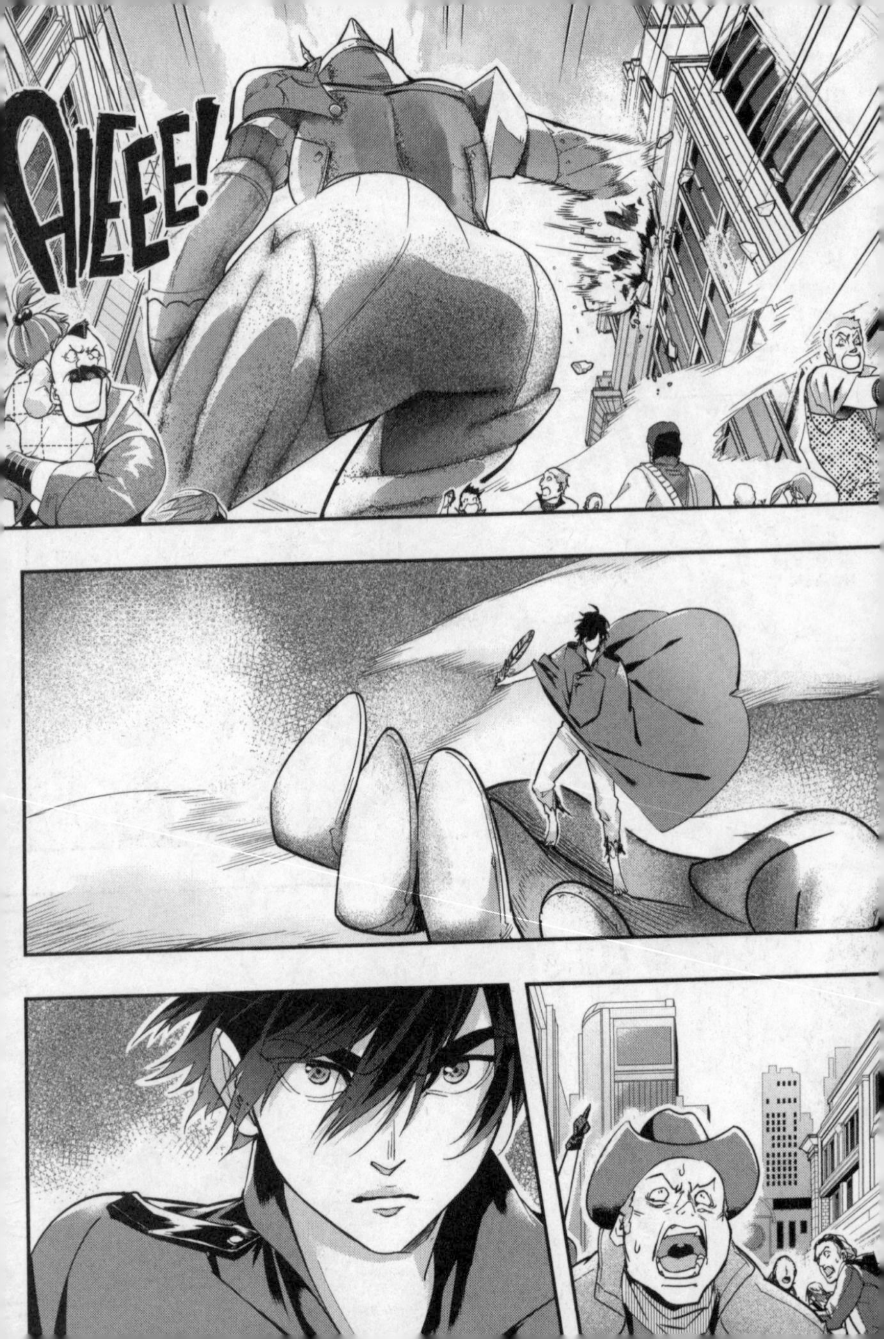
AIEEE!

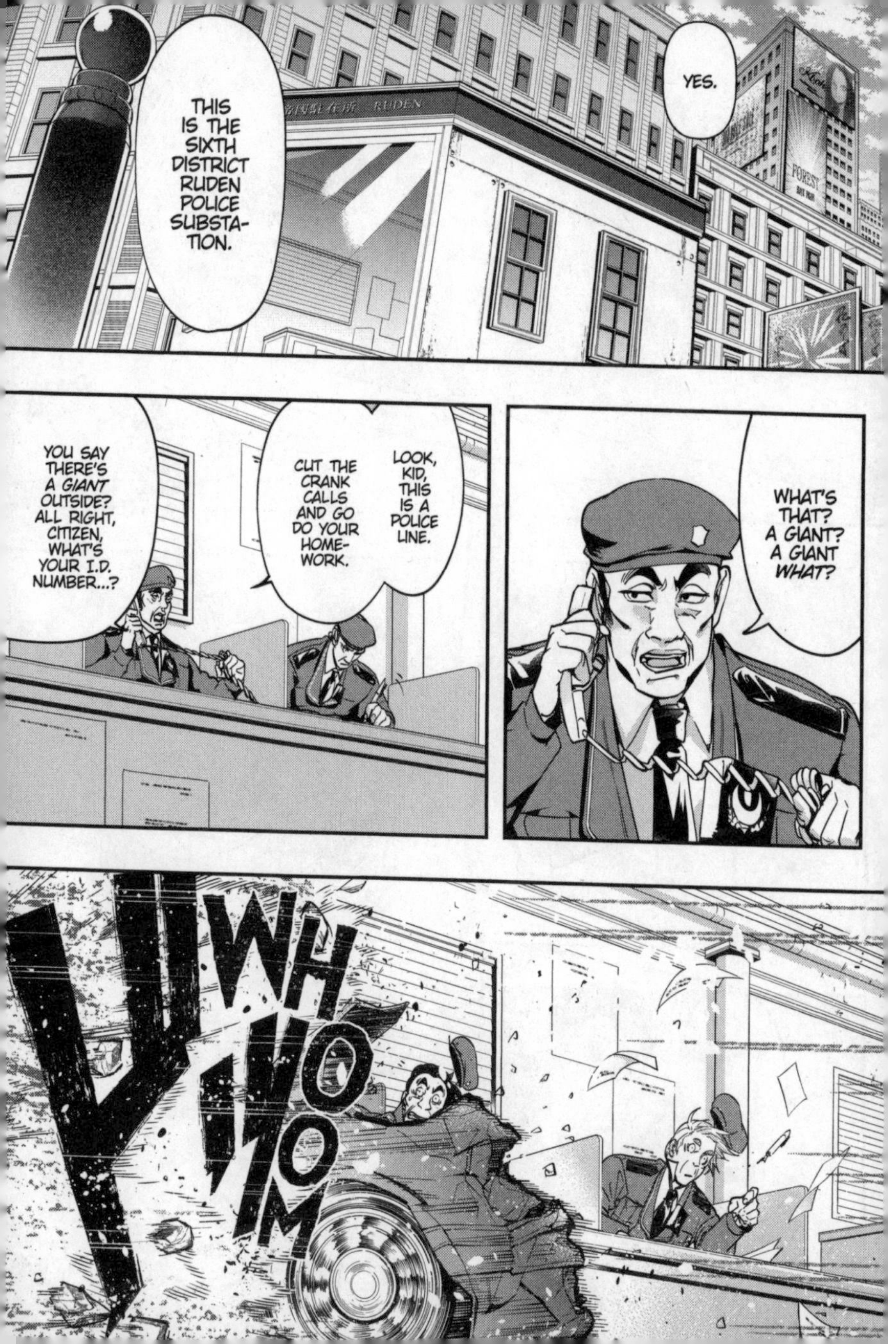
YES.
THIS IS THE SIXTH DISTRICT RUDEN POLICE SUBSTATION.
WHAT'S THAT? A GIANT? A GIANT *WHAT?*
LOOK, KID, THIS IS A POLICE LINE.
CUT THE CRANK CALLS AND GO DO YOUR HOME-WORK.
YOU SAY THERE'S A *GIANT* OUTSIDE? ALL RIGHT, CITIZEN, WHAT'S YOUR I.D. NUMBER...?
VWHOOM

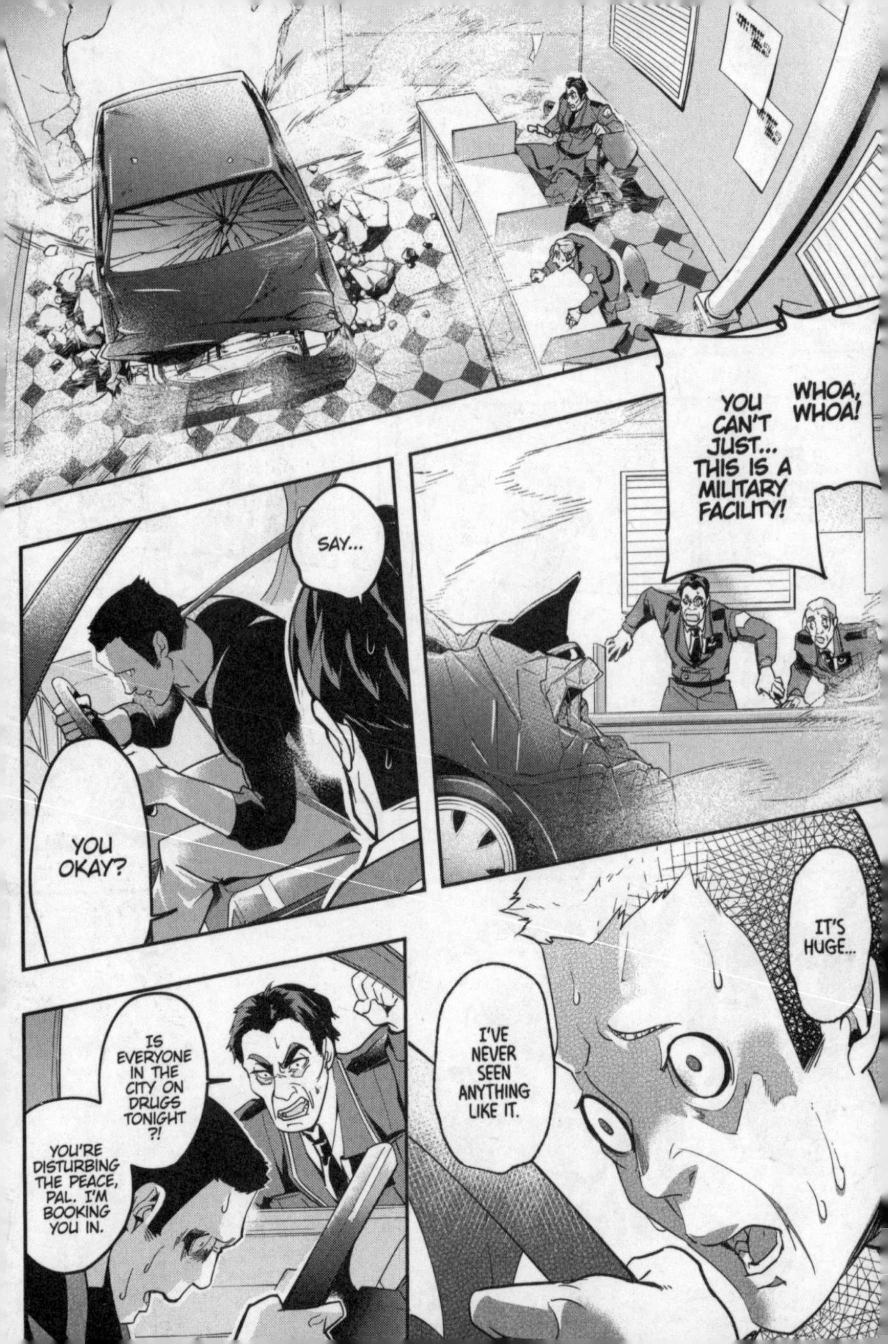
WHOA, WHOA!
YOU CAN'T JUST... THIS IS A MILITARY FACILITY!
SAY...
YOU OKAY?
IT'S HUGE...
I'VE NEVER SEEN ANYTHING LIKE IT.
IS EVERYONE IN THE CITY ON DRUGS TONIGHT?!
YOU'RE DISTURBING THE PEACE, PAL. I'M BOOKING YOU IN.

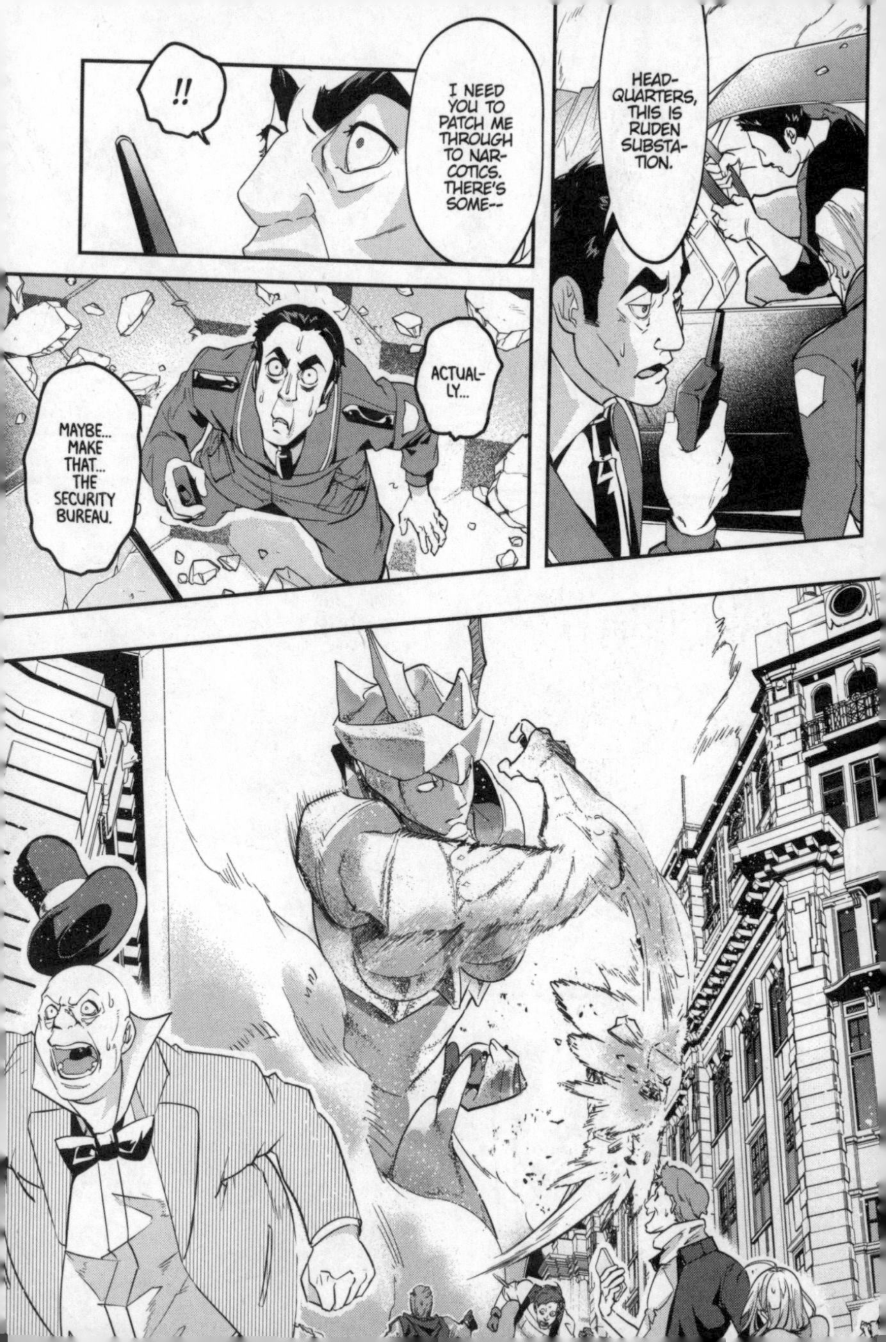
HEAD-QUARTERS, THIS IS RUDEN SUBSTA-TION.
I NEED YOU TO PATCH ME THROUGH TO NAR-COTICS. THERE'S SOME--
!!
ACTUAL-LY...
MAYBE... MAKE THAT... THE SECURITY BUREAU.

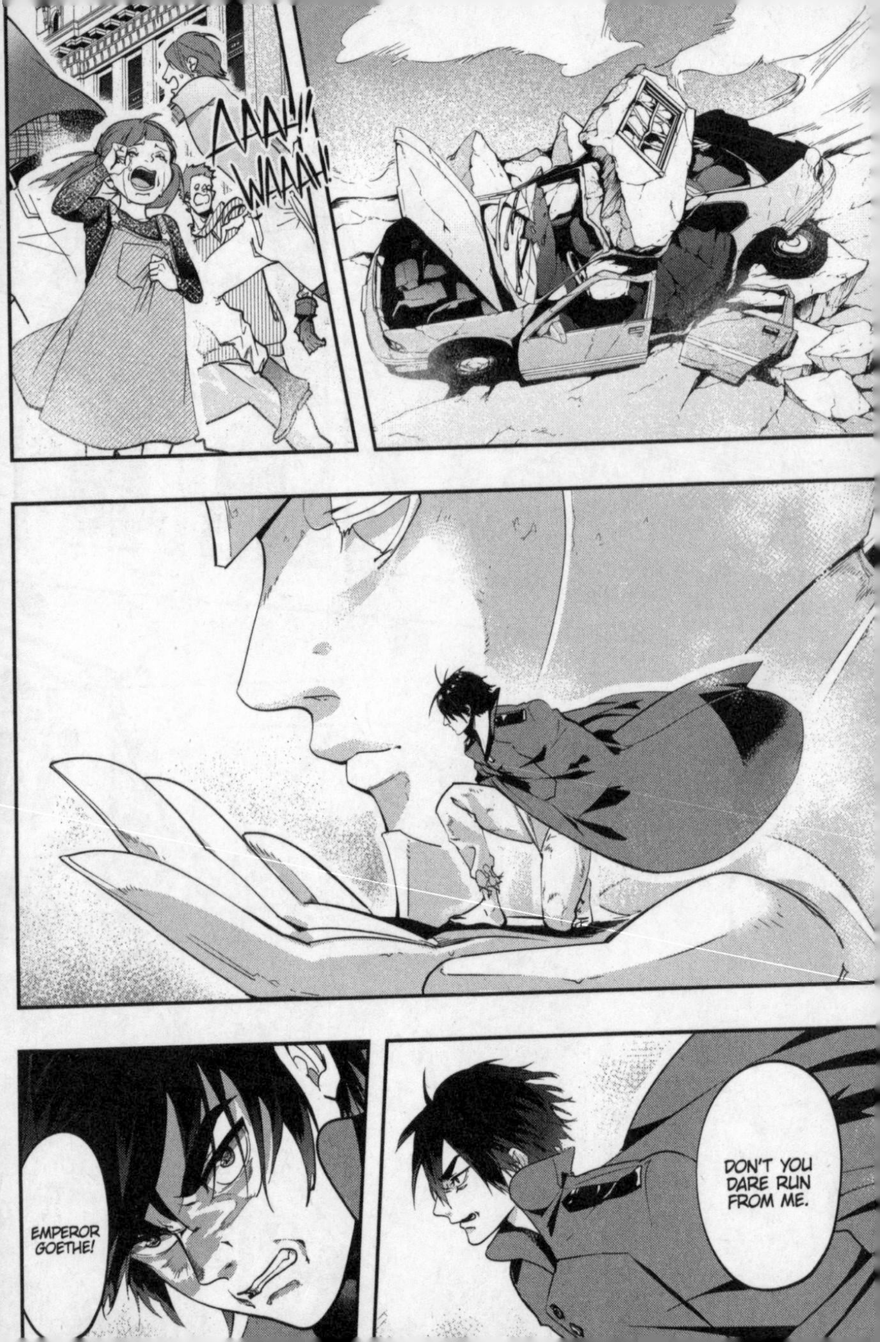
DAAH!! WAAAH!
DON'T YOU DARE RUN FROM ME.
EMPEROR GOETHE!

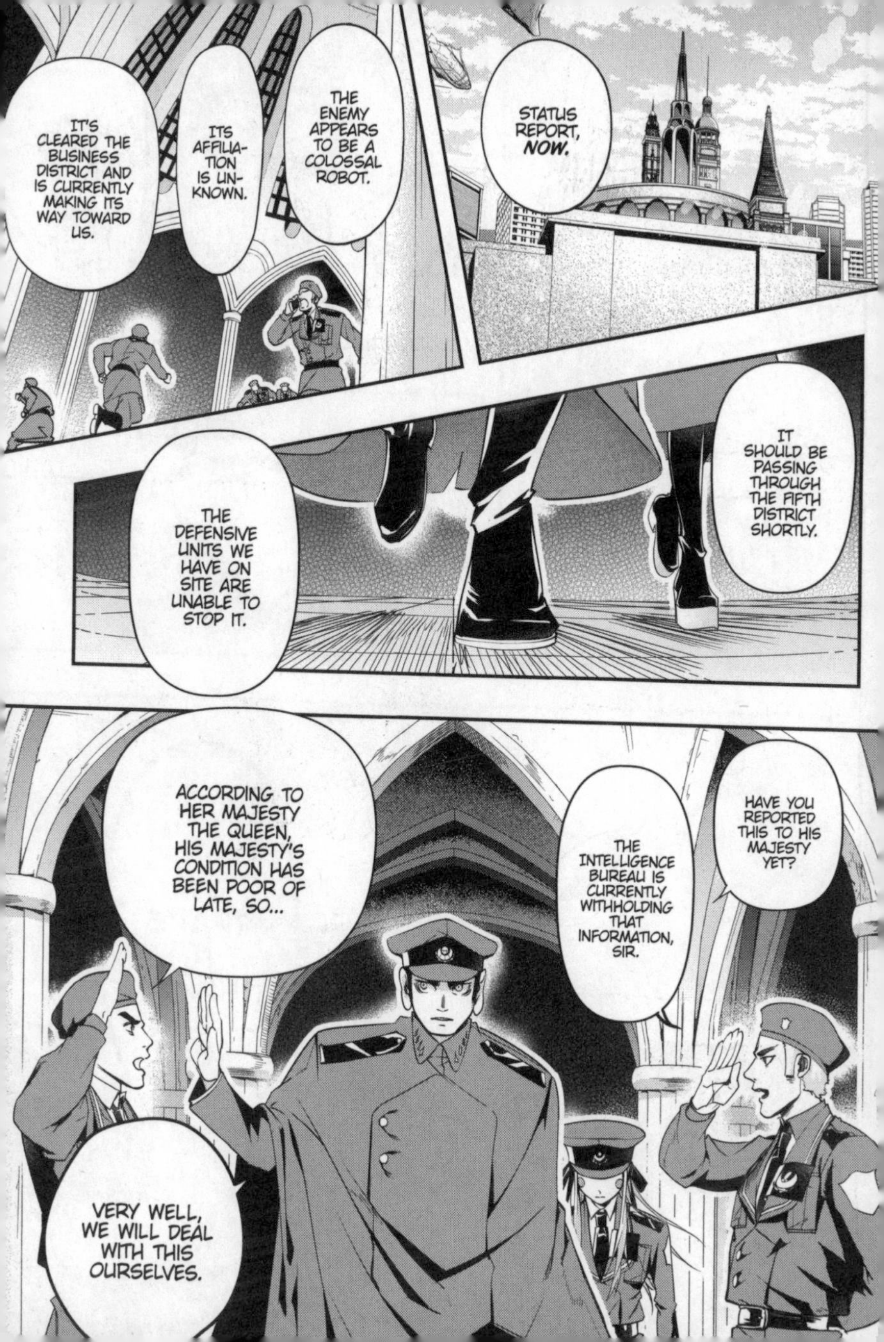
STATUS REPORT, *NOW.*
THE ENEMY APPEARS TO BE A COLOSSAL ROBOT.
ITS AFFILIATION IS UNKNOWN.
IT'S CLEARED THE BUSINESS DISTRICT AND IS CURRENTLY MAKING ITS WAY TOWARD US.
IT SHOULD BE PASSING THROUGH THE FIFTH DISTRICT SHORTLY.
THE DEFENSIVE UNITS WE HAVE ON SITE ARE UNABLE TO STOP IT.
HAVE YOU REPORTED THIS TO HIS MAJESTY YET?
THE INTELLIGENCE BUREAU IS CURRENTLY WITHHOLDING THAT INFORMATION, SIR.
ACCORDING TO HER MAJESTY THE QUEEN, HIS MAJESTY'S CONDITION HAS BEEN POOR OF LATE, SO...
VERY WELL, WE WILL DEAL WITH THIS OURSELVES.

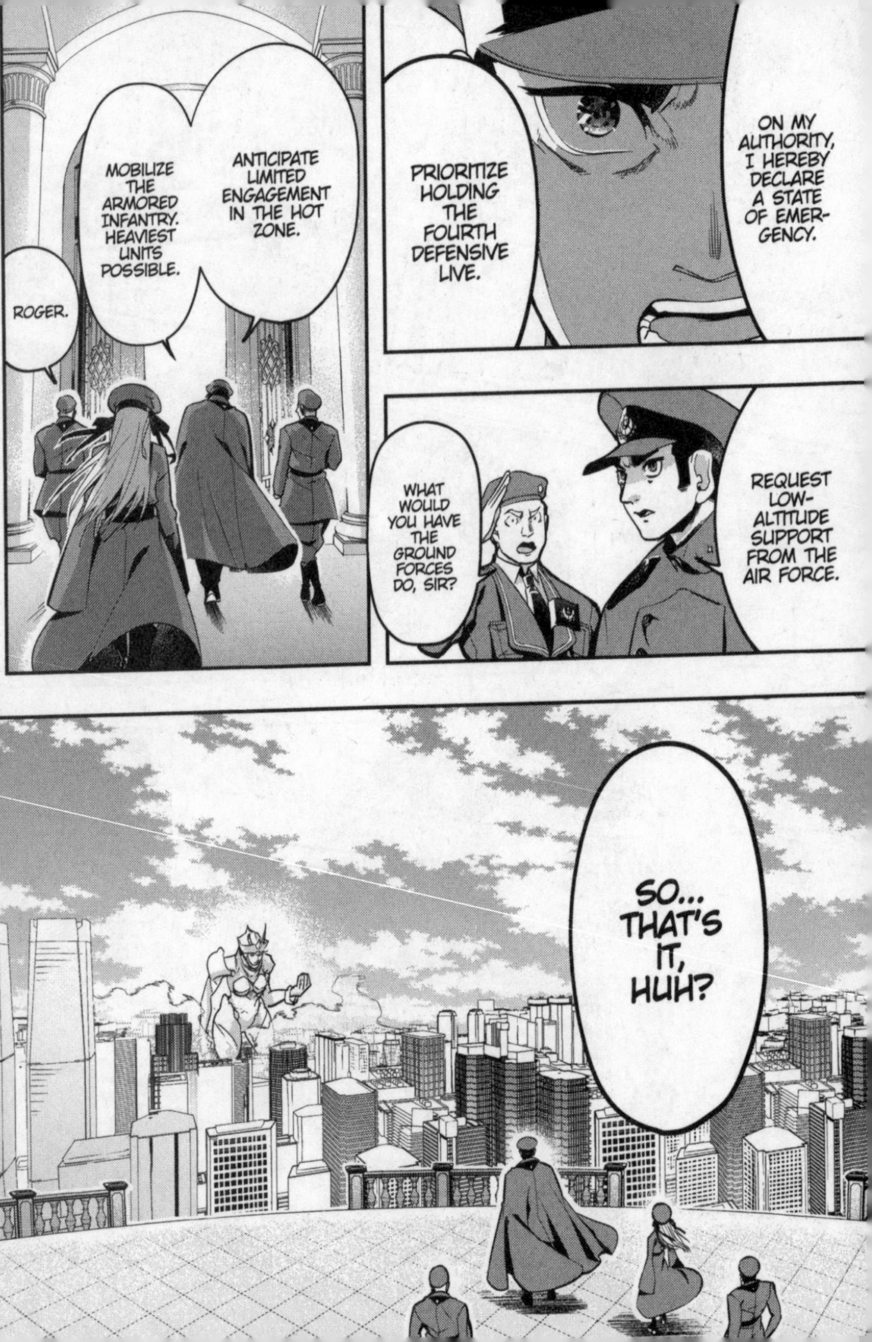
ON MY AUTHORITY, I HEREBY DECLARE A STATE OF EMERGENCY.
PRIORITIZE HOLDING THE FOURTH DEFENSIVE LIVE.
REQUEST LOW-ALTITUDE SUPPORT FROM THE AIR FORCE.
WHAT WOULD YOU HAVE THE GROUND FORCES DO, SIR?
ANTICIPATE LIMITED ENGAGEMENT IN THE HOT ZONE.
MOBILIZE THE ARMORED INFANTRY. HEAVIEST UNITS POSSIBLE.
ROGER.
SO... THAT'S IT, HUH?

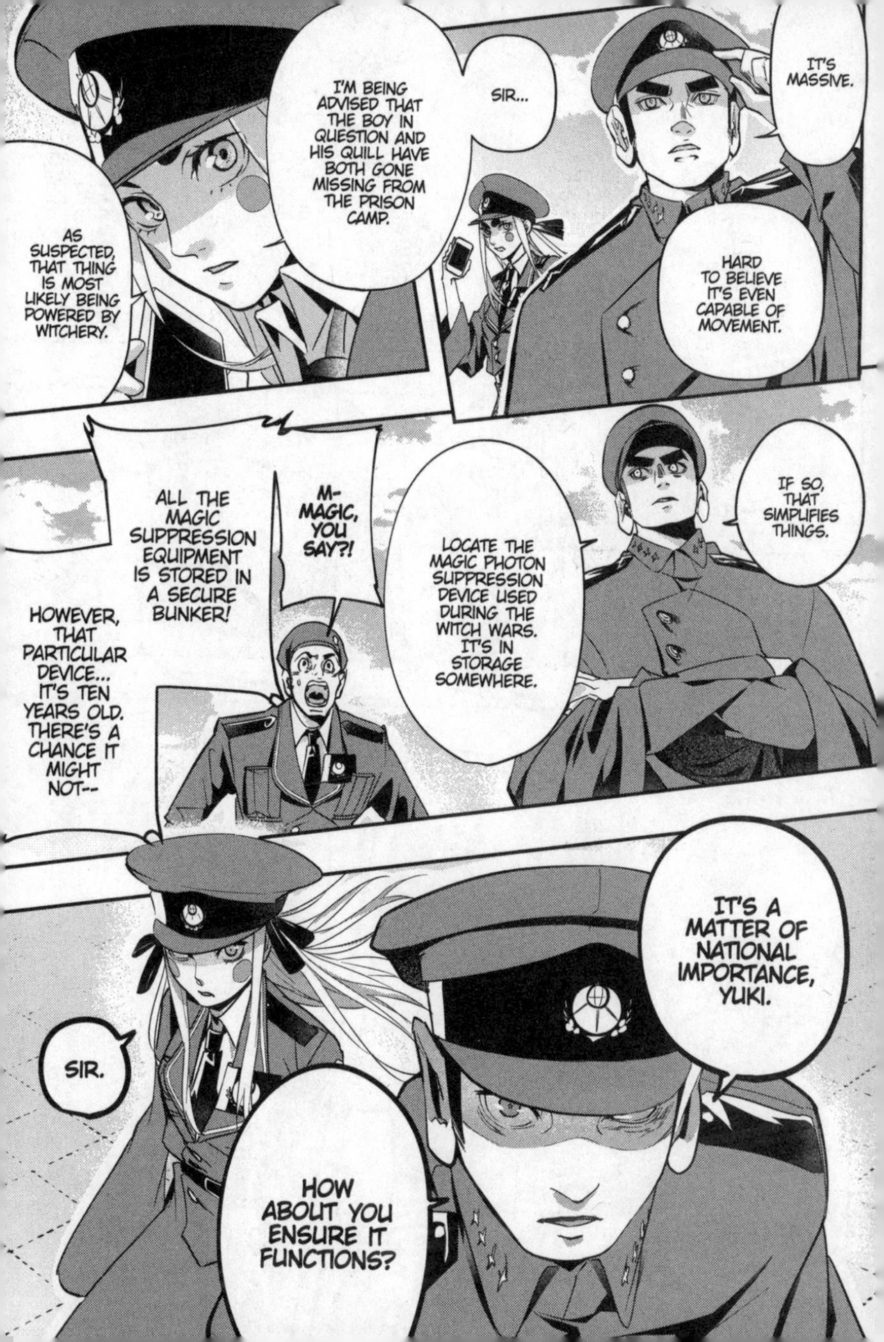
IT'S MASSIVE.
HARD TO BELIEVE IT'S EVEN CAPABLE OF MOVEMENT.
SIR...
I'M BEING ADVISED THAT THE BOY IN QUESTION AND HIS QUILL HAVE BOTH GONE MISSING FROM THE PRISON CAMP.
AS SUSPECTED, THAT THING IS MOST LIKELY BEING POWERED BY WITCHERY.
IF SO, THAT SIMPLIFIES THINGS.
LOCATE THE MAGIC PHOTON SUPPRESSION DEVICE USED DURING THE WITCH WARS. IT'S IN STORAGE SOMEWHERE.
M-MAGIC, YOU SAY?!
ALL THE MAGIC SUPPRESSION EQUIPMENT IS STORED IN A SECURE BUNKER!
HOWEVER, THAT PARTICULAR DEVICE... IT'S TEN YEARS OLD. THERE'S A CHANCE IT MIGHT NOT--
IT'S A MATTER OF NATIONAL IMPORTANCE, YUKI.
HOW ABOUT YOU ENSURE IT FUNCTIONS?
SIR.

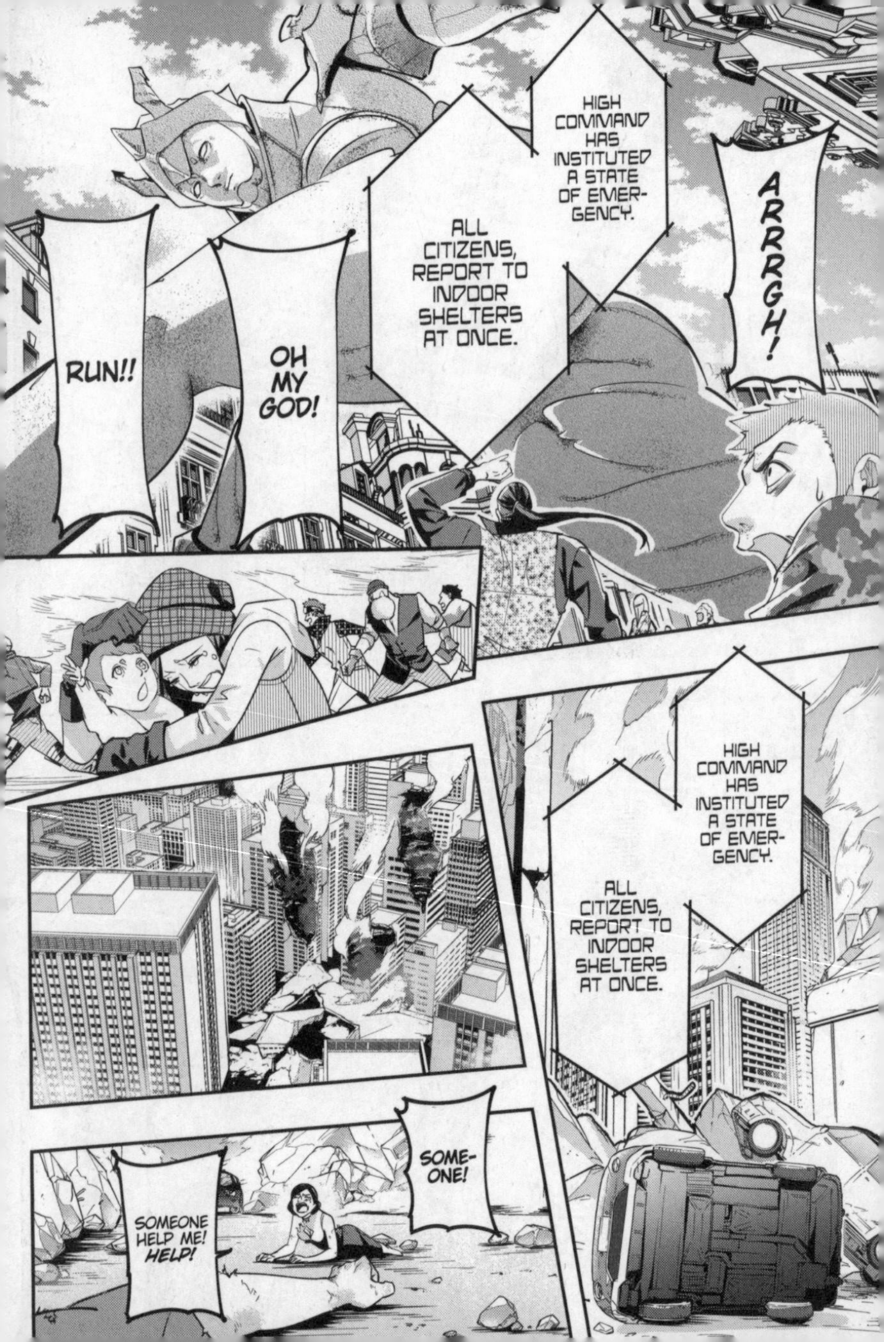
ARRRGH!
HIGH COMMAND HAS INSTITUTED A STATE OF EMER-GENCY.
ALL CITIZENS, REPORT TO INDOOR SHELTERS AT ONCE.
OH MY GOD!
RUN!!
HIGH COMMAND HAS INSTITUTED A STATE OF EMER-GENCY.
ALL CITIZENS, REPORT TO INDOOR SHELTERS AT ONCE.
SOME-ONE!
SOMEONE HELP ME! *HELP!*

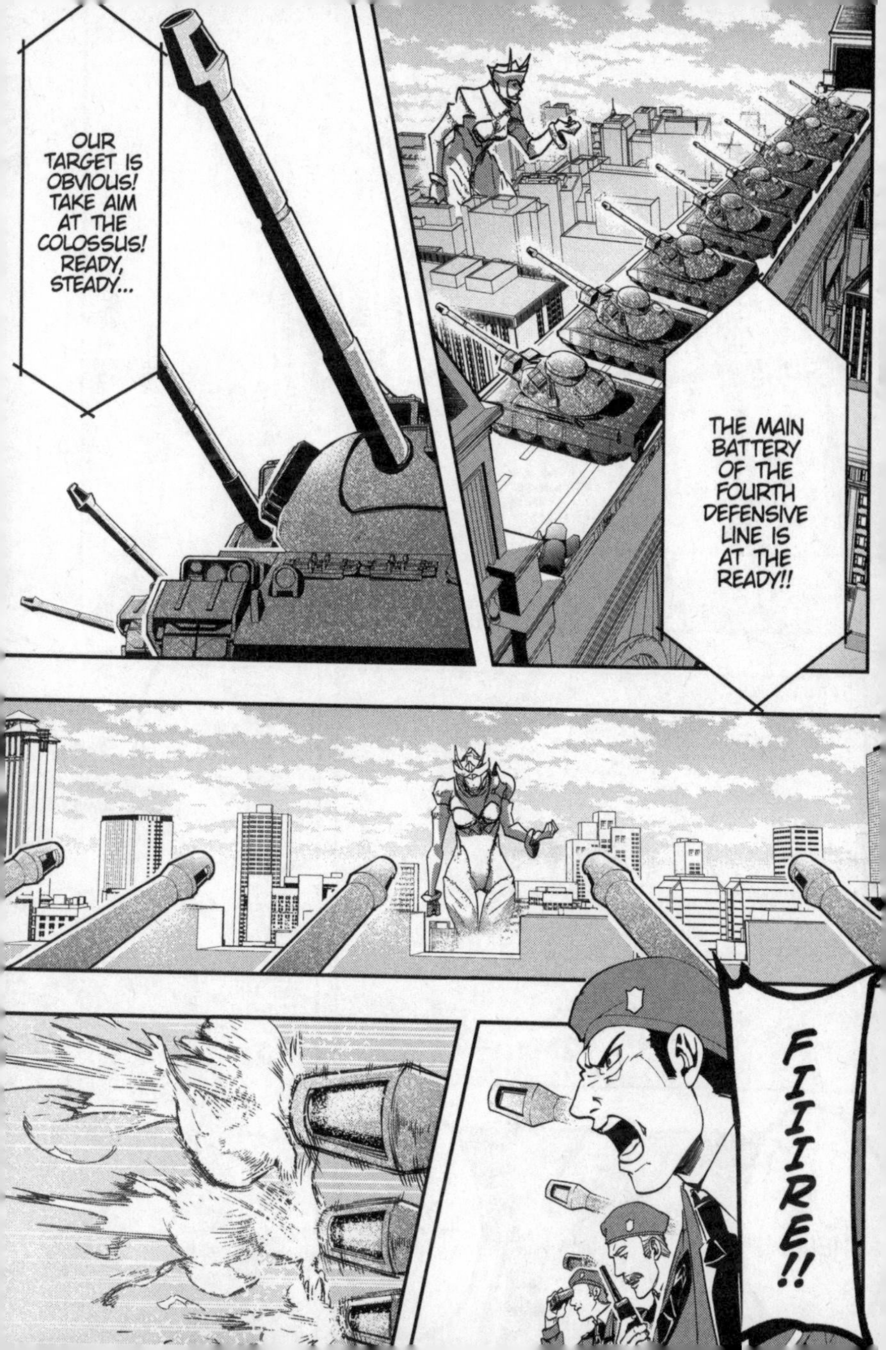
THE MAIN BATTERY OF THE FOURTH DEFENSIVE LINE IS AT THE READY!!
OUR TARGET IS OBVIOUS! TAKE AIM AT THE COLOSSUS! READY, STEADY...
FIIIRE!!

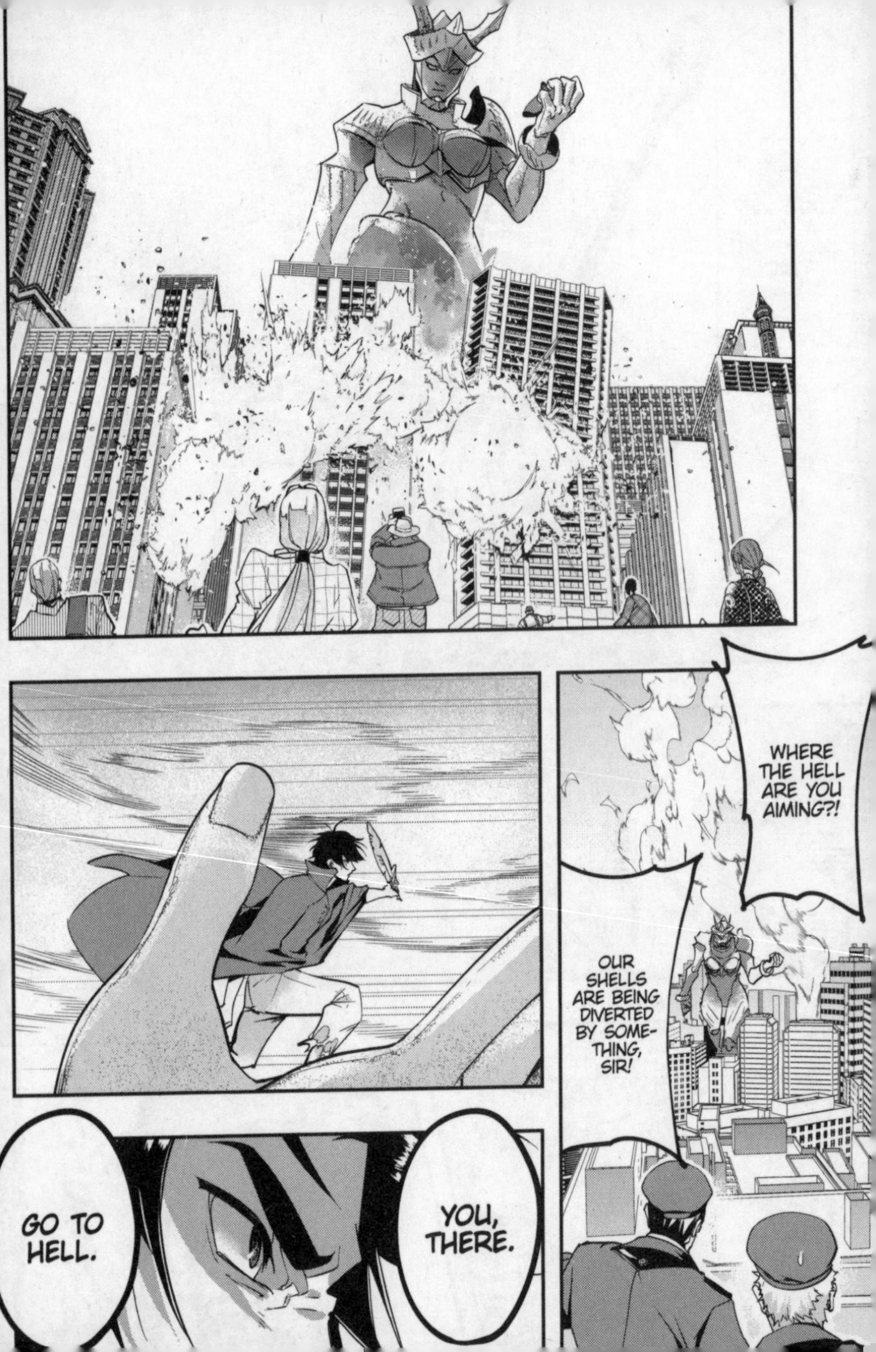
WHERE THE HELL ARE YOU AIMING?!
OUR SHELLS ARE BEING DIVERTED BY SOME-THING, SIR!
YOU, THERE.
GO TO HELL.

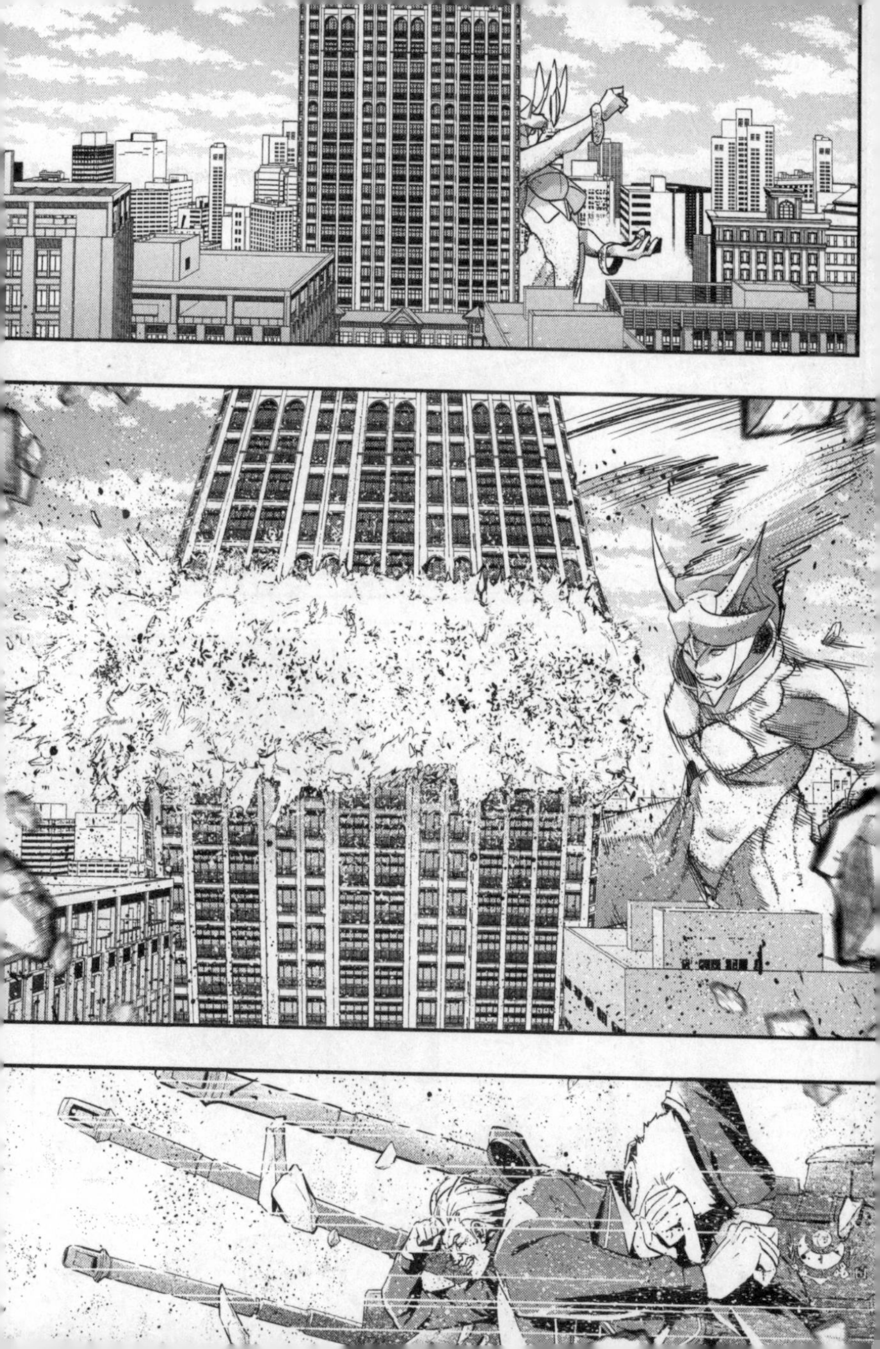

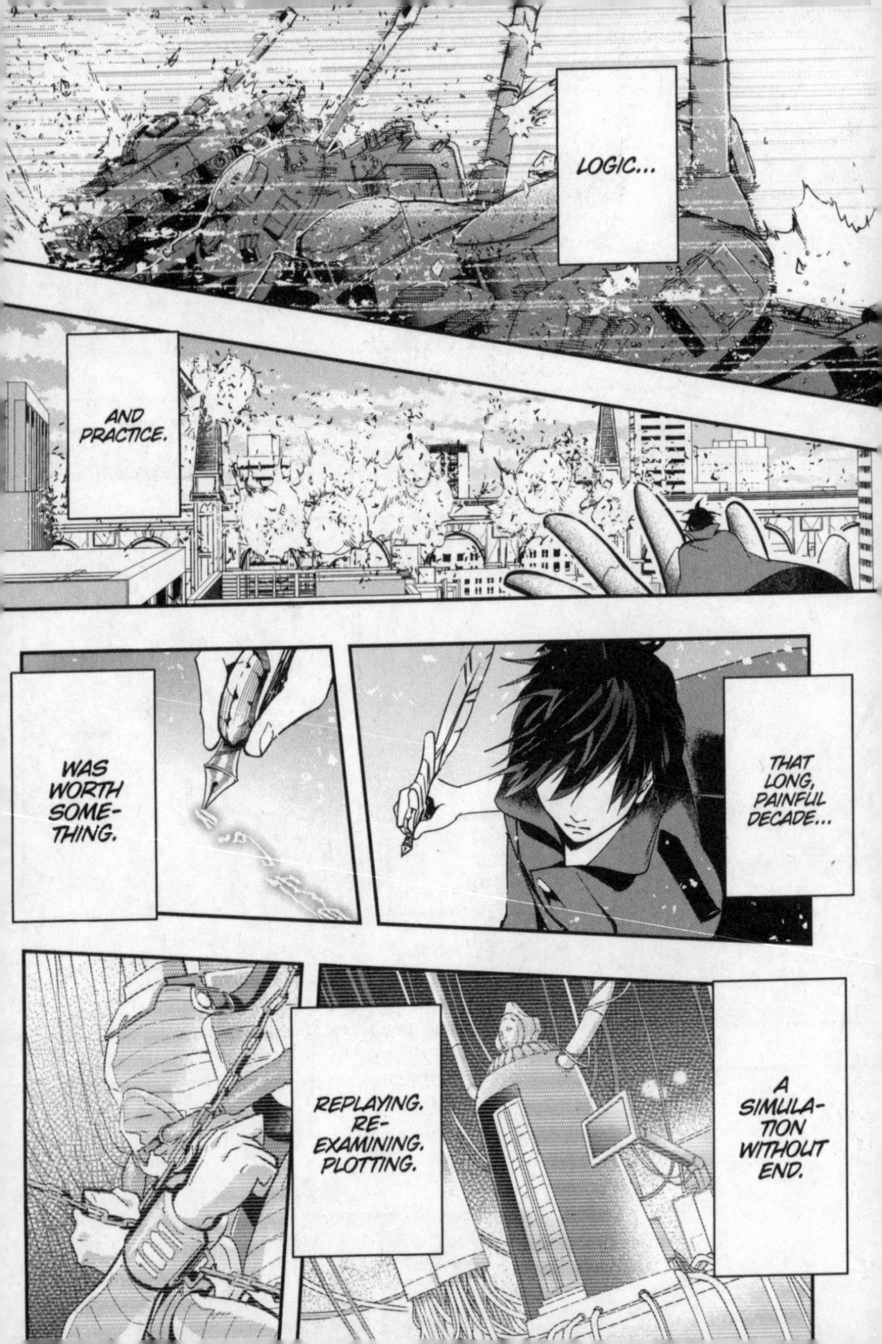
LOGIC...
AND PRACTICE.
THAT LONG, PAINFUL DECADE...
WAS WORTH SOME-THING.
A SIMULA-TION WITHOUT END.
REPLAYING. RE-EXAMINING. PLOTTING.

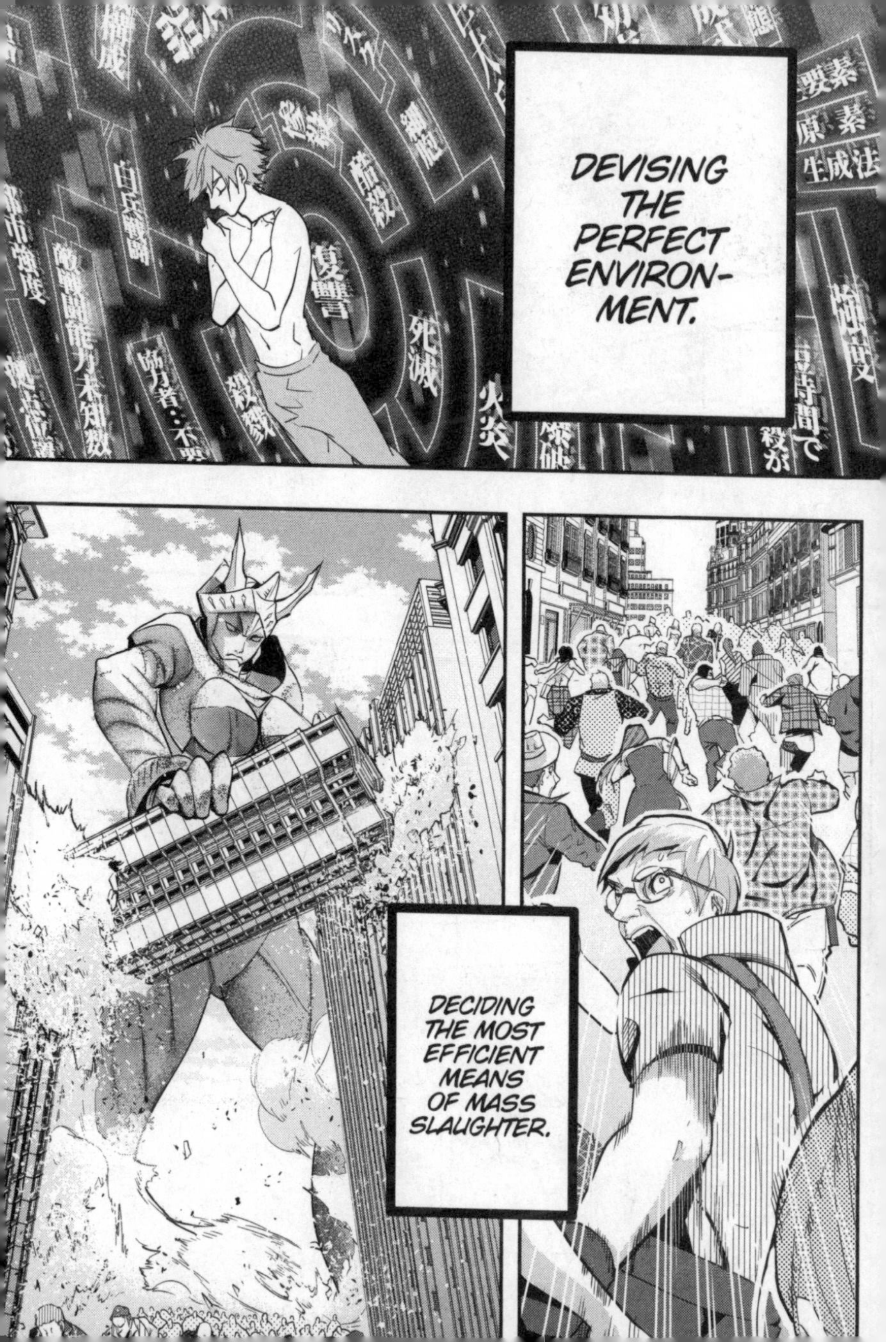
DEVISING THE PERFECT ENVIRON-MENT.
DECIDING THE MOST EFFICIENT MEANS OF MASS SLAUGHTER.

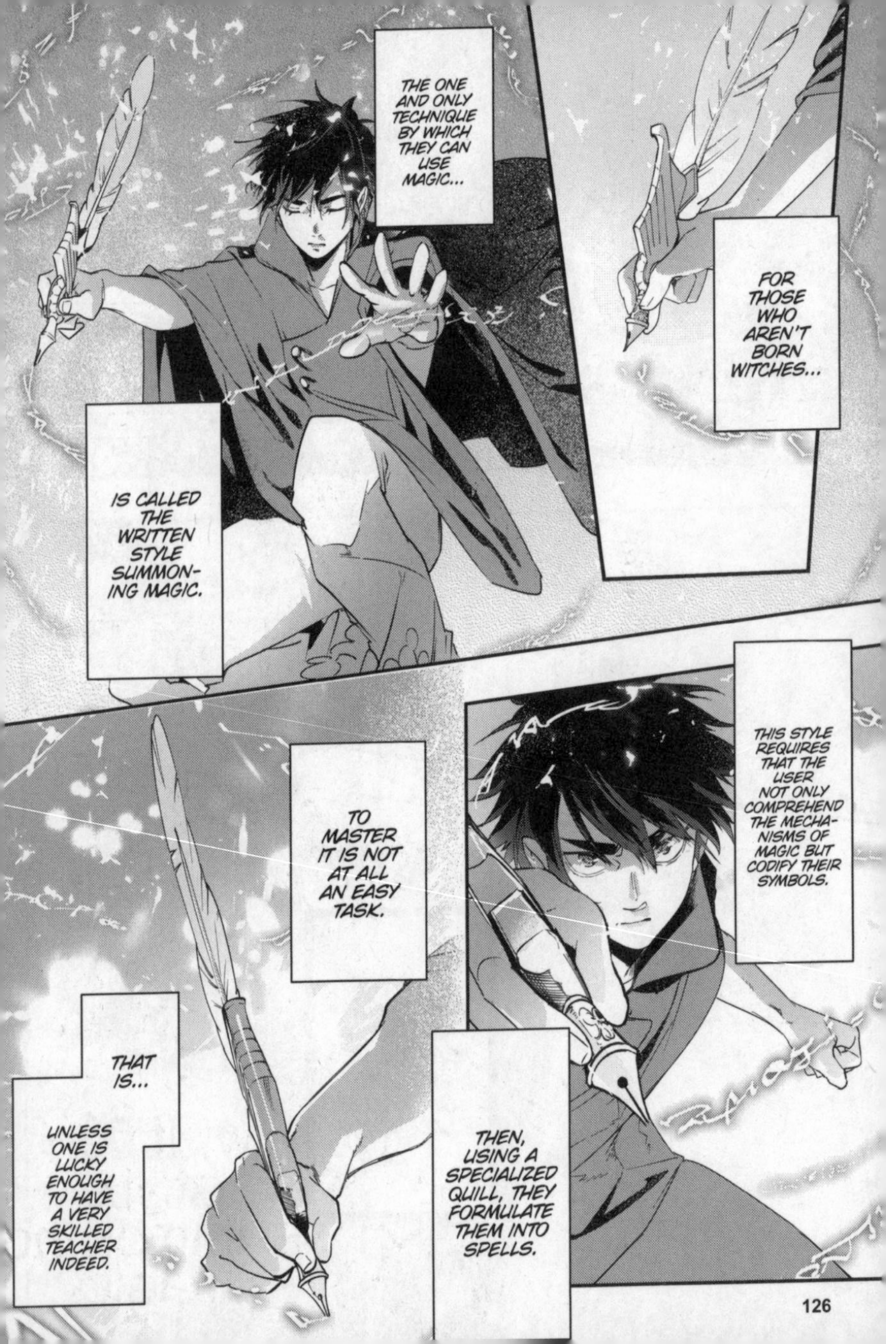
FOR THOSE WHO AREN'T BORN WITCHES...
THE ONE AND ONLY TECHNIQUE BY WHICH THEY CAN USE MAGIC...
IS CALLED THE WRITTEN STYLE SUMMONING MAGIC.
THIS STYLE REQUIRES THAT THE USER NOT ONLY COMPREHEND THE MECHANISMS OF MAGIC BUT CODIFY THEIR SYMBOLS.
THEN, USING A SPECIALIZED QUILL, THEY FORMULATE THEM INTO SPELLS.
TO MASTER IT IS NOT AT ALL AN EASY TASK.
THAT IS...
UNLESS ONE IS LUCKY ENOUGH TO HAVE A VERY SKILLED TEACHER INDEED.

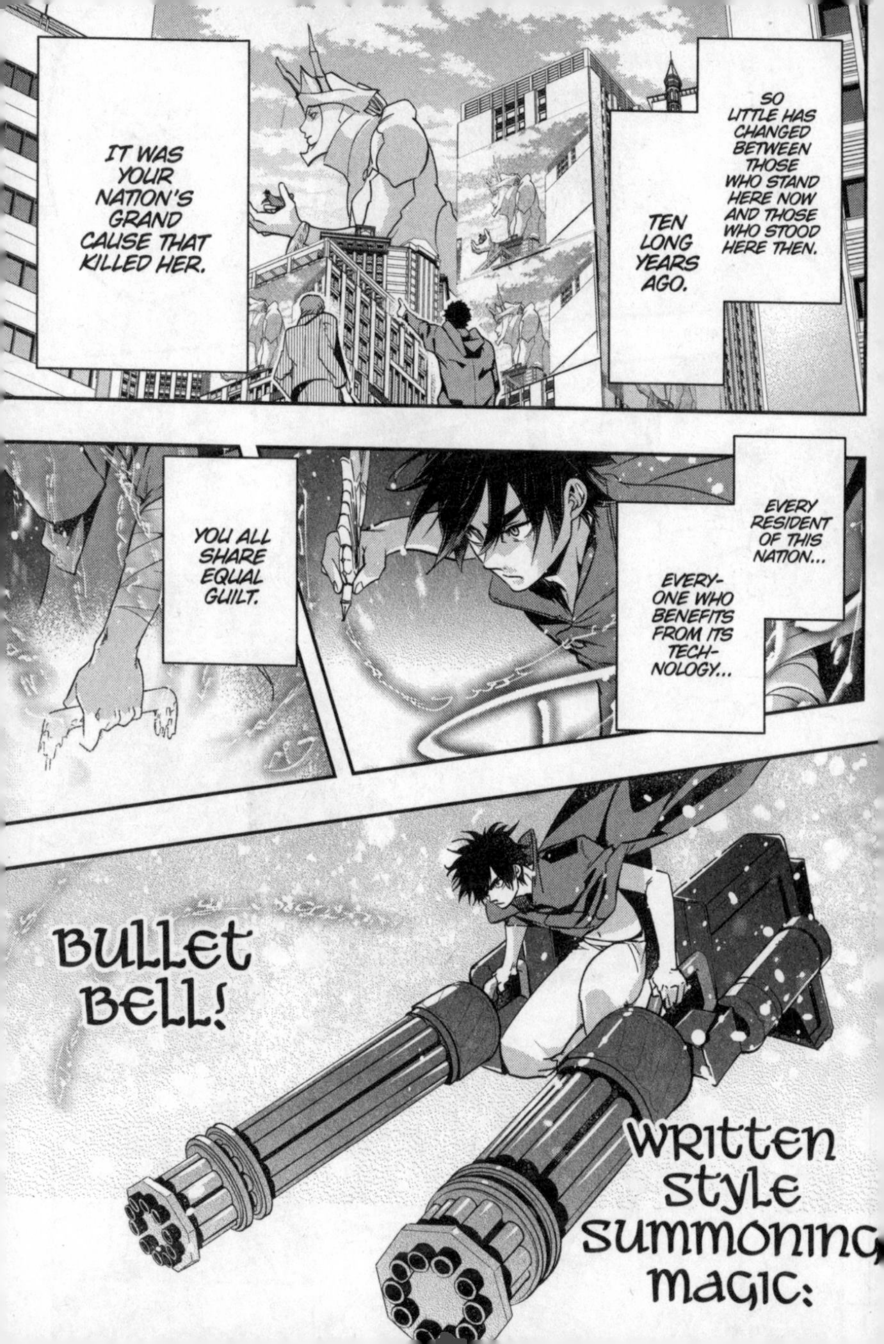
SO LITTLE HAS CHANGED BETWEEN THOSE WHO STAND HERE NOW AND THOSE WHO STOOD HERE THEN.
TEN LONG YEARS AGO.
IT WAS YOUR NATION'S GRAND CAUSE THAT KILLED HER.
EVERY RESIDENT OF THIS NATION...
EVERY-ONE WHO BENEFITS FROM ITS TECH-NOLOGY...
YOU ALL SHARE EQUAL GUILT.
WRITTEN STYLE SUMMONING MAGIC:
BULLET BELL!

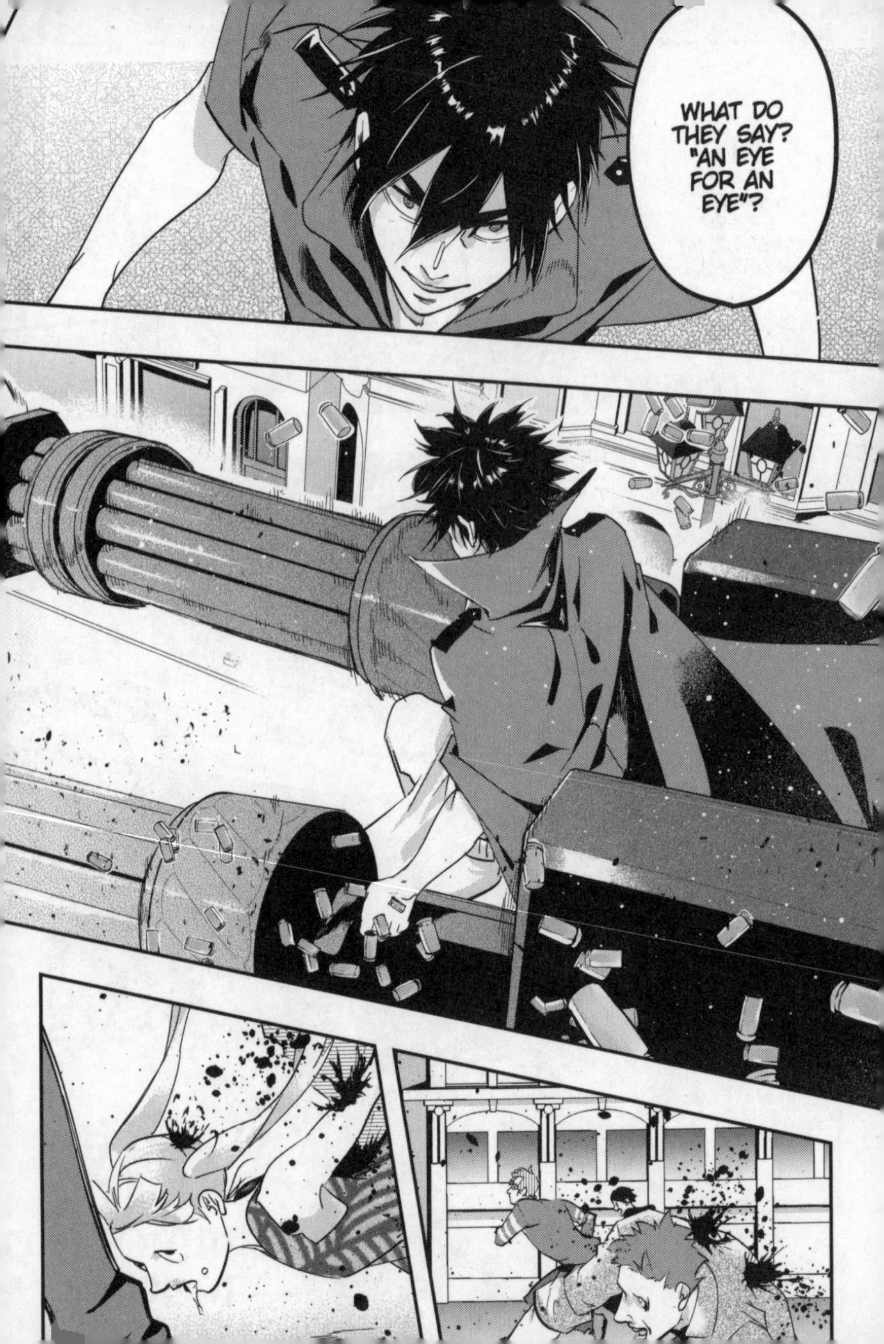
WHAT DO THEY SAY? "AN EYE FOR AN EYE"?

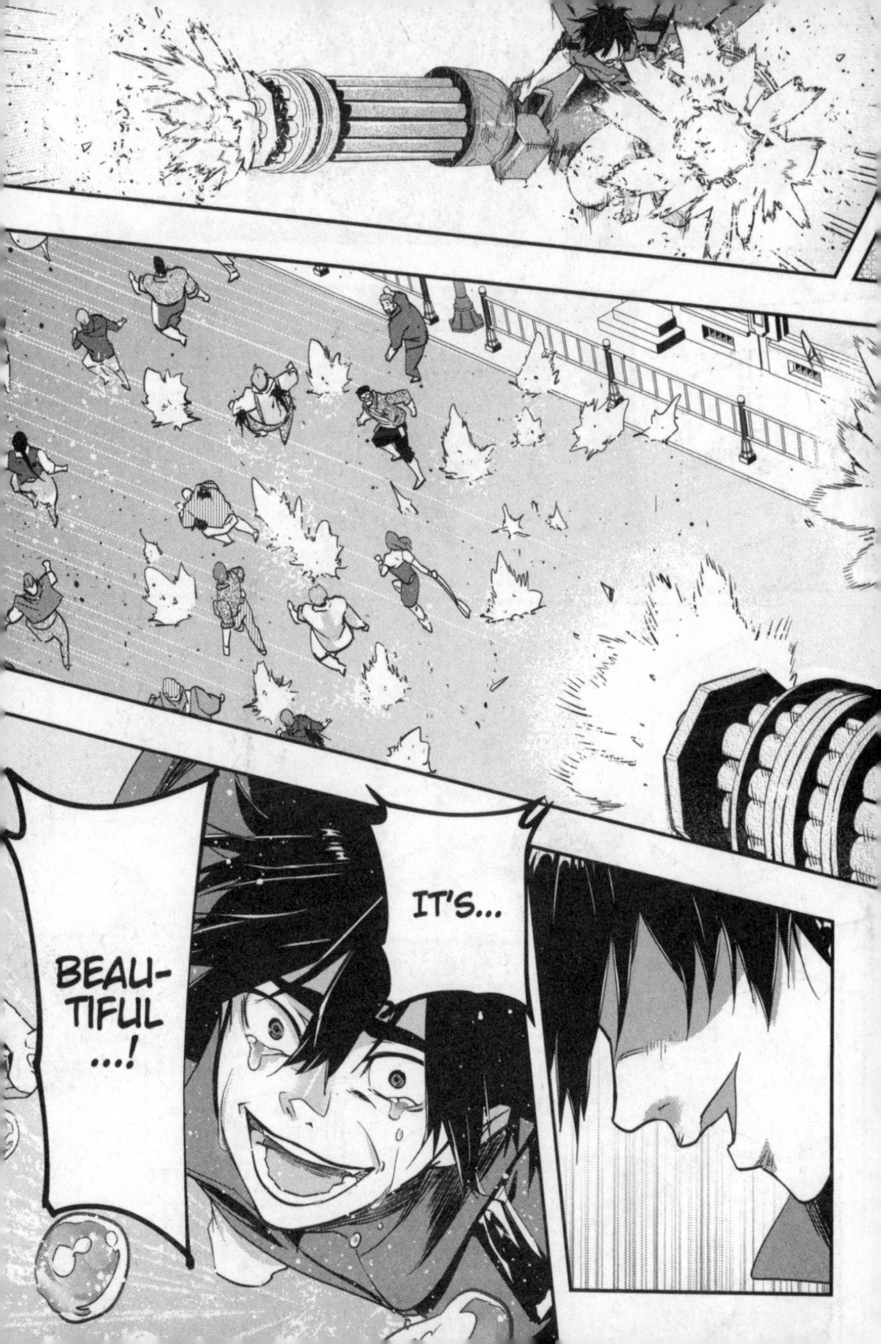
IT'S...
BEAU-TIFUL ...!

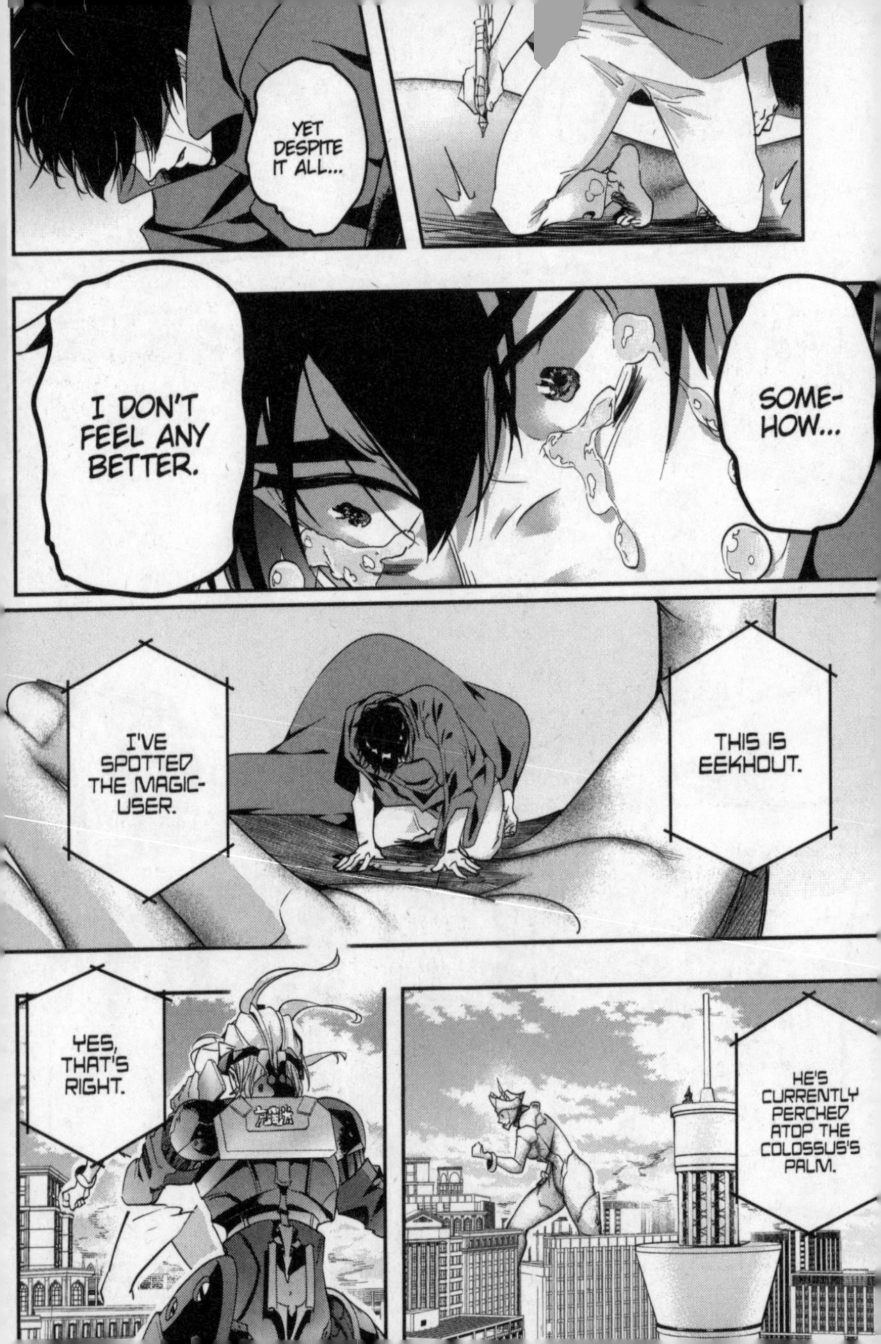
YET DESPITE IT ALL...
SOME-HOW...
I DON'T FEEL ANY BETTER.
THIS IS EEKHOUT.
I'VE SPOTTED THE MAGIC-USER.
HE'S CURRENTLY PERCHED ATOP THE COLOSSUS'S PALM.
YES, THAT'S RIGHT.

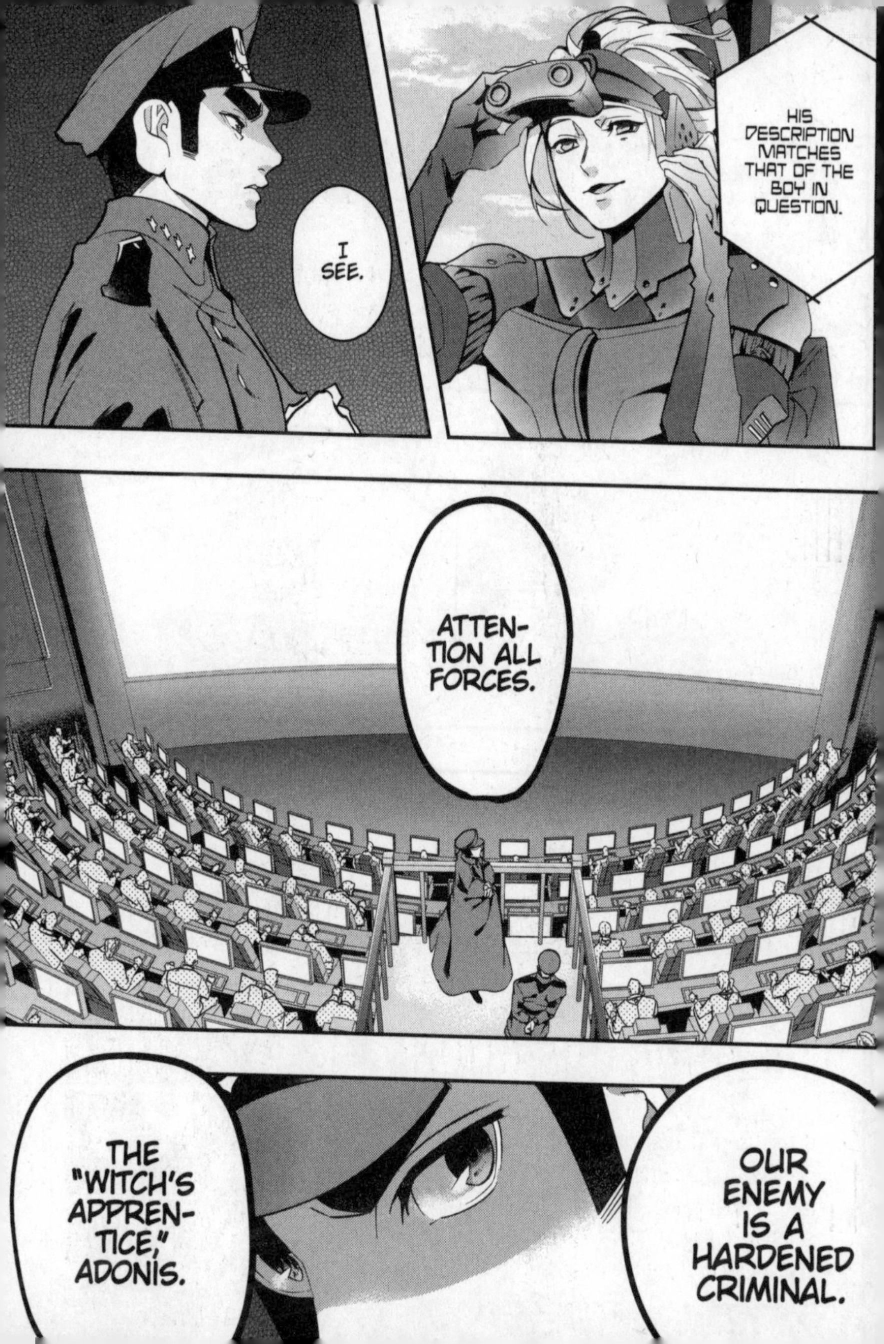
HIS DESCRIPTION MATCHES THAT OF THE BOY IN QUESTION.
I SEE.
ATTEN-TION ALL FORCES.
OUR ENEMY IS A HARDENED CRIMINAL.
THE "WITCH'S APPREN-TICE," ADONIS.

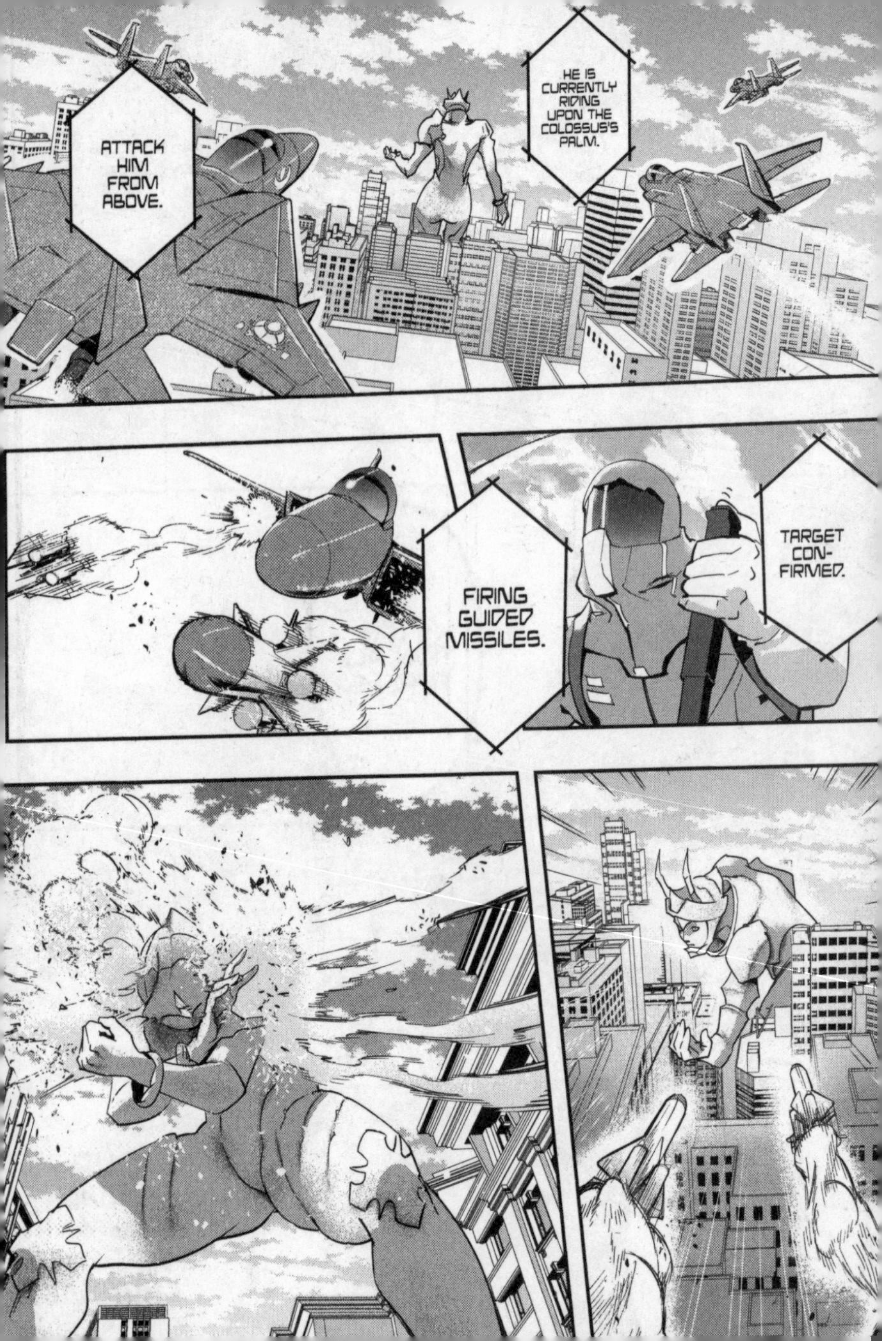
HE IS CURRENTLY RIDING UPON THE COLOSSUS'S PALM.
ATTACK HIM FROM ABOVE.
TARGET CON-FIRMED.
FIRING GUIDED MISSILES.

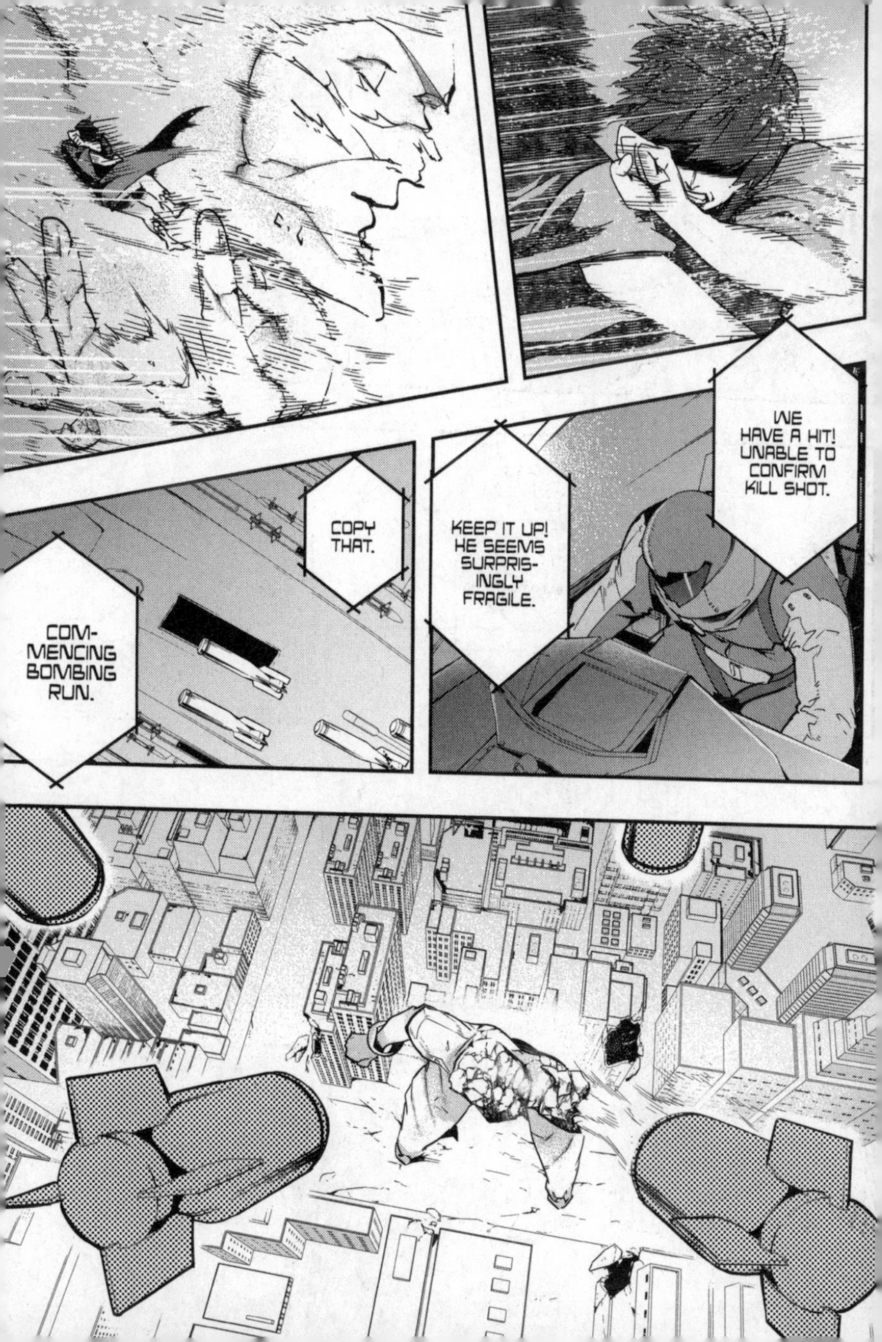
WE HAVE A HIT! UNABLE TO CONFIRM KILL SHOT.
KEEP IT UP! HE SEEMS SURPRIS-INGLY FRAGILE.
COPY THAT.
COM-MENCING BOMBING RUN.

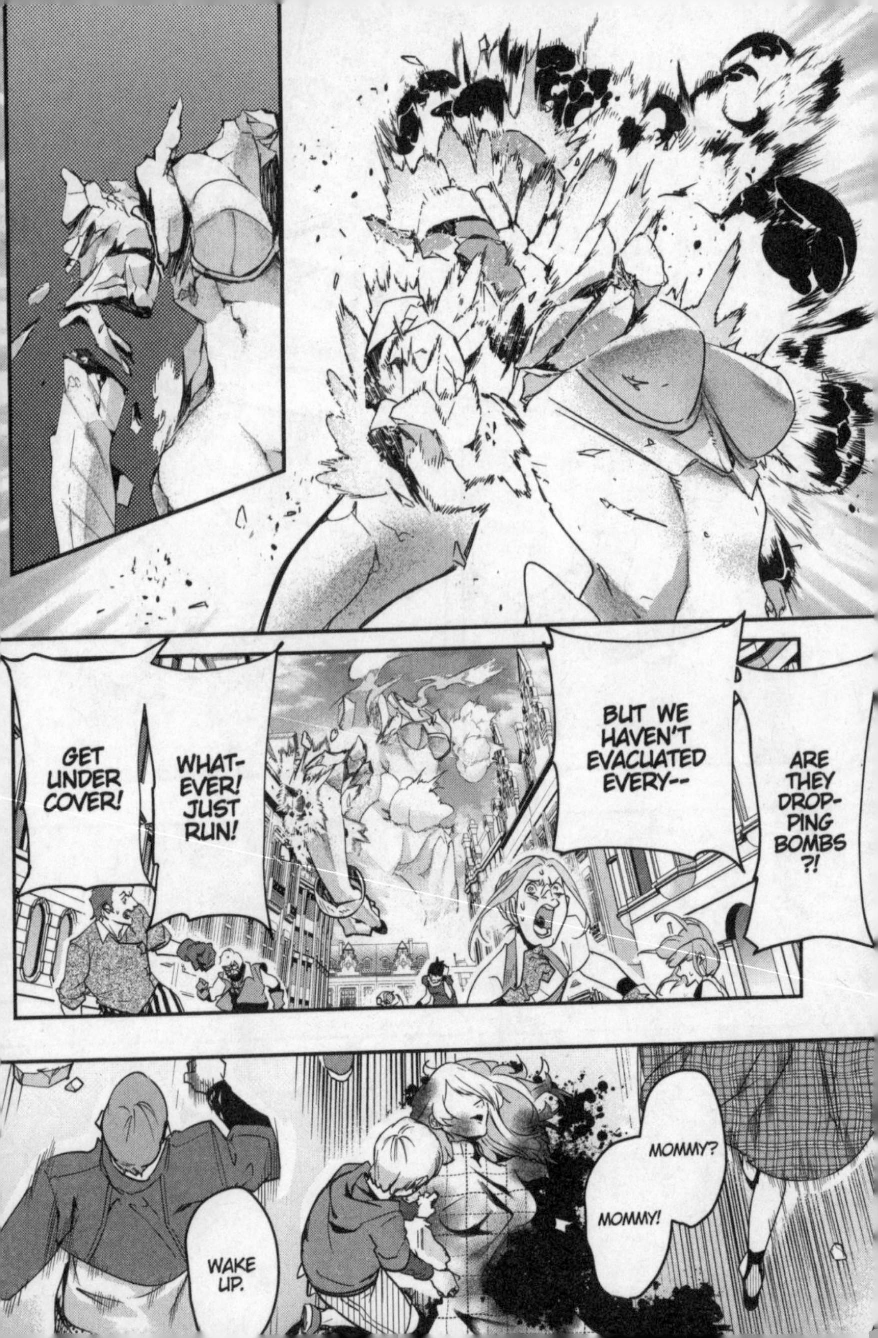
ARE THEY DROP-PING BOMBS?!
BUT WE HAVEN'T EVACUATED EVERY--
WHAT-EVER! JUST RUN!
GET UNDER COVER!
MOMMY?
MOMMY!
WAKE UP.

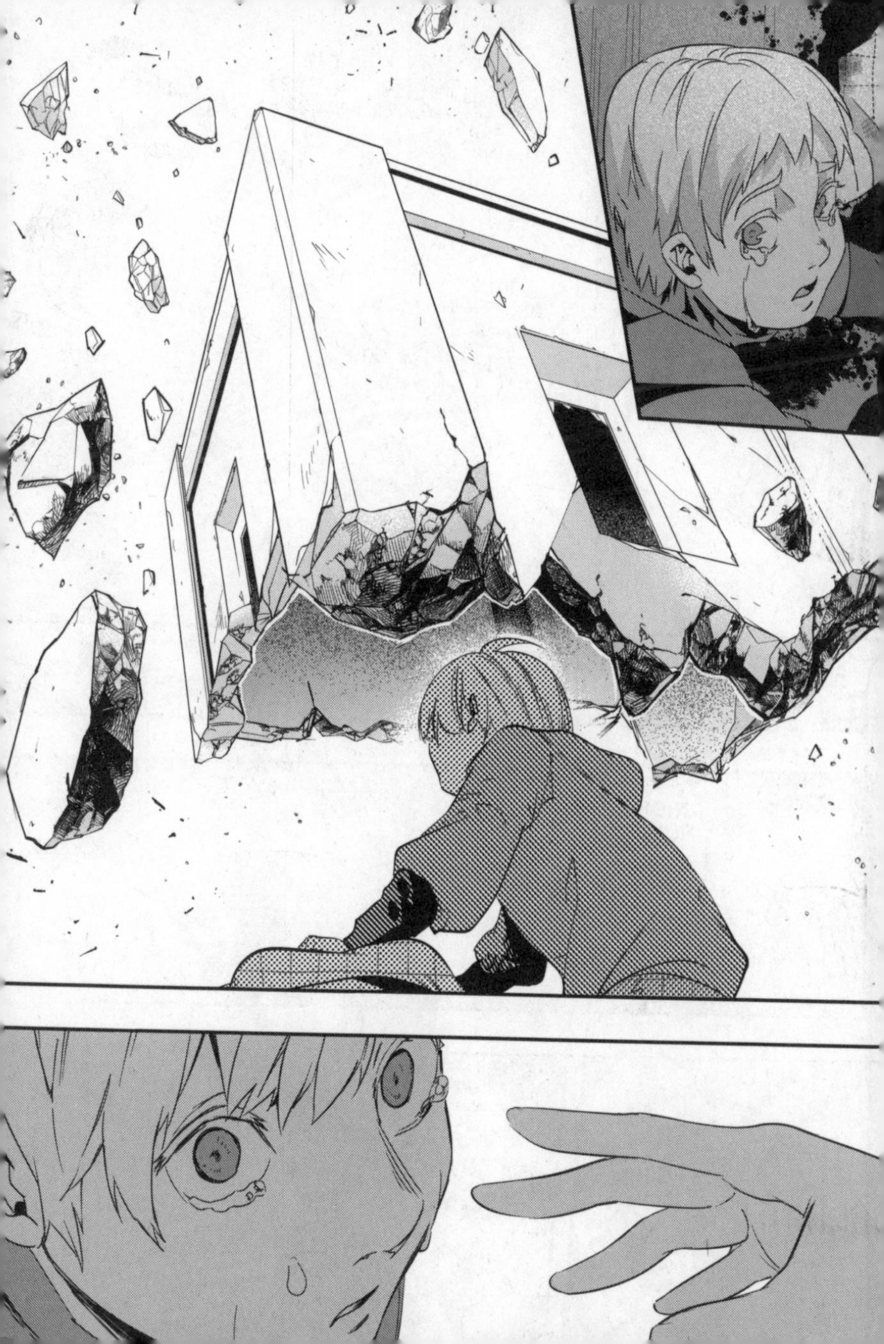

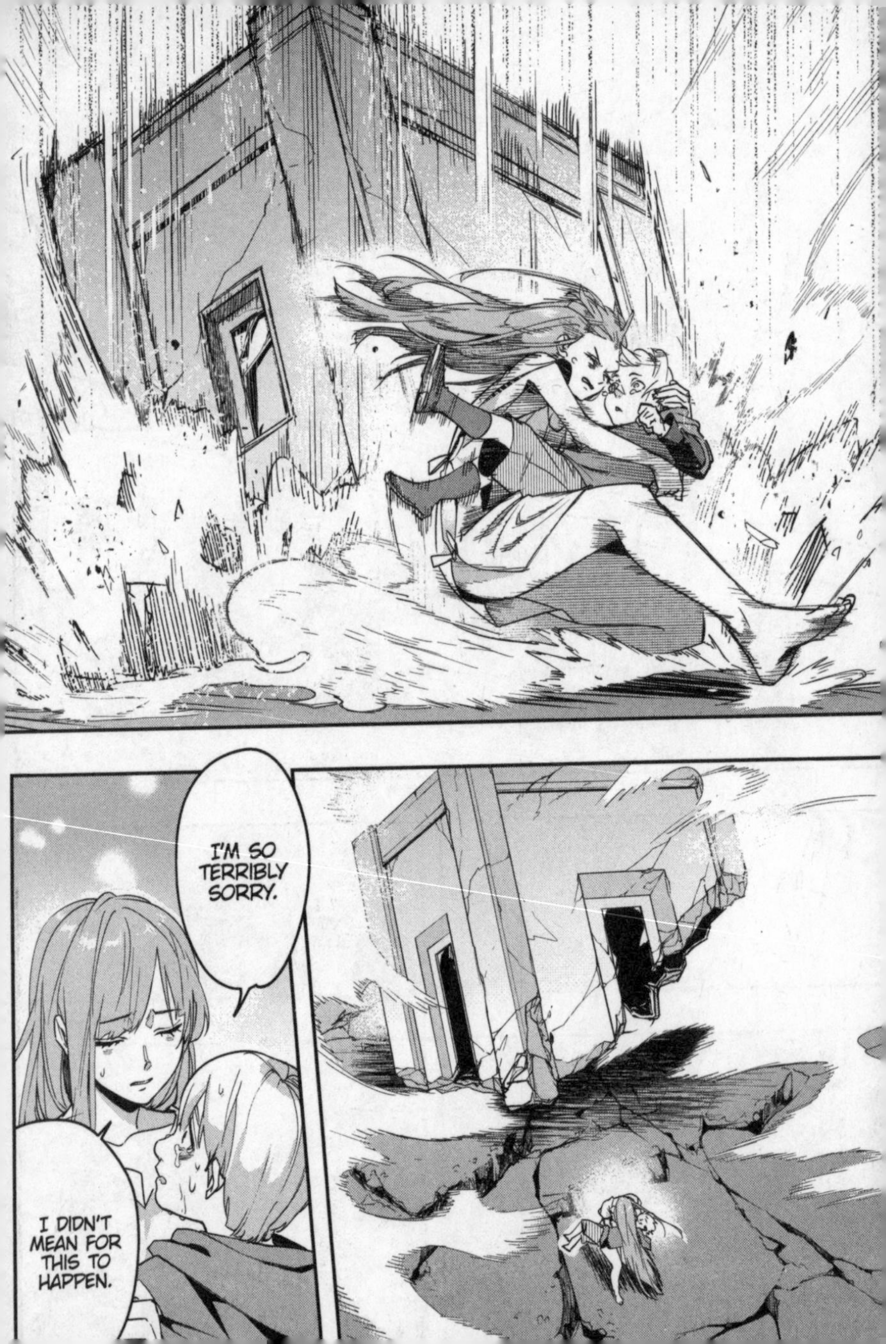
I'M SO TERRIBLY SORRY.
I DIDN'T MEAN FOR THIS TO HAPPEN.

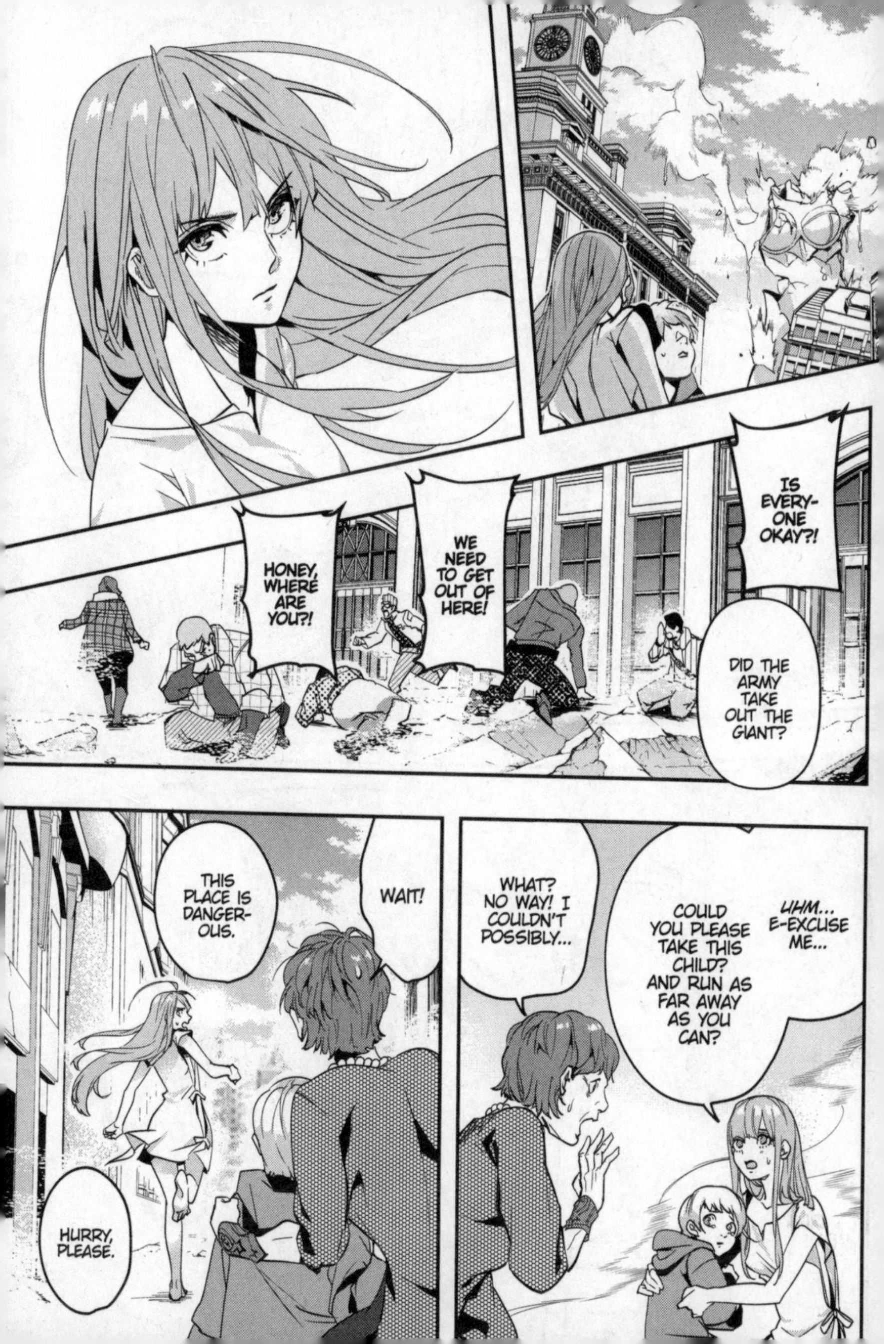
IS EVERY-ONE OKAY?!
DID THE ARMY TAKE OUT THE GIANT?
WE NEED TO GET OUT OF HERE!
HONEY, WHERE ARE YOU?!
UHM... E-EXCUSE ME...
COULD YOU PLEASE TAKE THIS CHILD? AND RUN AS FAR AWAY AS YOU CAN?
WHAT? NO WAY! I COULDN'T POSSIBLY...
WAIT!
THIS PLACE IS DANGER-OUS.
HURRY, PLEASE.

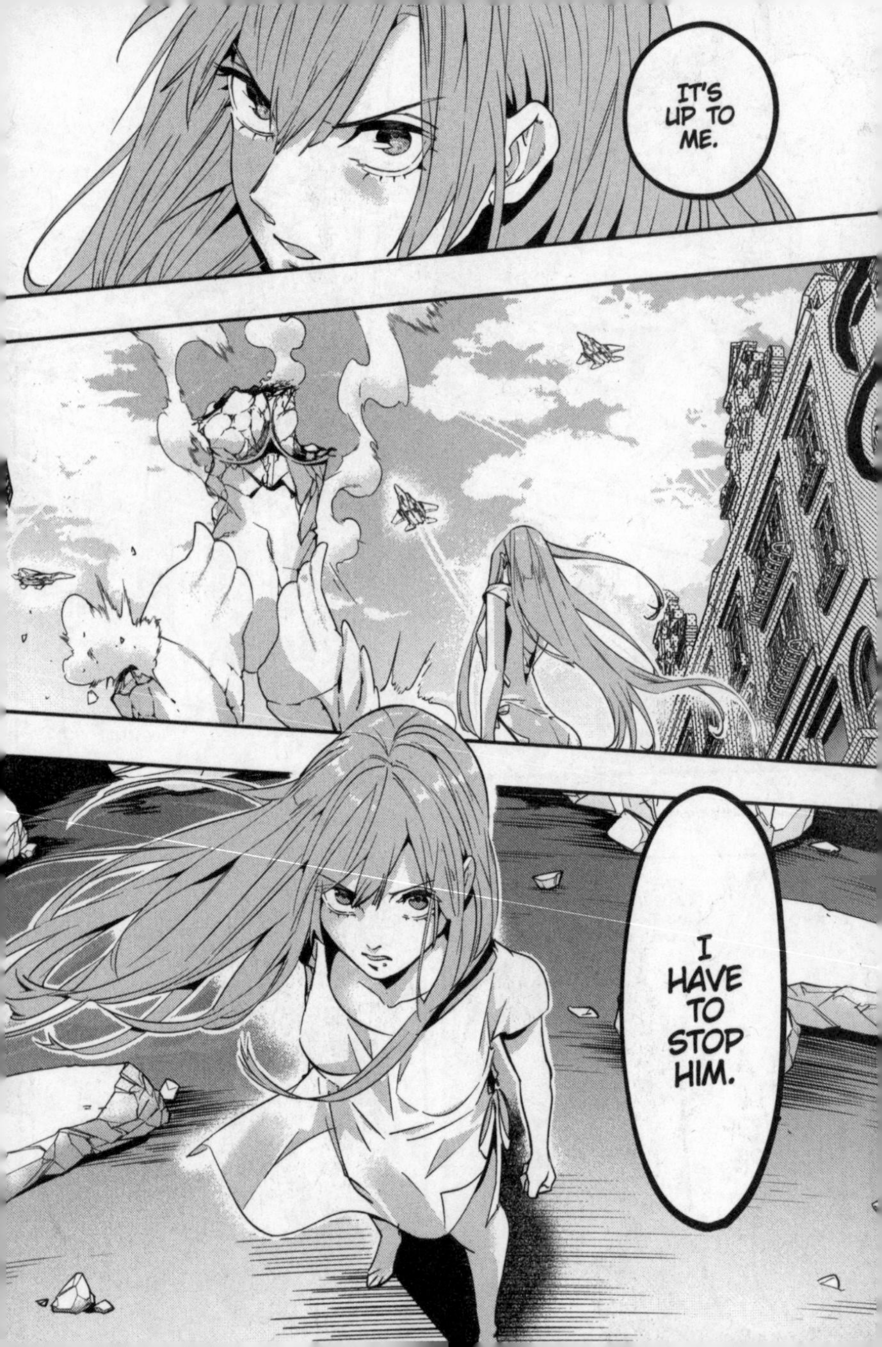
IT'S UP TO ME.
I HAVE TO STOP HIM.

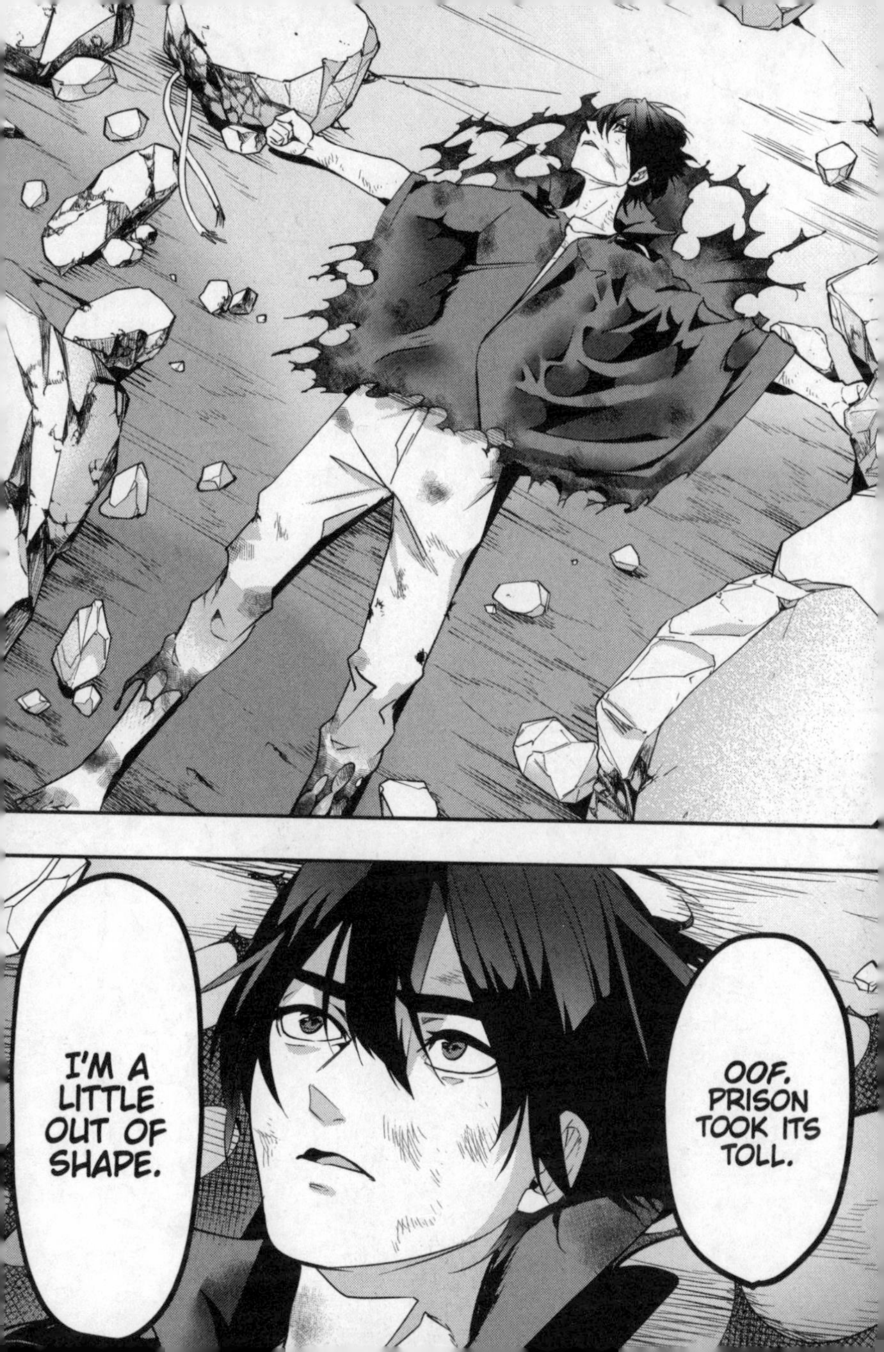
OOF. PRISON TOOK ITS TOLL.
I'M A LITTLE OUT OF SHAPE.

THE
KINGDOMS
OF RUIN

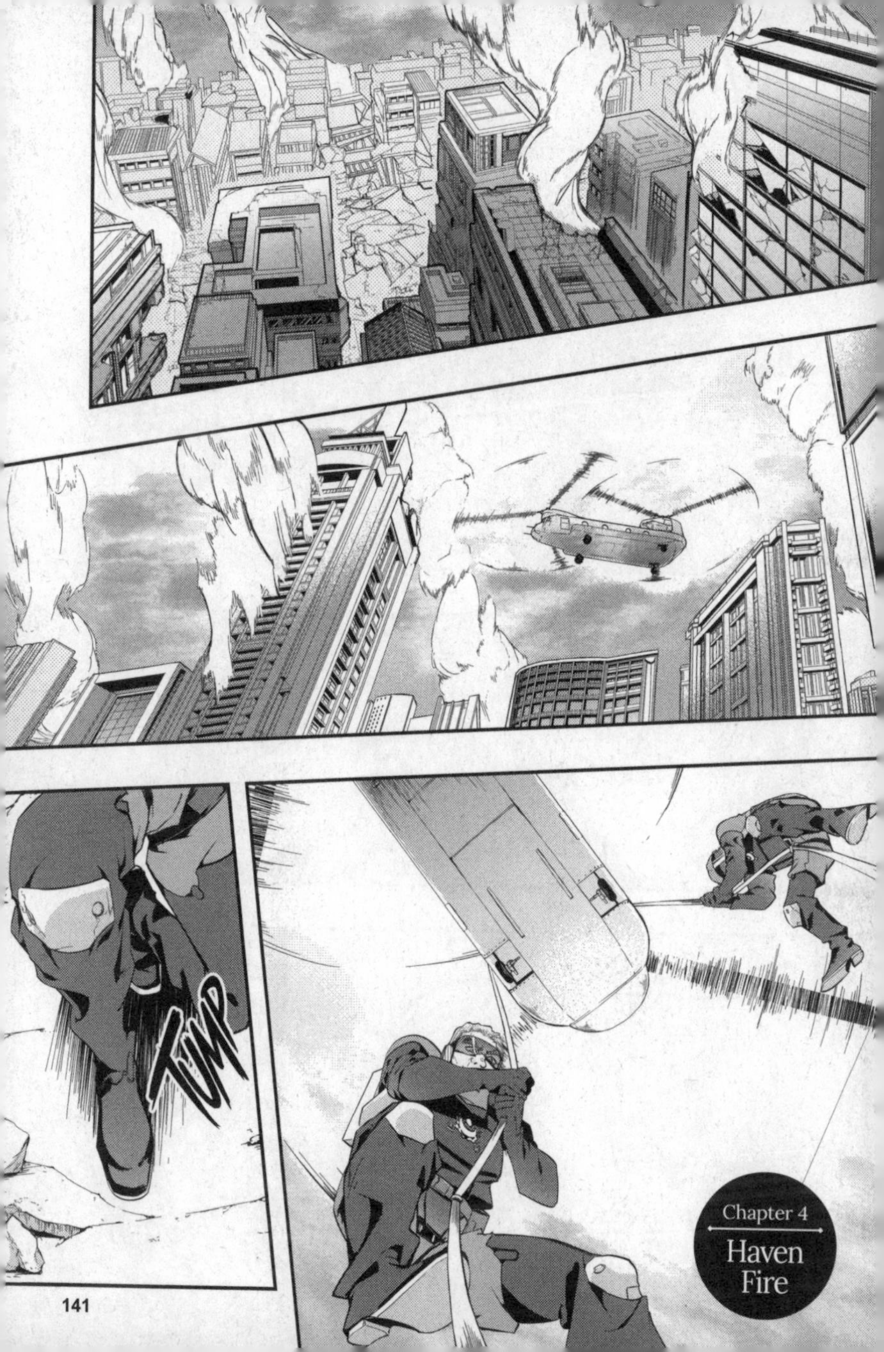
THMP
Chapter 4
Haven Fire

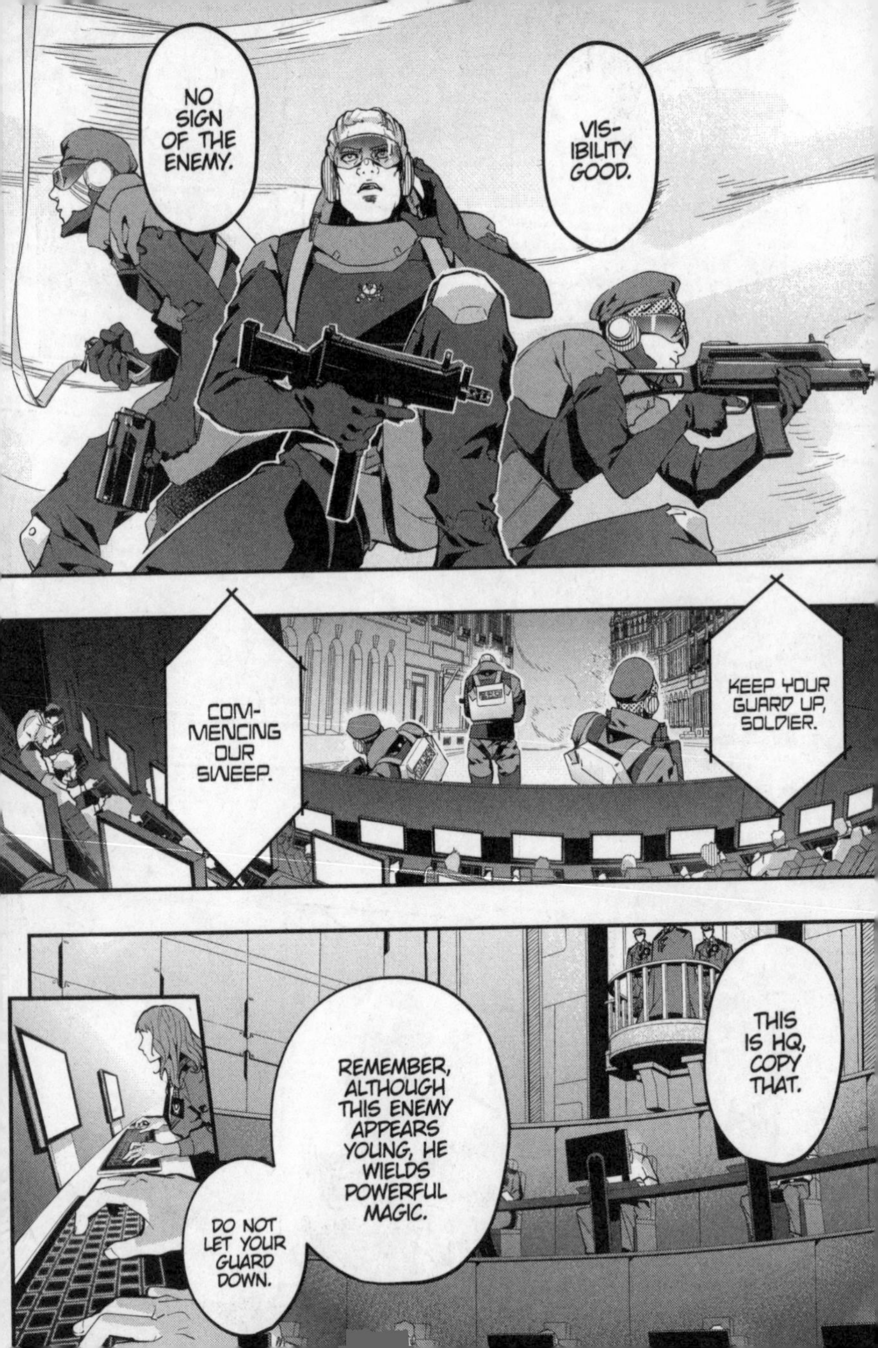
VIS-IBILITY GOOD.
NO SIGN OF THE ENEMY.
KEEP YOUR GUARD UP, SOLDIER.
COM-MENCING OUR SWEEP.
THIS IS HQ, COPY THAT.
REMEMBER, ALTHOUGH THIS ENEMY APPEARS YOUNG, HE WIELDS POWERFUL MAGIC.
DO NOT LET YOUR GUARD DOWN.

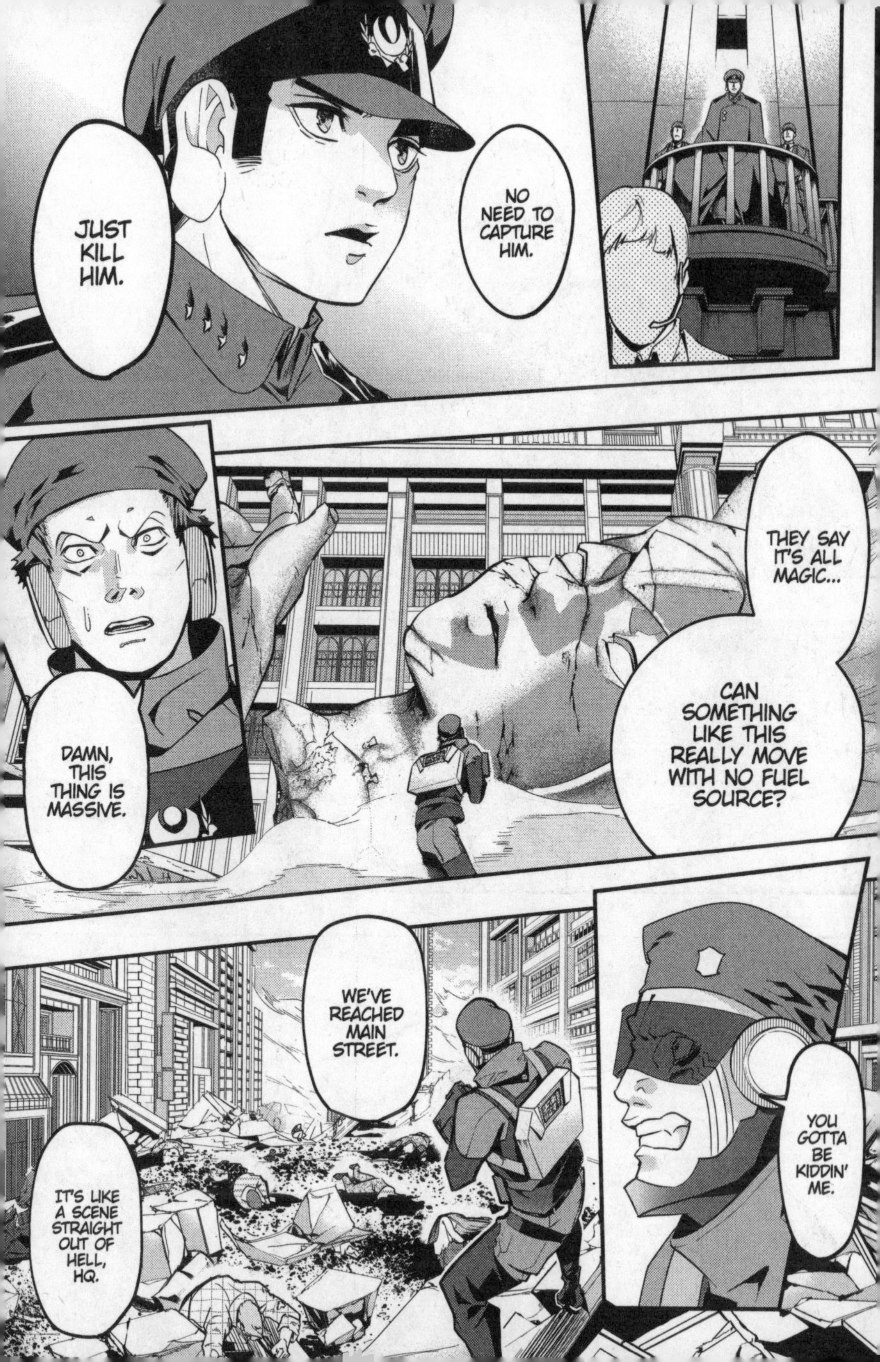
NO NEED TO CAPTURE HIM.
JUST KILL HIM.
THEY SAY IT'S ALL MAGIC...
CAN SOMETHING LIKE THIS REALLY MOVE WITH NO FUEL SOURCE?
DAMN, THIS THING IS MASSIVE.
YOU GOTTA BE KIDDIN' ME.
WE'VE REACHED MAIN STREET.
IT'S LIKE A SCENE STRAIGHT OUT OF HELL, HQ.

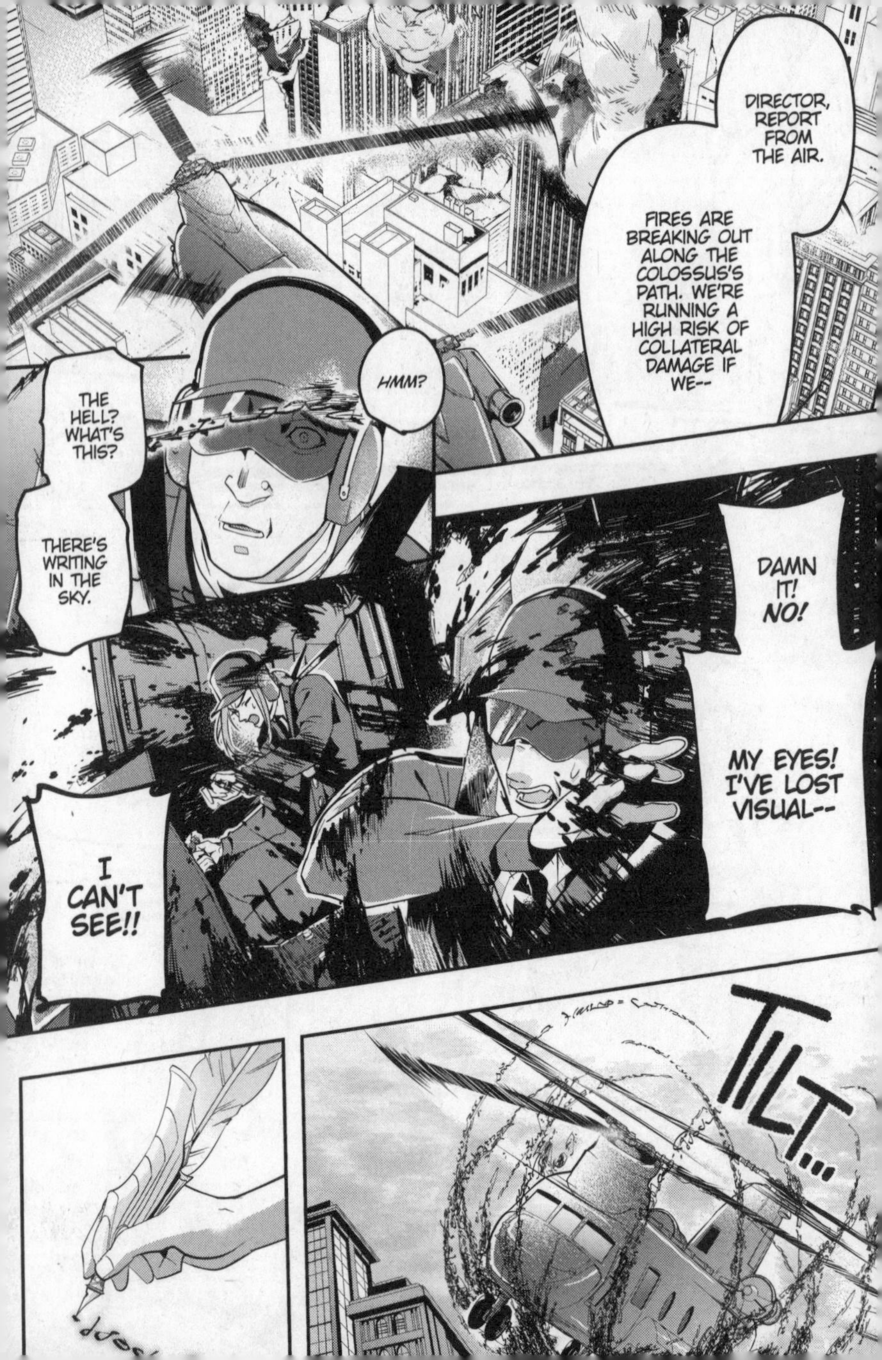

DIRECTOR, REPORT FROM THE AIR.
FIRES ARE BREAKING OUT ALONG THE COLOSSUS'S PATH. WE'RE RUNNING A HIGH RISK OF COLLATERAL DAMAGE IF WE--
HMM?
THE HELL? WHAT'S THIS?
THERE'S WRITING IN THE SKY.
DAMN IT! NO!
MY EYES! I'VE LOST VISUAL--
I CAN'T SEE!!
TILT...

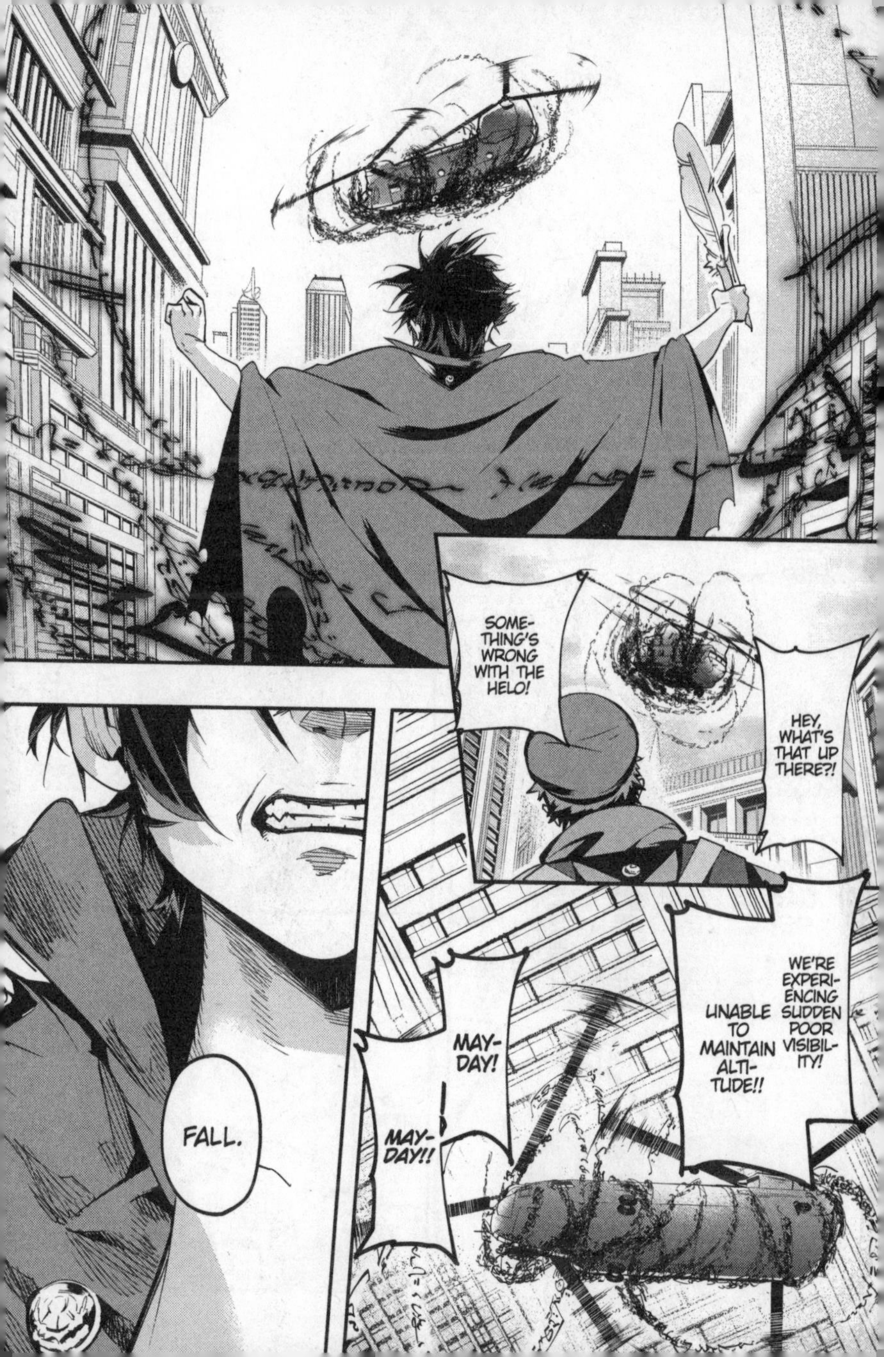
HEY, WHAT'S THAT UP THERE?!
SOMETHING'S WRONG WITH THE HELO!
WE'RE EXPERIENCING SUDDEN POOR VISIBILITY!
UNABLE TO MAINTAIN ALTITUDE!!
MAYDAY!
MAYDAY!!
FALL.

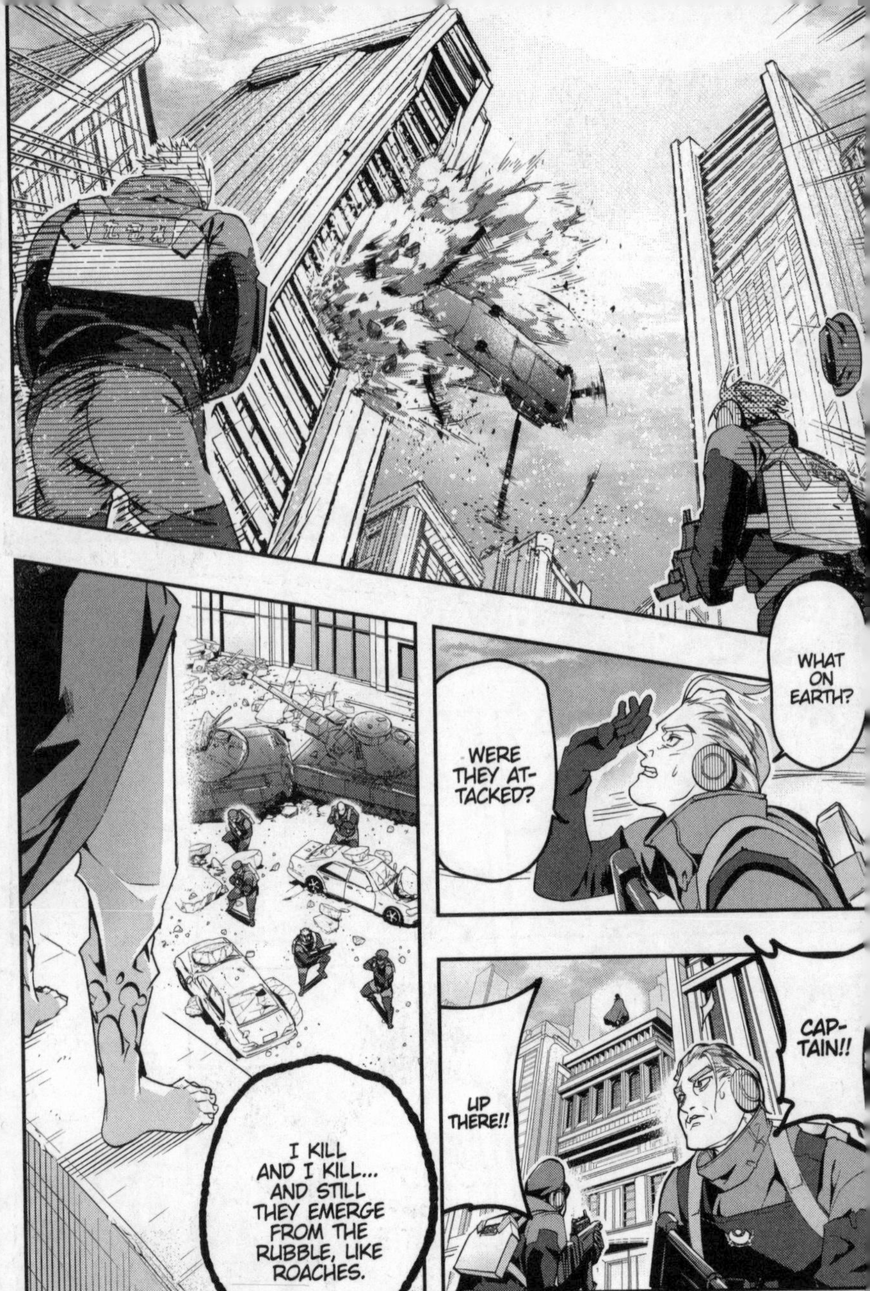
WHAT ON EARTH?
WERE THEY ATTACKED?
CAPTAIN!!
UP THERE!!
I KILL AND I KILL... AND STILL THEY EMERGE FROM THE RUBBLE, LIKE ROACHES.

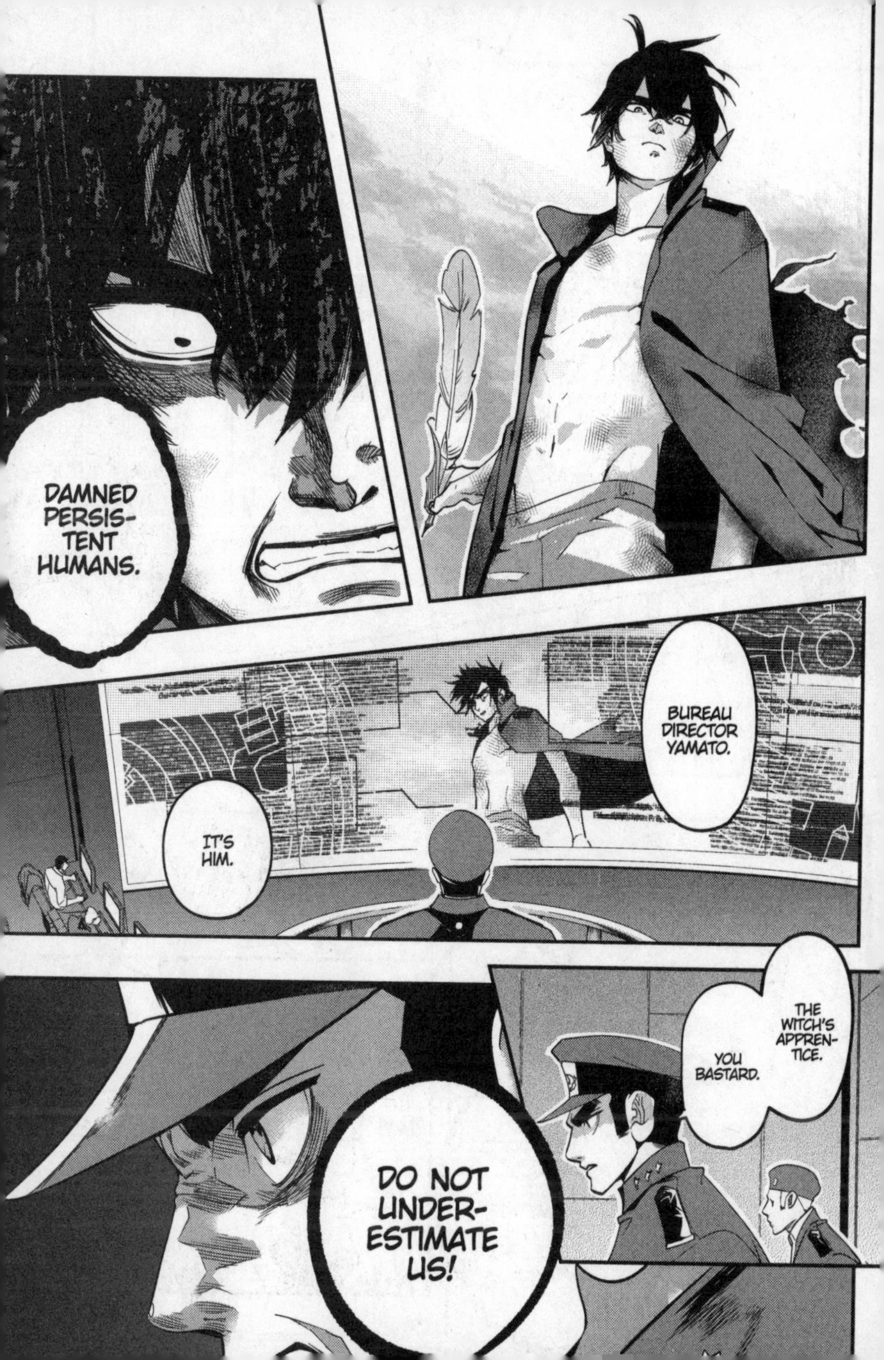
DAMNED PERSISTENT HUMANS.
BUREAU DIRECTOR YAMATO.
IT'S HIM.
THE WITCH'S APPRENTICE.
YOU BASTARD.
DO NOT UNDERESTIMATE US!

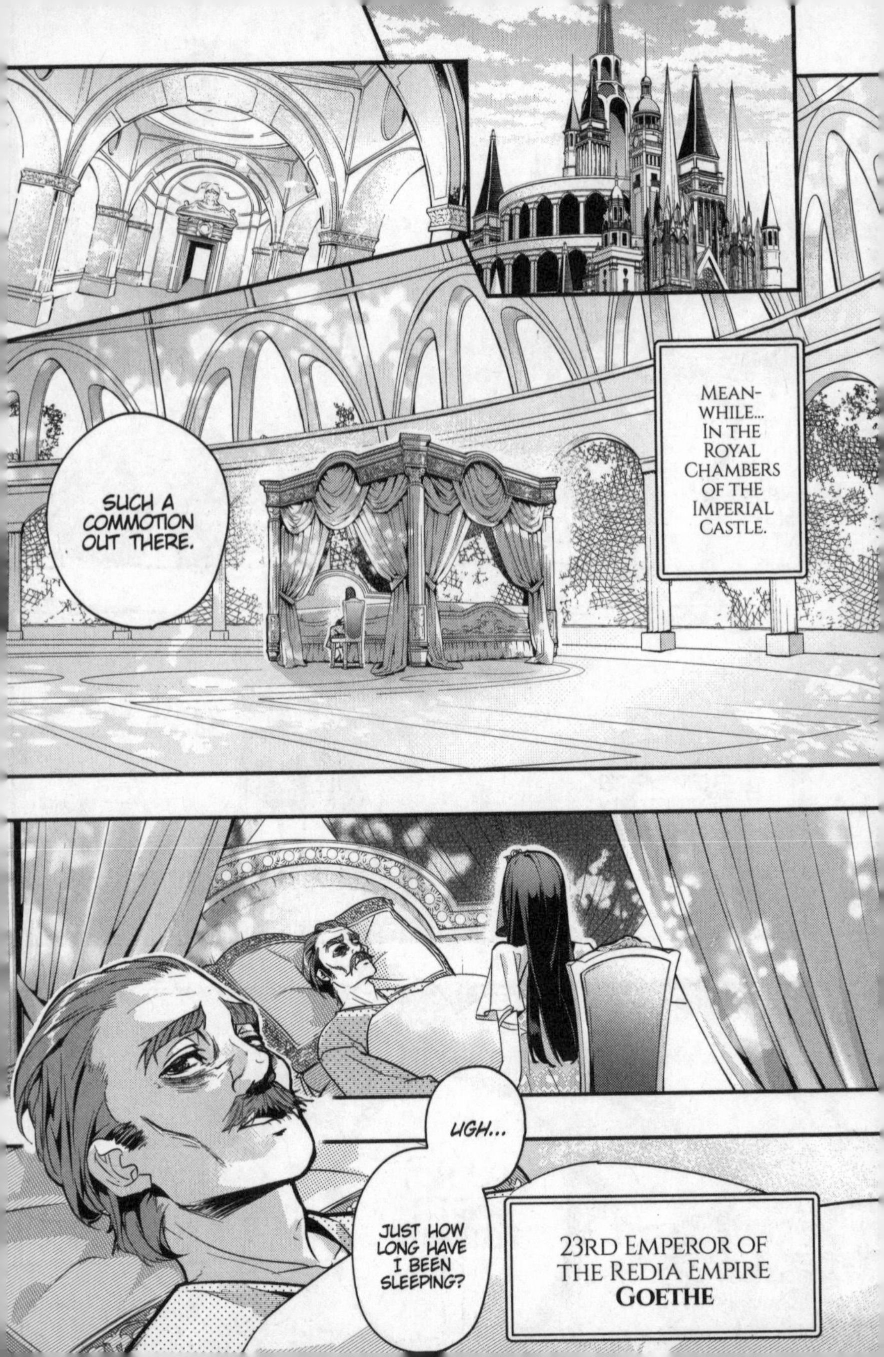
MEAN-WHILE... IN THE ROYAL CHAMBERS OF THE IMPERIAL CASTLE.
SUCH A COMMOTION OUT THERE.
UGH...
JUST HOW LONG HAVE I BEEN SLEEPING?
23RD EMPEROR OF THE REDIA EMPIRE **GOETHE**

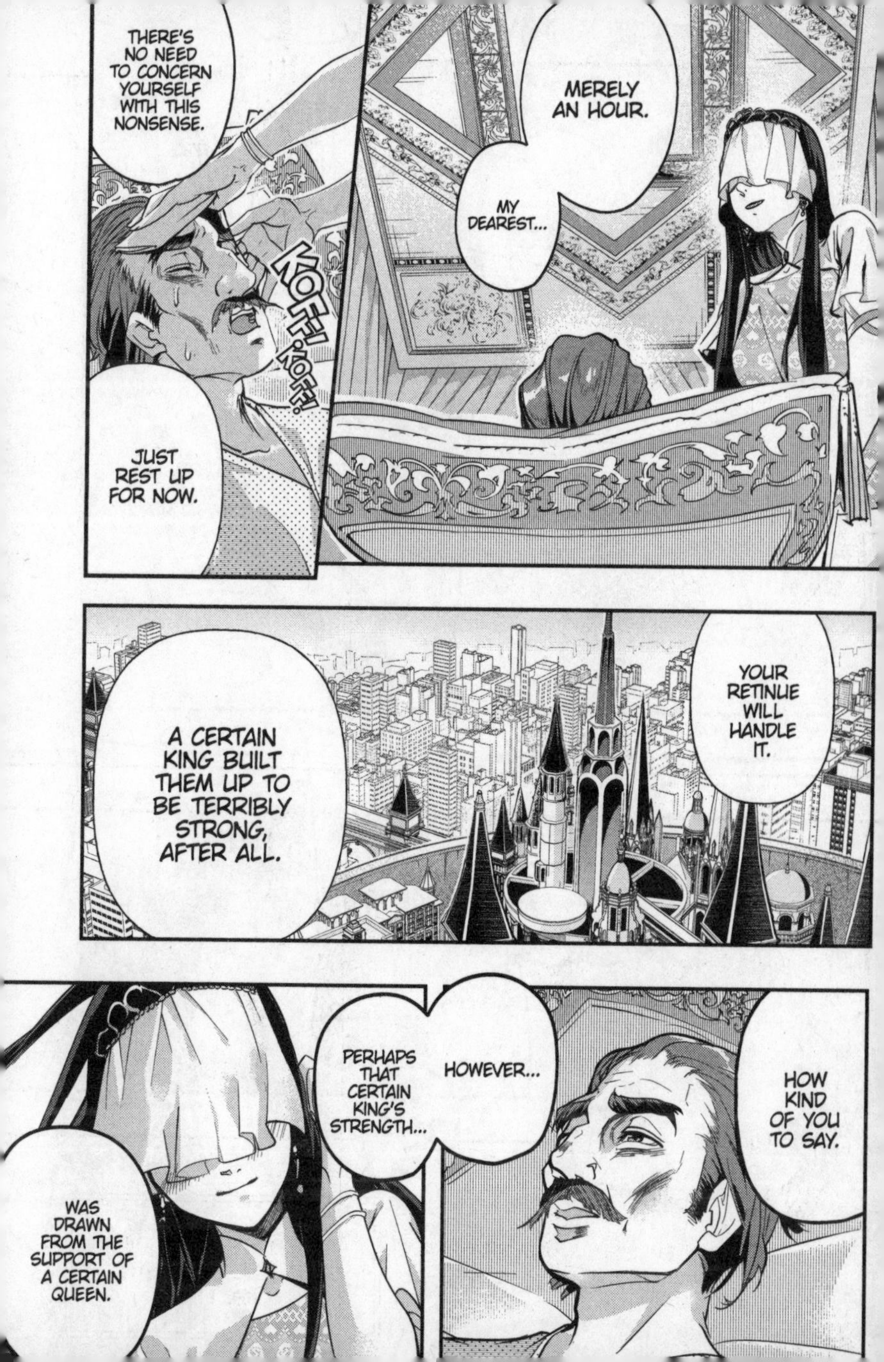
MERELY AN HOUR.
MY DEAREST...
THERE'S NO NEED TO CONCERN YOURSELF WITH THIS NONSENSE.
KOFF! KOFF!
JUST REST UP FOR NOW.
YOUR RETINUE WILL HANDLE IT.
A CERTAIN KING BUILT THEM UP TO BE TERRIBLY STRONG, AFTER ALL.
HOW KIND OF YOU TO SAY.
HOWEVER...
PERHAPS THAT CERTAIN KING'S STRENGTH...
WAS DRAWN FROM THE SUPPORT OF A CERTAIN QUEEN.

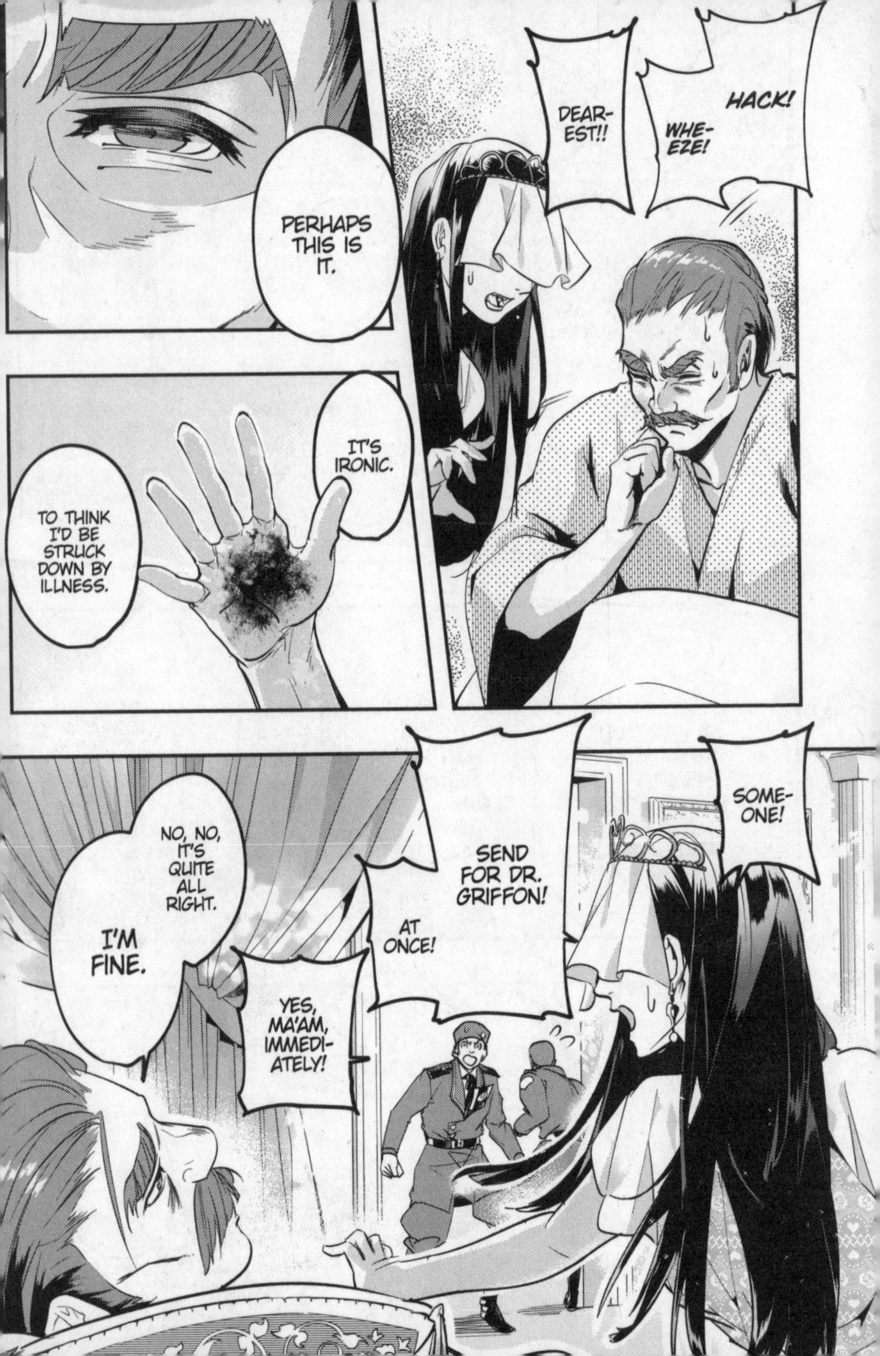
HACK!
WHE-EZE!
DEAREST!!
PERHAPS THIS IS IT.
IT'S IRONIC.
TO THINK I'D BE STRUCK DOWN BY ILLNESS.
SOME-ONE!
SEND FOR DR. GRIFFON!
AT ONCE!
YES, MA'AM, IMMEDIATELY!
NO, NO, IT'S QUITE ALL RIGHT.
I'M FINE.

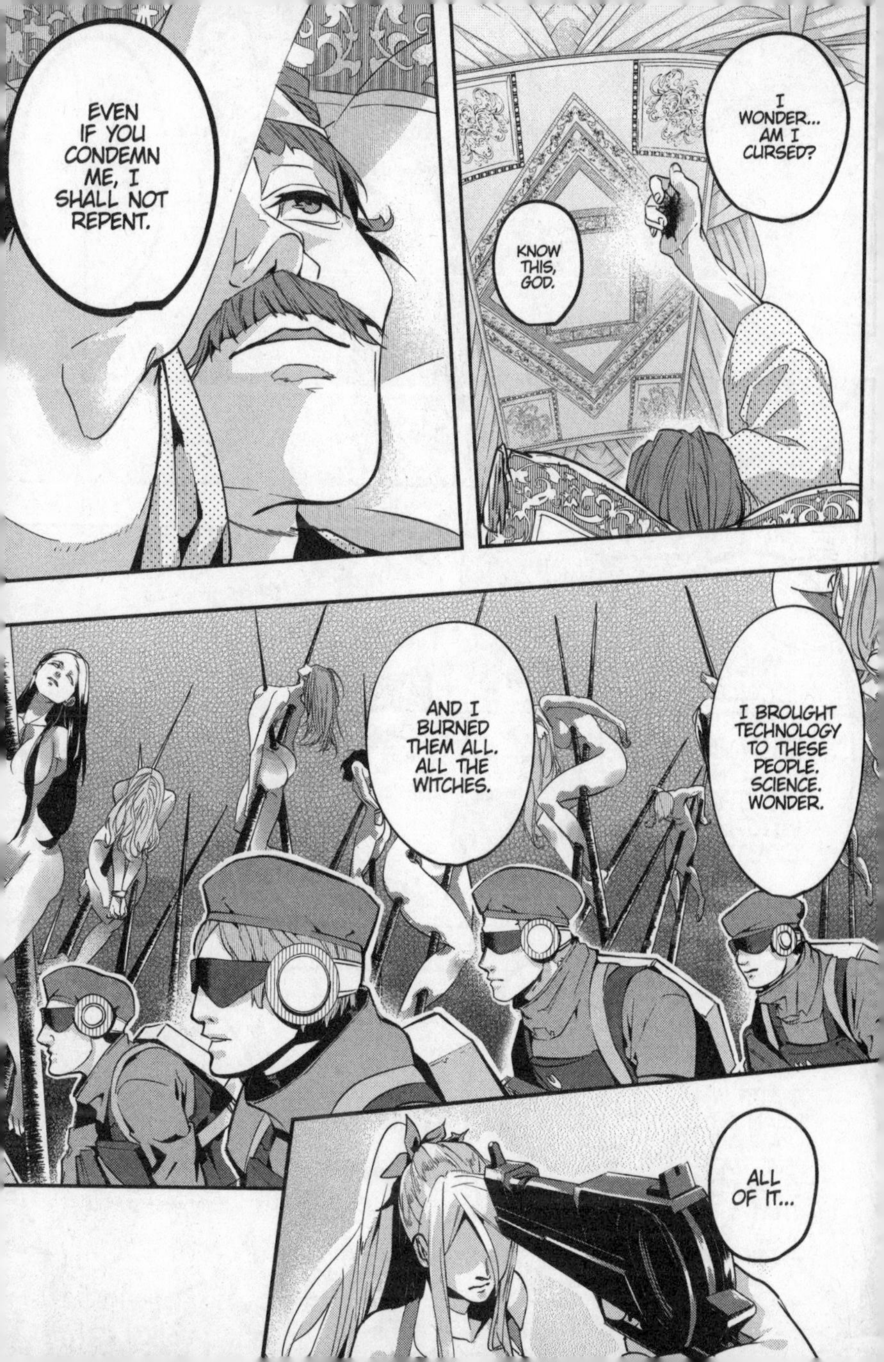
I WONDER... AM I CURSED?
KNOW THIS, GOD.
EVEN IF YOU CONDEMN ME, I SHALL NOT REPENT.
I BROUGHT TECHNOLOGY TO THESE PEOPLE. SCIENCE. WONDER.
AND I BURNED THEM ALL. ALL THE WITCHES.
ALL OF IT...

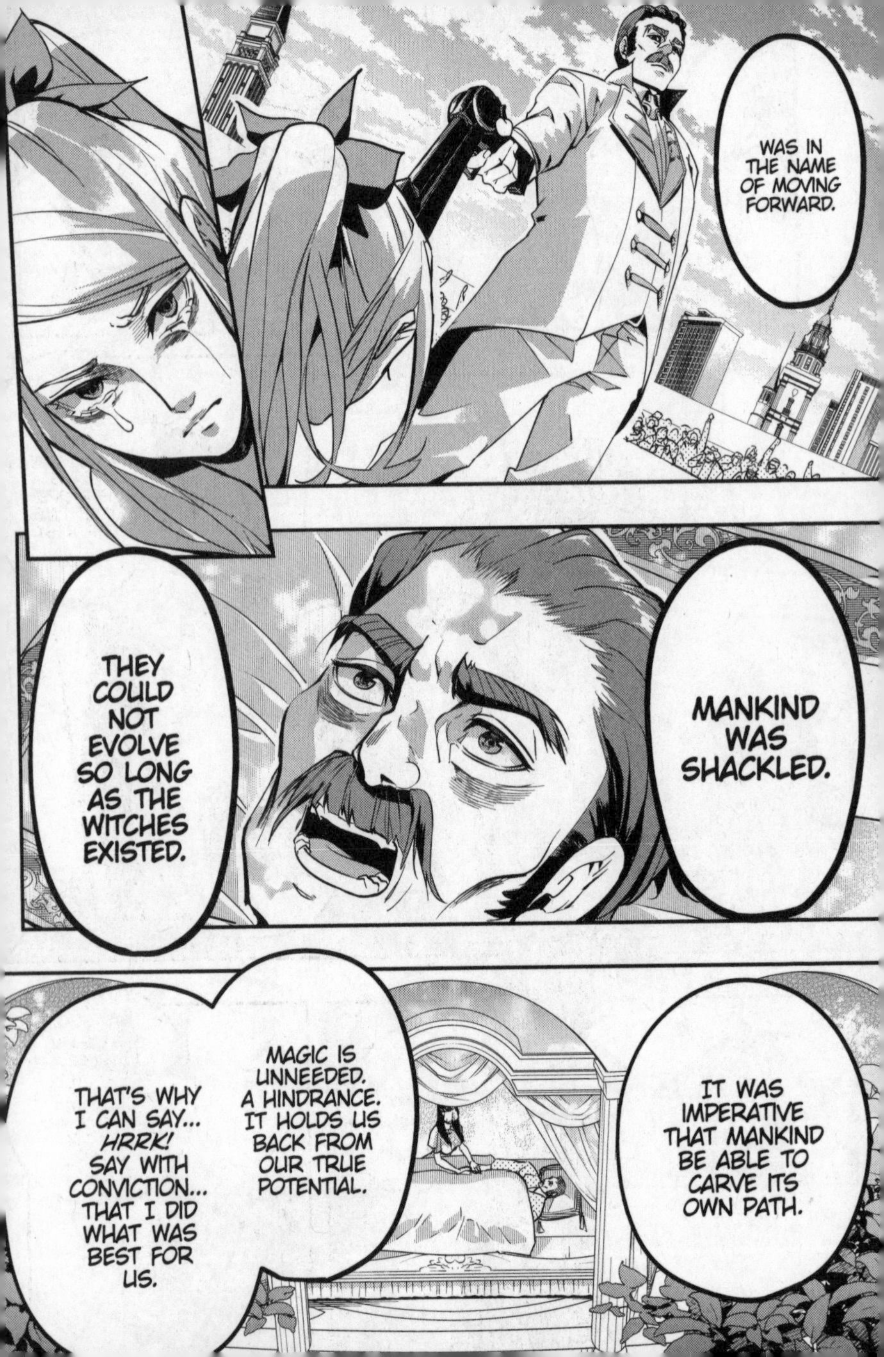
WAS IN THE NAME OF MOVING FORWARD.
MANKIND WAS SHACKLED.
THEY COULD NOT EVOLVE SO LONG AS THE WITCHES EXISTED.
IT WAS IMPERATIVE THAT MANKIND BE ABLE TO CARVE ITS OWN PATH.
MAGIC IS UNNEEDED. A HINDRANCE. IT HOLDS US BACK FROM OUR TRUE POTENTIAL.
THAT'S WHY I CAN SAY... *HRRK!* SAY WITH CONVICTION... THAT I DID WHAT WAS BEST FOR US.

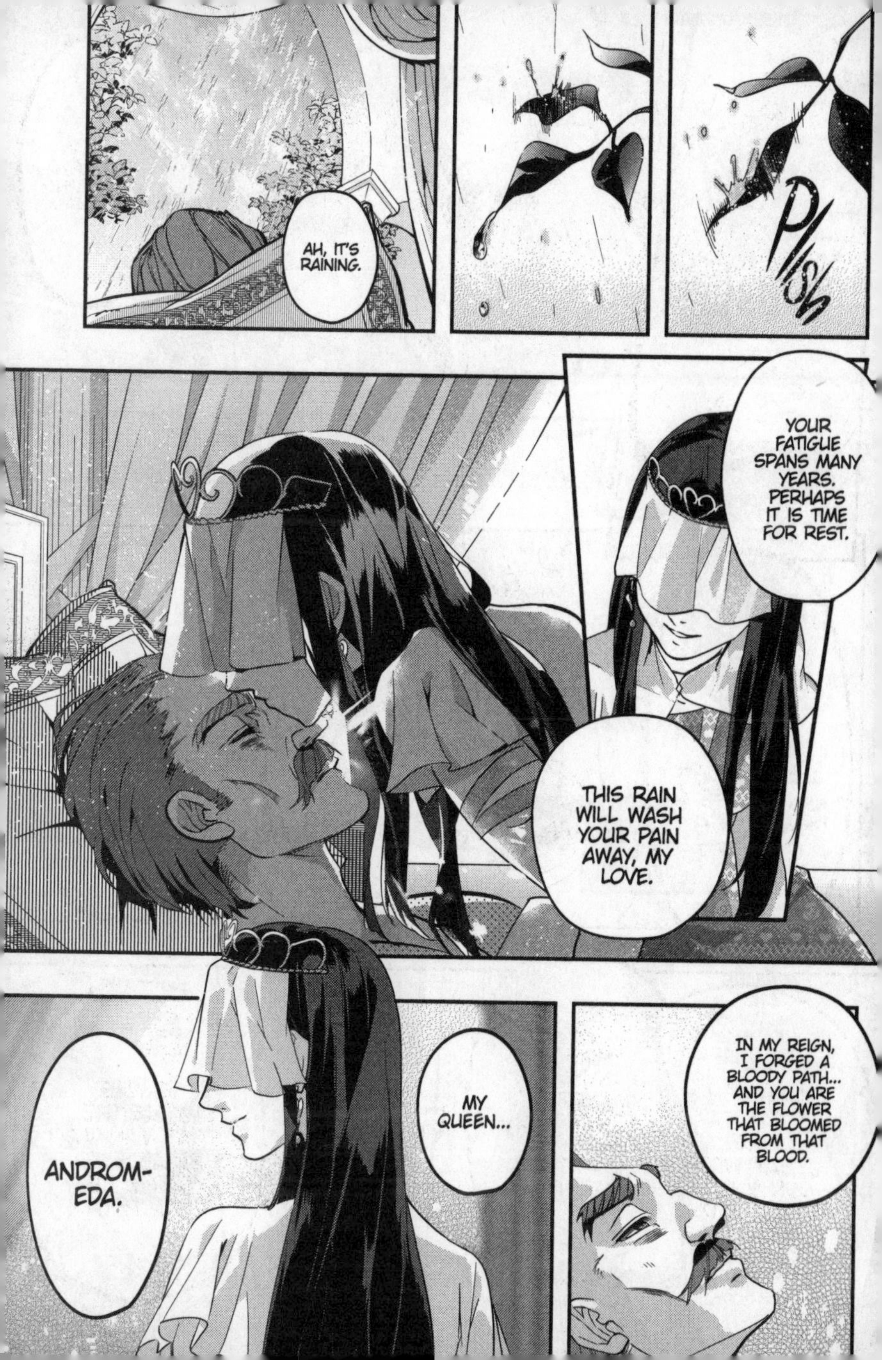
PISH
AH, IT'S RAINING.
YOUR FATIGUE SPANS MANY YEARS. PERHAPS IT IS TIME FOR REST.
THIS RAIN WILL WASH YOUR PAIN AWAY, MY LOVE.
IN MY REIGN, I FORGED A BLOODY PATH... AND YOU ARE THE FLOWER THAT BLOOMED FROM THAT BLOOD.
MY QUEEN...
ANDROM-EDA.

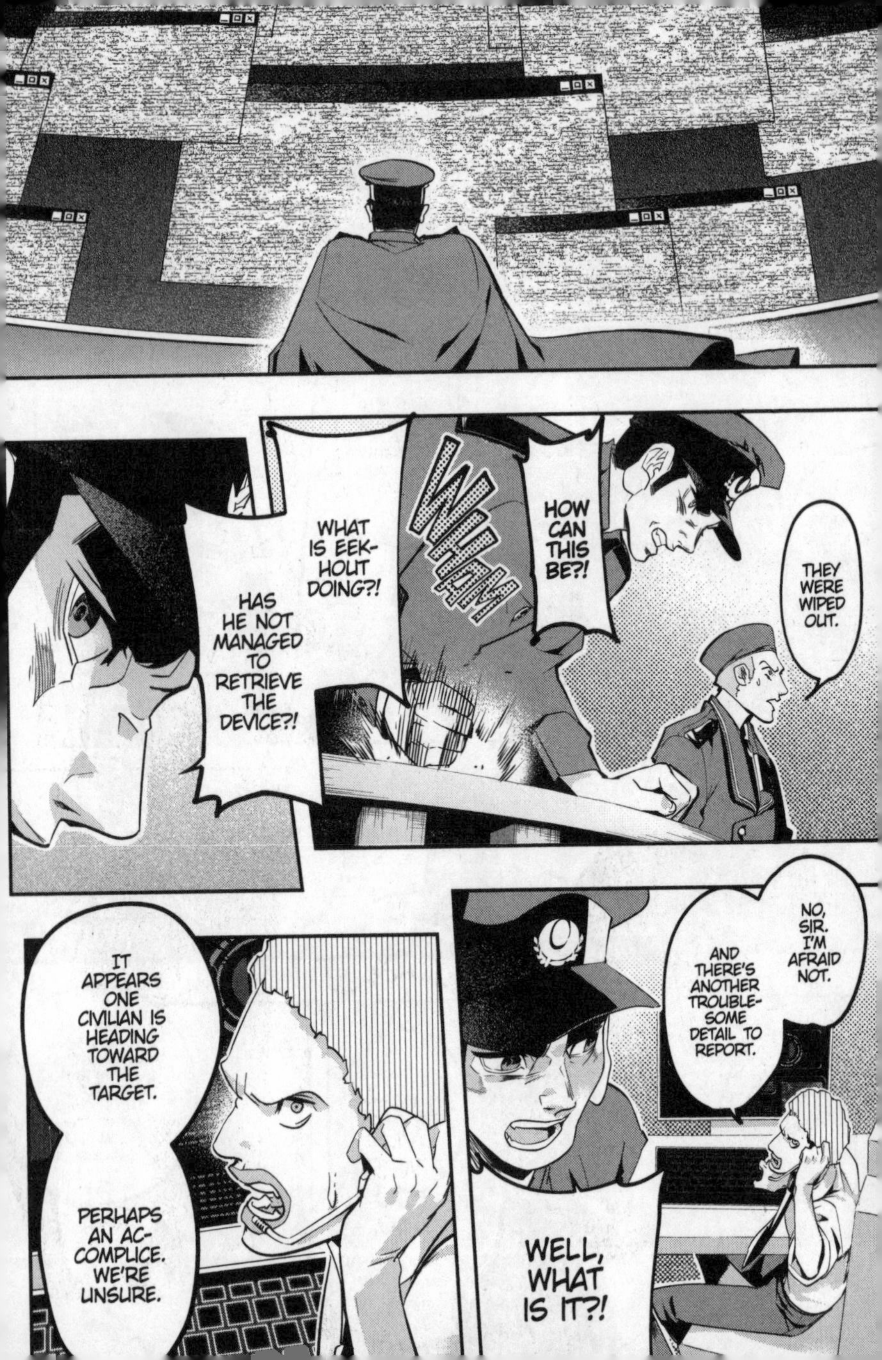
THEY WERE WIPED OUT.
HOW CAN THIS BE?!
WHAM!
WHAT IS EEK-HOUT DOING?!
HAS HE NOT MANAGED TO RETRIEVE THE DEVICE?!
NO, SIR. I'M AFRAID NOT.
AND THERE'S ANOTHER TROUBLE-SOME DETAIL TO REPORT.
WELL, WHAT IS IT?!
IT APPEARS ONE CIVILIAN IS HEADING TOWARD THE TARGET.
PERHAPS AN AC-COMPLICE. WE'RE UNSURE.

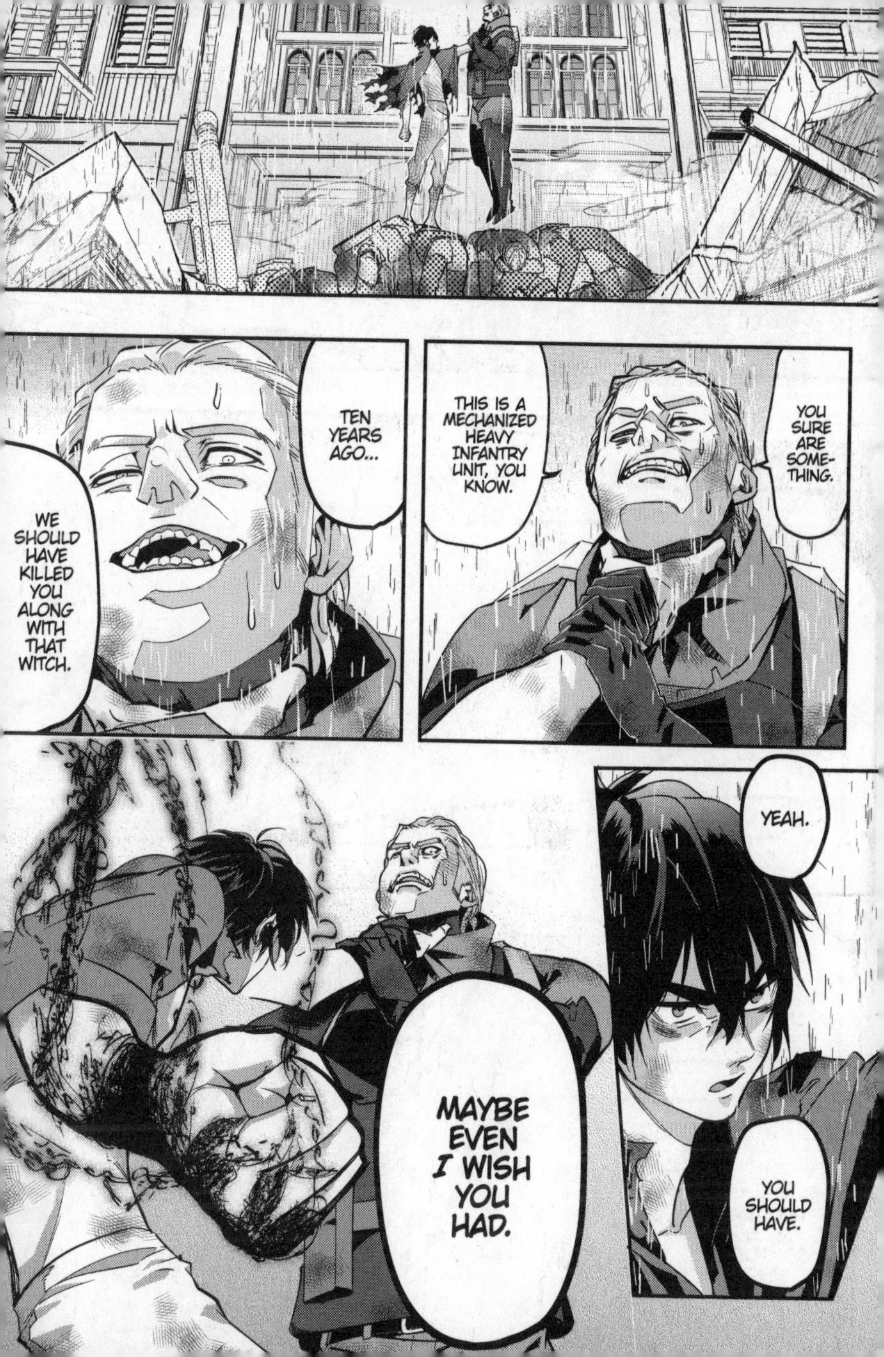
YOU SURE ARE SOME-THING.
THIS IS A MECHANIZED HEAVY INFANTRY UNIT, YOU KNOW.
TEN YEARS AGO...
WE SHOULD HAVE KILLED YOU ALONG WITH THAT WITCH.
YEAH.
YOU SHOULD HAVE.
MAYBE EVEN *I* WISH YOU HAD.

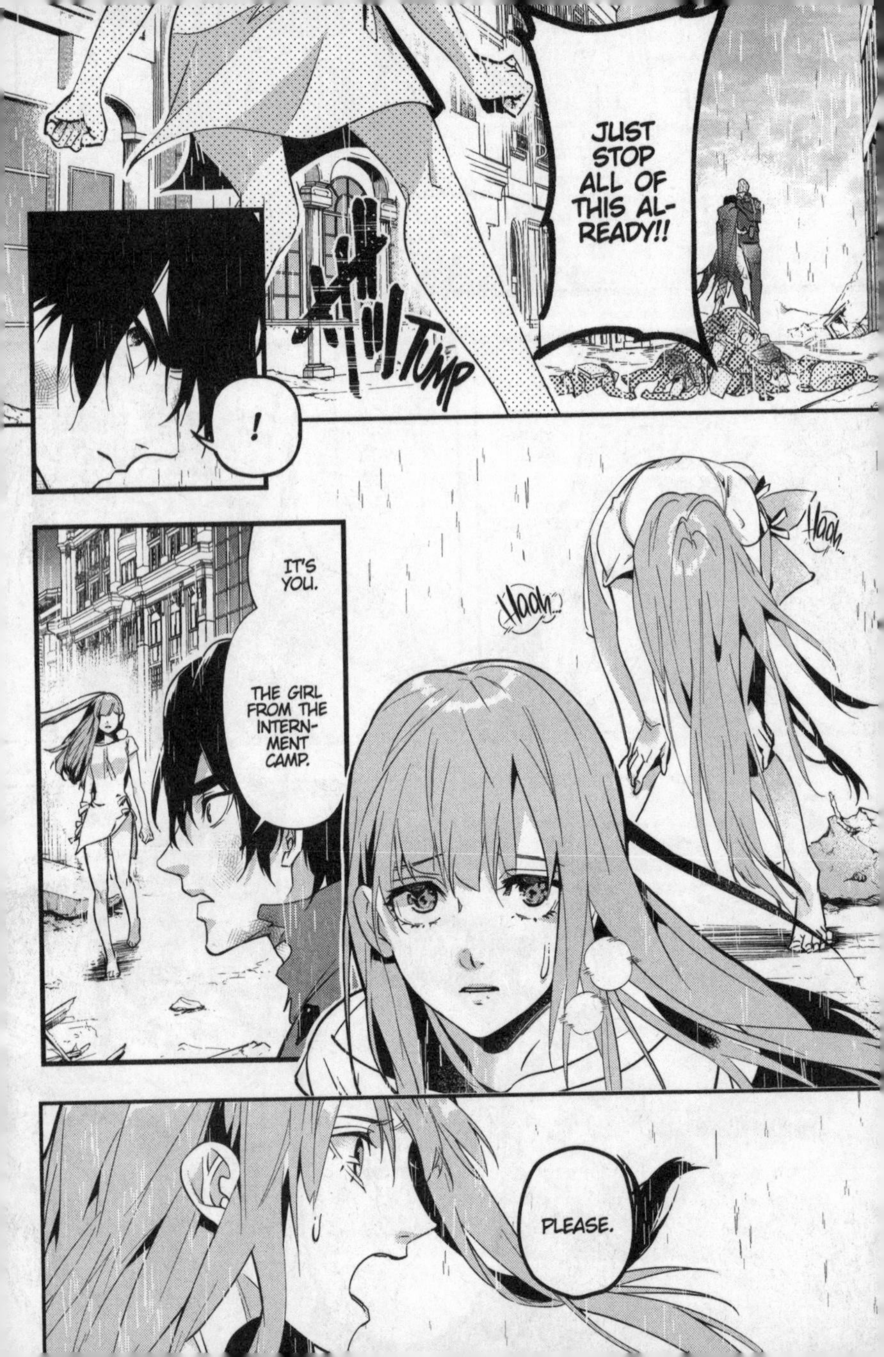
JUST STOP ALL OF THIS AL-READY!!
THUMP
!
Haah...
Haah...
IT'S YOU.
THE GIRL FROM THE INTERN-MENT CAMP.
PLEASE.

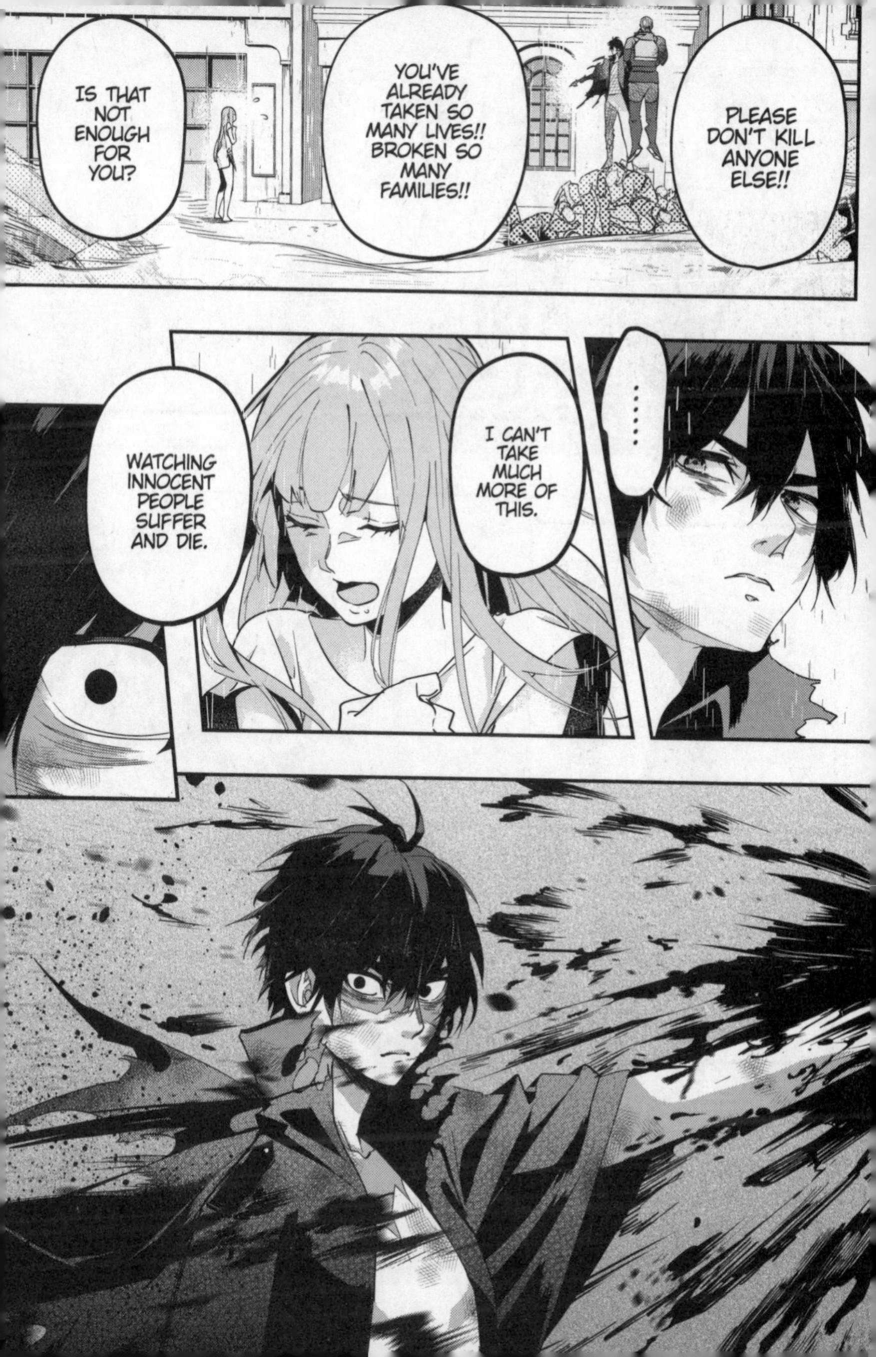
PLEASE DON'T KILL ANYONE ELSE!!
YOU'VE ALREADY TAKEN SO MANY LIVES!! BROKEN SO MANY FAMILIES!!
IS THAT NOT ENOUGH FOR YOU?
......
I CAN'T TAKE MUCH MORE OF THIS.
WATCHING INNOCENT PEOPLE SUFFER AND DIE.

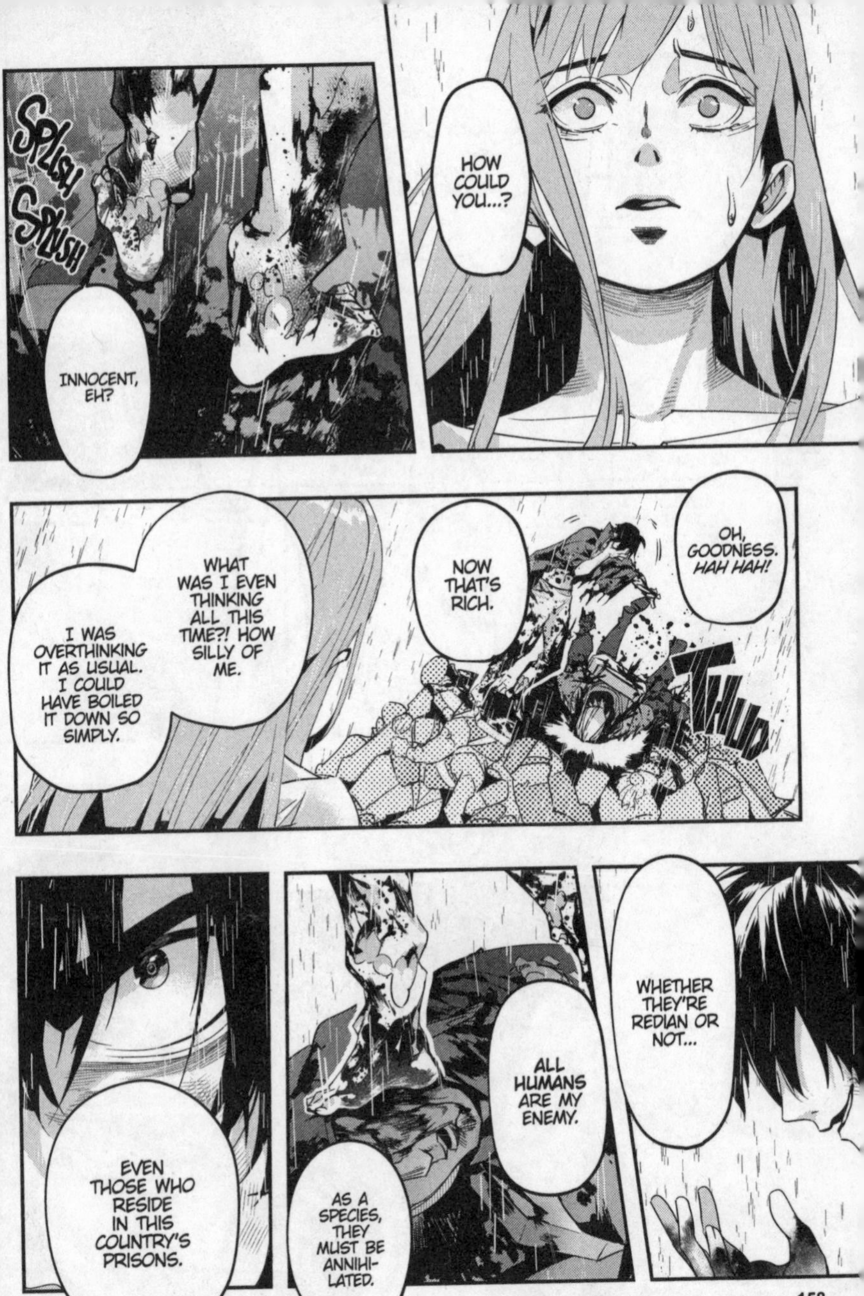
HOW COULD YOU...?
SPLISH SPLISH
INNOCENT, EH?
OH, GOODNESS. HAH HAH!
NOW THAT'S RICH.
THUD
WHAT WAS I EVEN THINKING ALL THIS TIME?! HOW SILLY OF ME.
I WAS OVERTHINKING IT AS USUAL. I COULD HAVE BOILED IT DOWN SO SIMPLY.
WHETHER THEY'RE REDIAN OR NOT...
ALL HUMANS ARE MY ENEMY.
AS A SPECIES, THEY MUST BE ANNIHILATED.
EVEN THOSE WHO RESIDE IN THIS COUNTRY'S PRISONS.

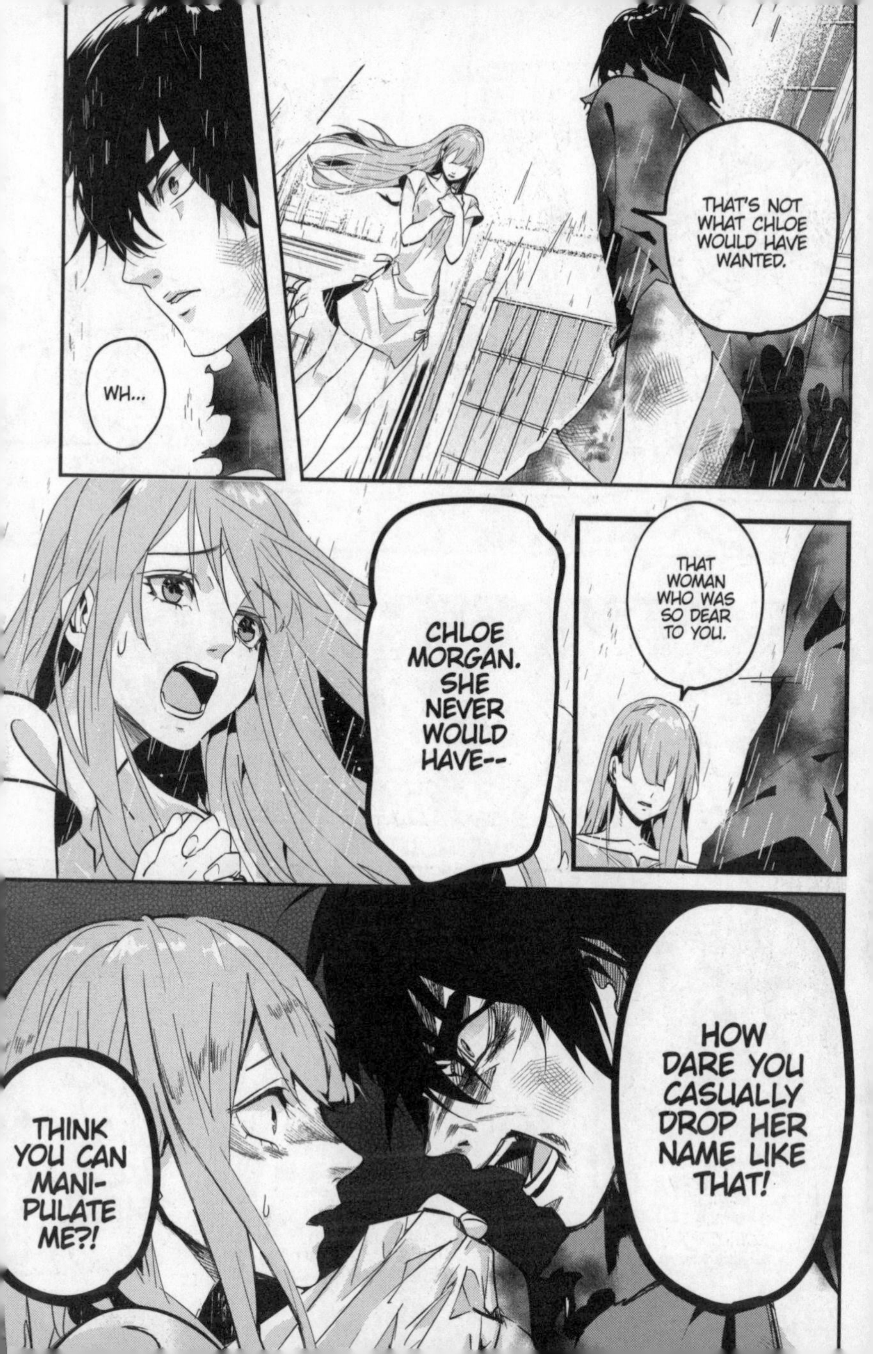
THAT'S NOT WHAT CHLOE WOULD HAVE WANTED.
WH...
THAT WOMAN WHO WAS SO DEAR TO YOU.
CHLOE MORGAN. SHE NEVER WOULD HAVE--
HOW DARE YOU CASUALLY DROP HER NAME LIKE THAT!
THINK YOU CAN MANI-PULATE ME?!

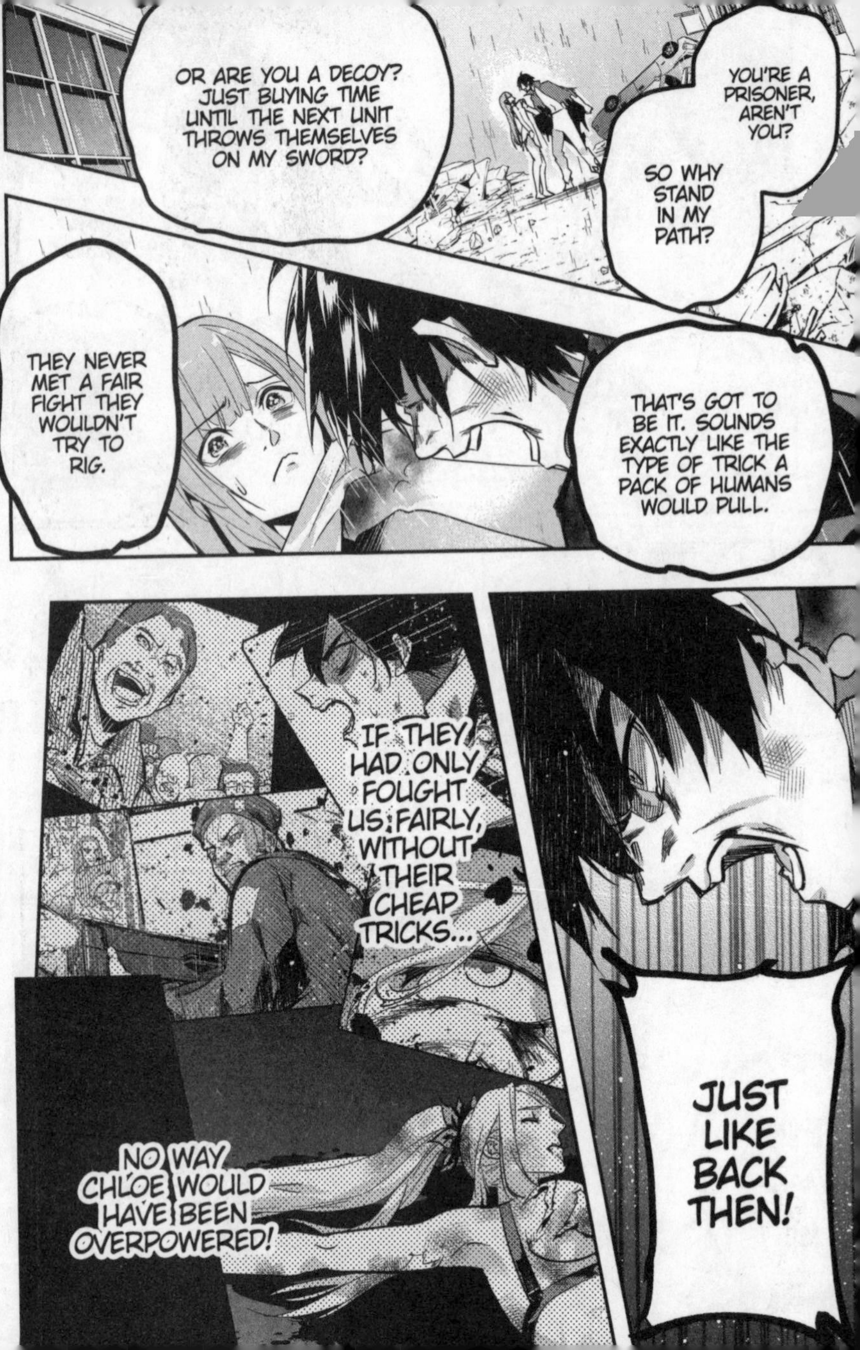
YOU'RE A PRISONER, AREN'T YOU?
SO WHY STAND IN MY PATH?
OR ARE YOU A DECOY? JUST BUYING TIME UNTIL THE NEXT UNIT THROWS THEMSELVES ON MY SWORD?
THAT'S GOT TO BE IT. SOUNDS EXACTLY LIKE THE TYPE OF TRICK A PACK OF HUMANS WOULD PULL.
THEY NEVER MET A FAIR FIGHT THEY WOULDN'T TRY TO RIG.
JUST LIKE BACK THEN!
IF THEY HAD ONLY FOUGHT US FAIRLY, WITHOUT THEIR CHEAP TRICKS...
NO WAY CHLOE WOULD HAVE BEEN OVERPOWERED!

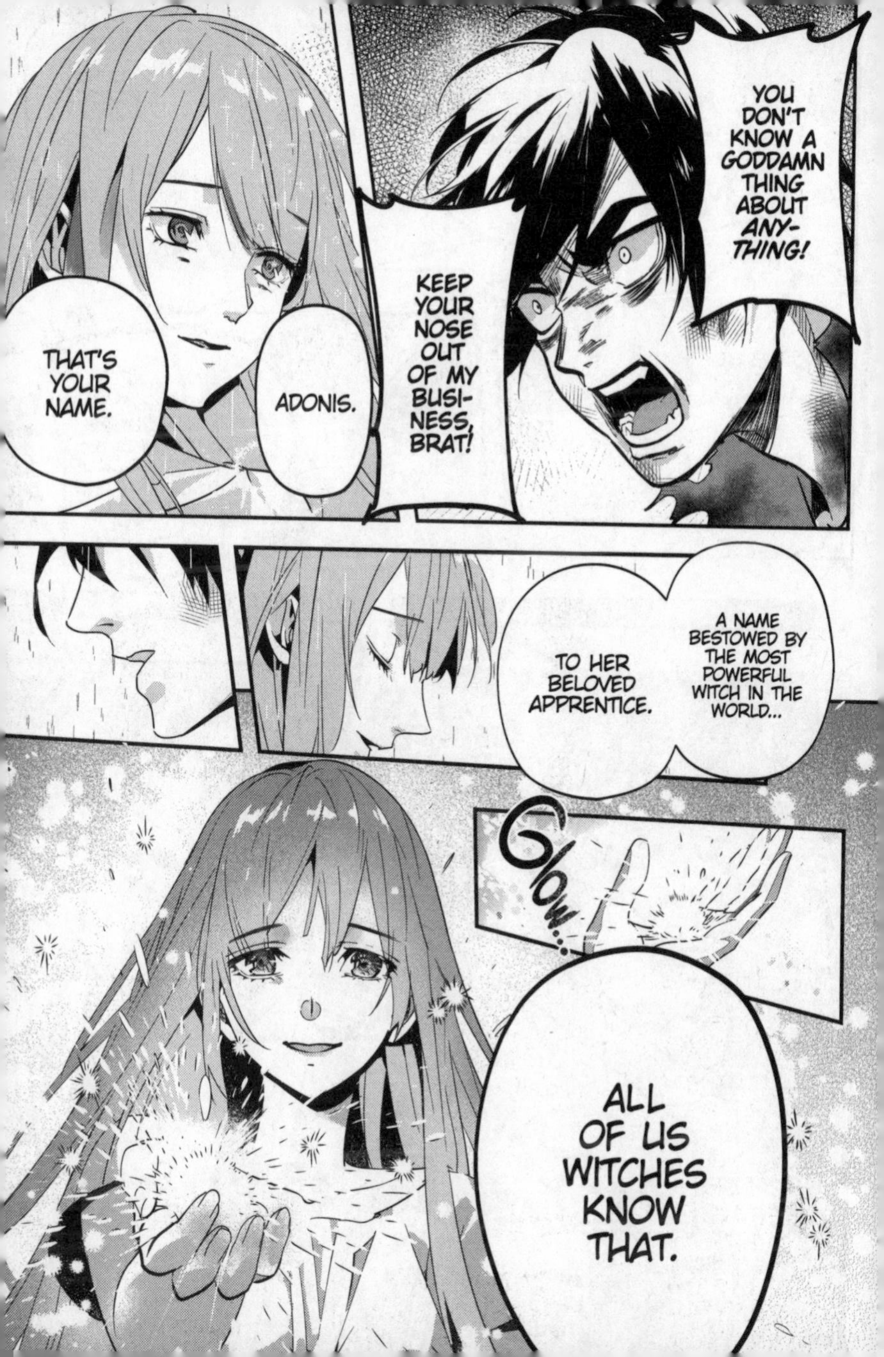
YOU DON'T KNOW A GODDAMN THING ABOUT ANYTHING!
KEEP YOUR NOSE OUT OF MY BUSINESS, BRAT!
ADONIS.
THAT'S YOUR NAME.
A NAME BESTOWED BY THE MOST POWERFUL WITCH IN THE WORLD...
TO HER BELOVED APPRENTICE.
Glow...
ALL OF US WITCHES KNOW THAT.

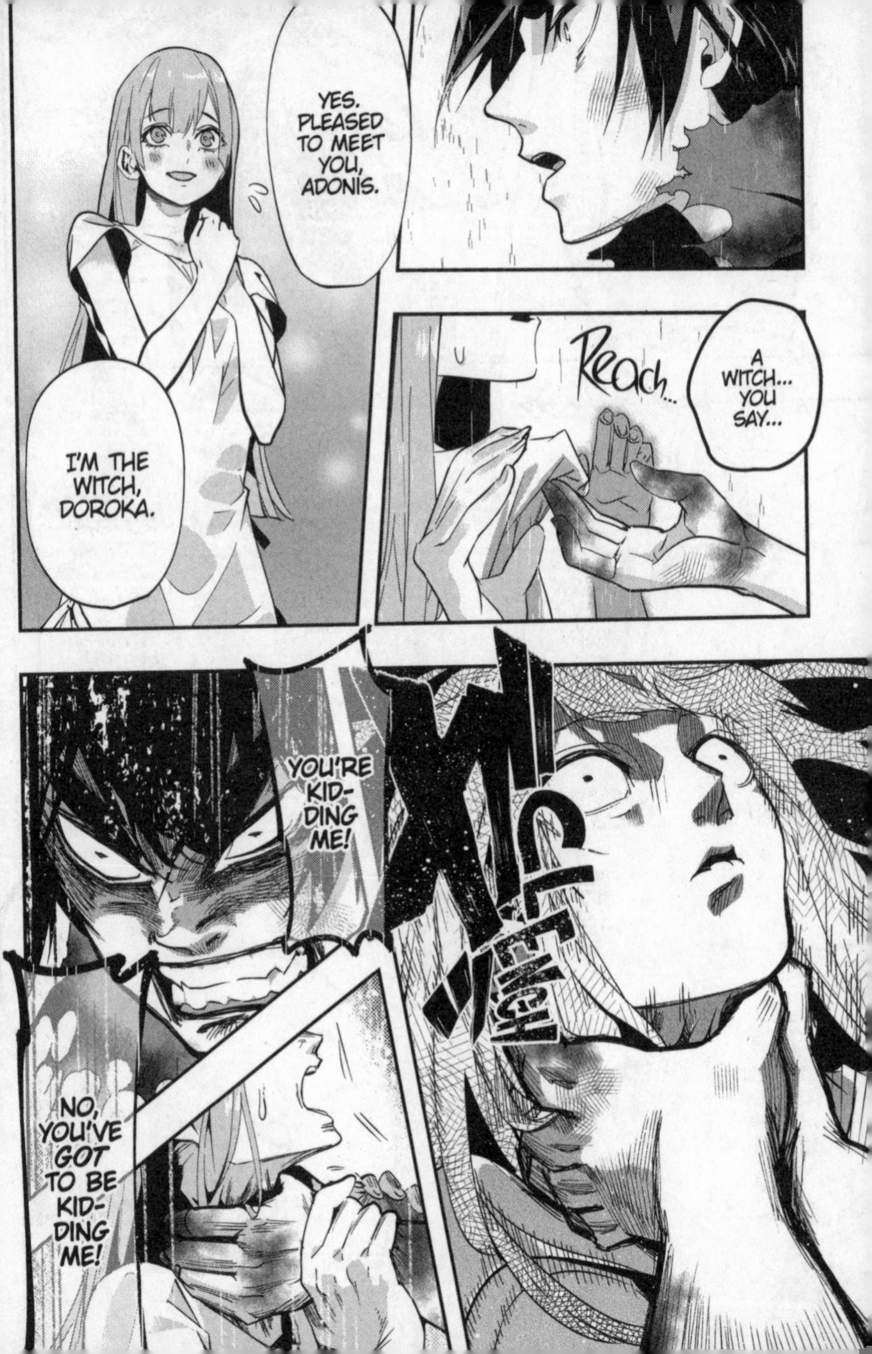
Reach...
A WITCH... YOU SAY...
YES. PLEASED TO MEET YOU, ADONIS.
I'M THE WITCH, DOROKA.
CLENCH
YOU'RE KID-DING ME!
NO, YOU'VE GOT TO BE KID-DING ME!

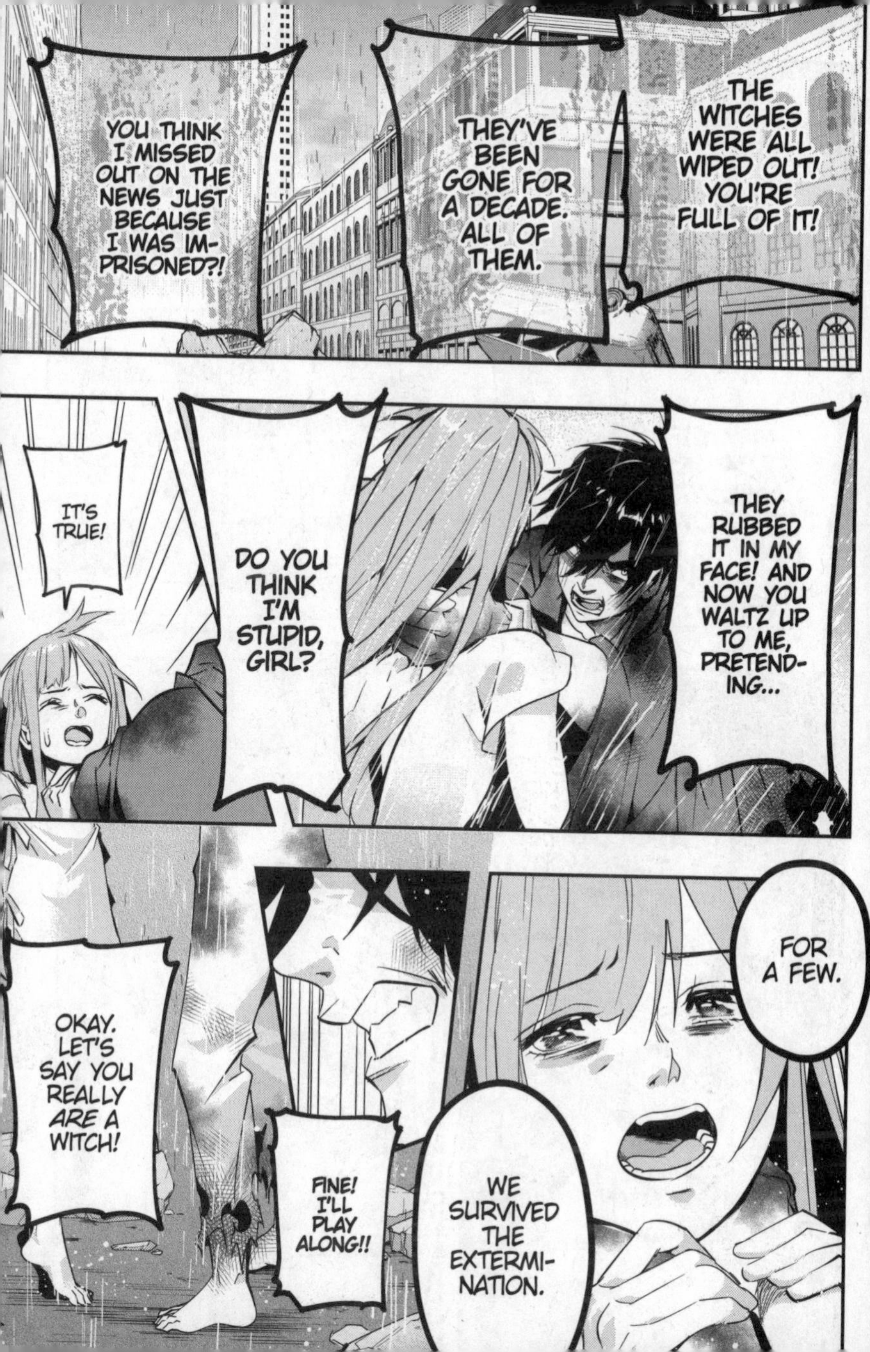
THE WITCHES WERE ALL WIPED OUT! YOU'RE FULL OF IT!
THEY'VE BEEN GONE FOR A DECADE. ALL OF THEM.
YOU THINK I MISSED OUT ON THE NEWS JUST BECAUSE I WAS IM-PRISONED?!
THEY RUBBED IT IN MY FACE! AND NOW YOU WALTZ UP TO ME, PRETEND-ING...
DO YOU THINK I'M STUPID, GIRL?
IT'S TRUE!
FOR A FEW.
WE SURVIVED THE EXTERMI-NATION.
FINE! I'LL PLAY ALONG!!
OKAY. LET'S SAY YOU REALLY ARE A WITCH!

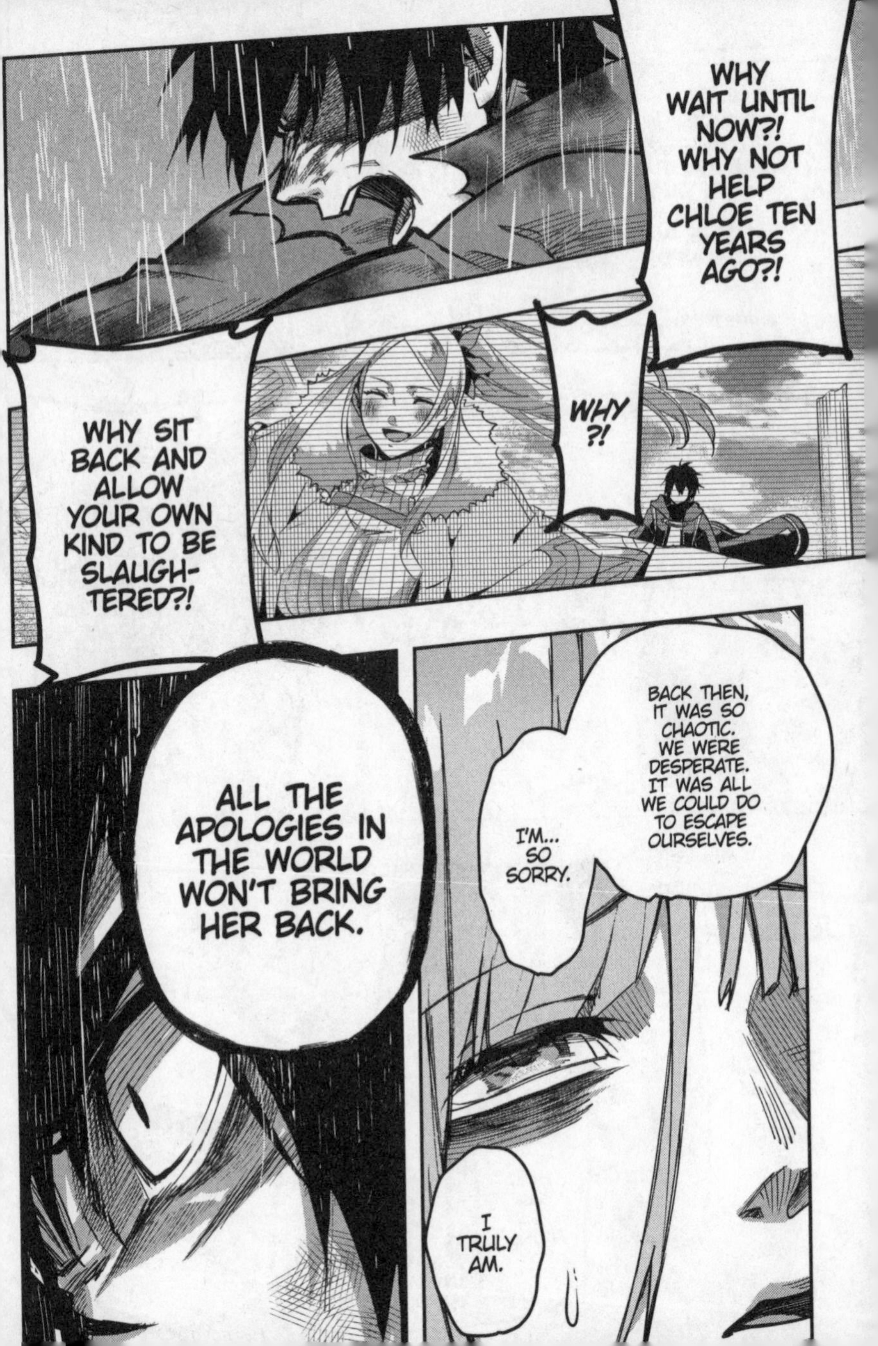
WHY WAIT UNTIL NOW?! WHY NOT HELP CHLOE TEN YEARS AGO?!
WHY ?!
WHY SIT BACK AND ALLOW YOUR OWN KIND TO BE SLAUGH-TERED?!
BACK THEN, IT WAS SO CHAOTIC. WE WERE DESPERATE. IT WAS ALL WE COULD DO TO ESCAPE OURSELVES.
I'M... SO SORRY.
I TRULY AM.
ALL THE APOLOGIES IN THE WORLD WON'T BRING HER BACK.

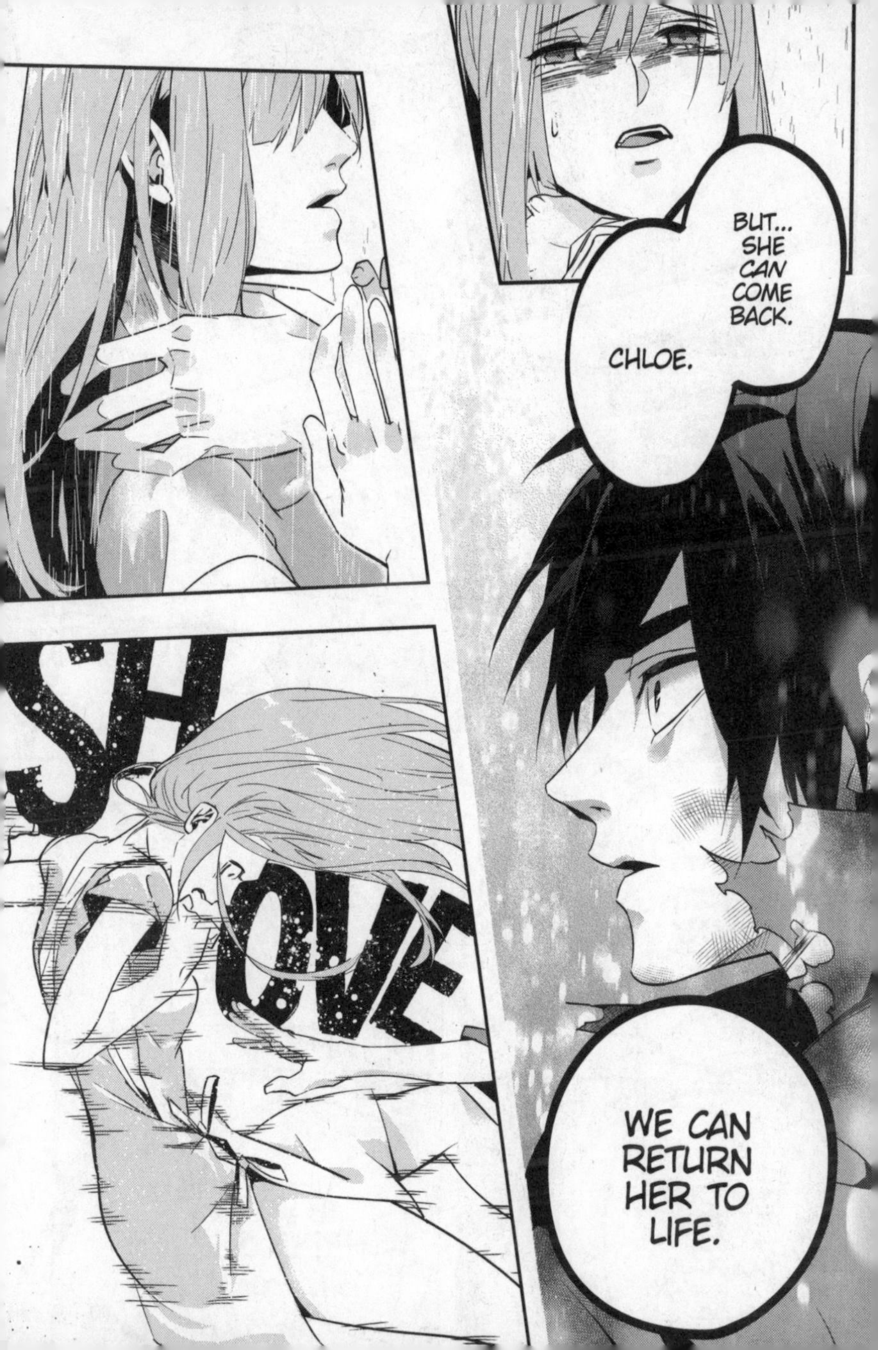
BUT... SHE CAN COME BACK.
CHLOE.
WE CAN RETURN HER TO LIFE.
SH
OVE

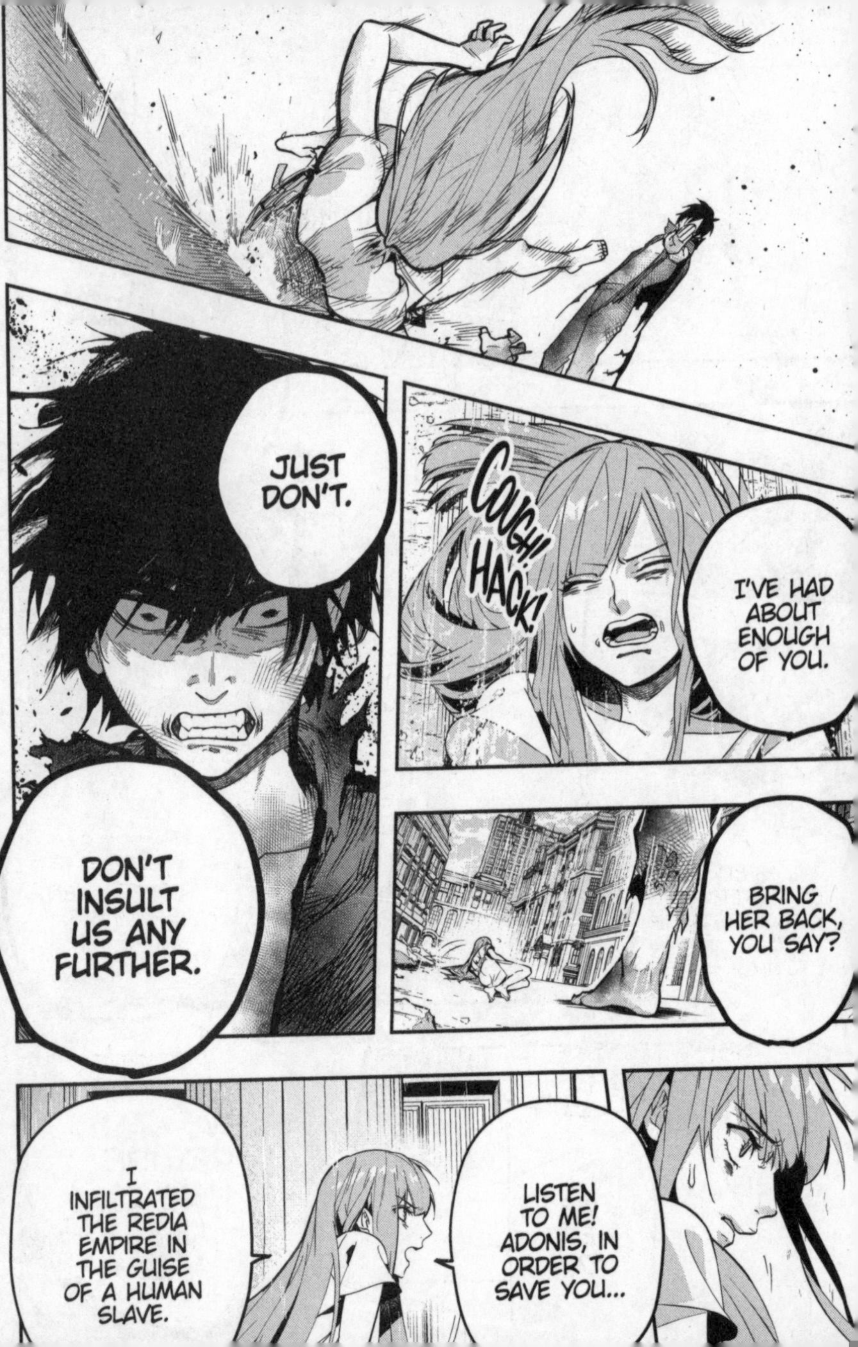
COUGH! HACK!
I'VE HAD ABOUT ENOUGH OF YOU.
BRING HER BACK, YOU SAY?
JUST DON'T.
DON'T INSULT US ANY FURTHER.
LISTEN TO ME! ADONIS, IN ORDER TO SAVE YOU...
I INFILTRATED THE REDIA EMPIRE IN THE GUISE OF A HUMAN SLAVE.

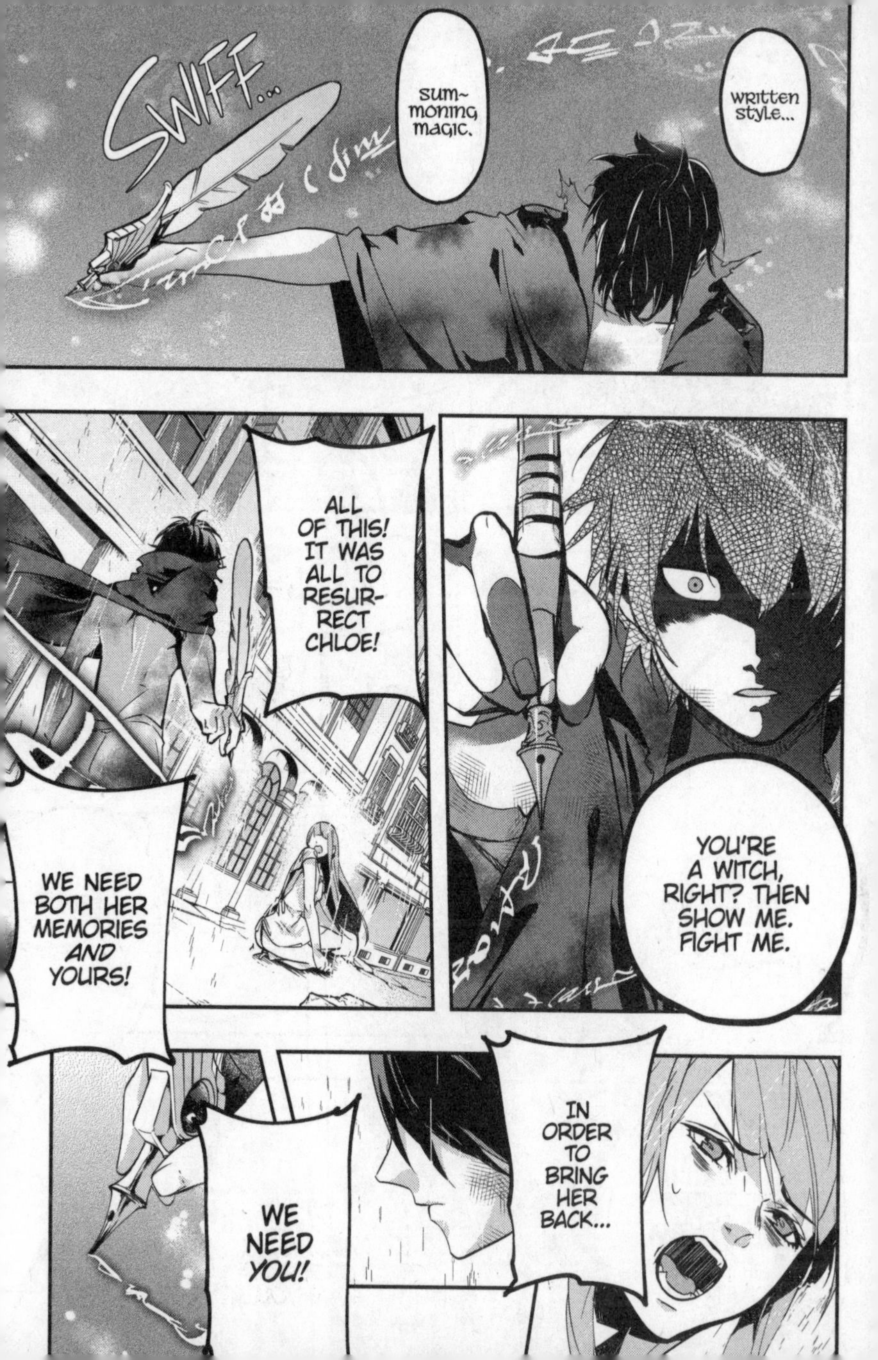
written style...
sum~moning magic.
SWIFF...
YOU'RE A WITCH, RIGHT? THEN SHOW ME. FIGHT ME.
ALL OF THIS! IT WAS ALL TO RESURRECT CHLOE!
WE NEED BOTH HER MEMORIES AND YOURS!
IN ORDER TO BRING HER BACK...
WE NEED YOU!

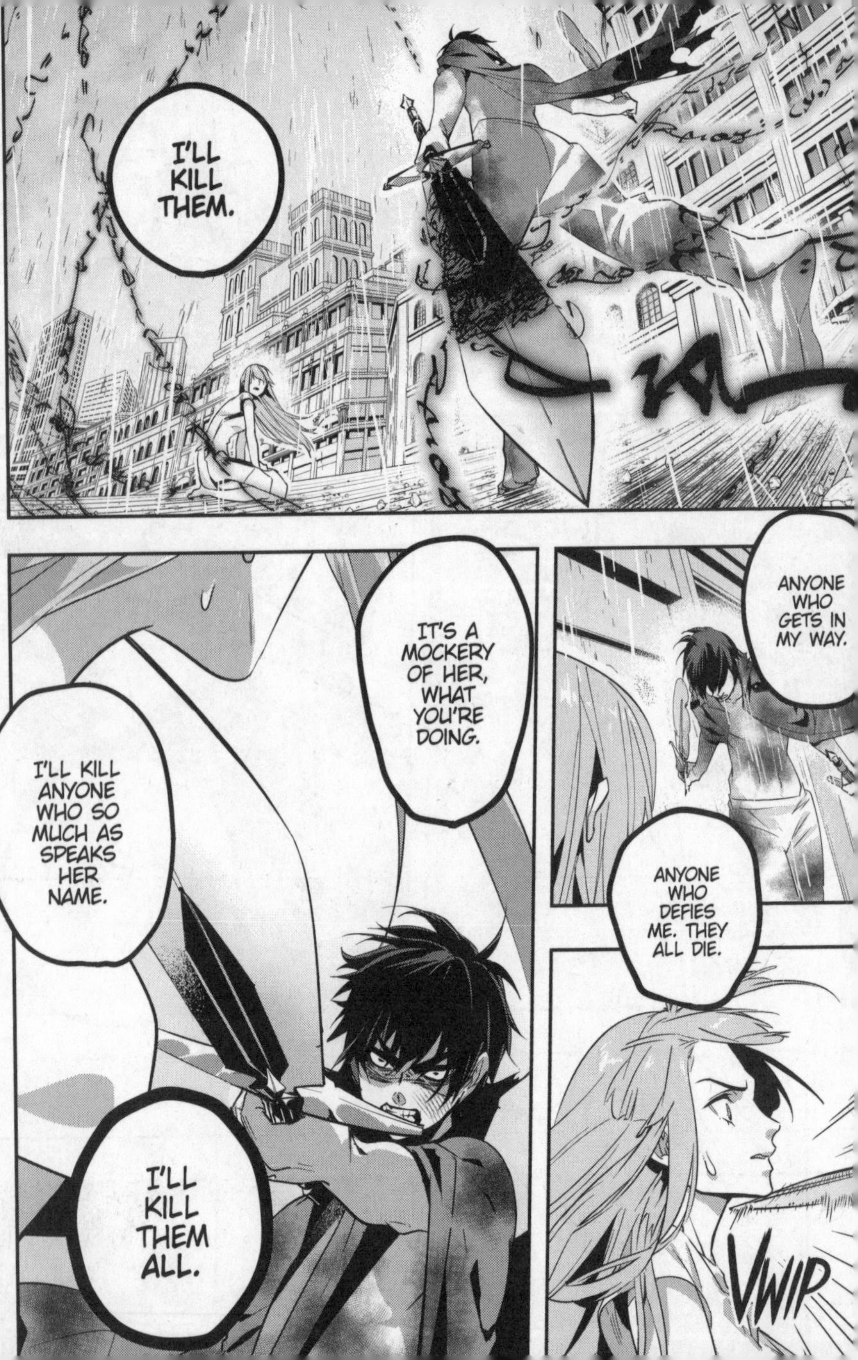
I'LL KILL THEM.
ANYONE WHO GETS IN MY WAY.
ANYONE WHO DEFIES ME. THEY ALL DIE.
VWIP
IT'S A MOCKERY OF HER, WHAT YOU'RE DOING.
I'LL KILL ANYONE WHO SO MUCH AS SPEAKS HER NAME.
I'LL KILL THEM ALL.

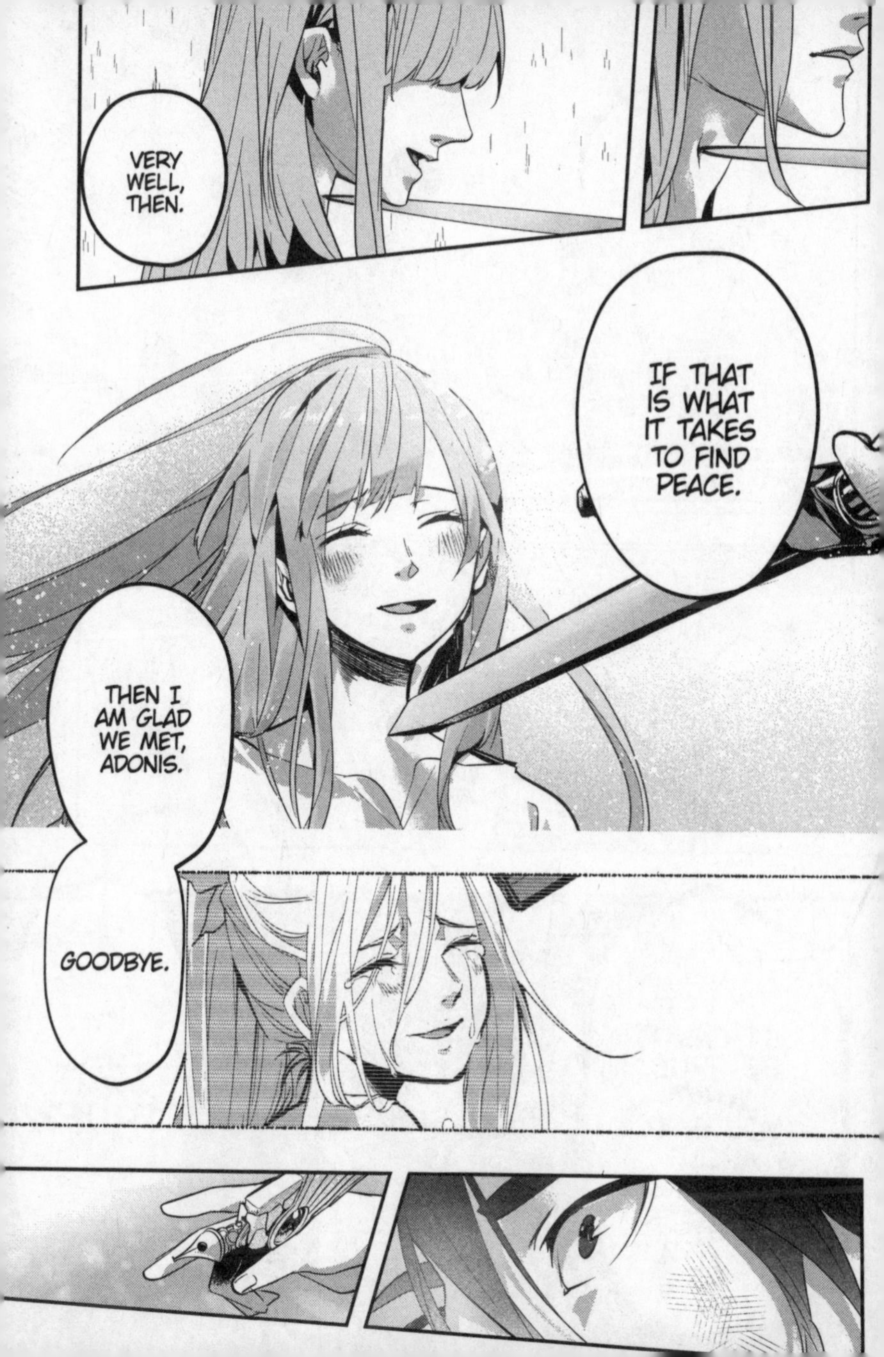
VERY WELL, THEN.
IF THAT IS WHAT IT TAKES TO FIND PEACE.
THEN I AM GLAD WE MET, ADONIS.
GOODBYE.

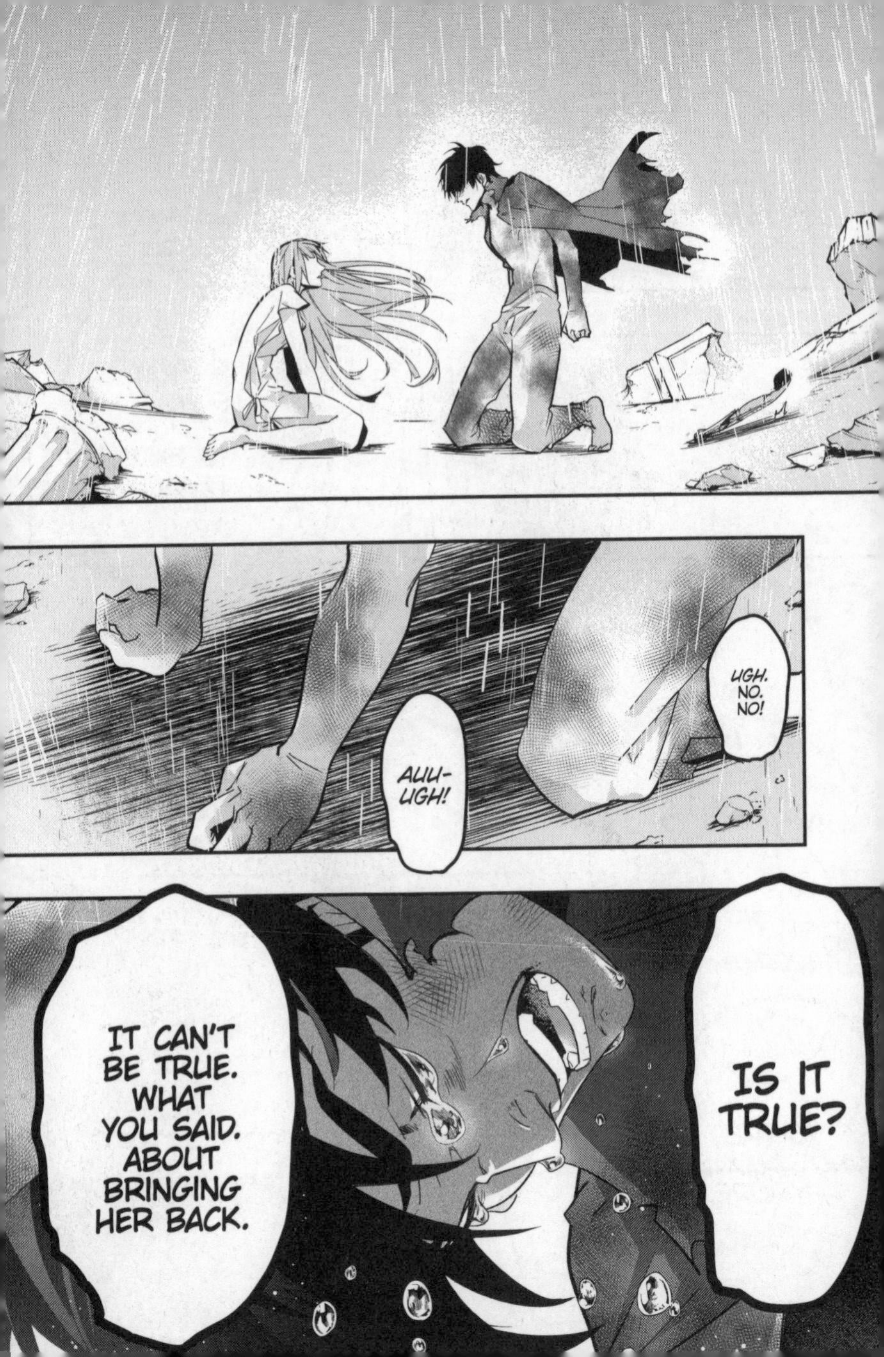
UGH. NO. NO!
AUU-UGH!
IS IT TRUE?
IT CAN'T BE TRUE. WHAT YOU SAID. ABOUT BRINGING HER BACK.

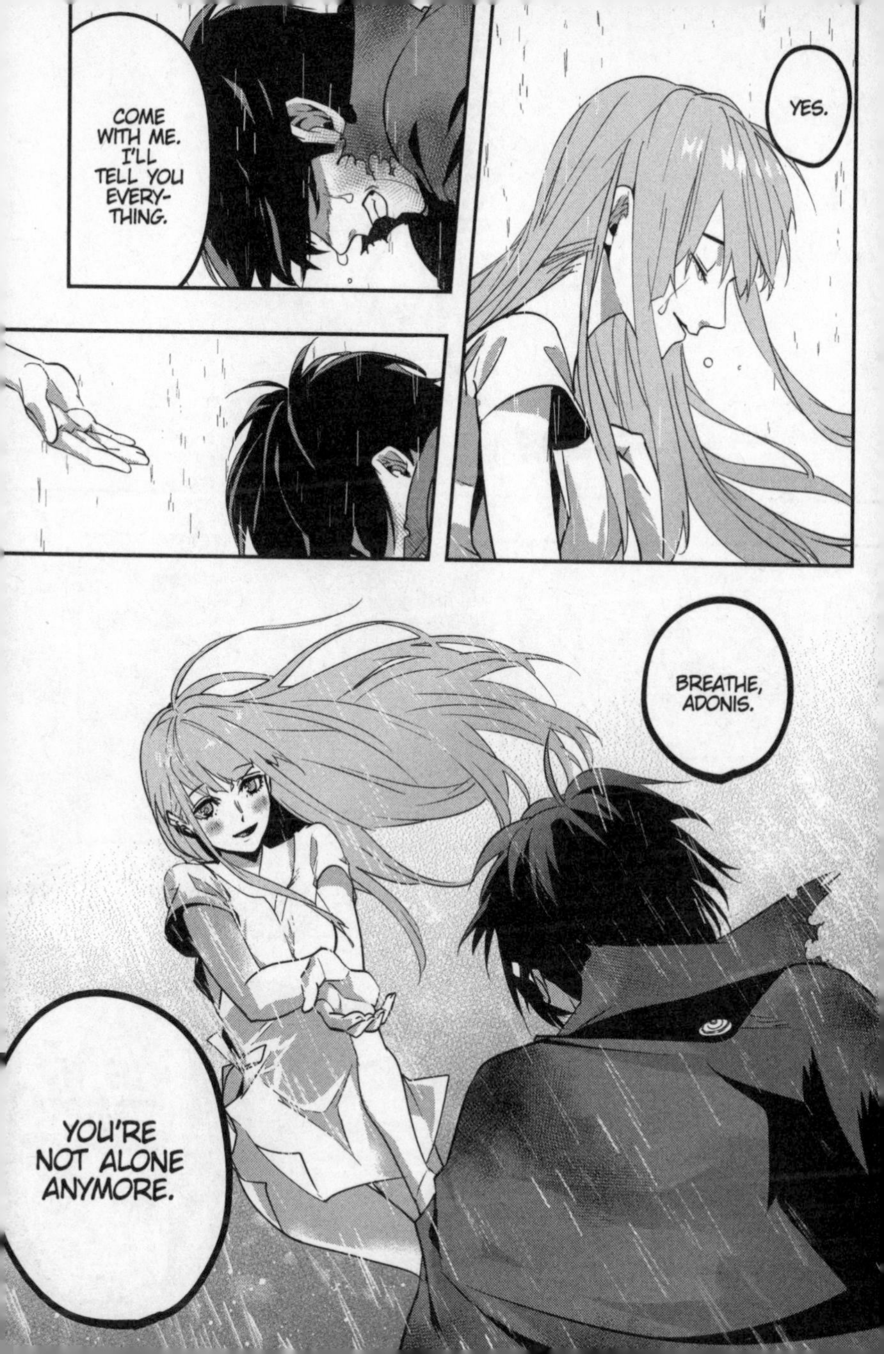
YES.
COME WITH ME. I'LL TELL YOU EVERY-THING.
BREATHE, ADONIS.
YOU'RE NOT ALONE ANYMORE.

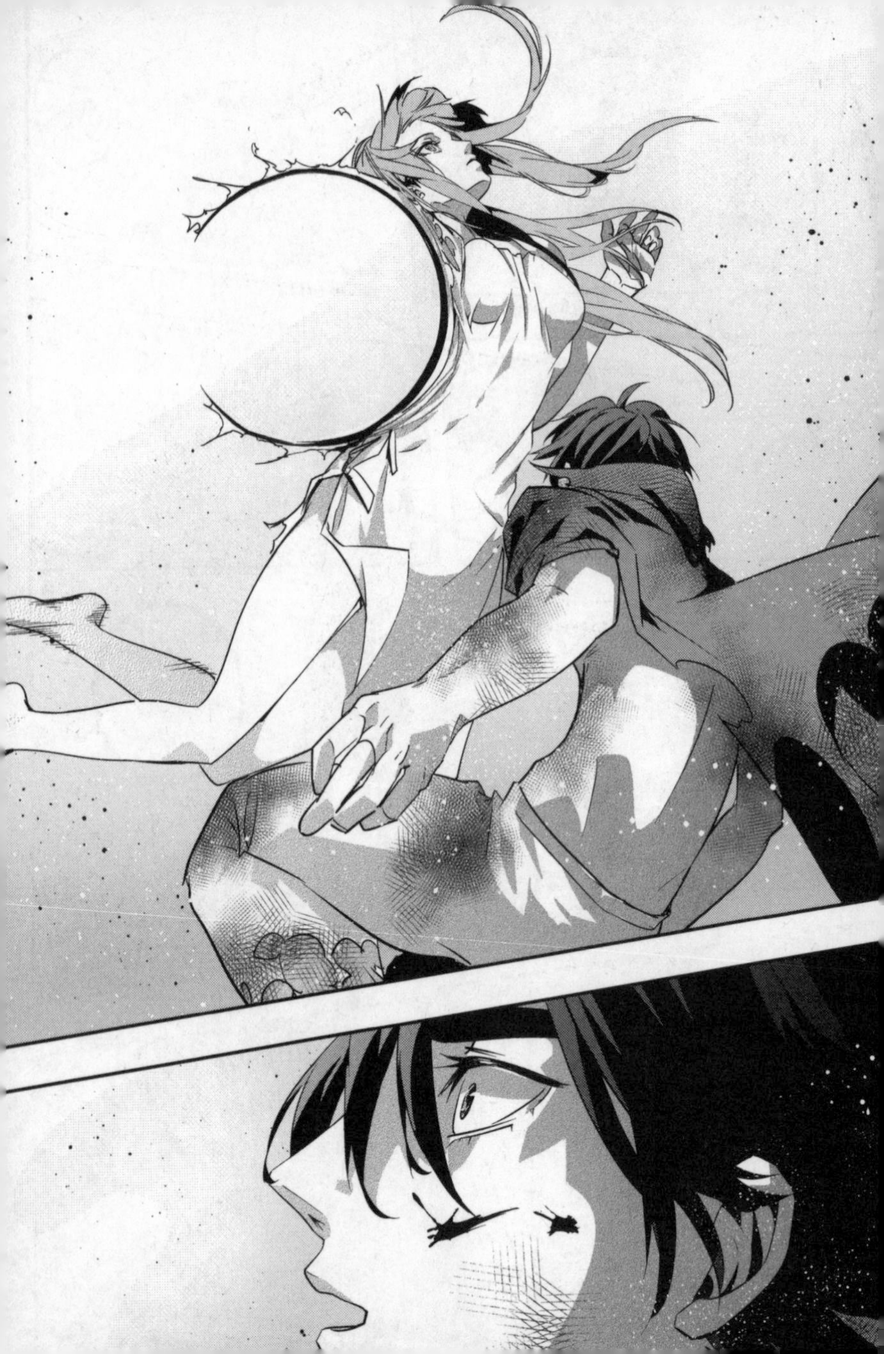

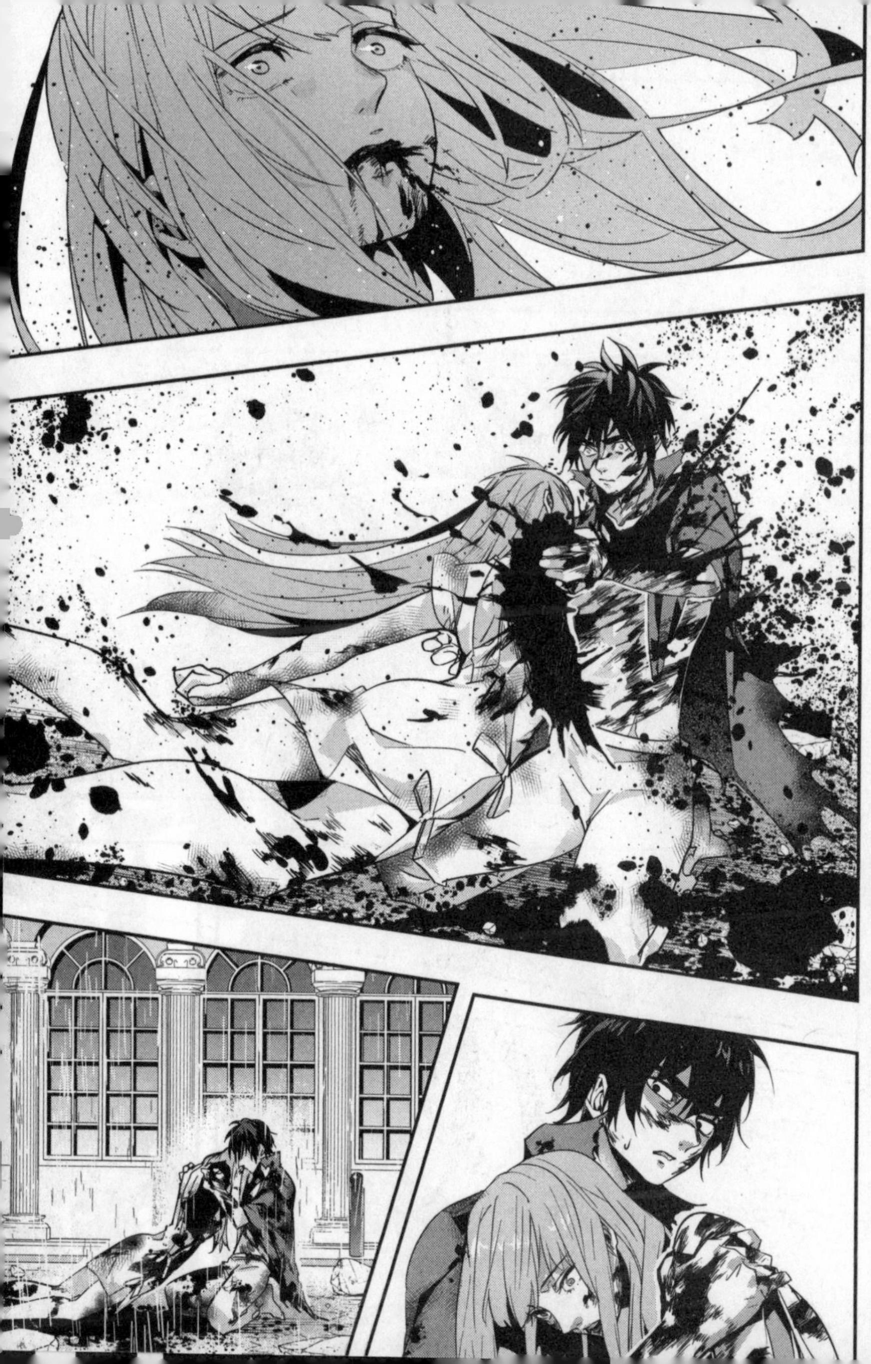

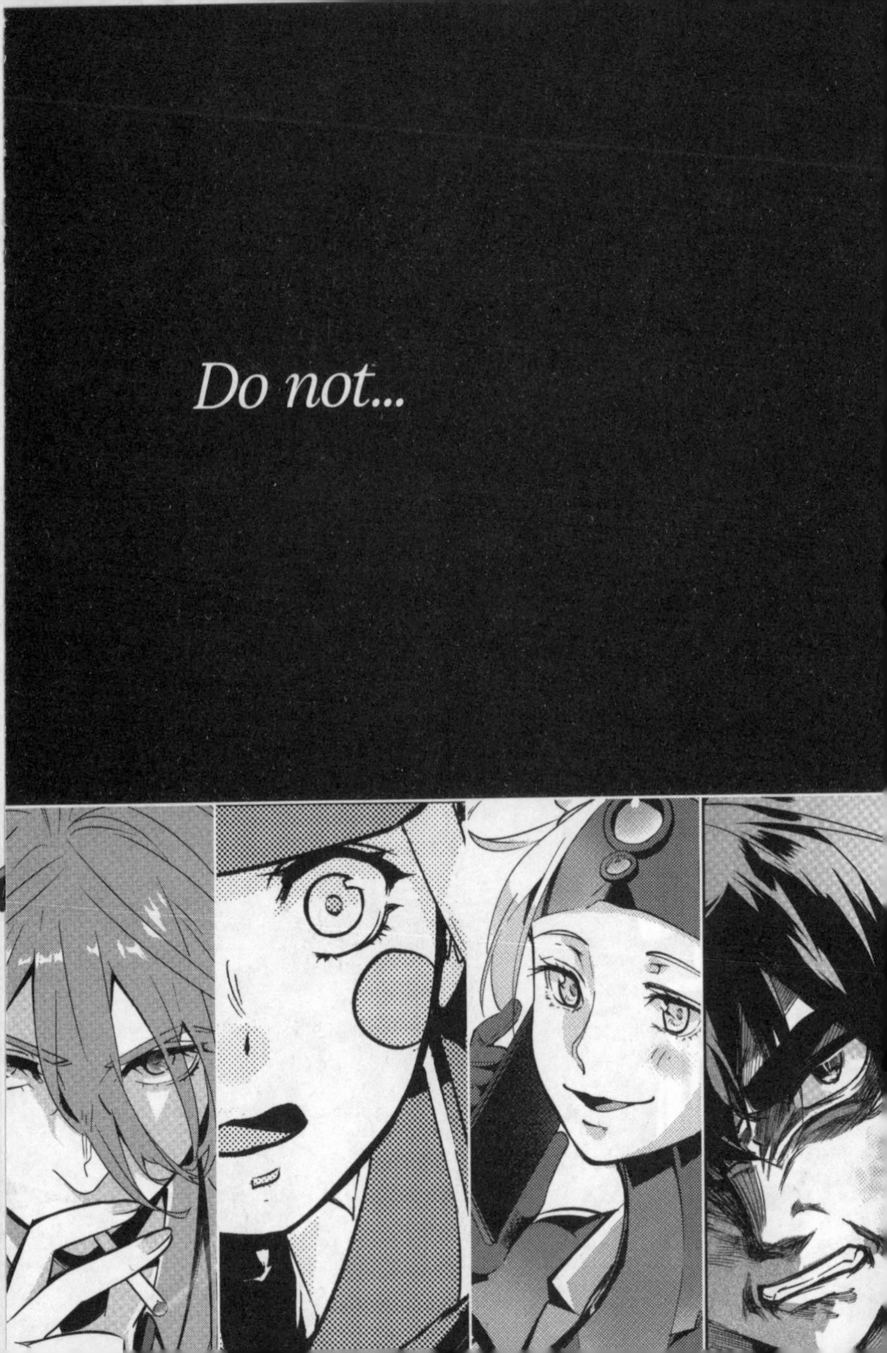
Do not...

lose your way.

THE KINGDOMS OF RUIN

2

The story continues!

SEVEN SEAS ENTERTAINMENT PRESENTS

THE KINGDOMS OF RUIN

story and art by YORUHASHI

VOLUME 1

TRANSLATION
Nan Rymer

ADAPTATION
Casey Lucas

LETTERING AND RETOUCH
Joseph Barr

COVER DESIGN
KC Fabellon

PROOFREADER
Brett Hallahan

EDITOR
J.P. Sullivan

PREPRESS TECHNICIAN
Rhiannon Rasmussen-Silverstein

PRODUCTION MANAGER
Lissa Pattillo

MANAGING EDITOR
Julie Davis

ASSOCIATE PUBLISHER
Adam Arnold

PUBLISHER
Jason DeAngelis

THE KINGDOMS OF RUIN VOL. 1
© yoruhashi 2019
Originally published in Japan in 2019 by MAG Garden Corporation, TOKYO.
English translation rights arranged through TOHAN CORPORATION, Tokyo.

Seven Seas press and purchase enquiries can be sent to Marketing Manager
Lianne Sentar at press@gomanga.com. Information regarding the distribution
and purchase of digital editions is available from Digital Manager CK Russell
at digital@gomanga.com.

Seven Seas and the Seven Seas logo are trademarks of
Seven Seas Entertainment. All rights reserved.

ISBN: 978-1-64505-855-7

Printed in Canada

First Printing: December 2020

10 9 8 7 6 5 4 3 2 1

FOLLOW US ONLINE: *www.sevenseasentertainment.com*

READING DIRECTIONS

This book reads from *right to left*, Japanese style.
If this is your first time reading manga, you start
reading from the top right panel on each page and
take it from there. If you get lost, just follow the
numbered diagram here. It may seem backwards at
first, but you'll get the hang of it! Have fun!!

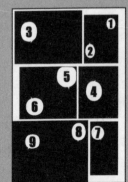